COMMENTARY
2025–2026
VOLUME 118

The lessons in this commentary are based on the International Uniform Sunday School Lesson Outlines, copyright ©2023, Division of Christian Education, the National Council of the Churches of Christ in the USA, and is used with permission.

Entered according to Act of Congress in the Office of Librarian of Congress in the year 1903 at Washington, DC, by R. H. Boyd, D.D., LL.D.

R. H. Boyd, D.D., LL.D., Founder (1896–1922)

H. A. Boyd, D.D. (1922–1959) • T. B. Boyd Jr., D.D. (1959–1979) • T. B. Boyd III, D.D. (1979–2017)

LaDonna Boyd, EdD
President/CEO (2017–Present)

LaDonna Boyd, EdD
President/CEO

EDITORIAL STAFF
Rev. Olivia M. Cloud, M.R.E.
Managing Editor

Monique Gooch, B.A.; Sinclaire Sparkman, M.A.B.T.S.
Brittany Batson, B.A.; Carla Davis, B.A.

**Dr. Eugene C. English • Rev. Nicole Tolliver • Dr. Claude Ellis Forehand II
Dr. Angela Miller • Dr. Nika Davis**
Writers

Jasmine Cole
Cover Design

www.rhboyd.com

For Customer Service
and Toll–Free Ordering,
Call
1–877–4RHBOYD (474–2693)
Hours: 24/7 Phone Support
or
Fax (615) 350–9018

6717 Centennial Blvd.• Nashville, Tennessee 37209–1017

FROM THE PUBLISHER...

Dear Faithful Reader,

As we turn the page into a new cycle of study and reflection, I welcome you to the 2025–2026 edition of *Boyd's Commentary*. In these turbulent times—marked by political unrest, cultural division, and uncertainty about the future—our faith remains an unshakable foundation. Isaiah and Jeremiah remind us that even in the midst of chaos, God is still calling us to renewal, restoration, and righteousness.

Isaiah's vision of a renewed Temple and a restored people speaks directly to our yearning for justice in an unjust world. Similarly, Jeremiah, the weeping prophet, challenges us to see beyond the ruins and to trust in the promises of a God who never abandons His people, even when exile seems imminent.

Faithful worship is the overarching theme of this annual study, taken from both Old and New Testament passages. Our testimony, rooted in the Gospel of Jesus Christ, must reflect God's unwavering love, His demand for justice, and His promise of redemption. We are not called to silence or despair, but to speak boldly, live righteously, and serve compassionately.

This edition of *Boyd's Commentary* invites readers to explore the Word deeply and to embody it boldly. Whether in the sanctuary, classroom, or community, let this be a tool that nourishes your spiritual journey and equips you to be a vessel of hope and healing.

As we continue to spread the gospel and stand for truth, may we remain anchored in the assurance that God is with us—guiding, refining, and renewing us daily.

In faith and service,

LaDonna Boyd, EdD
Fifth-generation President/CEO

FROM THE MANAGING EDITOR...

Greetings!

It is with pleasure that we present this labor of love to you, the 2025–2026 edition of *Boyd's Commentary for the Sunday School*. Celebrating 119 years of publication, this trusted resource continues to uphold its legacy of delivering biblical insights that illuminate the truth of God's Word and its relevance to contemporary and timeless human experiences.

Each lesson is crafted to achieve theological and practical synergy—delving into Scripture while offering life applications that empower you to live its teachings. Our writers and editors have worked thoughtfully to ensure that the Bible's wisdom speaks clearly into the complexities of our contemporary landscape.

Boyd's Commentary invites you to explore the rich depths of exegetical and theological discovery. Whether you're preparing a sermon, leading a class, or engaged in personal study, this holistic resource is your companion for meaningful engagement with Scripture.

May the Lord bless your ministry as you seek His face and guide others to do the same.

With gratitude,

Rev. Olivia M. Cloud, MRE
Managing Editor, R.H. Boyd

NOTES FROM THE EDITOR

The layout of the *2025–2026 Boyd's Commentary* has been formatted for easy use in the classroom. In keeping with our rich history of publishing quality Christian literature, we include the Unifying Principle as a feature to enhance your study while using our commentary. Listed below is an explanation of each feature and the intended use of each.

Lesson Setting: Gives the basic time line and place for the events in the lesson.

Lesson Outline: Provides the topics used in the exposition of the lesson.

Unifying Principle: States the main idea for the lesson across age groups. This feature allows the teacher to understand exactly what each lesson is about.

Introduction: Gives the thesis and any background information that will be useful in the study of the lesson.

Exposition: Provides the exegetical study done by the writer, breaking down the text for discussion.

The Lesson Applied: Provides possible life applications of the biblical text for today's learners.

Let's Talk About It: Highlights ideas, thoughts, and questions from the text. Visit the R.H. Boyd website, *www.rhboyd.com*, for followup information and in-depth discussion.

Home Daily Devotional Readings: Located at the end of each lesson, the topics are designed to lead into the following lesson.

Meet Your Writers

REV. NICOLE HARRIS TOLLIVER

Rev. Tolliver is a native of Cleveland, Ohio currently residing in Nashville. A graduate of Fisk University, she earned her Master of Theological Studies degree with emphasis in Black Church Studies from Vanderbilt University Divinity School. She has previously served in full-time ministry as a youth pastor and later as pastor of assimilation at a Nashville church. Currently, she works as an operations associate for Faith Matters Network and as director of student success at American Baptist College in Nashville. She is an associate minister at Nashville's historic Jefferson Street Baptist Church.

REV. DR. EUGENE C. ENGLISH

Pastor English, a native of Cincinnati, Ohio, served twenty years as a commissioned officer in the United States Army, earning numerous awards, including a Bronze Star for combat duty during Operation Desert Shield. Pastor English leads Little Elk Missionary Baptist Church in Athens, Alabama, and holds Master of Divinity and Doctor of Ministry degrees. Dr. English has been married to his wife Kathy for forty-six years. They have reared three daughters and are the proud grandparents of four grandchildren.

REV. DR. CLAUDE ELLIS FOREHAND II

Dr. Forehand is a native of Lakewood, New Jersey who has been residing in Charlotte, N.C. for more than eighteen years. Throughout his years as a North Carolina resident, he served nine of them in the United States Marine Corps and earned a Bachelor of Science degree from Johnson C. Smith University, and Master of Divinity and Doctor of Ministry degrees from Hood Theological Seminary. He is married to Ulinda V. Forehand and serves as pastor of Buncombe Baptist Church in Lexington, North Carolina. He also is an adjunct professor for Queen City Bible College in Charlotte.

DR. ANGELA MILLER

Dr. Angela Miller earned her Doctor of Education degree in Educational Leadership. Throughout her career in higher education, Dr. Miller has served in various leadership positions at public and private universities. She is also the founder of Purpose Ministries, providing sound biblical teaching and mentorship to help others grow in their personal relationship with Christ.

REV. DR. NIKA DAVIS

Dr. Nika Davis is pastor of the Second Missionary Baptist Church in Waco, Texas where the church has implemented numerous ministries that serve the community. He holds a Doctor of Ministry degree from Houston Graduate School of Theology, a Master of Divinity degree from Southwestern Theological Seminary, Fort Worth, Texas, and a Master of Arts degree in history. For twelve years Dr. Davis was a public school educator, and during that time received the honor of Teacher of the Year at Lufkin High School. He is author of *The Beauty of the Christian Faith*. He and his wife, Beverly, are parents to three children.

2025–2026 Lesson Overview

Looking Back, Looking Forward

The 2025–2026 lessons honor the historic work of the Committee on the Uniform Series, which has been developing Sunday school lesson outlines for more than 150 years. The 2025-2026 scope and sequence is based on a series of Scripture readings selected from the 1929–1930 lessons.

FALL: *Judah, From Isaiah to the Exile*—The fall quarter invites us to discover and appreciate how God, through prophets and other leaders, gave help and guidance to the people of Judah, so that we may come to see the hand of God in our own lives and in all human affairs. The unit studies include "Isaiah and the Renewal of the Temple," "Jeremiah and the Promise of Renewal," and "Ezekiel and the Exile of Judah."

WINTER: *Enduring Beliefs of the Christian Faith*—The winter quarter highlights essential teachings of the Bible in relation to defining elements of our Christian faith. The three units of study are "Our Holy God and the Holy Scriptures," "Grace and Reconciliation," and "The Church and Its Teachings."

SPRING: *Social Teachings of the Church*—The spring quarter is an intriguing study of social issues that faithful Christians confronted in the early 1900s and gives an opportunity to consider how the church brings Christ to bear on these issues in our day and time. The three unit titles for this quarter are: "Fulfilling Our Obligations to Neighbors," "Fulfilling Our Obligations to Family and Community," and "Fulfilling Our Obligations to God and Society."

SUMMER: *The Testimony of Faithful Witnesses*—The summer quarter introduces women and men in the Bible who heard the call of God, responded in faith, and through their words and deeds, spread the Good News. The three units of study include the following titles: "Faithful Witnesses Testify to God's Promises," "Faithful Witnesses Say 'Yes' to Jesus Christ," and "Faithful Witnesses Spread the Good News."

Boyd's Commentary for the Sunday School (2025–2026)

Copyright © 2025 by R.H. Boyd

6717 Centennial Blvd., Nashville, TN 37209-1017

Scripture passages marked KJV are taken from the Holy Bible, *King James Version*, which is in the public domain.

Scriptures taken from the Holy Bible, *New International Version*. Copyright © 1984 by International Bible Society. Used by permission of Zondervan Publishing House. All rights reserved worldwide. The NIV and *New International Version* trademarks are registered in the United States Patent and Trademark Office by International Bible Society. Use of either trademark requires the permission of the International Bible Society.

Scriptures marked *NRSVue* are taken from the *New Revised Standard Version Updated Edition* of the Bible © 2021 by the Division of Christian Education of the National Council of Churches of Christ in the United States of America. Used by permission. All rights reserved.

Scripture quotations are from The *Holy Bible, English Standard Version*® (ESV®), copyright © 2001 by Crossway, a publishing ministry of Good News Publishers. Used by permission. All rights reserved.

All rights reserved. This book may not be reproduced in part or in whole in any form or by any means without prior written permission from the publisher.

Printed in the United States of America.

The publisher, R.H. Boyd Publishing Corporation, bears no responsibility or liability for any claim, demand, action, or proceeding related to its content, including but not limited to claims of plagiarism, copyright infringement, defamation, obscenity, or the violation of the rights of privacy, publicity, or any other right of any person or party, and makes no warranties regarding the content.

PREFACE

The 2025–2026 *Boyd's Commentary* has been formatted and written with you in mind. This format is to help you further your preparation and study of Sunday school lessons over the next twelve months.

We have presented parallel Scripture lesson passages using the *New Revised Standard Version Updated Edition* (NRSVue) alongside the timeless and revered *King James Version* (KJV). This allows you to have a clear and contemporary approach to the Scripture passages each week. These versions are reliable and reputable. They will bless you as you rightly divide the word of truth (2 Timothy 2:15, KJV).

The abbreviations used throughout the commentary are as follows:

    KJV — King James Version
    NIV — New International Version
    NKJV — New King James Version
    NLT — New Living Translation
    NRSVue — New Revised Standard Version Updated Edition
    RSV — Revised Standard Version
    TLB — The Living Bible
    NEB — New English Bible
    JB — Jerusalem Bible
    ESV — English Standard Version

To the Pastor: Our hope is that this commentary will provide context and insight for your sermons. Also, we hope this commentary will serve as a preparatory aid for the message of God.

To the Bible Teacher: This commentary also has you in mind. You can use it as a ready reference to the background of the text and difficult terms that are used in the Bible. Boyd's Commentary will provide your lesson study with the historical context that will enable you to interpret the text for yourself and your students more effectively.

To the Layperson: This resource is for anyone who wants to get a glimpse at the glory of God. This commentary seeks to highlight and lift the workings of God with His people and to make God's history with humanity ever present.

We hope and pray God will bless and keep you as you diligently study His mighty and majestic Word. Remain ever steadfast to our one eternal God. Keep the faith, and pray always.

CONTENTS

First Quarter 2025 (Fall)
Judah, From Isaiah to Exile

UNIT THEME: Isaiah and the Renewal of the Temple

Lesson 1	September 7—The Ministry of Isaiah (Isaiah 6:1–8; 38:1–5)	12
Lesson 2	September 14—Hezekiah Leads the People Back to God (2 Chronicles 30:1–9, 26–27)	18
Lesson 3	September 21—What Hilkiah Found in the Temple (2 Chronicles 34:15–22, 26–27)	24
Lesson 4	September 28—The Suffering Servant of the Lord (Isaiah 53:1–7)	30

UNIT THEME: Jeremiah and the Renewal of the Temple

Lesson 5	October 5—The Early Ministry of Jeremiah (Jeremiah 1:6–10; 26:8–9, 12–15)	36
Lesson 6	October 12—Jeremiah Calls the People to Obedience (Jeremiah 7:1–11, 21–23)	42
Lesson 7	October 19—The Story of the Rechabites (Jeremiah 35:5–11)	48
Lesson 8	October 26—God's Law in the Heart (Jeremiah 31:29–34; John 1:17)	54

UNIT THEME: Ezekiel and the Exile of Judah

Lesson 9	November 2—Later Experiences of Jeremiah (Jeremiah 38:7–13)	60
Lesson 10	November 9—Judah Taken Captive (2 Kings 24:18–25:9)	66
Lesson 11	November 16—The Story of Ezekiel (Ezekiel 3:10–11; 24:15–24, 27)	72
Lesson 12	November 23—Ezekiel Teaches Personal Responsibility (Ezekiel 33:7–16)	78
Lesson 13	November 30—Ezekiel's Vision of Hope (Ezekiel 47:1–9, 12)	83

CONTENTS

Second Quarter 2025–2026 (Winter)
Enduring Beliefs of the Christian Faith

UNIT THEME: Our Holy God and the Holy Scriptures

Lesson 1	December 7—The Holy Scriptures (Psalm 19:7-13; 2 Timothy 3:14-15)	89
Lesson 2	December 14—Our Heavenly Father (Matthew 6:24-34)	95
Lesson 3	December 21—Christ the Savior (Luke 15:3-7; Romans 5:6-10)	101
Lesson 4	December 28—The Holy Spirit (Romans 8:12-17, 26-27)	107

UNIT THEME: Grace and Reconciliation

Lesson 5	January 4—Sin (1 John 1:5–2:6)	113
Lesson 6	January 11—Repentance and Faith (Luke 15:11-24; Acts 2:38-39)	119
Lesson 7	January 18—Prayer (Genesis 18:25-27; Luke 18:9-14; 1 John 5:14-15)	125
Lesson 8	January 25—Christian Growth (Matthew 4:18-20; 16:16-18; John 21:15-18; 2 Peter 3:14-15, 18)	131

UNIT THEME: The Church and Its Teachings

Lesson 9	February 1—Working Together Makes Us Better (Mark 4:26-32; Ephesians 4:4-6, 11-18)	137
Lesson 10	February 8—Baptism and the Lord's Supper (Matthew 3:13-17; 28:19-20; 1 Corinthians 11:23-29)	143
Lesson 11	February 15—The Lord's Day (Exodus 20:8-11; Romans 14:4-6; Revelation 1:10)	148
Lesson 12	22—Stewardship and Mission (Acts 1:6-8; 2 Corinthians 8:3-9)	153

CONTENTS

Third Quarter 2026 (Spring)
Social Teachings of the Church

UNIT THEME: Fulfilling Our Obligations to Neighbors

Lesson 1	March 1—Recognizing Our Debt to Others (Mark 12:28-34; James 2:14-17)	159
Lesson 2	March 8—Keeping Fit for the Sake of Others (Daniel 1:8-17; 1 Timothy 4:7-8)	165
Lesson 3	March 15—Helping Neighbors in Need (Deuteronomy 15:4-11; Matthew 25:42-45)	171
Lesson 4	March 22—All Are One in Christ (Acts 10:9-15, 30-35; Galatians 3:28-29)	177
Lesson 5	March 29—World Peace through Mutual Understanding (Isaiah 2:2-4; Acts 17:26-28)	183

UNIT THEME: Fulfilling Our Obligations to Family and Community

Lesson 6	April 5—The Future Life (1 Corinthians 15:13-20, 51-58)	189
Lesson 7	April 12—Respect for Rightful Authority (Mark 12:17; Romans 13:1, 6-8; 1 Peter 2:13-17)	195
Lesson 8	April 19—The Child in a Christian World (Mark 9:36-37, 42; 10:13-16)	201
Lesson 9	April 26—The Christian Home in a Modern World (Deuteronomy 6:3-9; Matthew 19:3-9)	207

UNIT THEME: Fulfilling Our Obligations to God and Society

Lesson 10	May 3—The Higher Patriotism (Jonah 1:1-3; 3:1-5; 4:6-11)	213
Lesson 11	May 10—Useful Work as Christian Duty (Genesis 2:15; Exodus 20:9; John 5:17; 9:4; Acts 20:33-35; 2 Thessalonians 3:6-12)	219
Lesson 12	May 17—The Christian Spirit in Industry (Deuteronomy 24:14-21; Ephesians 6:5-9; 1 Timothy 6:17-19)	225
Lesson 13	May 24—The Christian View of Recreation (Mark 2:18-28)	231
Lesson 14	May 31—Fellowship through Worship (Matthew 28:18-20; Hebrews 10:22-25)	237

CONTENTS

Fourth Quarter 2026 (Summer)
The Testimony of Faithful Witnesses

UNIT THEME: Faithful Witnesses Testify to God's Promises

Lesson 1	June 7—Deborah, a Leader in a National Emergency (Judges 4:4–10, 14, 21–22)	245
Lesson 2	June 14—Hannah, a Godly Mother (1 Samuel 1:9–20, 25)	251
Lesson 3	June 21—Jonathan and David, a Noble Friendship (1 Samuel 18:1–4; 20:16–17, 32–34, 42; 2 Samuel 1:26–27; 21:7)	257
Lesson 4	June 28—Amos, a Herdsman Called of God to Be a Prophet (Amos 1:1; 2:11–12; 3:7–8; 7:10–15)	263

UNIT THEME: Faithful Witnesses Say "Yes" to Jesus

Lesson 5	July 5—The Believing Centurion, a Gentile Whose Faith Jesus Commended (Matthew 8:5–13)	269
Lesson 6	July 12—Simon Peter, from Weakness to Strength (Mark 8:27–29; Luke 22:31–34; John 18:25–27; 21:15–17)	275
Lesson 7	July 19—Zacchaeus, the Publican (Luke 19:1–10)	281
Lesson 8	July 26—Mary, the Mother of Jesus (Luke 2:15–19; John 2:1–5; 19:25–27)	287

UNIT THEME: Faithful Witnesses Spread the Good News

Lesson 9	August 2—Thomas, the Honest Doubter (John 11:14–16; 14:5–8; 20:24–29; 21:1–2)	293
Lesson 10	August 9—Stephen, an Early Interpreter of Christianity (Acts 6:7–10; 7:54–60)	299
Lesson 11	August 16—Saul of Tarsus, How a Pharisee Became a Christian (Acts 22:3–15)	304
Lesson 12	August 23—Timothy, the Influence of Home Training (2 Timothy 1:1–6; 3:14–16)	309
Lesson 13	August 30—Lydia, Judged to Be Faithful (Acts 16:11–15, 40)	314

FIRST QUARTER

September
October
November

Lesson material is based on International Sunday School Lessons and International Bible Lessons for Christian Teaching, copyrighted by the International Council of Religious Education, and is used by its permission.

Lesson I — September 7, 2025

The Ministry of Isaiah

Adult Topic: Here I Am! What Now?
Background Scripture: Isaiah 6:1–13; 7:1–7; 20:1–6; 38:1–22
Lesson Passage: Isaiah 6:1–8; 38:1–5

ISAIAH 6:1–8; 38:1–5

KJV

IN the year that king Uzziah died I saw also the Lord sitting upon a throne, high and lifted up, and his train filled the temple.
2 Above it stood the seraphims: each one had six wings; with twain he covered his face, and with twain he covered his feet, and with twain he did fly.
3 And one cried unto another, and said, Holy, holy, holy, is the Lord of hosts: the whole earth is full of his glory.
4 And the posts of the door moved at the voice of him that cried, and the house was filled with smoke.
5 Then said I, Woe is me! for I am undone; because I am a man of unclean lips, and I dwell in the midst of a people of unclean lips: for mine eyes have seen the King, the Lord of hosts.
6 Then flew one of the seraphims unto me, having a live coal in his hand, which he had taken with the tongs from off the altar:
7 And he laid it upon my mouth, and said, Lo, this hath touched thy lips; and thine iniquity is taken away, and thy sin purged.
8 Also I heard the voice of the Lord, saying, Whom shall I send, and who will go for us? Then said I, Here am I; send me.

••• 38:1–5 •••

1 In those days was Hezekiah sick unto death. And Isaiah the prophet the son of Amoz came unto him, and said unto him, Thus saith the Lord, Set thine house in order: for thou shalt die, and not live.

NRSVue

IN the year that King Uzziah died, I saw the Lord sitting on a throne, high and lofty, and the hem of his robe filled the temple.
2 Seraphs were in attendance above him; each had six wings: with two they covered their faces, and with two they covered their feet, and with two they flew.
3 And one called to another and said, "Holy, holy, holy is the Lord of hosts; the whole earth is full of his glory."
4 The pivots on the thresholds shook at the voices of those who called, and the house filled with smoke.
5 And I said, "Woe is me! I am lost, for I am a man of unclean lips, and I live among a people of unclean lips, yet my eyes have seen the King, the Lord of hosts!"
6 Then one of the seraphs flew to me, holding a live coal that had been taken from the altar with a pair of tongs.
7 The seraph touched my mouth with it and said, "Now that this has touched your lips, your guilt has departed and your sin is blotted out."
8 Then I heard the voice of the Lord saying, "Whom shall I send, and who will go for us?" And I said, "Here am I; send me!"

••• 38:1–5 •••

1 In those days Hezekiah became sick and was at the point of death. The prophet Isaiah son of Amoz came to him and said to him, "Thus says the Lord: Set your house in order, for you shall die; you shall not recover."

MAIN THOUGHT: I heard the voice of the Lord saying, "Whom shall I send, and who will go for us?" And I said, "Here am I; send me!" (Isaiah 6:8, NRSVue)

ISAIAH 6:1-8; 38:1-5

KJV	NRSVue
2 Then Hezekiah turned his face toward the wall, and prayed unto the Lord, 3 And said, Remember now, O Lord, I beseech thee, how I have walked before thee in truth and with a perfect heart, and have done that which is good in thy sight. And Hezekiah wept sore. 4 Then came the word of the Lord to Isaiah, saying, 5 Go, and say to Hezekiah, Thus saith the Lord, the God of David thy father, I have heard thy prayer, I have seen thy tears: behold, I will add unto thy days fifteen years.	2 Then Hezekiah turned his face to the wall and prayed to the Lord: 3 "Remember now, O Lord, I implore you, how I have walked before you in faithfulness with a whole heart and have done what is good in your sight." And Hezekiah wept bitterly. 4 Then the word of the Lord came to Isaiah: 5 "Go and say to Hezekiah, Thus says the Lord, the God of your ancestor David: I have heard your prayer; I have seen your tears; I will add fifteen years to your life.

LESSON SETTING
Time: 742 or 733 BC
Place: Judah

LESSON OUTLINE
I. Isaiah's Vision (Isaiah 6:1-4)
II. Isaiah's Confession and Commission (Isaiah 6:5-8)
III. Hezekiah's Illness and Divine Intervention (Isaiah 38:1-5)

UNIFYING PRINCIPLE
People experience increased anxiety when leaders do not provide clear direction, especially in challenging situations. Who is positioned to offer a moral compass to national leaders in times of crisis? At a pivotal point in Israel's history, God called Isaiah to deliver a message that led to health for King Hezekiah and political stability for Jerusalem.

INTRODUCTION

The book of Isaiah is one of the richest prophetic texts in the Hebrew Bible, offering profound theological themes about God. Specifically, Isaiah provides insights relating to God's holiness, judgment, mercy, and redemption. The prophet Isaiah—who served during the reigns of Uzziah, Jotham, Ahaz, and Hezekiah—was both a messenger to and intercessor for Judah. Isaiah 6:1-8 and 38:1-5 encapsulate critical moments in his ministry, offering unique perspectives on his call along with a demonstration of God's power and mercy.

Isaiah 6 records Isaiah's transformative vision of God's glory, culminating in his commission as a prophet. In Isaiah 38, the narrative shifts to an account of King Hezekiah's illness and miraculous healing, where Isaiah served as the intermediary between the king and God. Together, these passages highlight the interplay between divine holiness, human inadequacy, and God's grace that empowers ministry.

EXPOSITION

I. Isaiah's Vision (Isaiah 6:1–4)

Isaiah 6 begins by noting the timeframe of the prophet's vision. Judah's King Uzziah, also known as Azariah, died sometime between 742–733 BC (2 Kings 15:1–7), though the exact date is uncertain. While Uzziah's reign had been one of stability and prosperity, his death ushered in a period of uncertainty. During the subsequent reigns of Uzziah's son, Jotham, and grandson, Ahaz, the Syro-Ephraimite Alliance of Aram and the Northern Kingdom of Israel first attempted to invade Judah, prompting Assyria to assert control over the region.

Amidst the national sadness and confusion of losing one of Judah's better kings, Isaiah had a vision and was commissioned as God's prophet. Visions—through which people experienced the divine—were typically associated with priests (Moses, Samuel, Jeremiah, Ezekiel) rather than prophets like Elijah, Amos, and Habakkuk. While he was not a priest, Isaiah was a royal adviser.

Call narratives in the Hebrew Bible are generally divided into two categories. While some were dominated by God's Word, others (like Isaiah's) involved a manifestation of Almighty God.

In verse 1, Isaiah stated that he "saw the Lord." This text does not contradict others declaring that humans cannot see God (e.g. Exod. 33:20), since several biblical witnesses encountered manifestations of God (Gen. 32:30; Judg. 13:22). Even so, the Lord's majesty and glory make it impossible for humans to fully behold Him. Note that Isaiah observed God's location and what was happening around Him—not His face or any identifying features. Thus, it can be inferred that Isaiah only saw God in part.

In Isaiah's vision, the Lord was "high and lofty," seated on a royal throne. This symbolizes God's sovereignty over all creation and reinforces His supreme authority. Especially during a time of political uncertainty, this description would reaffirm for Isaiah's audience that God should be exalted as the sovereign king and that humanity should humble itself before Him. The enormous "hem" or train of God's royal robe affirms His majesty and power.

Surrounding God's throne, Isaiah saw seraphim, angelic beings with six wings (v. 2). Two wings covered their faces, signifying reverence. Two wings covered their feet, possibly indicating humility and modesty. They used the final two wings for flight, symbolizing their readiness to serve God. Their name—derived from the Hebrew word *saraph,* which means "burning ones"—suggests a fiery nature. This reflects not only their zeal for God but also their role in purifying those who stand before Him. Their presence underscores the intensity of divine holiness and the necessity of purification before entering God's service.

The seraphim called to one another: "Holy, holy, holy is the LORD of hosts; the whole earth is full of his glory" (v. 3). The triple repetition of "holy" emphasizes God's absolute purity, supreme righteousness, uniqueness, and transcendence. At their words, the Temple filled with smoke and its foundations shook. This imagery, recalling God's presence at Mount Sinai (Exod. 19:18), signifies divine majesty and judgment.

II. Isaiah's Confession and Commission (Isaiah 6:5–8)

Overwhelmed by the vision, Isaiah cried out: "Woe is me! I am lost" (v. 5). This lament acknowledged his own unworthiness in God's presence. Isaiah then reflected on his condition, confessing that he had "unclean lips." With this powerful metaphor, Isaiah not only acknowledged his individual failings but also associated with the sinfulness of his society. His words convey deep despair, which was typical of prophetic figures who were acutely aware that judgment was coming on their community. By confessing his and his people's impurity, Isaiah underscored a critical and collective need for divine cleansing and redemption.

In response to Isaiah's confession, a seraph took a burning coal from the altar and touched it to Isaiah's lips (v. 6). The altar was a place of atonement, where sacrifices were offered to cleanse humans from sin and reconcile them with the Lord. The burning coal symbolized divine purification. By touching it to Isaiah's lips, through which he would proclaim God's Word, the action both cleansed and empowered him for his prophetic mission. This event emphasizes a biblical theme that God does not call those who are qualified or deemed worthy by human standards; instead, He qualifies those whom He calls, equipping them with the grace they need to fulfill their mission.

In verse 7, the seraph declared that Isaiah's guilt was removed, and his sin was "blotted out." Afterward, he was completely reconciled with God; any barriers that may have hindered his mission were removed. Thus, Isaiah was worthy to stand in God's presence and ready to serve as His messenger.

Isaiah's profound experience with God is similar to the transformative encounters of other biblical figures. For instance, Moses was called to lead the Israelites after encountering God in the burning bush (Exod. 3); Jeremiah received his prophetic commission amidst divine assurance (Jer. 1); and Paul experienced a radical transformation after encountering the risen Christ (Acts 9). Each of these occurrences highlights the transforming power of God's grace, preparing ordinary individuals for extraordinary purposes in His service.

Following his purification, Isaiah heard God ask, "Whom shall I send, and who will go for us?" (v. 8) The plural "us" in this question could refer to the divine council—a heavenly assembly of beings who stand before God—suggesting a communal aspect of divine decision-making. Alternatively, as some Christian theologians propose, this might be an early indication of the Holy Trinity: God the Father, Jesus Christ the Son, and the Holy Spirit.

God's call was not directed only to Isaiah; it is a general invitation to anyone who is willing to engage in service. This reflects a biblical principle that God desires human cooperation in His divine plan.

Emboldened by his purification, Isaiah answered enthusiastically: "Here am I; send me!" (v. 8) His reply exhibits the ideal attitude of God's servant: available, willing, and obedient to God's directives.

In stark contrast to others, such as Moses (Exod. 3:11) or Jeremiah (Jer. 1:6), who initially resisted their divine assignment with doubts and excuses, Isaiah's immediate acceptance highlights his unique character. He demonstrated an unwavering faith in the Lord and surrender to God's will, without hesitation or self-doubt.

Isaiah's willingness to heed God's call offers an enduring reminder of the importance of readiness and commitment in the service of God. His attitude provides a powerful example for those who are called to ministry, inspiring them to embrace their calling with confidence and enthusiasm. Those who exhibit this characteristic also encourage future generations to respond eagerly to God's call.

III. Hezekiah's Illness and Divine Intervention (Isaiah 38:1-5)

Isaiah 38:1-5 presents a remarkable account of divine mercy and the power of prayer. The chapter begins with Isaiah's solemn declaration about King Hezekiah's impending death. "Set your house in order" (v. 1) implies that Hezekiah should make necessary arrangements for his kingdom and personal affairs. In biblical times, a king's untimely death without a successor could result in political upheaval and national instability. This moment likely tested Hezekiah's trust in God's sovereignty.

Instead of responding in despair, however, Hezekiah answered with a fervent prayer. Turning his "face to the wall" (v. 2) signified the king's intense focus on God and the desperation of his plea. By removing all external distractions, Hezekiah demonstrated the earnestness of his supplication.

As he prayed, Hezekiah recounted his past faithfulness to God. Rather than a claim to sinlessness, the king's words reflected his sincere devotion to God's Law. The phrase "with a whole heart" (v. 3) signifies integrity and commitment. The king's tears showed his profound sorrow and desire for mercy. This appeal illustrates the biblical principle that righteousness and obedience to God invite His favor (cf. Deut. 28:1-14). While salvation comes only by grace, living righteously brings God's blessings (Ps. 1:1-3).

Hezekiah's prayer of faith recognized that only divine intervention could alter his fate. His response encourages believers to persist in prayer even in dire circumstances.

Remarkably, before Isaiah even left the palace, God spoke to the prophet. The Lord acknowledged that He had heard Hezekiah's prayer and would add fifteen years to the king's life. This immediate response highlights God's attentiveness to sincere prayer and demonstrates that He is deeply involved in the lives of His people.

This passage presents a balance between God's justice and His mercy. While Isaiah's prophetic warning was firm, it was not an unchangeable decree. Hezekiah's plea shows that heartfelt prayers can prompt God to respond, reinforcing the biblical theme of divine responsiveness to faith (James 5:16).

The mention of "the God of your ancestor David" (v. 5) would have reminded Hezekiah of the Lord's covenant faithfulness. The God of the covenant abounds in "steadfast love and faithfulness" (Exod. 34:6; Ps. 86:15). He desires to provide hope and restoration for His people.

Isaiah 38:1-5 stands as a powerful example of God's authority over human affairs, the efficacy of prayer, and divine mercy. Hezekiah's response to his impending death—turning to God in sincere supplication—provides a model of faith in action. This passage reassures believers that God hears prayers, sees tears, and can alter circumstances according to His will. Furthermore, this story affirms God's sovereignty over life and death, while emphasizing the importance of living a righteous life that is devoted to Him. These verses offer encouragement for contemporary faith, reminding believers that God is compassionate, responsive, and ever-present in times of need. Just as He extended Hezekiah's life, He continues to work in the lives of those who earnestly seek Him.

THE LESSON APPLIED

Isaiah 6:1-8 and 38:1-5 both offer powerful lessons related to personal growth, leadership, and faith. In Isaiah 6:1-8, the prophet Isaiah had a vision of God's holiness. Because of this overwhelming vision, he became keenly aware of his own unworthiness. However, God purified him and commissioned him to speak the Lord's message. This passage underscores the importance of recognizing one's own limitations while highlighting the transformative power of God's grace. It also challenges individuals to acknowledge their faults and surrender to God's purpose, trusting that God will equip them to fulfill His calling despite their shortcomings.

Similarly, in Isaiah 38:1–5, King Hezekiah faced a life-threatening illness and turned to God in prayer, pleading for mercy. God heard his plea and extended Hezekiah's life. This passage emphasizes the importance of relying on God during a crisis and the power of prayer in seeking divine intervention. It also teaches the value of repentance and humility, as Hezekiah acknowledged his dependence on God for healing.

Together, these passages remind individuals of the necessity of humility, faith, and a willingness to accept God's will. They encourage a deep reliance on God, trusting that He will guide, purify, and provide—whether during challenges or opportunities—helping individuals to grow into the people and leaders they are meant to be.

LET'S TALK ABOUT IT...

Discuss the following questions and visit www.rhboyd.com for more information.

How can recognizing our own limitations, similar to Isaiah in Isaiah 6:1–8, aid our spiritual growth and enable us to embrace God's calling in our lives despite the flaws we may have?

In Isaiah 38:1–5, King Hezekiah went to God in prayer during a life-threatening crisis. How can we cultivate a habit of turning to God in prayer, particularly in challenging times, and trust in His ability to intervene?

Both passages emphasize the themes of repentance, humility, and divine mercy. How might these themes shape the way we lead and serve others, especially when we have positions of responsibility?

Get Social

Share your views and tag us
@rhboydco and use #rhboydco

@rhboydco

Home Daily Devotional Readings
September –14, 2025

Monday	Tuesday	Wednesday	Thursday	Friday	Saturday	Sunday
An Everlasting Kingdom	A Call to Bear Good Fruit	A Summons to Repent	A Ministry of Care and Comfort	A Feast of Remembrance	A Dwelling for God's Name	An Act of Repentance and Renewal
Psalm 145:13–21	Matthew 3:4–12	Acts 3:12–20	James 5:12–18	Exodus 12:3–14	Deuteronomy 12:5–12	2 Chronicles 30:1–9, 26–27

Lesson II September 14, 2025

Hezekiah Leads the People Back to God

Adult Topic: Celebrating the Past
Background Scripture: 2 Chronicles 30:1–27
Lesson Passage: 2 Chronicles 30:1–9, 26–27

2 CHRONICLES 30:1-9, 26-27

KJV

AND Hezekiah sent to all Israel and Judah, and wrote letters also to Ephraim and Manasseh, that they should come to the house of the Lord at Jerusalem, to keep the passover unto the Lord God of Israel.

2 For the king had taken counsel, and his princes, and all the congregation in Jerusalem, to keep the passover in the second month.

3 For they could not keep it at that time, because the priests had not sanctified themselves sufficiently, neither had the people gathered themselves together to Jerusalem.

4 And the thing pleased the king and all the congregation.

5 So they established a decree to make proclamation throughout all Israel, from Beersheba even to Dan, that they should come to keep the passover unto the Lord God of Israel at Jerusalem: for they had not done it of a long time in such sort as it was written.

6 So the posts went with the letters from the king and his princes throughout all Israel and Judah, and according to the commandment of the king, saying, Ye children of Israel, turn again unto the Lord God of Abraham, Isaac, and Israel, and he will return to the remnant of you, that are escaped out of the hand of the kings of Assyria.

7 And be not ye like your fathers, and like your brethren, which trespassed against the Lord God of their fathers, who therefore gave them up to desolation, as ye see.

8 Now be ye not stiffnecked, as your fathers

NRSVue

HEZEKIAH sent word to all Israel and Judah and wrote letters also to Ephraim and Manasseh, that they should come to the house of the Lord at Jerusalem, to keep the Passover to the Lord the God of Israel.

2 For the king and his officials and all the assembly in Jerusalem had taken counsel to keep the Passover in the second month

3 (for they could not keep it at its proper time because the priests had not sanctified themselves in sufficient number, nor had the people assembled in Jerusalem).

4 The plan seemed right to the king and all the assembly.

5 So they decreed to make a proclamation throughout all Israel, from Beer-sheba to Dan, that the people should come and keep the Passover to the Lord the God of Israel, at Jerusalem, for they had not kept it in great numbers as prescribed.

6 So couriers went throughout all Israel and Judah with letters from the king and his officials, as the king had commanded, saying, "O people of Israel, return to the Lord, the God of Abraham, Isaac, and Israel, so that he may turn again to the remnant of you who have escaped from the hand of the kings of Assyria.

7 Do not be like your ancestors and your kindred, who were faithless to the Lord God of their ancestors, so that he made them a desolation, as you see.

8 Do not now be stiff-necked as your ancestors

MAIN THOUGHT: There was great joy in Jerusalem, for since the time of Solomon, son of King David of Israel, there had been nothing like this in Jerusalem. (2 Chronicles 30:26, NRSVue)

2 CHRONICLES 30:1-9, 26-27

KJV

were, but yield yourselves unto the Lord, and enter into his sanctuary, which he hath sanctified for ever: and serve the Lord your God, that the fierceness of his wrath may turn away from you.

9 For if ye turn again unto the Lord, your brethren and your children shall find compassion before them that lead them captive, so that they shall come again into this land: for the Lord your God is gracious and merciful, and will not turn away his face from you, if ye return unto him.

••• 26-27 •••

26 So there was great joy in Jerusalem: for since the time of Solomon the son of David king of Israel there was not the like in Jerusalem.

27 Then the priests the Levites arose and blessed the people: and their voice was heard, and their prayer came up to his holy dwelling place, even unto heaven.

NRSVue

were, but yield yourselves to the Lord and come to his sanctuary, which he has sanctified forever, and serve the Lord your God, so that his fierce anger may turn away from you.

9 For as you return to the Lord, your kindred and your children will find compassion with their captors and return to this land. For the Lord your God is gracious and merciful and will not turn away his face from you, if you return to him."

••• 26-27 •••

26 There was great joy in Jerusalem, for since the time of Solomon son of King David of Israel there had been nothing like this in Jerusalem.

27 Then the priests and the Levites stood up and blessed the people, and their voice was heard; their prayer came to his holy dwelling in heaven.

LESSON SETTING

Time: Hezekiah's reign (around 715 BC)
Place: Jerusalem
Setting: The events recorded in 2 Chronicles Chapter 30 take place in Jerusalem, the capital of the Kingdom of Judah, during the reign of King Hezekiah, the thirteenth king of Judah. His reign is dated to approximately 715-686 BC, following the death of his father Ahaz, an idolatrous king. Hezekiah's reign marked a significant religious reform as he sought to restore the worship of Yahweh, which had been severely neglected under his father's rule.

LESSON OUTLINE

I. Invitation to Celebrate the Passover (2 Chronicles 30:1-9)
II. The Extension of Passover Festival (2 Chronicles 30:26-27)

UNIFYING PRINCIPLE

In times of crisis, people desire national leadership that provides the most effective means for restoring the health and wholeness of society. What methods of leadership promote national stability? Hezekiah restored the nation's stability by leading their return to the Lord through worship and reinstituting the Passover celebration.

INTRODUCTION

Judah's King Hezekiah was notable among the Israelite kings. He succeeded his father, Ahaz, a wicked king who promoted foreign deities and neglected appropriate worship practices. These led to the desecration of the Temple in Jerusalem and continued idolatry among the people of Judah.

Nevertheless, King Hezekiah recognized the need for renewal and worked to rectify Judah's spiritual decline. Second Kings 18:1-4 highlights how he dismantled the pagan worship places that promoted and supported idolatry in Judah. Second Chronicles 29 elaborates on his efforts to cleanse the Temple, reinstate the Levitical priesthood, and restore proper worship of Yahweh, the one true God. His actions sought to renew the covenantal relationship between God and His chosen people.

With an unwavering commitment to the Lord, Hezekiah sought to lead the nation back to spiritual vitality and divine favor, ensuring that the legacy of their faith would be conveyed to future generations.

EXPOSITION

I. Invitation to Celebrate the Passover (2 Chronicles 30:1-9)

Passover was one of the three principal pilgrimage festivals of ancient Israel, alongside Pentecost (The Festival of Weeks) and Tabernacles (The Festival of Booths). The annual Passover festival commemorated the time when God liberated the Israelites from servitude in Egypt—the commencement of their exodus (Exod. 12:1-13). Known in Hebrew as *Pesach*, which means "to pass over," the festival recalls the night in Egypt when the Lord passed over the houses of the Israelites on which they had painted the doorposts and lintels with the blood of a lamb. Yet for the Egyptians whose doorposts had no blood applied, the Lord killed all of the firstborn as judgment on that nation.

Passover was to be a perpetual reminder for the Israelites (Exod. 12:14-27, 43-49) that God—and only He—was their protector, liberator, sustainer, and guide. As part of the religious calendar, Passover celebrated the Lord's mighty act of salvation. In addition, it sought to unify the people of Israel as they shared a meal that recalled the foundational narrative of their nation and served as a collective expression of their faith and gratitude.

By the time that Hezekiah became king of Judah, the Passover observance had significantly declined. With Israel's division following King Solomon's death, the northern tribes stopped celebrating Passover. As verse 5 emphasizes, all the tribes together "had not kept it [Passover] in great numbers as prescribed." The disunity between the Northern and Southern Kingdoms, along with the theological drift toward idolatry in both regions, contributed to the neglect of this important religious observance.

After restoring the Temple, King Hezekiah extended a heartfelt call for "all Israel and Judah" to join in the Passover celebration "at Jerusalem" (v. 1). Couriers were sent "from Beer-sheba to Dan"—all of Israel from the extreme south to the far north (Judg. 20:1)—to communicate the king's proclamation. The festival would occur a month after the date that God had decreed, primarily since not enough priests had "sanctified themselves" (v. 3). Even so, this later observance was in accordance with the Law (Num. 9:10-11).

Hezekiah intended this Passover observance to be a significant step toward restoring proper worship of the one true God as well as initiating a possible reunification between the northern and southern tribes.

The Northern Kingdom (Israel), having fallen to the Assyrian invasion in 721 BC, was in a state of disarray and devastation. Many of the Israelites had been displaced from their ancestral lands, while those who remained had intermingled with the cultures of people whom Assyria brought in from other countries to repopulate the region. This cultural and religious fusion threatened the identity and faith of the Israelite "remnant" (v. 5) who were still living in the land.

Despite these challenges, Hezekiah's appeal was infused with hope. It was a genuine plea for unity and restoration of the people's covenantal relationship with Yahweh, the God of Israel.

The king's invitation included a call for self-examination and repentance. This was Hezekiah's primary message. He urged the people to "return to the LORD" (v. 6)—to their spiritual roots—and renew their commitment to the God who had previously guided their ancestors. Hezekiah challenged them not to be "faithless" (v. 7) or "stiff-necked" (v. 8) as their predecessors had been. As a result of their disobedience, God poured out His "fierce anger" (v. 8) on His people and "made them a desolation" (v. 7). While Hezekiah's words certainly applied to the northern tribes, they were applicable to people from the southern tribes, who had also suffered because of their ancestors' sins.

Hezekiah then reminded the people of God's promises of restoration for those whom He has disciplined. This restoration is noted in passages like Leviticus 26:40–42 and 2 Chronicles 7:13–14. As Hezekiah emphasized in his letters, the Lord will be "gracious and merciful" (v. 9) to His disobedient people who humble themselves, repent, and return to Him (Exod. 34:6–7).

The response from the northern tribes, however, was limited and lackluster. Verses 10–22 indicate that only a few individuals responded positively to Hezekiah's appeal and traveled to Jerusalem for Passover. Despite this disappointment, the small number who returned to Jerusalem signified the beginning of a slow and arduous process of spiritual restoration and reunification for the tribes of Israel. This endeavor, while hopeful, was not fully realized during the reign of Hezekiah.

II. The Extension of the Passover Festival (2 Chronicles 30:26–27)

Though Hezekiah and other leaders encountered setbacks during the early stages of their planning, the seven-day Passover celebration (which included the "Festival of Unleavened Bread," 2 Chron. 30:13) was successful. God's people from both the northern and southern tribes, along with non-Israelites who lived among them and also worshiped Yahweh, observed the festival with remarkable enthusiasm. A spirit of generosity resonated deeply among everyone who participated in the extraordinary event, which had not occurred among all Israel in over two centuries.

Second Chronicles 30:23–27 provides a vivid account of how the people, overwhelmed by the profound "joy" and sanctity of this occasion, came together to express their heartfelt desire for the festivities to be extended for another week. This enthusiastic request not only bolstered their sense of community but also highlighted the significance of the event.

Verse 26 emphasizes that "since the time of Solomon son of King David of Israel there had been nothing like this in

Jerusalem." The people's request to prolong the Passover festivities beautifully echoes the occasion when King Solomon brought all Israel together to dedicate the Temple (as detailed in 1 Kings 8:1-66 and 2 Chron. 7:1-10). In that earlier consecration ceremony, a similar spirit of celebration permeated Jerusalem. The connection between these two significant events stresses a profound appreciation for the spiritual importance of the Passover and its role in the life of the community.

Hezekiah, along with the priests and Levites, recognized the depth of this moment and responded to the people's joy and enthusiasm with liberal generosity. Together, the leaders ensured that all participants not only engaged in the spiritual experience but also had the fellowship offerings that they needed to offer appropriate sacrifices to the Lord.

At the end of the event, the spiritual leaders "blessed the people" (v. 27) in accordance with Moses' instruction about the priestly blessing in Numbers 6:22-27. As a result, the writer states that "their voice was heard" (v. 27)—God heard their prayer in His heavenly dwelling. Implied in this response is that the Lord indeed blessed His people, just as the priests had requested. Their petition recalls King Solomon's prayer during the Temple dedication—he asked the Lord to hear and respond (2 Chron. 6:19-40), and the Lord affirmed that He heard the king's prayer (2 Chron. 7:12).

The extension of the Passover festival emphasized the people's renewed faith and desire to worship God. Furthermore, it highlighted the leadership's commitment to nurturing a vibrant, unified spiritual community that was centered on their covenant relationship with God.

Following that extended Passover, the people demonstrated their renewed dedication to the Lord. Second Chronicles 31:1 records how they eradicated the idols and pagan altars in Judah and Benjamin (the Southern Kingdom) as well as in parts of the former Northern Kingdom. This significant act solidified their commitment to worship God alone.

Hezekiah's actions in revitalizing the Temple and restoring one of Israel's primary festivals serve as a model of spiritual leadership. Though he did not fully reunite all of Israel, he successfully inspired many from both the southern and northern tribes to renew their commitment to the Lord as His covenant people.

God's original ordinance (Exod. 12:14) related to the annual Passover observance highlights the importance of communal worship that focuses on God's work and His Word. The restoration of this pilgrimage festival (Deut. 16:5-8) during King Hezekiah's reign emphasizes the need for constant renewal in the life of God's people. Both of these ancient events challenge contemporary faith communities to remember God's past acts of mercy and grace, return to their roots in God's covenant, embrace unity, and prioritize the importance of shared worship.

THE LESSON APPLIED

Hezekiah's Passover reform reveals several important principles for God's people in every time period. First, the passage calls for individuals to prioritize the worship of God, recognizing it as fundamental and essential for their spiritual lives. Worship, in its many forms, serves as a bridge to a deeper understanding of and connection with the Lord. Genuine worship often prompts God's people to recommit themselves to their covenant Lord. In addition, worship strengthens the bonds within a faith community.

Likewise, the biblical text emphasizes the importance of unity within God's family, highlighting the necessity of coming together as a collective, regardless of individual backgrounds or differences. Unity is crucial—especially within a church—as it fosters an environment where love and understanding can flourish. Furthermore, the passage highlights the blessings that God pours out on His people when they worship and obey Him.

Hezekiah's life reminds us of the importance of examining our relationship with God. His actions challenge us to pursue reconciliation—with God and with others. This will foster a community that glorifies God and works together to advance His Kingdom.

Finally, Hezekiah's example encourages us to create communities where all can participate freely, share in the joy of worship, and live out their faith in practical ways. In so doing, we can build a community that reflects the love and unity that Hezekiah championed, paving the way for a more profound spiritual transformation in our lives and in the lives of those around us.

LET'S TALK ABOUT IT...

Discuss the following questions and visit www.rhboyd.com for more information.

In what areas of your life do you feel a need for spiritual renewal? How could you restore those areas by prioritizing the worship of God?

How can you contribute to unity and reconciliation in your community, church, or family, especially in times of division or conflict?

What steps can you take to embrace repentance in your daily life? How can you encourage others to do the same in their spiritual journey?

In what ways can you practice generosity and support others—particularly in times of need or celebration—to strengthen a sense of community and shared joy?

Get Social

Share your views and tag us
@rhboydco and use #rhboydco

@rhboydco

Home Daily Devotional Readings
September 15–21, 2025

Monday	Tuesday	Wednesday	Thursday	Friday	Saturday	Sunday
The Command to Love	Keep God's Laws and Do Good	Promised Restoration	Choose Life	A Greater Message	Hidden Treasure	Sorrow Leads to Joy
Matthew 22:36–40	Romans 2:9–16	Deuteronomy 30:1–10	Deuteronomy 30:11–21	Hebrews 1:13–2:4	Matthew 13:44–52	2 Chronicles 34:15–22, 26–27

Lesson III   **September 21, 2025**

What Hilkiah Found in the Temple

Adult Topic: Finders Keepers!
Background Scripture: 2 Chronicles 33:1–33
Lesson Passage: 2 Chronicles 34:15–22, 26–27

2 CHRONICLES 34:15-22, 26-27

KJV

AND Hilkiah answered and said to Shaphan the scribe, I have found the book of the law in the house of the Lord. And Hilkiah delivered the book to Shaphan.

16 And Shaphan carried the book to the king, and brought the king word back again, saying, All that was committed to thy servants, they do it.

17 And they have gathered together the money that was found in the house of the Lord, and have delivered it into the hand of the overseers, and to the hand of the workmen.

18 Then Shaphan the scribe told the king, saying, Hilkiah the priest hath given me a book. And Shaphan read it before the king.

19 And it came to pass, when the king had heard the words of the law, that he rent his clothes.

20 And the king commanded Hilkiah, and Ahikam the son of Shaphan, and Abdon the son of Micah, and Shaphan the scribe, and Asaiah a servant of the king's, saying,

21 Go, enquire of the Lord for me, and for them that are left in Israel and in Judah, concerning the words of the book that is found: for great is the wrath of the Lord that is poured out upon us, because our fathers have not kept the word of the Lord, to do after all that is written in this book.

22 And Hilkiah, and they that the king had appointed, went to Huldah the prophetess, the wife of Shallum the son of Tikvath, the son of Hasrah, keeper of the wardrobe; (now she dwelt

NRSVue

HILKIAH said to the secretary Shaphan, "I have found the book of the law in the house of the Lord," and Hilkiah gave the book to Shaphan.

16 Shaphan brought the book to the king and further reported to the king, "All that was committed to your servants they are doing.

17 They have emptied out the silver that was found in the house of the Lord and have delivered it into the hand of the overseers and the workers."

18 The secretary Shaphan informed the king, "The priest Hilkiah has given me a book." Shaphan then read it aloud to the king.

19 When the king heard the words of the law, he tore his clothes.

20 Then the king commanded Hilkiah, Ahikam son of Shaphan, Abdon son of Micah, the secretary Shaphan, and the king's servant Asaiah,

21 "Go, inquire of the Lord for me and for those who are left in Israel and in Judah, concerning the words of the book that has been found, for the wrath of the Lord that is poured out on us is great, because our ancestors did not keep the word of the Lord, to act in accordance with all that is written in this book."

22 So Hilkiah and those whom the king had sent went to the prophet Huldah, the wife of Shallum son of Tokhath son of Hasrah, keeper of the wardrobe (who lived in Jerusalem in the Second

MAIN THOUGHT: Hilkiah said to the secretary Shaphan, "I have found the book of the law in the house of the LORD," and Hilkiah gave the book to Shaphan.
(2 Chronicles 34:15, NRSVue)

2 CHRONICLES 34:15-22, 26-27

KJV
in Jerusalem in the college:) and they spake to her to that effect.

••• 26-27 •••

26 And as for the king of Judah, who sent you to enquire of the Lord, so shall ye say unto him, Thus saith the Lord God of Israel concerning the words which thou hast heard;

27 Because thine heart was tender, and thou didst humble thyself before God, when thou heardest his words against this place, and against the inhabitants thereof, and humbledst thyself before me, and didst rend thy clothes, and weep before me; I have even heard thee also, saith the Lord.

NRSVue
Quarter) and spoke to her to that effect.

••• 26-27 •••

26 But as to the king of Judah, who sent you to inquire of the Lord, thus shall you say to him: Thus says the Lord, the God of Israel: 'Regarding the words that you have heard,

27 because your heart was penitent and you humbled yourself before God when you heard his words against this place and its inhabitants, and you have humbled yourself before me and have torn your clothes and wept before me, I also have heard you, says the Lord.

LESSON SETTING
Time: 622 BC
Place: Jerusalem
Setting: The setting is Jerusalem, the capital of Judah, with the initial events occurring in the temple of the Lord, which was undergoing restoration at the time. The temple had fallen into disrepair and neglect due to the idolatrous practices of Josiah's grandfather (King Manasseh) and father (King Amon). During King Josiah's reign, he initiated a national religious reform, which included restoring the temple and purging the land of idolatry.

LESSON OUTLINE
I. Discovering the Book of the Law (2 Chronicles 34:15-18)
II. Josiah's Conviction and Confession (2 Chronicles 34:19-22)
III. Huldah's Prophetic Pronouncement (2 Chronicles 34:26-27)

UNIFYING PRINCIPLE
People lose a sense of meaning and purpose if they neglect practices or traditions that have helped establish their identity. What triggers a return to meaningful practices or traditions? When Hilkiah found the book of the Law, it opened the path to a restoration of Israel's proper worship practices.

INTRODUCTION
King Josiah's reign, as recounted in 2 Chronicles 34–35, offers a profound account of religious reform, divine covenant renewal, and prophetic fulfillment. As the last good king of Judah, Josiah is remembered for his intense zeal for the Lord. His rule followed a time of significant spiritual decline in Judah under the leadership of his two predecessors—King Manasseh and King Amon (Josiah's grandfather and father, respectively). Manasseh was notori-

ous for his apostasy, which included placing altars to foreign gods in the Temple. Amon continued his father's ways and furthered the nation's spiritual decay.

Josiah ascended the throne at age eight, following his father's assassination. When he was sixteen years old, Josiah began to seek the Lord. Four years later, he set out to eradicate the idolatry that was rampant in both Judah and parts of the former Northern Kingdom of Israel.

By purging the land of idolatry, restoring the temple, and emphasizing the proper observance of the Law, Josiah set an exemplary model of faithfulness to God. Josiah's life highlights the enduring impact of leadership that is rooted in spiritual conviction, and demonstrates how even a young leader can effect transformation when guided by faith in and a commitment to the Lord.

EXPOSITION

I. Discovering the Book of the Law (2 Chronicles 34:15–18)

A turning point in the spiritual life of the nation of Judah occurred in the "eighteenth year" of Josiah's reign (2 Kings 22:3). The pivotal moment came when the high priest Hilkiah found "the book of the law of the LORD given through Moses" in the Temple (2 Chron. 34:14). Biblical scholars once proposed that this was the book of Deuteronomy. However, more recent scholarship suggests that it could refer to the entire Pentateuch, since the description in verse 14 is similar to Persian-era descriptions of the five books of Moses.

The high priest evidently read and recognized the book. He took it to Shaphan, the king's "secretary" or scribe, who may have supervised the Temple restoration.

The secretary then went to King Josiah and briefly updated him on the repairs to "the house of the LORD" (v. 17). Almost as an afterthought, Shaphan added that Hilkiah had found "a book" during the renovation. Shaphan had already read the book (2 Kings 22:8), and thus he "read it aloud to the king" (v. 18). Perhaps Shaphan read only selected portions of the book, which could have included the blessings and curses noted in Leviticus chapter 26 or Deuteronomy chapter 28.

For generations, the people in Judah had lived without the Lord's guidance. God had given them the Law to govern their lives as His covenant people. Likewise, the Lord has given us "all Scripture" (2 Tim. 3:16–17) to guide our thinking and acting as His people living under the New Covenant. Yet, whenever God's people neglect His Word, the ultimate result will be ruined lives and a crumbling society.

II. Josiah's Conviction and Confession (2 Chronicles 34:19–22)

Upon hearing the words that Shaphan read, the king immediately "tore his clothes" (v. 19). This was a traditional expression of mourning, grief, distress, and repentance. Josiah was convicted as he recognized his nation's spiritual and moral failures—they had forsaken the Lord and His covenant with them. The insightful king realized that "the wrath of the LORD" was already being "poured out" (v. 21) on him, the remnant of Israel, and the people of Judah. Because their "ancestors did not keep the word of the LORD," Josiah may have expected that he and the rest of God's people would suffer consequences as a result of their predecessors' disobedience (Exod. 20:5).

Therefore, Josiah sent messengers to find someone who could "inquire of the LORD" (v. 21) about what he had heard in God's Law. Perhaps the king needed an explanation for something he heard that he did not understand. Or, he may have understood it completely, thus he sought a word from the Lord about what, if anything, could be done about the impending crisis.

The king's desire to know God's will, particularly after the discovery of the book of the Law, highlights his genuine concern for his nation and his commitment to restoring the covenant between God and His people.

Verse 22 explains that the delegation went to the prophet Huldah. Unlike other prophets who ministered at that time in Judah (including Jeremiah and Zephaniah), little is known about Huldah. She is only mentioned here and in the companion account of this event preserved in 2 Kings chapter 22. The biblical text explains that Huldah's husband, Shallum, had responsibility for the "wardrobe" (the priestly or Levitical garments) at the temple. While she lived in Jerusalem, the location of the "Second Quarter" is otherwise unknown. Mentioned also in Zephaniah 1:10, this area may have been part of an earlier extension on the northern or western side of Jerusalem.

The events noted in 2 Chronicles 34:19–22 emphasize several important principles. One is that a leader's life can have a profound influence on the spiritual direction of his or her people. Josiah's response to the discovery of the law and to God's impending judgment was not only a personal matter but also a national one. As king, Josiah's repentance served as a model for the people of Judah, and his spiritual leadership set the tone for the entire nation's potential renewal. Josiah's personal humility and sorrow over Judah's sin were transformative.

This passage also highlights the importance of divine guidance—through God's Word and His Spirit—for God's people and their community. It encourages believers to consider what they know of God's Word, reflect on their obedience to Him, and respond in confession and repentance whenever they become aware of disobedience and unfaithfulness to the Lord.

III. Huldah's Prophetic Pronouncement (2 Chronicles 34:26–27)

In speaking to the emissaries, three times Huldah reiterated the common prophetic declaration: "Thus says the LORD" (vv. 23–24, 26). Huldah spoke for God, and the Lord's message was for the king—the one who sent the envoys to seek God's word.

Unlike other kings who ignored divine guidance, Josiah sought God's will for his life and his nation. This was rare among Judah's kings, many of whom championed the idolatry and moral decay of the nation.

Huldah's response emphasizes the importance of the prophetic voice throughout the Old Testament. Especially in times of crisis—when the people had forsaken their covenant responsibilities to Yahweh, "the God of Israel"—the prophet was a vehicle for divine intervention.

God's word through Huldah (vv. 24–25) first confirmed the coming "disaster," noting "all the curses that are written in the book" that Shaphan read to King Josiah. Because God's covenant people had forsaken Him, they would experience His unquenchable wrath that was going to be poured out on Jerusalem and Judah.

Verse 27 records the focus of God's response to Josiah. First, the Lord commended Josiah's attitude: his "heart was penitent." The Hebrew word translated "penitent" means "tender" or "soft." Unlike previous kings who hardened their hearts toward God, Josiah's heart was receptive to the Lord's message.

The phrase "you humbled yourself before God" further describes Josiah's attitude. Humility, in the biblical sense, is not self-deprecation. Rather, it reflects an acknowledgment of dependence on God and a willingness to submit to His will.

Josiah's initial response to what he heard in the book of the Law was one of brokenness and conviction. The imagery of him tearing his clothes and weeping in God's presence underscores the depth of Josiah's grief over Judah's sin and judgment. These were not merely performative gestures; because God truly knows what is in a person's heart (1 Sam. 16:7), the Lord acknowledged that Josiah's response was a genuine act of contrition. Josiah truly desired to align himself and the nation with God's will, and sought to restore their covenant relationship with their Lord.

In response to Josiah's humble and contrite heart, God promised a reprieve for the king and the nation. The declaration, "I also have heard you, says the LORD" (v. 27), signifies that God accepted Josiah's repentance. This moment of divine favor on one man contrasts sharply with the judgment that God pronounced against the nation. Because of Josiah's repentance and faith, he would completely escape the calamity that was coming on Judah—it would not occur during his lifetime.

In addition, Josiah's repentance brought a temporary reprieve of God's judgment on the nation. Throughout Scripture, God often responds to sincere repentance with mercy and forgiveness. One prominent example is Nineveh's repentance following Jonah's preaching; in mercy, the Lord averted the calamity that He had planned for that wicked nation (Jon. 3:3–10).

While believers should never presume on God's mercy, they should likewise never be surprised by it. Mercy is one of the Lord's primary attributes. David declared that God's mercy is "great" (2 Sam. 24:14; 1 Chron. 21:13). David also emphasized that the Lord "crowns you with steadfast love and mercy" (Ps. 103:4).

In addition to highlighting God's mercy, 2 Chronicles 34:26–27 underscores the profound positive impact that a godly, humble leader can have on a nation.

THE LESSON APPLIED

Second Chronicles 34:15–22, 26–27 offers timeless lessons that are highly applicable to the lives of believers today. First, this lesson highlights the importance of good leadership in the spiritual life of a nation. Despite the prominent examples of wickedness and unfaithfulness from his father and grandfather, Josiah sought the Lord wholeheartedly. From an early age, Josiah followed the example of his ancestor David, who was "a man after [God's] own heart" (1 Sam. 13:14).

Second, King Josiah's response to the discovery of the book of the Law serves as a powerful reminder of how a leader's personal faith, humility, and commitment to God can bring about transformation in both individuals and communities.

Third, Josiah's heartfelt, emotional response to the sins of his people—tearing his robes, weeping, and humbling himself before God—point to the power of repentance. In a culture that often emphasizes self-sufficiency and denial of guilt, Josiah's example challenges believers to respond to our own shortcomings and sins with genuine remorse. Repentance is not only about feeling regret but also about turning away from actions or attitudes that dishonor God and instead seeking God's will and following His way. In both our personal lives and in our leadership, embracing true repentance can lead to spiritual renewal.

This fosters the blessings that we and others can experience when we live in closer relationship with our Lord. Some of these blessings are noted in John 15:5, Galatians 5:22–23, and Ephesians 1:3.

In addition, Josiah's sincere inquiry of the Lord through the prophet Huldah illustrates the importance of seeking divine guidance, especially when facing difficult decisions. In today's fast-paced world, it's easy to rely solely on human wisdom or our own personal experience, but Josiah's example shows the value of actively seeking God's direction through prayer, Scripture, and wise counsel. Leaders, in particular, can learn from Josiah's humility and willingness to seek and follow God's word, rather than acting out of self-reliance or haste.

Finally, God's promise to Josiah reveals that the Lord responds to sincere repentance with mercy. No matter how far one has fallen or how broken a situation may seem, God is always ready to extend mercy and grace to those who seek Him with a contrite heart. For individuals and communities grappling with the consequences of sin or failure, this lesson provides hope and assurance that renewal is possible.

Josiah's example calls believers today to lead with humility, seek God's guidance, and approach repentance with sincerity, trusting in God's grace for renewal and restoration.

LET'S TALK ABOUT IT...

Discuss the following questions and visit www.rhboyd.com for more information.

In what ways can we, as individuals and leaders, actively seek God's guidance in making decisions? What role does humility play in this process?

How can Josiah's example of repentance and sorrow for the sins of his people inspire us to address our own shortcomings in addition to the problems within our communities?

When confronted with the consequences of our sins, how can we respond to God in sincere repentance and seek His mercy and restoration?

Get Social

Share your views and tag us
@rhboydco and use #rhboydco

@rhboydco

Home Daily Devotional Readings
September 22–28, 2025

Monday	Tuesday	Wednesday	Thursday	Friday	Saturday	Sunday
The Humble Servant Exalted by God	The Faithful Servant	The Resurrected and Glorified Servant	A Light for the World	A Doorkeeper in God's House	God's Servant Obeys	The Suffering Servant
Philippians 2:5–10	Isaiah 42:1–7	Acts 2:25–31	Acts 13:44–49	Psalm 84	Isaiah 50:4–9	Isaiah 53:1–7

Lesson III – What Hilkiah Found in the Temple – September 21, 2025

Lesson IV September 28, 2025

The Suffering Servant of the Lord

Adult Topic: How Do You Spell "Relief"?
Background Scripture: Isaiah 52:13–53:12
Lesson Passage: Isaiah 53:1–7

ISAIAH 53:1-7

KJV

WHO hath believed our report? and to whom is the arm of the Lord revealed?

2 For he shall grow up before him as a tender plant, and as a root out of a dry ground: he hath no form nor comeliness; and when we shall see him, there is no beauty that we should desire him.

3 He is despised and rejected of men; a man of sorrows, and acquainted with grief: and we hid as it were our faces from him; he was despised, and we esteemed him not.

4 Surely he hath borne our griefs, and carried our sorrows: yet we did esteem him stricken, smitten of God, and afflicted.

5 But he was wounded for our transgressions, he was bruised for our iniquities: the chastisement of our peace was upon him; and with his stripes we are healed.

6 All we like sheep have gone astray; we have turned every one to his own way; and the Lord hath laid on him the iniquity of us all.

7 He was oppressed, and he was afflicted, yet he opened not his mouth: he is brought as a lamb to the slaughter, and as a sheep before her shearers is dumb, so he openeth not his mouth.

NRSVue

WHO has believed what we have heard? And to whom has the arm of the Lord been revealed?

2 For he grew up before him like a young plant and like a root out of dry ground;

he had no form or majesty that we should look at him, nothing in his appearance that we should desire him.

3 He was despised and rejected by others; a man of suffering and acquainted with infirmity,

and as one from whom others hide their faces he was despised, and we held him of no account.

4 Surely he has borne our infirmities and carried our diseases, yet we accounted him stricken, struck down by God, and afflicted.

5 But he was wounded for our transgressions, crushed for our iniquities; upon him was the punishment that made us whole, and by his bruises we are healed.

6 All we like sheep have gone astray; we have all turned to our own way,

and the Lord has laid on him the iniquity of us all.

7 He was oppressed, and he was afflicted, yet he did not open his mouth; like a lamb that is led to the slaughter and like a sheep that before its shearers is silent, so he did not open his mouth.

MAIN THOUGHT: All we like sheep have gone astray; we have all turned to our own way, and the Lord has laid on him the iniquity of us all. (Isaiah 53:6, NRSVue)

LESSON SETTING

Time: Eighth century BC
Place: Judah
Setting: The passage is believed to have been written in the eighth century BC, during the ministry of the prophet Isaiah. This was a period in which all of Israel experienced turmoil—including threats from foreign powers such as Assyria and Babylon—because of their apostasy. During this time of political instability, Isaiah's prophecies spoke not only of judgment but also of hope. Isaiah was active in Judah, the Southern Kingdom of Israel, particularly in Jerusalem. He served as God's spokesperson during the reigns of several kings, including Uzziah, Jotham, Ahaz, and Hezekiah. The events of this passage occurred in Judah, and the prophecy addresses the future of the nation and individuals, mainly focusing on the coming of a servant who would bear the sins of the people.

LESSON OUTLINE

I. The Suffering Servant's Rejection (Isaiah 53:1-3)
II. Purpose in Suffering (Isaiah 53:4-5)
III. Silent Submission (Isaiah 53:6-7)

UNIFYING PRINCIPLE

People want relief from the results of their wrongful actions. But what alleviates the consequences of wrongdoing? Isaiah described a "suffering servant" as the one who carried the iniquity of all God's people so they could be made righteous.

INTRODUCTION

Isaiah 53:1-7, often termed the "Suffering Servant" passage, is one of the most profound passages in the Hebrew Bible. It is set against the backdrop of the Babylonian exile, when the people of Judah were displaced from their land because of their unfaithfulness to God.

During this period of darkness and despair, Isaiah prophesied hope and restoration. He spoke of a figure who would be despised, rejected, and misunderstood, yet would suffer for the people's sins. Through his sacrificial suffering, he would bring about their redemption.

Written during a time of political and social upheaval in Judah, the passage offers a striking contrast between the expectations of worldly power and the divine plan for salvation that would come through humility and sacrifice.

Isaiah 53:1-7 is an insightful exploration of suffering, injustice, and the paradox of redemptive love. It has been interpreted in both Jewish and Christian traditions as a pivotal passage that points to a future hope and restoration. Whether viewed as a representation of Israel, a prophetic figure, or the Messiah, this passage continues to challenge and inspire readers, inviting reflection on the nature of suffering, sacrifice, and the path to redemption.

EXPOSITION

I. The Suffering Servant's Rejection (Isaiah 53:1–3)

Isaiah 52:13—53:12 describes the suffering and ultimate vindication of a Servant who is despised and rejected by mortals, yet who is exalted by God. This passage, along with the other "Servant Songs" in Isaiah (42:1-9; 49:1-13; and 50:4-11), depicts the Servant as a figure through whom God's redemptive purposes for Israel and the world will be accomplished.

Several times in the book of Isaiah, God referred to Israel as His Servant, chosen to fulfill His purposes (e.g., Isa. 41:8-9; 44:1-2; 45:4; 48:20). The people of Israel were called to be a "light to the nations" (Isa. 42:6; 49:6)—revealing God's character and plan to the world. However, Israel's failure to achieve this purpose led to their exile.

Through the "Suffering Servant," however, God's people would be restored and would fulfill their mission. Isaiah 53 portrays this Servant, not as a triumphant conqueror, but rather as one who was wounded and crushed for the transgressions of others. His suffering was not punishment for His own wrongdoing; rather, it was a redemptive act on behalf of the people.

Isaiah 53:1 sets the stage for the description of the Servant. Throughout verses 1-3, "we" may refer to the prophet Isaiah and the faithful remnant of Israel, who recognized and understood the importance of the Servant's role. The initial question indicates that the message about the Servant was met with skepticism. Many people struggled to accept the truth about this Servant, especially since the revelation of God's "arm"—a symbol of His power and activity—was not immediately obvious.

Verse 2 describes the Servant's physical appearance and humble origin. The metaphors of a "young plant" and "root" suggest something fragile and unremarkable. The "dry ground" metaphor indicates a barren and hostile environment—implying that His appearance and background were not noteworthy in the eyes of the world.

Likewise, "no form or majesty that we should look at him" and "nothing in his appearance that we should desire him" highlight that the Servant did not command attention due to His outward appearance or status. In a time when physical attractiveness and noble lineage were linked to significance and divine favor, God's Servant defied those expectations. Human beings are no different today. The mortal eye looks for physical appeal, but this is not God's way. Though unassuming, he was the chosen instrument of God's salvation. God's selection process is affirmed in His choosing David to become king of Israel (1 Samuel 16:7).

Not only was he disregarded because of his humble appearance, the Servant was also actively rejected by the people. Verse 3 describes Him as "despised and rejected by others," emphasizing the emotional and social isolation that he experienced. He was "a man of suffering and acquainted with infirmity." The Hebrew word translated "infirmity" (*choli*) suggests something chronic or constant. Thus, the Servant experienced pain and grief—both physical and emotional—throughout his life.

The phrase "as one from whom others hide their faces" reveals the depth of shame and dishonor that He experienced. The phrase "he was despised, and we held him of no account" underscores the deep level of rejection he faced.

Ultimately, this passage pictures a man who was socially marginalized, misunderstood, and scorned despite his important role in God's plan.

II. Purpose in Suffering (Isaiah 53:4–5)

Verse 4 introduces the idea that the Servant would not suffer for anything he had done. Both "infirmities" and "diseases" can be understood metaphorically—symbolizing emotional, spiritual, and physical suffering. The Hebrew word for "borne" (*nasa*) means to "carry" or "take away." Thus, like the scapegoat on the Day of Atonement (Lev. 16:22), the Servant would take away what actually belonged to others.

Even so, the last part of verse 4 reveals that the people thought God gave the Servant what He deserved because of his own wrongdoing. This reflects a common (but incorrect) mindset that suffering is a sign of personal sin or divine disfavor.

Verse 5 emphasizes the Servant's physical agony—both "wounded" and "crushed" describe severe pain and suffering. This was directly connected to the people's sin—specifically, their "transgressions" (willful wrongdoings) and "iniquities" (moral failures). While the people deserved this suffering, God's Servant willingly endured it.

The second part of verse 5 clarifies that the Servant's suffering has a redemptive purpose. This "punishment" ("chastisement," KJV) reconciles people to God. It makes them "whole," which is the Hebrew word *shalom* that encompasses completeness, soundness, and renewal.

"Bruises" (v. 5) are the physical wounds that the Servant endured. Through those injuries, people can experience healing—both physical and spiritual. The Servant's suffering brings restoration to the brokenness of humanity, repairing the rift between God and His people that was caused by sin.

These verses present a powerful paradox: The Servant was not afflicted for his own wrongdoing, but for the people's iniquities. Taking their place, he willingly accepted the suffering that they deserved. Thus, his redemptive suffering brought healing, wholeness, and reconciliation.

For Christians, this passage is a prophecy of Jesus Christ's atoning sacrifice on the cross. The concept of Christ's suffering for the sins of all humanity is integral to Christian theology. Thus, Isaiah 53:4–5 is often cited as foretelling Jesus' role as the Suffering Servant who bears the penalty for human sin, providing a way for humanity to be healed and reconciled to God.

III. Silent Submission (Isaiah 53:6–7)

Isaiah 53:6 offers a metaphor describing not only the people of Israel in that time but also all of humanity across the ages—they are like "sheep" who have "gone astray." This vivid image highlights the persistent waywardness and stubborn rebellion of God's people, who turned away from Him to their own way. This picture reinforces the biblical teaching of human sinfulness—the natural tendency of humans to turn away from God and reject His direction, as noted elsewhere throughout Scripture (e.g., Gen. 6:5; 1 Kings 8:46; Ps. 14:2–3; Eccl. 7:20; Jer. 17:9; John 3:19; Rom. 3:23).

The phrase "we have all turned to our own way" further emphasizes the universality of human rebellion. This collective defiance also emphasizes that people have not merely made mistakes or strayed from the Lord in minor ways; instead, they have deliberately chosen to reject God's guidance and follow what seems right in their own eyes. Disobedience to God is a fundamental characteristic of fallen human nature throughout all times and cultures.

Despite this universal rebellion, the Servant will bear the weight of all the people's sin, as the prophet noted: "the LORD has laid on him the iniquity of us all" (v. 6). The Hebrew word for "iniquity" (*avon*) encompasses the entire catalog of human sin—anything and everything that falls short of God's standard of righteousness. In addition, the word can reflect the guilt that people experience as a result of their sinful actions. Even so, in an extraordinary act of grace, God placed the burden of the people's sins upon the Servant, who carried them and suffered the consequences that all humans deserved. Once again, we see the vicarious nature of the Servant's suffering: he does not suffer for his own wrongdoings but for the transgressions of others.

The opening phrase of verse 7 further describes his mistreatment and suffering. "Oppressed" expresses brutal, demanding treatment; the same Hebrew word is used for the "taskmasters" who tyrannized the Israelites during their slavery in Egypt (Exod. 3:7; 5:6, 10, 13-14). In addition, "afflicted" means to be "bowed down" or "humbled." Together, these terms describe the intense physical and emotional suffering that the Servant endured on behalf of others.

Despite the severity of his oppression, the Servant neither retaliated nor resisted. He remained silent in the face of relentless mistreatment. Such silence offers a remarkable contrast to our human tendency to lash out at oppressors or defend ourselves when we have been wronged. The Servant's restraint and submission are essential elements of his redemptive role: he endures the suffering willingly, without protest, to fulfill God's will and bring about the healing of the people.

The comparison to a "lamb that is led to the slaughter" and a "sheep that before its shearers is silent" further emphasizes the Servant's meekness and willing submission to God's will. Even so, while a lamb being led to slaughter doesn't know what is coming, the Suffering Servant knew and humbly accepted it. Just as a sheep goes before the shearers without hesitation, so the Servant willingly accepted the suffering that he experienced.

The Servant's silence in the face of injustice and oppression presents a profound reflection on the mystery of suffering and God's plan to redeem or restore a broken world. For Jewish readers, Isaiah 53:6-7 resonates with the broader concept of Israel's suffering for the sake of the nations, as noted elsewhere in the book of Isaiah.

For Christians, however, this passage foretells the suffering and sacrifice of Jesus Christ (Acts 8:26-35) during His trials, flogging, and crucifixion. Throughout those agonizing events, Jesus remained silent before His accusers and endured suffering without defending Himself (Matt. 27:12-14; Mark 15:5). Though Jesus was without sin, He willingly surrendered His life (John 10:14-18), taking the place of sinful humans (Rom. 8:3; 2 Cor. 5:21; Gal. 3:13; 1 Pet. 2:24) who deserved to die for their sins. Therefore, His sacrificial death made it possible for humans to be forgiven and restored in their relationship to God.

THE LESSON APPLIED

The Suffering Servant's humility is a key attribute noted in this lesson. Though humans often scorn humility, God highly values this trait (Ps. 138:6; Isa. 57:15; James 4:6), especially in human beings. Humility is essential for all who want to live in right relationship to God, experience His blessings, and fulfill His purposes. Thus, believers should focus on humility (Phil. 2:3) instead of seeking recognition.

The Servant's willingness to sacrifice for

others encourages believers to give ourselves—especially in service to others—with the same selfless attitude (Rom. 15:1–2).

Another major emphasis in Isaiah 53 is the Servant's extraordinary response to undeserved oppression and suffering. His example challenges us to choose silence or restraint whenever we experience personal hardship (1 Pet. 2:19, 21), letting our actions speak louder than words.

The Servant's suffering brought peace and healing, which is God's desire for humanity. As believers, we are called to be God's agents of peace (Rom. 14:19), striving to reconcile relationships and heal divisions, even when this requires sacrifice on our part.

Finally, this lesson teaches us the value of enduring suffering for the sake of others. This highlights the importance of believers bearing one another's burdens (Gal. 6:2). Just as the Servant took on the sins of others, we too can stand with and support those who are struggling, recognizing that our efforts can contribute to healing and restoration in their lives.

LET'S TALK ABOUT IT...

Discuss the following questions and visit www.rhboyd.com for more information.

How can we apply the concept of "suffering for the sake of others" in our modern relationships and communities, particularly when standing up for those who are marginalized or oppressed?

In Isaiah 53:3, the servant is described as being "despised and rejected." How can we respond with humility and grace when we experience rejection or criticism? What does this teach us about the nature of authentic leadership and influence?

Isaiah 53 highlights the servant's willingness to endure suffering without retaliation. How can this example of silent endurance in the face of injustice be practically applied in today's world, where speaking out against injustice is often seen as a necessary response?

Get Social

Share your views and tag us
@rhboydco and use #rhboydco

@rhboydco

Home Daily Devotional Readings
September 29–October 5, 2025

Monday	Tuesday	Wednesday	Thursday	Friday	Saturday	Sunday
Passion for God's Laws	The Piercing Word of God	Return to the Father	Cleanse Yourselves and Be Saved	God's Discipline Proves God's Love	God Is a Consuming Fire	A Defiant Prophet
2 Chronicles 34:1–7	Hebrews 4:12–16	Jeremiah 3:12–19	Jeremiah 4:5–14	Hebrews 12:3–17	Hebrews 12:18–29	Jeremiah 1:6–10; 26:8–9, 12–15

Lesson V — October 5, 2025

The Early Ministry of Jeremiah

Adult Topic: Who? Me?
Background Scripture: Jeremiah 1:1–10; 6:10–11; 8:18; 9:2; 26:1–24
Lesson Passage: Jeremiah 1:6–10; 26:8–9, 12–15

JEREMIAH 1:6–10; 26:8–9, 12–15

KJV

THEN said I, Ah, Lord God! behold, I cannot speak: for I am a child.
7 But the Lord said unto me, Say not, I am a child: for thou shalt go to all that I shall send thee, and whatsoever I command thee thou shalt speak.
8 Be not afraid of their faces: for I am with thee to deliver thee, saith the Lord.
9 Then the Lord put forth his hand, and touched my mouth. And the Lord said unto me, Behold, I have put my words in thy mouth.
10 See, I have this day set thee over the nations and over the kingdoms, to root out, and to pull down, and to destroy, and to throw down, to build, and to plant.

•••Jeremiah 26:8–9•••

8 Now it came to pass, when Jeremiah had made an end of speaking all that the Lord had commanded him to speak unto all the people, that the priests and the prophets and all the people took him, saying, Thou shalt surely die.
9 Why hast thou prophesied in the name of the Lord, saying, This house shall be like Shiloh, and this city shall be desolate without an inhabitant? And all the people were gathered against Jeremiah in the house of the Lord.

••••••

12 Then spake Jeremiah unto all the princes and to all the people, saying, The Lord sent me to prophesy against this house and against this city all the words that ye have heard.
13 Therefore now amend your ways and your doings, and obey the voice of the Lord your God;

NRSVue

THEN I said, "Ah, Lord God! Truly I do not know how to speak, for I am only a boy."
7 But the Lord said to me, "Do not say, 'I am only a boy,' for you shall go to all to whom I send you, and you shall speak whatever I command you.
8 Do not be afraid of them, for I am with you to deliver you, says the Lord."
9 Then the Lord put out his hand and touched my mouth, and the Lord said to me, "Now I have put my words in your mouth.
10 See, today I appoint you over nations and over kingdoms, to pluck up and to pull down, to destroy and to overthrow, to build and to plant."

•••Jeremiah 26:8–9•••

8 And when Jeremiah had finished speaking all that the Lord had commanded him to speak to all the people, then the priests and the prophets and all the people laid hold of him, saying, "You shall die!
9 Why have you prophesied in the name of the Lord, saying, 'This house shall be like Shiloh, and this city shall be desolate, without inhabitant'?" And all the people gathered around Jeremiah in the house of the Lord.

••••••

12 Then Jeremiah spoke to all the officials and all the people, saying, "It is the Lord who sent me to prophesy against this house and this city all the words you have heard.
13 Now therefore amend your ways and your doings, and obey the voice of the Lord your

MAIN THOUGHT: But the Lord said to me, "Do not say, 'I am only a boy,' for you shall go to all to whom I send you, and you shall speak whatever I command you." (Jeremiah 1:7, NRSVue)

JEREMIAH 1:6-10; 26:8-9, 12-15

KJV
and the Lord will repent him of the evil that he hath pronounced against you.

14 As for me, behold, I am in your hand: do with me as seemeth good and meet unto you.

15 But know ye for certain, that if ye put me to death, ye shall surely bring innocent blood upon yourselves, and upon this city, and upon the inhabitants thereof: for of a truth the Lord hath sent me unto you to speak all these words in your ears.

NRSVue
God, and the Lord will change his mind about the disaster that he has pronounced against you.

14 But as for me, here I am in your hands. Do with me as seems good and right to you.

15 Only know for certain that if you put me to death, you will be bringing innocent blood upon yourselves and upon this city and its inhabitants, for in truth the Lord sent me to you to speak all these words in your ears."

LESSON SETTING

Time: Around 626 and 609-608 BC
Place: Jerusalem
Setting: The events in this lesson happened during a turbulent time in the history of Judah. In Jeremiah 1:6-10, God commissioned the prophet Jeremiah to deliver a message to Israel and the surrounding nations. This call occurred in Jerusalem around 626 BC, during the reign of King Josiah. Even as religious reforms were underway during this period, tensions were rising because foreign powers posed a growing threat to God's people. Despite Jeremiah's initial reluctance to God's call, the Lord assured His prophet that he would indeed have all that he needed to speak on God's behalf. In Jeremiah 26:8-9, 12-15, the setting shifts to a later time in Judah's history—possibly about 609-608 BC, which was Jehoiakim's first year as king. As the Babylonian influence increased in the region and Judah faced political instability, Jeremiah delivered a prophecy of doom, declaring Jerusalem's imminent destruction. His message enraged the people, thus he was taken before the authorities. The setting is Jerusalem, specifically in the Temple and royal court, where Jeremiah defended his words and asserted that his message came from God. While the people and religious leaders were enraged and ready to kill Jeremiah, the royal officials intervened because they recognized that his prophecy might actually have been inspired by God. This event captured a moment of intense political and religious crisis as the leaders of Judah grappled with the looming Babylonian threat and the potential destruction of Jerusalem.

LESSON OUTLINE

I. Jeremiah's Call (Jeremiah 1:6-10)
II. Conflict between Prophet and People (Jeremiah 26:8-9)
III. Jeremiah Defends His Prophecy (Jeremiah 26:12-15)

UNIFYING PRINCIPLE

Sometimes we are called to lead in situations for which we do not have adequate experience. How should people respond when they lack the necessary experience to carry out a task? When God called Jeremiah, he objected that he was too young to fulfill the prophetic task. Nevertheless, God's sufficiency and purpose came to bear despite Jeremiah's reservations.

INTRODUCTION

The prophet Jeremiah was born into a priestly family from Anatoth. This town was in the territory of Benjamin, which along with Judah became known as the Southern Kingdom (or the Kingdom of Judah) during the division that occurred in Israel after King Solomon's death.

Jeremiah served God during the late seventh and early sixth centuries BC—a time of significant political and spiritual turmoil in Judah that ultimately led to its downfall.

Although Jeremiah's ministry lasted more than forty years, most people rejected his message. He is known as the "weeping prophet" because of his grief over God's message of judgment on Judah. Ultimately, Jeremiah witnessed the destruction of Jerusalem at the hands of the Babylonians and later was forced to go to Egypt, where he likely died. Based on these outcomes, many people might consider Jeremiah a failure. In God's eyes, however, Jeremiah was a faithful servant because he obeyed God's word regardless of the cost.

This lesson first offers insights into Jeremiah's calling and mission. Initially, he raised objections to the Lord's call for him to be "a prophet to the nations" (Jer. 1:4). Like other biblical figures—including Moses and Gideon—Jeremiah felt inadequate to fulfill the role to which God was calling him. Even so, God responded and promised that His presence, power, plan, and purpose would prevail through Jeremiah's ministry.

Jeremiah chapter 26 reveals some of the consequences that the prophet experienced as he foretold Jerusalem's impending destruction. His messages evoked intense hostility from leaders and people alike. The threats against Jeremiah's life demonstrate the perilous nature of prophetic work, especially during a time when the political climate was fraught with insecurity.

Jeremiah's life offers a profound lesson on the importance of steadfastness and courage in the face of persecution, and emphasizes the importance of prophetic voices who communicate God's message.

EXPOSITION

I. Jeremiah's Call (Jeremiah 1:6–10)

In response to God's call, Jeremiah expressed a natural sense of inadequacy about an overwhelming assignment. Verse 6 relates: "Ah, Lord GOD! Truly I do not know how to speak, for I am only a boy." Whether Jeremiah lacked confidence in his communication skills or simply felt like he was too young, he effectively said, "I can't."

The Hebrew word translated "boy" (na'ar) is used of Moses as an infant (Ex. 2:6) and of Joshua as an adult male (Ex. 33:11). The Hebrew word naʿar (נַעַר), commonly translated as "boy" or "lad," is used throughout the Old Testament to describe males of various ages—from infants to young adults. Though Jeremiah's age at that time is unknown, some scholars suggest that he was in his late teens or early 20s. Whatever his age, Jeremiah thought that it would hinder his effectiveness as a prophet. He might have questioned how he, as a young man, could command the attention of kings, priests, and people. In the ancient world, age was often associated with wisdom and authority, so a young person might have struggled to gain respect in such a significant role. This feeling speaks to the insecurities of many people who are called to an important task, especially when they feel unprepared or ill-equipped.

In response to Jeremiah's doubts and fears, God issued a command: "Do not say, 'I am only a boy.'" Rather than a rebuke, this was a gentle correction, directing Jeremiah's focus away from his perceived limitations. With these words, God invalidated any thoughts that age, skill, or readiness are barriers to fulfilling His purpose. This statement urged Jeremiah to trust in God's plan rather than relying on his assessment of his qualifications.

Then, God assured Jeremiah of divine support: "you shall go to all to whom I send you, and you shall speak whatever I command you." Jeremiah was to be obedient and faithful. He did not have to invent a message or act according to his own judgment; instead, he was called to speak God's word with divine authority.

Verse 8 continues God's reassurance: "Do not be afraid of them, for I am with you to deliver you." This is a profound promise of God's presence and protection. Like many other of God's servants, Jeremiah's mission would be filled with opposition and hostility. To address the root of Jeremiah's reluctance, God promised not only to be with him but also to deliver him from harm. Jeremiah's success did not depend on his talent or strength but instead on God's ongoing presence and intervention. No matter what Jeremiah faced—ridicule, rejection, or persecution—he would not face those challenges alone.

The Lord then "touched" Jeremiah and put His "words" into the prophet's mouth (v. 9). Through this symbolic gesture, God empowered Jeremiah for his ministry.

Afterward, God noted the dual nature of Jeremiah's task. In verse 10, the imagery of destructive actions ("pluck up … pull down … destroy … overthrow") and constructive ones ("build … plant") indicates Jeremiah's future messages of judgment and hope. God wanted to build up and restore Israel, but to do so, He would first have to tear down and remove the impurities from both His land and His people.

II. Conflict Between Prophet and People (Jeremiah 26:8–9)

Jeremiah 26 presents a moment of heightened tension for the prophet. Jeremiah delivered God's message (vv. 1–6), which promised destruction for the temple and Jerusalem. Yet, Jeremiah noted an alternative: If the people repented of their disobedience and obeyed the Lord, He would change His mind about the coming disaster.

Instead, the priests, prophets, and people who heard Jeremiah's words were outraged. Believing that his words were false and blasphemous, they violently "laid hold of him" (v. 8). They sought to kill Jeremiah (in accordance with Lev. 24:16 and Deut. 18:20), likely because they considered him a false prophet who had blasphemed the Lord and the temple.

In verse 9, the angry listeners questioned, "Why have you prophesied in the name of the Lord saying, 'This house shall be like Shiloh, and this city shall be desolate, without inhabitant'?" Shiloh was the first permanent location for the tabernacle (Josh. 18:1). Thus, that place reflected God's presence with His people before the temple was built. While Shiloh's destruction is not expressly noted in Scripture, it probably occurred around 1050 BC when the Philistines defeated Israel and captured the ark of the covenant (1 Sam. 4:1–10; Ps. 78:56–64). Undoubtedly, no one in Israel at that time could have imagined that a holy place like Shiloh would ever be destroyed.

Jeremiah had warned the people that the same fate that befell Shiloh was also coming for Jerusalem. Even so, most of those who heard his words (especially the priests and prophets) could not comprehend that God would bring judgment on the place that symbolized His presence on earth. Because they believed false prophecies of peace and prosperity (Jer. 6:13–14), Jeremiah's dire prophecy was unwelcome and unacceptable.

III. Jeremiah Defends His Prophecy (Jeremiah 26:12–15)

As the violent mob in the Temple wanted to put Jeremiah to death, "the officials of Judah" (v. 10) intervened. These civil officials apparently had judicial authority, because they immediately convened a trial at the New Gate in the Temple.

After the religious leaders presented their charges, Jeremiah began his defense. Though his life was at stake, he didn't cower, apologize, or retract his words. Instead, he boldly asserted that his prophecy was not his own. God alone was responsible for the prophet's dire message "against this house and this city" (v. 12). Just as God had commanded him, Jeremiah faithfully declared God's words (7:1–15) about the judgment that was coming as a result of the people's disobedience and unfaithfulness to the Lord.

Even so, there was a way for the people and their leaders to escape the impending destruction. Jeremiah urged them to amend their ways and obey the voice of the LORD your God (v. 13). These words emphasized that God's judgment was neither final nor irreversible. If the people would change their behavior and return to God, He would "change his mind" and forgo the "disaster" that He promised. This was a message of hope, which demonstrated God's characteristic mercy even in the face of wrath.

Despite the seriousness of his situation, Jeremiah exhibited a remarkable sense of courage, personal resolve, and faith in God. He remained steadfast in his mission to convey the truth, regardless of the potential repercussions. In verse 14, Jeremiah acknowledged that his life was in the hands of the officials and the people. He said that they could do to him whatever they thought was "good" and "right." But while Jeremiah knew that they had power over his immediate circumstances, he trusted that God had ultimate control of his situation and his life.

Concluding his defense, Jeremiah added a word of warning: "If you put me to death, you will be bringing innocent blood upon yourselves and upon this city and its inhabitants" (v. 15). He wanted them to realize that if they carried out the death sentence, they would be guilty of killing an innocent man because his prophecy came directly from the Lord. By shedding his blood, they would bring guilt upon themselves and further incur God's wrath. Hopefully, this warning would cause the leaders to consider the gravity of their actions.

Jeremiah was ready to accept whatever consequences the officials decided that he deserved. This indicated not only the depth of his commitment to his prophetic duty but also the profound relationship he had with God—Jeremiah showed an unwavering faith in the Lord even when his life was in grave danger.

THE LESSON APPLIED

God often calls individuals who feel inadequate or unqualified, as revealed in Jeremiah's initial reluctance because of his age and inexperience. This is a reminder that personal limitations—whether perceived or real—do not disqualify us from pursuing and fulfilling God's purpose. God equips those He calls, offering His guidance and strength that far exceed our abilities (2 Cor. 12:9; Eph. 3:20).

Similarly, this lesson underscores the importance of trusting the Lord, especially in difficult situations. Jeremiah was willing to die for delivering God's unpopular message because he trusted in God's protection and guidance. God's truth usually challenges societal norms, thus it often brings backlash for those who hold to it. And yet, God gives His people courage to stand for Him even in the face of opposition.

Finally, Jeremiah's example shows the value of speaking truth with humility, especially when responding to critics. Because "a soft answer turns away wrath" (Prov. 15:1), even some people who oppose God's truth may be willing to consider and accept it when we speak gently (2 Tim. 2:25).

LET'S TALK ABOUT IT...

Discuss the following questions and visit www.rhboyd.com for more information.

How can we reconcile feelings of inadequacy or fear when we are asked to take on leadership roles or speak difficult truths, as Jeremiah did, both in his calling and in his defense?

What are some contemporary "Shilohs"—places or structures in which people place their trust rather than in God? How can we challenge or confront their false hopes about those places, much like Jeremiah confronted the people's false sense of security related to Jerusalem and the temple?

How can we, as individuals or communities, remain faithful to our convictions and trust in God's protection when we face opposition for speaking out against injustice or offering unpopular truths?

Get Social

Share your views and tag us
@rhboydco and use #rhboydco

@rhboydco

Home Daily Devotional Readings
October 6–12, 2025

Monday	Tuesday	Wednesday	Thursday	Friday	Saturday	Sunday
Endure to the End	God Will Protect God's People	To Obey Is Better than Sacrifice	Keep Christ's Commandments	An Indestructible Temple	The Sacrifice That Pleases God	Amend Your Ways!
Mark 13:1–13	Mark 13:14–27	1 Samuel 15:20–26	John 14:12–17	John 2:12–22	Psalm 51:15–19	Jeremiah 7:1–11, 21–23

Lesson VI   **October 12, 2025**

Jeremiah Calls the People to Obedience

Adult Topic: Walk the Talk
Background Scripture: Jeremiah 7:1–26
Lesson Passage: Jeremiah 7:1–11, 21–23

JEREMIAH 7:1-11, 21-23

KJV

THE word that came to Jeremiah from the Lord, saying,
2 Stand in the gate of the Lord's house, and proclaim there this word, and say, Hear the word of the Lord, all ye of Judah, that enter in at these gates to worship the Lord.
3 Thus saith the Lord of hosts, the God of Israel, Amend your ways and your doings, and I will cause you to dwell in this place.
4 Trust ye not in lying words, saying, The temple of the Lord, The temple of the Lord, The temple of the Lord, are these.
5 For if ye throughly amend your ways and your doings; if ye throughly execute judgment between a man and his neighbour;
6 If ye oppress not the stranger, the fatherless, and the widow, and shed not innocent blood in this place, neither walk after other gods to your hurt:
7 Then will I cause you to dwell in this place, in the land that I gave to your fathers, for ever and ever.
8 Behold, ye trust in lying words, that cannot profit.
9 Will ye steal, murder, and commit adultery, and swear falsely, and burn incense unto Baal, and walk after other gods whom ye know not;
10 And come and stand before me in this house, which is called by my name, and say, We are delivered to do all these abominations?
11 Is this house, which is called by my name, become a den of robbers in your eyes? Behold, even I have seen it, saith the Lord.

NRSVue

THE word that came to Jeremiah from the Lord:
2 Stand in the gate of the Lord's house, and proclaim there this word, and say, Hear the word of the Lord, all you people of Judah, you who enter these gates to worship the Lord.
3 Thus says the Lord of hosts, the God of Israel: Amend your ways and your doings, and let me dwell with you in this place.
4 Do not trust in these deceptive words: "This is the temple of the Lord, the temple of the Lord, the temple of the Lord."
5 For if you truly amend your ways and your doings, if you truly act justly one with another,
6 if you do not oppress the alien, the orphan, and the widow or shed innocent blood in this place, and if you do not go after other gods to your own hurt,
7 then I will dwell with you in this place, in the land that I gave to your ancestors forever and ever.
8 Here you are, trusting in deceptive words to no avail.
9 Will you steal, murder, commit adultery, swear falsely, make offerings to Baal, and go after other gods that you have not known
10 and then come and stand before me in this house, which is called by my name, and say, "We are safe!"—only to go on doing all these abominations?
11 Has this house, which is called by my name, become a den of robbers in your sight? I, too, am watching, says the Lord.

MAIN THOUGHT: This command I gave them: "Obey my voice, and I will be your God, and you shall be my people; and walk only in the way that I command you, so that it may be well with you." (Jeremiah 7:23, NRSVue)

JEREMIAH 7:1-11, 21-23

KJV

21 Thus saith the Lord of hosts, the God of Israel; Put your burnt offerings unto your sacrifices, and eat flesh.

22 For I spake not unto your fathers, nor commanded them in the day that I brought them out of the land of Egypt, concerning burnt offerings or sacrifices:

23 But this thing commanded I them, saying, Obey my voice, and I will be your God, and ye shall be my people: and walk ye in all the ways that I have commanded you, that it may be well unto you.

NRSVue

21 Thus says the Lord of hosts, the God of Israel: Add your burnt offerings to your sacrifices, and eat the flesh.

22 For in the day that I brought your ancestors out of the land of Egypt, I did not speak to them or command them concerning burnt offerings and sacrifices.

23 But this command I gave them, "Obey my voice, and I will be your God, and you shall be my people; walk only in the way that I command you, so that it may be well with you."

LESSON SETTING

Time: Likely between 626–586 BC
Place: Jerusalem
Setting: The passage reflects a time of religious and political crisis for Judah. King Josiah had attempted to reform the nation by purging idolatry and restoring proper worship practices (as detailed in 2 Kings 22–23). Still, these reforms were often superficial and not followed by an actual heart change among the people. Although Josiah had reformed the country and pushed for religious revival, the people still clung to rituals and external religious practices rather than genuine repentance and devotion to God. Thus, Jerusalem was a city in political instability. The threat of the Babylonians was looming; they eventually captured Judah and destroyed Jerusalem in 586 BC. The setting was a time of spiritual decay and impending judgment, with a call to true repentance and righteousness. The people of Judah, especially those in Jerusalem, had become complacent in their faith, relying on the temple rather than living in accordance with God's commands.

LESSON OUTLINE

I. Jeremiah Receives God's Command (Jeremiah 7:1-4)
II. True Repentance and Living Justly (Jeremiah 7:5-11)
III. God Desires Obedience (Jeremiah 7:21-23)

UNIFYING PRINCIPLE

Some people will act a certain way in one setting, but in another place they live by a different set of standards. What can we say to people who pretend to be something they are not? Jeremiah was compelled by God to speak out against Judah's duplicity because they stood in God's house and said, "We are safe," but they continued in their sin once they left their place of worship.

INTRODUCTION

In this lesson, Jeremiah conveyed a powerful message from God to the people of Judah. The words in Jeremiah 7 present a stark contrast between people who merely go through the motions of outward religious practices versus those who truly love and obey the Lord.

While King Josiah led significant reforms that eliminated idolatry in Judah and restored proper worship, those changes were only temporary. Likewise, the reforms had little (if any) effect on the people's hearts—their attitudes and motivations. They evidently thought that their covenant relationship with God was only about external actions—the rituals they performed in the Temple.

Thus, God confronted not only the people's wrong beliefs but also their wrong behavior. Through the prophet Jeremiah, the Lord rebuked His people and encouraged them to change both their thinking and their actions. Then, after emphasizing the most important aspect of the covenant—obedience to His words—God reminded them of the blessing that He offered to His faithful covenant people.

EXPOSITION

I. Jeremiah Receives God's Command (Jeremiah 7:1-4)

The Lord instructed Jeremiah to "stand in the gate of the LORD's house" (v. 2). This "house" was the Temple in Jerusalem, which was considered the dwelling place of God among His people and a symbol of God's presence (Deut. 12:5, 11). While the location of the "gate" is uncertain, it may have separated the Temple's outer and inner courts. Regardless, the spot allowed Jeremiah to address everyone who entered the Temple "to worship the LORD" (v. 2).

The people of Judah believed that their presence in the Temple guaranteed God's blessing, regardless of their behavior. They thought that merely participating in religious rituals would earn them God's favor. But Jeremiah challenged that mindset with succinct words: "Amend your ways and your doings" (v. 3). Here, "amend" carries the sense of correction, reformation, and return to a right path. Their worship and sacrifices would not be accepted unless they abandoned their wrong actions and attitudes and turned back to God with sincerity. If they did so, God promised that they would be allowed to remain in that "place"—possibly a reference to their land, which signified God's blessing to His covenant people.

While the New Revised Standard Version translates the end of verse 3 as "let me dwell with you in this place," other versions translate it "I will let you live (or dwell) in this place" (NIV, ESV, RSV). Either way, the people's continued presence in Jerusalem and Judah depended upon their repentance.

God's covenant relationship with His people was conditional on their faithfulness to His commands. In disobeying, they would experience the curses Moses noted in Deuteronomy 28, which included being removed from the Promised Land and being scattered among the nations.

In verse 4, Jeremiah warned against the people's false confidence in "deceptive words" spoken by the false prophets. This phrase—"the temple of the LORD, the temple of the LORD, the temple of the LORD"—was likely a chant that the people repeated. It reflected their belief that they could continue their sinful ways while relying on the Temple as some type of good-luck charm that would protect them. That thinking was deceitful because it would lead to the people's destruction. While the Temple was holy and central to Israel's worship, it was not a magical place that would shield them from God's judgment if they sinned.

II. True Repentance and Living Justly (Jeremiah 7:5–11)

Jeremiah then clarified what true repentance entails and how the people could live justly—in accordance with God's commands. The conditional phrases in verse 5—"if you truly amend your ways and your doings, if you truly act justly one with another"—were calls to right action. The words in verses 6–7 were a harsh critique of the people's behavior, and highlighted their need for genuine transformation.

Jeremiah emphasized God's command for His people to practice justice in their relationships, especially toward the marginalized or vulnerable in society—such as widows, orphans, and foreigners. Such people were often powerless in the ancient world, and mistreating them indicated a clear breakdown in covenant faithfulness. Social justice and righteousness were to be cornerstones of the people's covenant with God. The implication here is that true repentance manifests itself not only in personal piety but also in how one treats others in the community.

Furthermore, God condemned the shedding of "innocent blood," which refers both to murder (Deut. 19:10) and unjust actions that harm the defenseless. To restore their relationship with the Lord, the people would have to end their idolatry (going "after other gods") and worship only the Lord God.

In verse 7, God promised that if the people heeded His call, they would continue to live in the land that He had given to their ancestors "forever and ever." This promise would only apply, however, if the people remained faithful to their covenantal responsibilities.

In verse 9, God again called out specific sins of His people: theft, murder, adultery, perjury, and idolatry. In one sentence, He noted that they had broken six of the Ten Commandments! Idolatry—making "offerings to Baal" and pursuing "other gods"—represented the ultimate betrayal of God's exclusive claim on His people's worship.

Despite participating in these practices, the people thought nothing of going into the temple to present their sacrifices and offerings. Verse 10 highlights the absurdity of their thinking. They believed that their religious rituals kept them "safe" from the consequences of their sins. So after leaving the Temple, they had no concern about continuing with their "abominations."

By continuing their sinful actions while clinging to the Temple as a symbol of protection, the people were treating that sacred space as a refuge for sin rather than a place for repentance and worship. The rhetorical question in verse 11 expresses this sad reality. As God noted in 1 Kings 9:3, the Temple was His "house, which is called by [His] name"—a symbol of God's holiness and justice. Nevertheless, the people of Judah were treating it like a "den of robbers"—a place where lawbreakers could hide and avoid the consequences of their actions until it was safe to continue their wrongdoing. Jesus echoed this verse when He condemned the corruption of the temple during His day (Matt. 21:13).

While the people of Judah may have thought they could hide their actions (and motivations) from God, He assured them they could not escape His watchful eye: "I, too, am watching" (v. 11). The Lord saw what they were doing and would respond appropriately if they did not change their ways.

III. God Desires Obedience (Jeremiah 7:21–23)

This passage presents a pivotal moment in God's message through Jeremiah. Like the previous passage, it also highlights the difference between meaningless religious rituals and true obedience to God's commandments.

In verse 21, God addressed the people's superficial understanding of worship. "Add your burnt offerings to your sacrifices" was a sarcastic response to their misguided belief that their sacrifices were an acceptable substitute for genuine repentance and obedience.

The burnt offering was one of the key sacrifices in the Levitical system (Lev. 1:3–17), symbolizing total commitment to God. However, while these and other offerings were indeed part of the Israelites' religious practice, they were meaningless when not accompanied by righteous living. Thus, God's command for the people of Judah to "eat the flesh" (of their sacrifices) was another sarcastic statement. The Lord suggested that rather than completely burning the sacrifices that were intended for Him, they might as well go ahead and eat those animals instead. Such sacrifices were unacceptable to God since the people's behavior (and their attitude toward Him) was unacceptable.

Verse 22 has been the subject of controversy regarding its interpretation. Some scholars think the verse suggests that the sacrificial system developed centuries after the people of Israel entered their land. This view, however, negates the instructions related to sacrifices in the books of Exodus and Leviticus, which God gave the Israelites soon after He delivered them from bondage in Egypt. Instead, the verse reflects a Hebrew idiom that denies one thing to emphasize another. After God led the Israelites out of Egypt, He focused on the people's covenantal relationship with Him—as defined by obedience to His moral commandments. Later, God instructed them about offerings and sacrifices during the year that they camped at Mount Sinai. Thus, when Jeremiah spoke God's words in verse 22, he was challenging the people's assumption that the sacrificial system was the core of their covenant relationship with God. While sacrifices were significant, they were not intended to be an end in themselves. Instead, sacrifices were meant to accompany lives lived in obedience to God's broader moral and ethical commands, particularly related to righteousness, justice, and mercy.

Verse 23 emphasizes not only this priority but also God's promise. The command to "Obey my voice" encapsulates the essence of Israel's covenant relationship with God. Even before Moses received the Ten Commandments, God emphasized that obedience was the foundational aspect of Israel's covenant with Him (Exod. 19:3–6).

God's promise, "I will be your God, and you shall be my people," reiterates the intimate relationship God desired to have with Israel (Exod. 6:7; Lev. 26:12). This exclusive relationship was to be characterized by their loyalty, trust in God, and faithfulness to Him. God's subsequent directive to "walk only in the way that I command you" emphasizes the holistic nature of this obedience. It was not enough to merely go through the motions of ritual worship; the people needed to follow God's instructions in every aspect of their lives.

The promise that "it may be well with you" signifies the blessings that result from living according to God's will, which include His protection and His presence. The idea that obedience to God leads to flourishing is a recurring theme in the Old Testament.

THE LESSON APPLIED

Worship without righteousness, ritual without repentance, and religious practices apart from moral integrity are unacceptable to God. The Lord rebuked the people of Judah who thought that such things would secure His favor. Thus, we should also consider whether our faith rests on religious rituals or a genuine relationship with the Lord. External actions are meaningless if not paired with a transformed heart and life.

Just as God required His people in Judah to obey Him, so He expects believers to do the same today. The Lord's call to "amend your ways" is also His call to us for repentance and inward transformation. In addition, God calls us to express our faith through acts of justice and mercy, especially toward those who are vulnerable.

God's blessings for the Israelites were contingent upon their obedience. Likewise, many of God's blessings for believers today require us to follow His Word faithfully.

By living according to these principles, we can ensure that our worship remains genuine, and our relationship with God is characterized by both devotion and justice, living in accordance with His will in every aspect of life.

LET'S TALK ABOUT IT...

Discuss the following questions and visit www.rhboyd.com for more information.

In what ways do we—whether individuals or communities—sometimes rely on religious practices (such as church attendance or rituals) to feel secure in our relationship with God, rather than focusing on obedience and a transformed heart?

How can we apply God's call for justice in Jeremiah 7:5-6 to contemporary issues—particularly in advocating for and supporting vulnerable populations like the poor, immigrants, or those facing systemic oppression?

Jeremiah 7:23 emphasizes obedience to God's commands as the foundation of a true covenant relationship. How can we cultivate a lifestyle where obedience to God's Word becomes the driving force in our everyday actions and decisions?

Get Social

Share your views and tag us
@rhboydco and use #rhboydco

@rhboydco

Home Daily Devotional Readings
October 13–19, 2025

Monday	Tuesday	Wednesday	Thursday	Friday	Saturday	Sunday
The Dangers of Strong Drink	Keep Earthly Pleasures in Perspective	Be Filled with the Spirit	The Nazirite	Called to Holiness	Keep Awake!	A Vow of Holiness
Proverbs 23:29–35	Ecclesiastes 9:4–10	Ephesians 5:11–19	Numbers 6:1–8	1 Thessalonians 4:1–7	1 Thessalonians 5:1–10	Jeremiah 35:5–11

Lesson VII   **October 19, 2025**

The Story of the Rechabites

Adult Topic: Promises, Promises
Background Scripture: Jeremiah 35:1–19
Lesson Passage: Jeremiah 35:5–11

JEREMIAH 35:5-11

KJV

AND I set before the sons of the house of the Rechabites pots full of wine, and cups, and I said unto them, Drink ye wine.

6 But they said, We will drink no wine: for Jonadab the son of Rechab our father commanded us, saying, Ye shall drink no wine, neither ye, nor your sons for ever:

7 Neither shall ye build house, nor sow seed, nor plant vineyard, nor have any: but all your days ye shall dwell in tents; that ye may live many days in the land where ye be strangers.

8 Thus have we obeyed the voice of Jonadab the son of Rechab our father in all that he hath charged us, to drink no wine all our days, we, our wives, our sons, nor our daughters;

9 Nor to build houses for us to dwell in: neither have we vineyard, nor field, nor seed:

10 But we have dwelt in tents, and have obeyed, and done according to all that Jonadab our father commanded us.

11 But it came to pass, when Nebuchadrezzar king of Babylon came up into the land, that we said, Come, and let us go to Jerusalem for fear of the army of the Chaldeans, and for fear of the army of the Syrians: so we dwell at Jerusalem.

NRSVue

THEN I set before the Rechabites pitchers full of wine and cups, and I said to them, "Have some wine."

6 But they answered, "We will drink no wine, for our ancestor Jonadab son of Rechab commanded us, 'You shall never drink wine, neither you nor your children,

7 nor shall you ever build a house or sow seed, nor shall you plant a vineyard or even own one, but you shall live in tents all your days, that you may live many days in the land where you reside.'

8 We have obeyed the charge of our ancestor Jonadab son of Rechab in all that he commanded us, to drink no wine all our days, ourselves, our wives, our sons, or our daughters,

9 and not to build houses to live in. We have no vineyard or field or seed,

10 but we have lived in tents and have obeyed and done all that our ancestor Jonadab commanded us.

11 But when King Nebuchadrezzar of Babylon came up against the land, we said, 'Come, and let us go to Jerusalem for fear of the army of the Chaldeans and the army of the Arameans.' That is why we are living in Jerusalem."

LESSON SETTING

Time: Unknown, but likely during the early years of the reign of King Jehoiakim, who ruled Judah from 609 to 598 BC
Place: Jerusalem

MAIN THOUGHT: They drink [no wine] to this day, for they have obeyed their ancestor's command. (Jeremiah 35:14, NRSVue)

Setting: Because the events in the book of Jeremiah are not always in chronological order, it is sometimes difficult to date a passage or know what else was happening at the time. Even so, the events in this passage likely occurred early in the reign of King Jehoiakim, who ruled Judah from 609 to 598 BC. This was a period of significant turmoil for the Kingdom of Judah, as it faced political and military pressure from powerful neighbors, particularly Babylon. The Babylonian Empire, led by Nebuchadnezzar II, was beginning to assert control over the region. The events in this passage, which occurred in the Temple in Jerusalem, primarily involve Jeremiah and the Rechabites—a nomadic group whose members were related to the Kenites (Judg. 1:16; 1 Chron. 2:55). God designed this event to present a lesson to the people of Judah. It was a living parable that illustrated the unfaithfulness of Judah, who had failed to follow God's commands despite repeated warnings. This passage is significant in the broader context of Jeremiah's prophetic ministry. Its purpose was to call the people of Judah to repentance as they faced impending destruction because of their disobedience. The passage also serves as a reminder of the importance of tradition and faithfulness to God's commands, even in the face of temptation or societal pressures.

LESSON OUTLINE

I. Obedience of the Rechabites (Jeremiah 35:5–7)

II. Disobedience of Judah (Jeremiah 35:8–11)

UNIFYING PRINCIPLE

People find it challenging to keep their promises. Who can we trust to keep their promises? The discipline of the Rechabites, who kept the promises made by their leader (see 1 Chron. 2:55), was presented as a contrast to Judah's disobedience to God.

INTRODUCTION

Jeremiah 35:5–11 presents a compelling narrative that contrasts the faithfulness of an obscure group with the disobedience of the people of Judah. Set against the backdrop of political instability and impending doom for the Kingdom of Judah, this passage serves as a stark reminder of the consequences of ignoring God's commands. Time and again throughout their history, the people of Judah had turned away from God's laws, engaging in idolatry, immorality, and rebellion. Thus, God called the prophet Jeremiah to warn them again about the disaster that was coming because of their disobedience.

In this passage, God instructed Jeremiah to perform a symbolic action, which he did on several occasions during his ministry. (For other symbolic actions, see Jer. 13:1–11; 16:1–9; 18:1–12; 19:1–15; 25:15–29; 32:1–15; 43:8–13; 51:59–64.) These dramatic events, which are also called enacted parables or object lessons, were designed to present a lesson to those who witnessed them. Their pattern was always the same: God commanded Jeremiah to do something (which was sometimes extreme or unusual), the prophet did as God had instructed, and then Jeremiah explained the message that God had for the people.

God first sent Jeremiah to meet with the Rechabites, a nomadic religious group. They were descended from a man named Jonadab (Jehonadab) son of Rechab, who is mentioned in 2 Kings 10:15-23. Jonadab was especially zealous for God and endeavored to rid Israel of Baal worship during the reign of King Jehu in Israel during the ninth century BC.

Through the Rechabites, Jeremiah would present a symbolic action that contrasted their faithfulness with the unfaithfulness of the people of Judah. God planned it as another reminder of the importance of obedience to His will and the consequences of turning away from His guidance, especially in times of crisis.

EXPOSITION

I. Obedience of the Rechabites (Jeremiah 35:5-7)

As God had instructed him (Jer. 35:1-4), Jeremiah brought the Rechabites into a side room of the Temple where he had placed "pitchers full of wine and cups" (v. 5). Then, Jeremiah invited the Rechabites to "have some wine."

When Jeremiah offered the wine to the Rechabites, it was a test. God planned this symbolic action to challenge the Rechabites' commitment to their forefather's command, which prohibited them from drinking wine. However, the Lord knew how they would respond. Thus, He would use the event to contrast the Rechabites' faithful actions with those of the people of Judah, who had been unfaithful to their covenant with God.

In response to Jeremiah, the Rechabites gave a firm refusal: "We will drink no wine" (v. 6). The reason, they explained, was that their ancestor had prohibited it. This was a permanent injunction that Jonadab instructed his family to maintain throughout their generations. Thus, the Rechabites of Jeremiah's time still honored their ancestor's command.

Drinking wine was culturally acceptable in ancient Israel, even in a religious setting like the Temple. Still, it was sometimes associated with idolatry and excess. While the Bible doesn't explain why Jonadab prohibited his family from drinking wine, likely it was to preserve a distinctive way of life.

In verse 7, the men provided more details about their lifestyle. Beyond abstaining from wine, they were to avoid activities that would tie them to a settled life. These pursuits—including owning land, planting vineyards, and establishing permanent houses—were also forbidden. Instead, the Rechabites were to be nomads, living "in tents all [their] days." This nomadic existence, which kept them mobile and distanced from the agricultural and urban practices of their neighbors, also helped preserve their unique identity.

Note the intensity of these phrases in verses 6-7: "you shall never" and "nor shall you ever." These reflected permanent prohibitions, which applied for all time for all of Jonadab's family members.

Jonadab's command to "live in tents" (v. 7) could be related to the Israelites' wilderness experience following the Exodus. Just as the people of Israel had to trust God for provisions before they reached the Promised Land, so the Rechabites' lifestyle may have been a reminder of their reliance on God—living as sojourners rather than settlers. This was a conscious choice to exist outside the typical societal norms of the time—a deliberate decision to remain distinct from the surrounding nations and cultures.

Whether or not the Rechabites knew their ancestor's original intention, they followed his commands without question. They wanted to experience the blessing that Jonadab promised—"that you may live many days in the land where you reside." This echoes the similar promise God made in the fifth commandment for those who honor their parents (Ex. 20:12).

II. Disobedience of Judah (Jeremiah 35:8-11)

In verse 8, the Rechabites continued to present their thoughtful and formal response to the challenge presented by the prophet Jeremiah. They declared their unwavering loyalty and obedience to the "charge" (command) of Jonadab, their esteemed ancestor. This commitment was not limited simply to their individual actions; it encompassed their entire households—including their wives, sons, and daughters. The language of their assertion emphasizes their complete adherence to Jonadab's instructions.

What stands out in this situation is the generational aspect of their obedience. Obviously, their commitment to those ancient principles was not merely a short-term decision made in the moment; rather, it reflected a long-standing family tradition that had been passed down through the ages—perhaps for as many as 250 years. Their deeply-rooted sense of duty underscores the strong values that were instilled within their lineage and reveals how Jonadab's commands had shaped their identity as a community.

Moreover, the Rechabites' response highlights a profound reverence for their forefather's directives. By refusing the wine that Jeremiah offered, they showed that their obedience went beyond mere ritualistic behavior. Rather, their conformity to community standards demonstrated their dedication to the values that defined their familial and spiritual identity. Their actions affirmed that such commitments were woven into the fabric of their lives, which reflected a powerful connection between faith, tradition, and family loyalty.

In verses 9-10, the Rechabites continued to champion their lifestyle—explaining that it had been consistent with what Jonadab commanded. They had not built permanent homes or engaged in agriculture by owning vineyards or fields. Their adherence to these commands speaks to their devotion to a way of life that is distinct from that of the people of Judah, who were focused on establishing secure homes and accumulating wealth through agricultural endeavors. The Rechabites' refusal to build houses or settle in one place demonstrates their commitment to live as sojourners, dedicated to their forefather's way of life.

The Rechabites' adherence to the commands of their ancestor represented a deep commitment to a lifestyle that was intentionally set apart from the surrounding culture, especially the settled, agricultural life of the people of Judah. By refraining from building permanent homes, planting vineyards, and owning fields, the Rechabites preserved a lifestyle rooted in simplicity, mobility, and separation from the pursuits of their neighbors.

For many in the ancient world, owning and cultivating land was a symbol of prosperity, success, and blessing. As such, Jonadab's instructions for his descendants to avoid building houses and to live in tents reflect a profoundly different perspective. As his people continued to live as sojourners—those who did not settle in one place but instead moved from location to location—they showed their dependence on God's provision rather than on what their hands could provide. Perhaps they believed they were placing their faith in the Lord to bless them instead of seeking blessings from fixed assets like land and crops.

This nomadic lifestyle was not simply about avoiding material wealth or comfort; it was deeply theological. By abstaining from activities like agriculture, which tied individuals to the land, the Rechabites kept their identity distinct from the Judahites, who had become more entrenched in an agricultural and even urban lifestyle. The Rechabites' choice to live as temporary residents rather than permanent settlers may have been seen as a way to honor God's command for His people to be faithful to Him. Whether they intended it or not, their lifestyle mirrored that of Abraham. Hebrews 11:10 emphasizes that the patriarch also lived "in tents" and was only a sojourner in the land God promised him, yet "he looked forward to the city that has foundations, whose architect and builder is God."

The Rechabites thus became a living reminder that earthly possessions and attachments are fleeting, and that one's true security and purpose lie in obedience to God. Their example also highlights a broader principle of religious and cultural preservation. By maintaining a lifestyle that was fundamentally different from that of their surrounding culture, the Rechabites ensured they could preserve their identity and values, passing them down from generation to generation. Their lifestyle was a testament to the idea that faithfulness to a standard could and should transcend the cultural values of the time.

For the Rechabites, faithfulness to their ancestors' commands was more than just about following traditions; it was part of a larger commitment to a divinely inspired way of life that preserved their distinctiveness as a people.

The final verse in this passage answers a question that some may have wondered: How did Jeremiah find the Rechabites so quickly if they were a nomadic people? In verse 11, the Rechabites explained why they were "living in Jerusalem," in houses rather than in tents, despite their lifelong commitment to a nomadic lifestyle. They told Jeremiah and those with him that they had moved to Jerusalem for their safety after the "army of the Chaldeans" (the Babylonians) and "the army of the Arameans" (the Syrians) invaded the land. As noted in 2 Kings chapter 24, those enemy nations, along with the Moabites and the Ammonites, allied together against Judah during the reign of King Jehoiakim. The Lord had decreed this attack to "remove [Judah] out of his sight, for the sins of Manasseh, for all that he had committed, and also for the innocent blood that he had shed, for he filled Jerusalem with innocent blood, and the Lord was not willing to pardon" (2 Kings 24:3-4).

Thus, the Rechabites' decision was pragmatic; in living outside of the city walls, they would have been vulnerable to invading armies. Although not explicitly stated, it is likely that their stay in Jerusalem was only temporary until the land was safe to travel in once again.

While not a part of this lesson, Jeremiah 35:12-19 reveals how the prophet used this symbolic action to confront the people of Judah. God used the episode to rebuke the disobedience of His people. He contrasted their continual unfaithfulness with the Rechabites' faithfulness for more than two centuries. In addition, while God sent multiple prophets to His disobedient people, Jonadab made only one decree, which his people obeyed continually.

THE LESSON APPLIED

The Rechabites' unwavering commitment encourages individuals to reflect on their own devotion to their beliefs. A related application highlights the significance of upholding one's values even when faced with pressures or temptations to compromise. Just as the ancient Rechabites resisted conforming to the accepted norms of the surrounding culture, believers today are called to preserve their integrity and remain true to their spiritual convictions, regardless of external influences.

Additionally, the passage highlights the importance of generational faithfulness. The Rechabites passed down their values and traditions for generations, setting a godly example to those who came after them. Lastly, the Rechabites' distinct lifestyle prioritized spiritual matters over material concerns. By not seeking security in wealth or possessions, believers show the value of trusting in God's provision and living with a sense of purpose that transcends the temporary things of this world.

Ultimately, this lesson calls all people to remain faithful to God and His commands, regardless of what others may do and despite outside variables.

LET'S TALK ABOUT IT...

Discuss the following questions and visit www.rhboyd.com for more information.

How can the example of the Rechabites' obedience to their ancestor's commands challenge us to remain faithful to our spiritual principles and practices, even when society pressures us to compromise?

What role does generational faithfulness play in shaping our lives? How can we intentionally pass down our values and traditions to the next generation, as the Rechabites did?

In a world that often values material success and security, how can we cultivate a lifestyle that prioritizes obedience to God's will over worldly pursuits, as exemplified by the Rechabites' nomadic way of life?

Get Social

Share your views and tag us @rhboydco and use #rhboydco

@rhboydco

Home Daily Devotional Readings
October 20–26, 2025

Monday	Tuesday	Wednesday	Thursday	Friday	Saturday	Sunday
A New Salvation	A New Heart	The Law's Essence	A New Covenant	A New Spirit	A New Freedom	A New Relationship with God
Joel 2:28-32	Ezekiel 36:25-35	Deuteronomy 10:12-21	2 Corinthians 3:1-6	2 Corinthians 3:7-11	2 Corinthians 3:12-17	Jeremiah 31:27-34

Lesson VIII   **October 26, 2025**

God's Law in the Heart

Adult Topic: The Heart Wants What the Heart Wants
Background Scripture: Jeremiah 31:1–40; John 1:17; Hebrews 8:7–13
Lesson Passage: Jeremiah 31:29–34; John 1:17

JEREMIAH 31:29–34; JOHN 1:17

KJV

IN those days they shall say no more, The fathers have eaten a sour grape, and the children's teeth are set on edge.

30 But every one shall die for his own iniquity: every man that eateth the sour grape, his teeth shall be set on edge.

31 Behold, the days come, saith the Lord, that I will make a new covenant with the house of Israel, and with the house of Judah:

32 Not according to the covenant that I made with their fathers in the day that I took them by the hand to bring them out of the land of Egypt; which my covenant they brake, although I was an husband unto them, saith the Lord:

33 But this shall be the covenant that I will make with the house of Israel; After those days, saith the Lord, I will put my law in their inward parts, and write it in their hearts; and will be their God, and they shall be my people.

34 And they shall teach no more every man his neighbour, and every man his brother, saying, Know the Lord: for they shall all know me, from the least of them unto the greatest of them, saith the Lord: for I will forgive their iniquity, and I will remember their sin no more.

• • • • • •

17 For the law was given by Moses, but grace and truth came by Jesus Christ.

NRSVue

IN those days they shall no longer say: "The parents have eaten sour grapes, and the children's teeth are set on edge."

30 But all shall die for their own sins; the teeth of the one who eats sour grapes shall be set on edge.

31 The days are surely coming, says the Lord, when I will make a new covenant with the house of Israel and the house of Judah.

32 It will not be like the covenant that I made with their ancestors when I took them by the hand to bring them out of the land of Egypt—a covenant that they broke, though I was their husband, says the Lord.

33 But this is the covenant that I will make with the house of Israel after those days, says the Lord: I will put my law within them, and I will write it on their hearts, and I will be their God, and they shall be my people.

34 No longer shall they teach one another or say to each other, "Know the Lord," for they shall all know me, from the least of them to the greatest, says the Lord, for I will forgive their iniquity and remember their sin no more.

• • • • • •

17 The law indeed was given through Moses; grace and truth came through Jesus Christ.

MAIN THOUGHT: I will put my law within them, and I will write it on their hearts, and I will be their God, and they shall be my people. (Jeremiah 31:33, NRSVue)

LESSON SETTING

Time: Jeremiah 31:29–34 was likely written around the sixth century BC. John 1:17 is traditionally dated to the late first century AD (around 90–100 AD).

Place: Jeremiah 31:29-34 was likely written from Jerusalem during the time of Babylonian exile. John 1:17 was likely written from Ephesus.

Setting: The book of Jeremiah was primarily written by the prophet Jeremiah, and much of it was written during Judah's exile in Babylon in the sixth century BC. The words in Jeremiah Chapter 31 were written either while the people of Judah were about to be taken to Babylon or were already in exile in that country. While Jeremiah likely wrote much of his prophecy from Jerusalem, his message often spoke to God's people in exile. So Jeremiah 31:29–34 may have been written with the exiled community in mind. The Gospel of John is traditionally believed to have been written by the Apostle John in the late first century AD. This Gospel is generally thought to have been composed in Ephesus (modern-day Turkey), although some scholars propose that it may have been written in another location in the Mediterranean region. Ephesus, an important commercial center in the first century, was a significant location for the initial spread of the Gospel during that time (Acts 19:10). Many scholars also believe that John spent much time in Ephesus during his later years.

LESSON OUTLINE

I. Promise of a New Covenant (Jeremiah 31:29–31)
II. Explanation of the New Covenant (Jeremiah 31:32–34)
III. The Fulfillment of the Law in Christ (John 1:17)

UNIFYING PRINCIPLE

People often blame others for their bad or evil behavior. What compels us to accept responsibility for our own behavior? God told Jeremiah that the people would be without excuse because, "I will put my law within them, and I will write it on their hearts," therefore God promised to forgive their iniquity, and remember their sin no more.

INTRODUCTION

Both the Old and New Testaments emphasize the themes of law, grace, and divine relationship, which are essential for understanding God's covenant with His people. Jeremiah 31:29–34 presents God's promise of a new covenant that transcends mere external Law observance, focusing instead on an internal transformation of the heart. Written during (or just before) the Babylonian exile—a time of great distress for the Israelites—these verses deliver a message of hope and restoration. Amid the consequences of their disobedience and separation from God, Jeremiah's prophecy envisioned a future where God restores His people and establishes a renewed, intimate relationship with them. This new covenant will not rely merely on external adherence to laws but will be inscribed on people's hearts. The passage reveals God's plan to foster a deep, personal connection with His people.

In the New Testament, John 1:17 builds on the prophetic hope of a new covenant by highlighting its ultimate fulfillment in Jesus Christ. John's Gospel reflects on the transition from the old covenant—which was given through Moses—to the new covenant, which came through Jesus, who embodied God's grace and truth. John 1:17 contrasts the Law with the grace that came through Christ, emphasizing a shift from an external, legalistic system to a relational, internal understanding of God's will. While the Law revealed God's expectations, the grace and truth embodied in Jesus Christ demonstrate the fulfillment of those expectations.

This lesson illustrates how God's redemptive plan moved from the promises of the Old Testament to their fulfillment in Jesus Christ. As such, God offered believers a new way of knowing and relating to Him.

EXPOSITION

I. Promise of a New Covenant (Jeremiah 31:29-31)

In this passage, the prophet Jeremiah promised a profound shift in the relationship between God and His people. This marked a change from the people's old way of relating to God—through external observances of the Law—to a new covenant that would be internalized within their hearts. To fully grasp these verses, it's essential to understand the context in which they were written and the more profound implications of the covenant that God promises.

Verse 29 begins with an apparently well-known proverb at that time. It expressed the people's belief that the consequences of a parent's sin were passed down to their children. This reflects the idea of collective or generational guilt, where one generation's wrongdoing affects the next. Such thinking may have been particularly applicable during the exile, when the people of Judah felt that their suffering resulted from the disobedience of their parents (Lam. 5:7).

In this passage, however, God proclaimed that the saying was invalid. Note that "in those days" refers to Jeremiah 31:23-28, where God promised a future restoration and blessing for His people.

Rather than collective guilt, God emphasized individual responsibility: "all shall die for their own sins; the teeth of the one who eats sour grapes shall be set on edge" (v. 30). In other words, each person will suffer the consequences of his or her own choices. The prophet Ezekiel, who ministered around the same time as Jeremiah, echoed these words as he emphasized individual accountability to the people of Judah (Ezek. 18:1-4).

The theological shift from generational guilt to personal responsibility had significant implications not only for Israel but also for all of humanity. It reflected a move toward personal accountability to God. This is more than just a focus on judgment; God's statement reflects how He will relate to individuals in the future. In the old covenant, the people of Israel were often defined by their collective identity as a nation. With the coming of a new covenant, however, the focus would instead be on the individual's relationship to God. This means that God will hold each person responsible for their own sin; He will judge a person based on that person's actions.

In verse 31, God promised His people that a "new covenant" was coming. It would replace the old covenant, which had been based on the Law given through Moses. This new covenant anticipates a future time when God will initiate a deeper and more intimate relationship with His people, moving beyond mere adherence to rules.

Note that this new covenant was promised not just to the people of Judah at that time. Rather, God's new covenant would be "with the house of Israel and the house of Judah." The Northern Kingdom, also known as Israel, ceased to exist after the Assyrians destroyed it and displaced its people around 722 BC. Though the tribes of Israel had been divided for around 200 years when God spoke through Jeremiah, the new covenant anticipates a time when the nation would be whole again. This pivotal moment will encompass all the people of God, uniting them under a singular divine plan.

II. Explanation of the New Covenant (Jeremiah 31:32-34)

In this passage, the Lord spoke through Jeremiah to contrast the old and new covenants. The old covenant was centered around the Law of Moses, which included commands, sacrifices, and rituals that the Israelites were expected to follow. God had entered into this covenant with the people of Israel after He "took them by the hand" (v. 32) and delivered them from slavery in Egypt. Then, God established a covenant relationship with Israel as His chosen people (Exod. 19–24). However, despite God's faithfulness in delivering and providing for them, the Israelites repeatedly broke their covenant with the Lord. Their disobedience, idolatry, and unfaithfulness led to repeated cycles of judgment and restoration. The people's failure to uphold their covenant responsibilities revealed the weakness of the old system—it was dependent on human obedience. While it might seem that God was surprised by His people's unfaithfulness, the Lord had foretold the people's apostasy centuries earlier, just before they entered the Promised Land (Deut. 31:16–20).

At the end of verse 32, God used the image of a "husband" to describe His relationship with Israel. This deeply personal metaphor reflects God's faithfulness, care, and commitment to His people. Although Israel's actions were often unfaithful, the Lord remained loving and steadfast. God also used the marriage metaphor—with Him as the husband of an unfaithful wife—on other occasions (Isa. 54:5–6; Jer. 2:2; 3:1) as He called His people to return to Him.

Because of the people's sinful nature that was bent toward unfaithfulness, the old covenant could not serve as the final solution for restoring their relationship with God.

In verse 33, God explained the new covenant. Unlike the old covenant, which was focused on external adherence to laws and rituals, the new covenant would involve an internal transformation. God promised to "put [His] law within them" and "write it on their hearts." Unlike the old covenant law that was written on tablets of stone (Exod. 24:12), God's Law in the new covenant will become part of His people's very being, guiding their thoughts, actions, and desires.

This promise signifies an intimate relationship with God. Under the new covenant, obedience will no longer be about external compliance to rules. Instead, it will become an internal motivation prompted by a heart transformation that is implemented by God's Spirit (Ezek. 36:27; 37:14). This forms the foundation for a relationship with God that is rooted not in fear of punishment or simply performing religious rituals, but in a genuine desire to honor and follow Him.

The promise that "I will be their God, and they will be my people" reflects the restoration of the intimate relationship that God originally intended with humanity. In the new covenant, God's presence and guidance are deeply personal, and the people's devotion to their Lord is authentic and heartfelt. This signifies a profound shift from the old covenant in which the Israelites were often distant from God, failing to uphold the covenant despite God's faithfulness.

Verse 34 describes the universal, intimate knowledge of God that will characterize the new covenant. Under the old covenant, the people of Israel were entrusted with teaching others about God, and there were clear distinctions between those who knew God and those who did not. Under the new covenant, however, there will be no need for anyone to say, "Know the LORD," because everyone will know God intimately. The Hebrew word for "know" (*yada*) goes beyond simply an intellectual understanding; rather, it stresses an intimate relationship—knowing by personal experience. From the "least" to the "greatest," everyone will have access to God and will experience His presence in a direct and personal way. This universal knowledge of God will contribute to the internal transformation that the new covenant brings.

As part of the new covenant, God also promised to forgive the "iniquity" (wickedness) of His people and "remember their sin no more." This is a profound promise of redemption—through the new covenant, sin will no longer separate God and His people. The sins of the past will be forgiven and erased, enabling humans to have a restored and unbroken relationship with God.

III. The Fulfillment of the Law in Christ (John 1:17)

This verse encapsulates the transition from the old covenant to the new covenant. Beyond simply contrasting Law and grace (which God emphasized throughout Jer. 31:29–34), John 1:17 also notes how Jesus Christ brought the fulfillment of both.

Verse 17 mentions the "law" that God gave to Israel through Moses. This included the moral, civil, and ceremonial laws that directed their relationship with God. The Law outlined God's righteous standards and His people's required obedience.

While the Law revealed God's holiness, it also highlighted humanity's inability to fully adhere to God's standards. The Law could identify sin but could not offer forgiveness, which indicated that salvation could not be achieved through human effort alone.

This verse also highlights the "grace and truth" that came through Jesus Christ. Grace refers to God's unmerited favor—His gift of salvation to humanity, offered not because of human merit, but only because of His love and mercy. Through Jesus, grace is made available to all people, providing forgiveness for sin and the possibility of reconciliation with God. Unlike the Law, which required strict adherence to rules, grace provides the means of salvation despite human failure.

In the Gospel of John, "truth" refers to the complete revelation of God, which is embodied in Jesus Christ. While the Law pointed to God's will, it could not fully reveal God's nature. Jesus, as the Word made flesh (John 1:14), is the ultimate revelation of God's truth. Jesus perfectly embodies God's righteous standards and His grace.

Thus, John 1:17 highlights the fulfillment of the Law in Christ. Jesus did not abolish the Law (Matt. 5:17) but fulfilled it by living a perfect life and offering grace through His sacrificial death. While the Law could show humans the way to live, it could not provide the way for them to obey God's will. The Law revealed the problem—sin—but Jesus is the solution. His coming marked the shift from focusing on external obedience to the Law to the internal transformation offered by grace and truth. Through Jesus, humanity is offered a new way of relating to God, not based on perfect rule-keeping but on faith in Christ, who embodies the fullness of both the Law and grace.

THE LESSON APPLIED

Jeremiah 31:29–34 reveals a new covenant in which God's Law is written on our hearts, rather than being mere external commands to follow. This reminds us that true obedience to God involves more than just outward actions; it's about an internal transformation that alters our hearts and desires. Consequently, we do not simply adhere to rules because we must; we do so because we genuinely want to honor God, reflecting His love and truth in our actions.

John 1:17 highlights the contrast between the Law, which merely points out sin, and the grace and truth brought by Jesus Christ. In our daily struggles, this verse is a reminder that although we may fall short and make mistakes, God extends grace—His unearned favor—not based on our actions, but based on what Jesus did. As we experience His grace, we are freed from the burden of perfection and empowered to show grace to others, forgiving their shortcomings. Collectively, these passages encourage us to live with integrity, embrace personal transformation, and rely on God's grace as we navigate life's challenges.

LET'S TALK ABOUT IT...

Discuss the following questions and visit www.rhboyd.com for more information.

How can we cultivate an internal transformation of the heart, as described in Jeremiah 31:29–34, in our daily interactions with others and in our relationship with God?

How can we apply the grace and truth that came through Jesus, as highlighted in John 1:17, to our struggles with guilt, failure, and forgiveness in our everyday lives?

How do the concepts of personal accountability in Jeremiah 31:29–30 and the grace offered through Jesus in John 1:17 intersect in how we view our responsibilities and the way we relate to others in our community?

Get Social

Share your views and tag us
@rhboydco and use #rhboydco

@rhboydco

Home Daily Devotional Readings
October 2–November 2, 2025

Monday	Tuesday	Wednesday	Thursday	Friday	Saturday	Sunday
Speak as the Spirit Leads	Do Not Fear Mortal Powers	Wait Patiently for the Lord	God Never Forsakes the Righteous	Overcome Evil with Good	Speak Even When the Message Stings	An Advocate Pleads for Justice
Matthew 10:16–27	Matthew 10:28–42	Psalm 37:1–13	Psalm 37:2528, 35–40	Romans 12:12–21	Jeremiah 38:1–6	Jeremiah 38:7–13

Lesson IX — **November 2, 2025**

Later Experiences of Jeremiah

Adult Topic: Well? That's a Deep Subject!
Background Scripture: Jeremiah 20:1–6; 37:1–38:28; 43:1–7
Lesson Passage: Jeremiah 38:7–13

JEREMIAH 38:7–13

KJV

NOW when Ebedmelech the Ethiopian, one of the eunuchs which was in the king's house, heard that they had put Jeremiah in the dungeon; the king then sitting in the gate of Benjamin;
8 Ebedmelech went forth out of the king's house, and spake to the king saying,
9 My lord the king, these men have done evil in all that they have done to Jeremiah the prophet, whom they have cast into the dungeon; and he is like to die for hunger in the place where he is: for there is no more bread in the city.
10 Then the king commanded Ebedmelech the Ethiopian, saying, Take from hence thirty men with thee, and take up Jeremiah the prophet out of the dungeon, before he die.
11 So Ebedmelech took the men with him, and went into the house of the king under the treasury, and took thence old cast clouts and old rotten rags, and let them down by cords into the dungeon to Jeremiah.
12 And Ebedmelech the Ethiopian said unto Jeremiah, Put now these old cast clouts and rotten rags under thine armholes under the cords. And Jeremiah did so.
13 So they drew up Jeremiah with cords, and took him up out of the dungeon: and Jeremiah remained in the court of the prison.

NRSVue

EBED-MELECH the Cushite, a eunuch in the king's house, heard that they had put Jeremiah into the cistern. The king happened to be sitting at the Benjamin Gate,
8 So Ebed-melech left the king's house and spoke to the king,
9 "My lord king, these men have acted wickedly in all they did to the prophet Jeremiah by throwing him into the cistern to die there of hunger, for there is no bread left in the city."
10 Then the king commanded Ebed-melech the Cushite, "Take three men with you from here, and pull the prophet Jeremiah up from the cistern before he dies."
11 So Ebed-melech took the men with him and went to the house of the king, to a wardrobe of the storehouse, and took from there old rags and worn-out clothes, which he let down to Jeremiah in the cistern by ropes.
12 Then Ebed-melech the Cushite said to Jeremiah, "Just put the rags and clothes between your armpits and the ropes." Jeremiah did so.
13 Then they drew Jeremiah up by the ropes and pulled him out of the cistern. And Jeremiah remained in the court of the guard.

Lesson Setting
Time: 586 BC
Place: Jerusalem

MAIN THOUGHT: Then the king commanded Ebed-melech the Cushite, "Take three men with you from here, and pull the prophet Jeremiah up from the cistern before he dies." (Jeremiah 38:10, NRSVue)

Setting: Jeremiah Chapter 38 reveals events that happened in Jerusalem during the Babylonians' siege of Jerusalem, in the final days before the city was destroyed. The prophet Jeremiah had previously prophesied the city's destruction and warned the people to surrender to the Babylonians. With the city under attack, the people of Judah were experiencing severe famine and hardship. Jeremiah's prophecy angered some of King Zedekiah's officials, who felt he was discouraging not only the people but also the soldiers from fighting against the Babylonians. Thus, the officials went to the king and sought to have Jeremiah put to death. The king consented, so they threw him into a cistern (a deep, well-like pit) and left him there to die. One man, however, acted to rescue Jeremiah from certain death.

LESSON OUTLINE
I. Jeremiah's Imprisonment (Jeremiah 38:7–9)
II. Ebed-melech's Intervention (Jeremiah 38:10–12)
III. Divine Protection and Faithfulness (Jeremiah 38:13)

UNIFYING PRINCIPLE
Sometimes those closest to us abandon us when we take a stand for what is right. Where can we look for support when those people turn against us? When Jeremiah's life was threatened because of his unpopular message, God sent Ebed-melech, a Cushite, to intervene on Jeremiah's behalf.

INTRODUCTION

Throughout his forty-year ministry, Jeremiah delivered God's message of judgment to the people of Judah. This was not a well-received message, especially for the nation's leaders, who preferred false assurances of security. By 586 BC, Jerusalem had been under siege by the Babylonians for more than two years. As the siege neared the end, Jeremiah encouraged the people to surrender to the Babylonians rather than facing destruction, famine, and death. He warned that resistance would only bring greater suffering, especially since God had already decided Jerusalem's fate. This was a bitter pill to swallow for King Zedekiah and other leaders in Judah. They resisted Jeremiah's message, believing that their own military strength, or perhaps the intervention of Egypt, could save them from the Babylonians. To these leaders, Jeremiah's calls for surrender were treasonous.

As Jeremiah's unpopular messages continued, some influential officials took more drastic actions in their efforts to silence him. Eventually they arrested Jeremiah and cast him into a cistern—a large, deep vessel in the ground that was dug out of the rock and used to store water for the city. One commentator stated that Jerusalem had many cisterns in which they stored the winter rain water to use during the hot, dry summers. (Feinberg, Charles L. *Jeremiah* in *The Expositor's Bible Commentary, Volume 6* [Grand Rapids: Zondervan, 1986], 616.) Often the rock was porous, which meant that any water remaining in it for an extended time would eventually drain out. But since the city was under siege, the water supply, like the food supply, may have been minimal. Jeremiah 38:6 notes that there was no water in the cistern, thus Jeremiah sank into the mud in this cold, dark "prison." Because of its shape and depth, it was nearly impossible for anyone to escape without help. This was a humiliating punishment by which Jeremiah would die and the officials would avoid being seen as guilty for shedding innocent blood.

EXPOSITION

I. Jeremiah's Imprisonment (Jeremiah 38:7–9)

The officials' decision to throw Jeremiah into the cistern was both a physical and symbolic act of rejection. By placing him in such a dire situation, the officials sought not only to silence Jeremiah but also to assert their authority. Perhaps they even believed that by punishing the prophet, they could stop the inevitable destruction he foretold.

What these leaders failed to understand, however, was that Jeremiah's message was not his own; it was God's word. Despite their resistance, Jeremiah's role as God's prophet required him to speak truth, no matter how unpopular or difficult the message was. Thus, Jeremiah's imprisonment was not an indication of his failure; rather, it reflected the spiritual blindness and hard hearts of the officials in Jerusalem. Their rejection of Jeremiah's prophecy was, in fact, a rejection of God's will.

Jeremiah 38:7 introduces a pivotal character: Ebed-melech, whose name means "servant of the king." This man was a "Cushite," that is, from the upper Nile region. While some translations (including the KJV) identify him as the "Ethiopian," this was not the same country of Ethiopia that today is located in Eastern Africa. Verse 7 noted that he was a "eunuch." The Hebrew word *sar* can also be translated "official" (as in Jer. 52:25), so it is uncertain exactly what role he served in the palace of King Zedekiah. Still, upon hearing of Jeremiah's imprisonment in the cistern, Ebed-melech decided to act. He went to the king and appealed for Jeremiah's release. At that moment the king was "sitting at the Benjamin Gate," where he went to arbitrate issues between people who sought justice from the king.

The Cushite's role in this event is significant for several reasons. First, as an outsider—both ethnically and socially—his intervention shows that God can work through unexpected people. Though Ebed-melech was a foreigner, he showed more compassion and courage than the officials in Judah, who should have been upholding justice. Second, as a eunuch serving in the royal palace, Ebed-melech held a position of responsibility but was still viewed as different in a culture that valued lineage and family. His willingness to do what was right and just, despite being an outsider, reveals that righteousness transcends ethnic and social boundaries. Ultimately, Ebed-melech's involvement highlights the biblical theme that God often uses unexpected individuals, regardless of their background, to fulfill His purposes.

Verse 9 relates how Ebed-melech confronted King Zedekiah, urging the king to take action against the injustices done to Jeremiah. The servant noted the cruelty of the officials, who "acted wickedly in all they did." Their wickedness was not merely the act of imprisoning Jeremiah; it included the greater injustice of condemning an innocent man for proclaiming the word of God.

Ebed-melech emphasized that Jeremiah was in a dire situation and would likely die from hunger. With the city under seige, the food supply had already been limited (Jer. 37:21), which was bad news. Here, however, the servant emphasized even worse news: "there is no bread left in the city." In speaking of Jeremiah's condition, Ebed-melech literally stated, "he is dead" or "he has died." In other words, Jeremiah was as good as dead if he remained imprisoned in the cistern, especially since any available food would not have been given to a prisoner. Ebed-melech's words reflect a genuine concern for Jeremiah's survival, not just a moral or religious argument.

This passage highlights the disparity between the wicked actions of the influential officials and the righteous compassion demonstrated by Ebed-melech, who recognized injustice and took decisive steps to rectify it. This took great courage, because the servant could have lost his position or his life for accusing the other officials. These verses reveal how God uses even the most unlikely individuals—like Ebed-melech—to stand up for justice and protect His messenger. While the king's officials vengefully conspired to silence Jeremiah, Ebed-melech's courage and moral clarity brought a moment of reprieve to the prophet. The verses also highlight the themes of injustice, righteousness, and God's provision in times of need, setting the stage for the rescue that will follow in the next verses.

II. Ebed-melech's Intervention (Jeremiah 38:10–12)

Notice that Ebed-melech did not make a request of King Zedekiah; the servant simply presented the dreadful facts. Implied in his words, however, was a request for the king to act immediately. The king, understanding the urgency of Ebed-melech's appeal, wasted no time in considering the matter.

Verse 10 notes the king's command to his servant. While some Hebrew manuscripts designate the number in this verse as "thirty men," one Hebrew text states "three men." Certainly 30 men would not be needed to pull Jeremiah from his cistern prison. Still, the extra men could have been used as guards for the mission in case the other officials tried to intervene and prevent the rescue.

No one knows why King Zedekiah decided to save Jeremiah at this time. Previously, he told the officials who wanted to kill the prophet: "he is in your hands, for the king is powerless against you" (Jer. 38:5). His words suggest a man who likely was not in charge—an ineffective leader. Still, perhaps Ebed-melech's courage in advocating for Jeremiah inspired the king to do the right thing. Thus, Zedekiah gave the order to save the prophet.

Ebed-melech's courageous actions were certainly a beacon of hope for Jeremiah. In addition, the servant's intervention points to the importance of leaders listening to input from all corners, especially from those who stand for justice and righteousness.

In verse 11, Ebed-melech enlisted a determined group of men to carry out the rescue mission. First, they went "to a wardrobe of the storehouse"—which was somewhere in the royal palace. Evidently Ebed-melech knew where he could find what the group needed. Then, they gathered the necessary tools—a strong set of ropes and some "old rags and worn-out clothes."

Ebed-melech was apparently a meticulous planner. His quick but thoughtful preparation underscores his value in service to the king. The servant's swift decision to act and his diligent efforts to ensure the success of the operation are a testament to the courage and compassion that drive some people even in the face of hardship.

Next, Ebed-melech took another courageous step by going directly to the cistern where Jeremiah was being held captive. Then, he lowered the rags and old clothes with the ropes, which were likely tied into a loop that Jeremiah could slip around his body. Despite the urgency of the situation, Ebed-melech kept a level head. Calling out with a sense of urgency and reassurance, Ebed-melech instructed the prophet to use the discarded clothing as cushioning under his arms before putting the ropes around him. This is another indication of Jeremiah's desperate condition—he may have been so weak that he could not hold on to the ropes that would be used to save him. Likewise, his body may have been so frail that the ropes would have cut into his skin.

Verse 12 again highlights Ebed-melech's compassion and forethought as he wanted to avoid further injury to the prophet during his extraction from the pit. The servant's words were also a profound gesture of emotional support. In speaking to Jeremiah, Ebed-melech offered hope and encouragement—needs that had been sorely lacking from others, especially the officials, in Jerusalem.

Ebed-melech's bravery, compassion, and practical wisdom set him apart as a unique person in the narrative. His willingness to act decisively and humanely, even in the bleakest of times, underscores an important lesson: A single individual, regardless of their background or societal status, can make a profound difference when they stand for what is just and right. The Cushite servant's example is a powerful reminder that one person's courage can inspire others, especially in situations where many people might choose inaction or self-preservation. This shows that integrity often shines brightest when faced with adversity.

III. Divine Protection and Faithfulness (Jeremiah 38:13)

Jeremiah was successfully extracted from the pit, thanks to the efforts of Ebed-melech and his men. While Ebed-melech was the agent of rescue, his actions are presented as part of God's providence. God used an outsider to save Jeremiah and ensure that the prophet's mission continued. Jeremiah might have echoed David's words: "I waited patiently for the Lord; he inclined to me and heard my cry. He drew me up from the desolate pit, out of the miry bog" (Ps. 40:1–2).

This act of rescue is a reminder of God's faithfulness to His people. The Lord's protection is greater than any adversary's plan.

The last part of verse 13 notes that while Jeremiah was free from the cistern, he was confined to "the court of the guard." Here, as before (Jer. 32:2; 37:21), he could have visitors (Jer. 32:8). Likewise, the prophet could continue speaking God's message.

Later, God commended Ebed-melech for his part in rescuing the prophet. In Jeremiah 39:15–18, the Lord promised to save the Cushite from the coming destruction of Jerusalem. Because Ebed-melech trusted in the Lord, the servant would not be handed over to those whom he feared, nor would he die in the battle.

THE LESSON APPLIED

Jeremiah 38:7–13 offers valuable lessons that can be applied to life today, especially related to standing up for justice, speaking truth in difficult times, and showing compassion in the face of adversity. In this lesson, Ebed-melech, an outsider, acted with moral courage to rescue the prophet Jeremiah from an unjust situation. His actions demonstrate the importance of doing what is right, even when it opposes the will of the majority or the established powers. Often in our world, believers are called to speak out against injustice, whether in the workplace, our communities, or in society at large. Like Ebed-melech, we can be instruments of change, advocating for those who are marginalized or oppressed.

Jeremiah's experience in the cistern also reminds us about the cost of standing firm in our convictions. Because the prophet's message was unpopular, it caused him to suffer. Even so, Jeremiah remained committed to the Lord and His word. Likewise, we may face rejection or ridicule when we stand for truth, especially in a world where conforming to the status quo is often more socially acceptable. This lesson encourages us to remain faithful, trusting that God will use our efforts for His purposes, just as He used Ebed-melech to rescue His prophet.

Ultimately, this story highlights the importance of compassion and taking action to help others, especially when they are vulnerable or mistreated. Ebed-melech's intervention serves as a powerful reminder that we are all called to serve others—using whatever influence or resources we have to make a positive difference. By practicing empathy and stepping into difficult situations, we can live out the values of justice, mercy, and righteousness in our daily lives.

LET'S TALK ABOUT IT...

Discuss the following questions and visit www.rhboyd.com for more information.

How can we, as individuals or communities, emulate Ebed-melech in standing up for justice and helping those who are marginalized or oppressed, especially when it may be unpopular or difficult?

In what ways does Jeremiah's unwavering commitment to speaking God's truth, despite facing rejection and suffering, challenge us to stay true to our values in today's world?

What are some modern-day "cisterns" where people are unjustly imprisoned or silenced? How can we as believers be more proactive in advocating for their release or providing support for them?

Get Social

Share your views and tag us @rhboydco and use #rhboydco

@rhboydco

Home Daily Devotional Readings
November 3–9, 2025

Monday	Tuesday	Wednesday	Thursday	Friday	Saturday	Sunday
The Master Is Coming Soon	The Purifying Fire of Change	The Lord's Purifying Purpose	Hope in the Lord	Faith Tested by Fire	Prepare for Action	God's Judgment Is Sure
Luke 12:42–48	Luke 12:49–53	Lamentations 2:17–22	Lamentations 3:21–36	1 Peter 1:1–12	1 Peter 1:13–25	2 Kings 24:18–25:9

Lesson X — November 9, 2025

Judah Taken Captive

Adult Topic: We've Fallen and We Can't Get Up!
Background Scripture: 2 Kings 23:1–25:21
Lesson Passage: 2 Kings 24:18–25:9

2 KINGS 24:18–25:9

KJV

ZEDEKIAH was twenty and one years old when he began to reign, and he reigned eleven years in Jerusalem. And his mother's name was Hamutal, the daughter of Jeremiah of Libnah.
19 And he did that which was evil in the sight of the Lord, according to all that Jehoiakim had done.
20 For through the anger of the Lord it came to pass in Jerusalem and Judah, until he had cast them out from his presence, that Zedekiah rebelled against the king of Babylon.

••• 2 Kings 25:1–9 •••
1 And it came to pass in the ninth year of his reign, in the tenth month, in the tenth day of the month, that Nebuchadnezzar king of Babylon came, he, and all his host, against Jerusalem, and pitched against it; and they built forts against it round about.
2 And the city was besieged unto the eleventh year of king Zedekiah.
3 And on the ninth day of the fourth month the famine prevailed in the city, and there was no bread for the people of the land.
4 And the city was broken up, and all the men of war fled by night by the way of the gate between two walls, which is by the king's garden: (now the Chaldees were against the city round about:) and the king went the way toward the plain.
5 And the army of the Chaldees pursued after the king, and overtook him in the plains of Jericho: and all his army were scattered from him.

NRSVue

ZEDEKIAH was twenty-one years old when he began to reign; he reigned eleven years in Jerusalem. His mother's name was Hamutal daughter of Jeremiah of Libnah.
19 He did what was evil in the sight of the Lord, just as Jehoiakim had done.
20 Indeed, Jerusalem and Judah so angered the Lord that he expelled them from his presence.

••• 2 Kings 25:1–9 •••
1 And in the ninth year of his reign, in the tenth month, on the tenth day of the month, King Nebuchadnezzar of Babylon came with all his army against Jerusalem and laid siege to it; they built siegeworks against it all around.
2 So the city was besieged until the eleventh year of King Zedekiah.
3 On the ninth day of the fourth month, the famine became so severe in the city that there was no food for the people of the land.
4 Then a breach was made in the city wall; the king with all the soldiers fled by night by the way of the gate between the two walls, by the King's Garden, though the Chaldeans were all around the city. They went in the direction of the Arabah.
5 But the army of the Chaldeans pursued the king and overtook him in the plains of Jericho; all his army was scattered, deserting him.

MAIN THOUGHT: Jerusalem and Judah so angered the Lord that he expelled them from his presence. (2 Kings 24:20, NRSVue)

2 KINGS 24:18-25:9

KJV

6 So they took the king, and brought him up to the king of Babylon to Riblah; and they gave judgment upon him.

7 And they slew the sons of Zedekiah before his eyes, and put out the eyes of Zedekiah, and bound him with fetters of brass, and carried him to Babylon.

8 And in the fifth month, on the seventh day of the month, which is the nineteenth year of king Nebuchadnezzar king of Babylon, came Nebuzaradan, captain of the guard, a servant of the king of Babylon, unto Jerusalem:

9 And he burnt the house of the Lord, and the king's house, and all the houses of Jerusalem, and every great man's house burnt he with fire.

NRSVue

6 Then they captured the king and brought him up to the king of Babylon at Riblah, who passed sentence on him.

7 They slaughtered the sons of Zedekiah before his eyes, then put out the eyes of Zedekiah; they bound him in fetters and took him to Babylon.

8 In the fifth month, on the seventh day of the month—which was the nineteenth year of King Nebuchadnezzar, king of Babylon—Nebuzaradan, the captain of the bodyguard, a servant of the king of Babylon, came to Jerusalem.

9 He burned the house of the Lord, the king's house, and all the houses of Jerusalem; every great house he burned down.

LESSON SETTING

Time: Around 586 BC
Place: Jerusalem
Setting: The larger passage from 2 Kings 24–25 describes the final events leading to the fall of Jerusalem, including the capture of King Zedekiah, the destruction of the city by the Babylonians, and the exile of the people of Judah. These chapters also record the death of King Jehoiakim in Jerusalem along with the exile and eventual release of King Jehoiachin from prison in Babylon. The events described in 2 Kings 24:18-25:9 took place in the early sixth century BC, particularly around 586 BC, when King Nebuchadnezzar led the Babylonian army in overthrowing Jerusalem. However, the book of Kings itself (which in Hebrew was originally one manuscript), was likely written or compiled much later. This is because the book reflects on the historical events with a theological perspective, understanding them as consequences of Israel's unfaithfulness to God. The final editing of the book of Kings is commonly believed to have occurred in Babylon during or shortly after the Babylonian exile, perhaps during the period between 560 and 540 BC. Jewish scribes and scholars who were exiled in Babylon would have written and compiled many historical records, including Kings, to reflect on not only the history of Israel as a whole (both the Northern and the Southern Kingdoms) but also God's judgment on His people's actions.

LESSON OUTLINE
I. Zedekiah Rules (2 Kings 24:18–20)
II. Fall of the Kingdom (2 Kings 25:1–7)
III. Burning the City and Temple (2 Kings 25:8–9)

UNIFYING PRINCIPLE
People seem to understand the consequences of bad behavior, yet they persist in living selfishly and irresponsibly. What are the consequences of our bad choices? The prophets understood Babylon as the instrument of God's judgment toward Judah for their blatant disregard of the covenant, though ultimately, God's love accompanied His people into their captivity and exile.

INTRODUCTION
Second Kings 24:18–25:9 marks the final stages of the Kingdom of Judah, detailing its collapse under the Babylonian conquest. This passage describes the events leading to the end of the Davidic dynasty in Jerusalem and the city's ultimate destruction.

Following Jehoiakim's rebellion against Babylon, he died and his son Jehoiachin succeeded him as king of Judah. Three months later, however, King Nebuchadnezzar led the Babylonian army into Jerusalem where they raided the Temple and took Jehoiachin and thousands of the notable citizens into exile in Babylon. Nebuchadnezzar then placed Zedekiah on Judah's throne as a puppet ruler. Zedekiah later rebelled against Babylon as well, culminating in a siege of Jerusalem that led to the city's ruin in 586 BC.

The Babylonian army, after a prolonged siege, finally breached the city walls, destroyed the Temple, burned down the royal palace, and captured Zedekiah, who was later blinded and exiled. The final scenes in the book of 2 Kings depict the people of Judah being taken into exile, the tragic fate of the governor whom Nebuchadnezzar left in charge of Judah, and Jehoiachin's release from prison in Babylon after thirty-seven years.

EXPOSITION

I. Zedekiah Rules (2 Kings 24:18–20)
After deposing and exiling Jehoiachin, King Nebuchadnezzar appointed Mattaniah, whom he renamed Zedekiah, as vassal king of Judah (2 Kings 24:17). This was a common practice by conquering empires to control subject people.

Zedekiah, a son of Josiah, was only twenty-one years old when he became king. His youth, combined with the circumstances of his installation, may explain his vulnerability to manipulation and the fact that he reigned only eleven years.

Hamutal, his mother, was the daughter of Jeremiah of Libnah. Her father, Jeremiah, could refer to the prophet Jeremiah, though it is unclear if this is the same person. While little is known about Hamutal, this notation also places Zedekiah in the royal lineage.

Verse 19 notes that Zedekiah's reign was characterized by evil. Like many of his predecessors, Zedekiah's actions displeased the Lord. Under his leadership, "All the leading priests and the people [of Judah] also were exceedingly unfaithful, following all the abominations of the nations, and they polluted the house of the LORD" (2 Chron.

36:14). The record in Chronicles (and Jer. 37:1–2) also notes that Zedekiah mocked, despised, and scoffed at God's words of warning and judgment through Jeremiah and the other prophets. Rather than following the example of his father—the good King Josiah—Zedekiah emulated the evil of his brother Jehoiakim.

The theological perspective behind the downfall of Jerusalem and Judah is revealed in verse 20. The phrase "expelled them from his presence" indicates that the people's sin led to God's abandonment—a devastating judgment. The exile was a result of God's just response to Judah's persistent rebellion. Zedekiah's reign is portrayed as the culmination of Judah's failure to remain faithful to God, leading to their exile.

The last sentence of verse 20 sets the scene for the Babylonian siege of Jerusalem: "Zedekiah rebelled against the king of Babylon." While the Bible doesn't specify the reason for Zedekiah's rebellion, he likely believed the false prophets who rejected Jeremiah's message (Jer. 27–28) and perhaps urged the king to rebel. Likewise, Zedekiah trusted that Egypt would help him, despite God's word to the contrary (Ezek. 17:15–18).

II. Fall of the Kingdom (2 Kings 25:1–7)

Jerusalem's fall began "in the ninth year of [Zedekiah's] reign" (v. 1), around 588 BC. The "tenth month ... tenth day" indicates the precise timing of the siege. The Bible often records exact dates to emphasize the fulfillment of prophecies and the weight of historical events.

Babylon's King Nebuchadnezzar led the "siege"—an extended military blockade designed to starve the city into submission. Babylon had already gained control over Judah prior to Zedekiah's reign, but the Judean king's rebellion compelled Nebuchadnezzar to intervene and end the revolt.

The siege lasted for about two and a half years—until the "eleventh year" (v. 2) of Zedekiah's reign (586 BC). This prolonged siege reflects the thoroughness of Babylon's military strategy. Eventually, the "famine became ... severe" (v. 3) after supplies from the outside world were cut off and any food that had previously been stored in the city was gone. This caused immense suffering for the inhabitants of Jerusalem.

As the siege continued, the Babylonian army finally breached "city wall" (v. 4), penetrating Jerusalem's defenses. As Babylonian troops and commanders poured into the city (Jer. 39:2–3), King Zedekiah realized that defeat was near. In a desperate move, he and his remaining soldiers tried to escape, even though the "Chaldeans [Babylonians] were all around the city." Under cover of darkness, they fled through a "gate between the two walls" that was near the royal garden. The group headed toward the Arabah—the desert region south of the Dead Sea.

Zedekiah's escape was short-lived, however. Verse 5 records that the Babylonian forces pursued him and eventually caught up with him in the "plains of Jericho," a region northeast of Jerusalem. In the same place where the Israelites victoriously entered the Promised Land (Josh. 5:10), the last king of Judah was left by himself after the soldiers scattered and deserted him.

Babylonian troops captured Zedekiah and took him to Riblah, a town in northern Syria where Nebuchadnezzar had his headquarters at that time. There, the Babylonian king "passed sentence on" Zedekiah (v. 6). He was no longer a ruler but a prisoner, at the mercy of the Babylonian king.

As verse 7 explains, the Babylonians brutally executed Zedekiah's sons in front of him; this horrific act was meant to break the king's spirit. Then after witnessing the slaughter of his sons, Zedekiah's eyes were gouged out. The final act of binding Zedekiah in "fetters" (shackles) and taking him to Babylon further humiliated the fallen king and sealed the fate of Judah.

These events serve as vivid symbols of God's judgment. The vicious actions fulfilled the prophecies of Jeremiah, who foretold that the Babylonians would capture Zedekiah and his family. Likewise, the events confirm God's promise through the prophet Ezekiel: "I will bring him [Zedekiah] to Babylon, the land of the Chaldeans, yet he shall not see it" (Ezek. 12:13).

III. Burning the City and Temple (2 Kings 25:8–9)

About a month after the Babylonians captured Jerusalem, they carried out the complete destruction of the city. Once again, the date is noted in detail: the fifth month and seventh day. According to the Babylonian calendar, this was August 14, 586 BC, which was during the 19th year of King Nebuchadnezzar's reign.

The Babylonian official who oversaw Jerusalem's destruction was Nebuzaradan, "the captain of the bodyguard" (v. 8). One scholar notes that this title (in Hebrew) literally means "the chief executioner" or "the slaughterer" (Dilday, Russell H., *The Communicator's Commentary: 1, 2 Kings* [Waco: Word Books, 1987], 505.) Nebuzaradan executed the king's orders to annihilate the city and its temple.

Verse 9 describes the strategic destruction of Jerusalem's most significant buildings. The "house of the LORD" refers to Solomon's Temple, the center of worship and the symbol of God's presence among His people. Setting fire to the Temple was a sacrilegious act that symbolized the complete abandonment of Jerusalem and the destruction of its religious identity. Burning the "king's house"—the royal palace—marked the collapse of the Davidic line in Jerusalem. The phrase "every great house" implies that the Babylonians also destroyed the homes of the wealthy and influential, further eradicating any remnants of Jerusalem's power and glory. Ultimately, nothing remained of the city's former splendor.

Jerusalem's total destruction had been foretold by the prophets (2 Kings 21:10-15; Jer. 7:12-14; 19:8). Both Jeremiah and Micah, for instance, warned that the city would become "a heap of ruins" (Jer. 9:11; Mic. 3:12) because of the people's sin and idolatry.

The destruction of Jerusalem also symbolized God's withdrawal of His presence from His people. The Temple, as the dwelling place of God on earth, represented the unique relationship between God and Israel. Its destruction signified that God was no longer with His people due to their ongoing disobedience, idolatry, and refusal to heed His prophetic warnings. The complete annihilation of Jerusalem serves as the ultimate expression of God's judgment on the Kingdom of Judah. It underscored the gravity of their disobedience and offered a cautionary tale for future generations.

THE LESSON APPLIED

This passage offers several valuable lessons applicable to modern life. First, we see the devastating impact of persistent disobedience to the Lord. This should remind believers that ignoring godly counsel and persisting in wrongdoing—either individually or as a society—can bring severe consequences. This also challenges us to consider the long-term effects that our choices can have on our lives and communities.

Furthermore, the passage highlights the repercussions of spiritual complacency and idolatry. In contemporary society, it's easy for people and institutions to place their faith in materialism, success, and power. This lesson emphasizes the importance of remaining faithful to God and following His standards as noted in the Bible. Likewise, we as believers should consider our priorities—assessing what is genuinely important and pursuing a life based on spiritual values rather than fleeting desires.

Finally, the destruction of Jerusalem and the exile of the people serve as a contemporary call to God's people for humility and repentance. The Israelites were exiled because they would not acknowledge their sin and turn back to God.

This story reminds us that restoration comes not through pride or denial, but through self-reflection, humility, and a commitment to greater personal responsibility and faithfulness to God. We can find hope in the message of redemption that comes from acknowledging our shortcomings and striving for positive change.

LET'S TALK ABOUT IT...

Discuss the following questions and visit www.rhboyd.com for more information.

How can the story of Judah's fall in 2 Kings 24:18–25:9 serve as a warning against ignoring the consequences of ongoing disobedience, both in our personal lives and in the context of societal issues?

In what ways can modern individuals or societies become like Judah—placing trust in materialism, power, or other "idols" instead of in the Lord? How can we address and overcome these challenges in our own lives?

The exile of the people of Judah reflects the importance of repentance and turning back to God. What are some practical steps that individuals or communities can take to seek restoration after a time of spiritual neglect or moral failure?

Get Social

Share your views and tag us
@rhboydco and use #rhboydco

@rhboydco

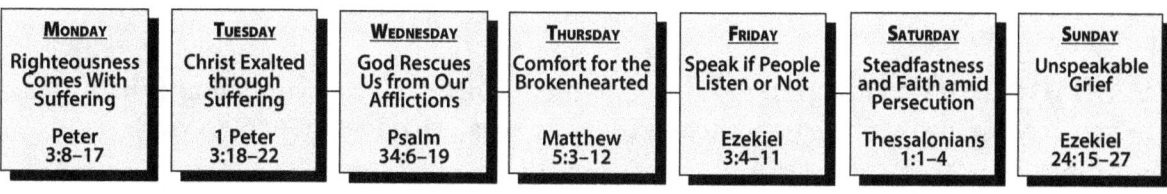

Lesson XI   **November 16, 2025**

The Story of Ezekiel

Adult Topic: The Medium Is the Message
Background Scripture: Ezekiel 1:1–3; 2:1–3:27; 8:1–4; 11:22–25; 24:15–24; 33:30–33
Lesson Passage: Ezekiel 3:10–11; 24:15–24, 27

EZEKIEL 3:10–11; 24:15–24, 27

KJV

MOREOVER he said unto me, Son of man, all my words that I shall speak unto thee receive in thine heart, and hear with thine ears.
11 And go, get thee to them of the captivity, unto the children of thy people, and speak unto them, and tell them, Thus saith the Lord God; whether they will hear, or whether they will forbear.

• • • • • •

15 Also the word of the Lord came unto me, saying,
16 Son of man, behold, I take away from thee the desire of thine eyes with a stroke: yet neither shalt thou mourn nor weep, neither shall thy tears run down.
17 Forbear to cry, make no mourning for the dead, bind the tire of thine head upon thee, and put on thy shoes upon thy feet, and cover not thy lips, and eat not the bread of men.
18 So I spake unto the people in the morning: and at even my wife died; and I did in the morning as I was commanded.
19 And the people said unto me, Wilt thou not tell us what these things are to us, that thou doest so?
20 Then I answered them, The word of the Lord came unto me, saying,
21 Speak unto the house of Israel, Thus saith the Lord God; Behold, I will profane my sanctuary, the excellency of your strength, the desire of your eyes, and that which your soul pitieth; and your sons and your daughters whom ye have left shall fall by the sword.

NRSVue

HE said to me, "Mortal, all my words that I shall speak to you receive in your heart and hear with your ears;
11 then go to the exiles, to your people, and speak to them. Say to them, 'Thus says the Lord God,' whether they hear or refuse to hear."

• • • • • •

15 The word of the Lord came to me:
16 Mortal, with one blow I am about to take away from you the delight of your eyes, yet you shall not mourn or weep, nor shall your tears run down.
17 Groan quietly; make no mourning for the dead. Bind on your turban, and put your sandals on your feet; do not cover your upper lip or eat the bread of mourners.
18 So I spoke to the people in the morning, and at evening my wife died. And on the next morning I did as I was commanded.
19 Then the people said to me, "Will you not tell us what these things mean for us, that you are acting this way?"
20 Then I said to them, "The word of the Lord came to me:
21 Say to the house of Israel: Thus says the Lord God: I will profane my sanctuary, the pride of your power, the delight of your eyes, and your heart's desire, and your sons and your daughters whom you left behind shall fall by the sword.

MAIN THOUGHT: [The Lord God] said to me, "Mortal, all my words that I shall speak to you receive in your heart and hear with your ears." (Ezekiel 3:10, NRSVue)

EZEKIEL 3:10-11; 24:15-24, 27

KJV

22 And ye shall do as I have done: ye shall not cover your lips, nor eat the bread of men.

23 And your tires shall be upon your heads, and your shoes upon your feet: ye shall not mourn nor weep; but ye shall pine away for your iniquities, and mourn one toward another.

24 Thus Ezekiel is unto you a sign: according to all that he hath done shall ye do: and when this cometh, ye shall know that I am the Lord God.

• • • • • •

27 In that day shall thy mouth be opened to him which is escaped, and thou shalt speak, and be no more dumb: and thou shalt be a sign unto them; and they shall know that I am the Lord.

NRSVue

22 And you shall do as I have done; you shall not cover your upper lip or eat the bread of mourners.

23 Your turbans shall be on your heads and your sandals on your feet; you shall not mourn or weep, but you shall pine away in your iniquities and groan to one another.

24 Thus Ezekiel shall be a sign to you; you shall do just as he has done. When this comes, then you shall know that I am the Lord God."

• • • • • •

27 On that day your mouth shall be opened to the one who has escaped, and you shall speak and no longer be silent. So you shall be a sign to them, and they shall know that I am the Lord.

Lesson Setting

Time: 593–571 BC, during the time of the Babylonian exile
Place: Babylon
Setting: Ezekiel 3:10–11 and 24:15–24, 27 were written during the Babylonian exile. Ezekiel, who was from a priestly family, was among the Jews who were taken as captives to Babylon in 597 BC. He received these messages from God while he lived in that foreign land. These passages are typically dated between 593 to 571 BC. Ezekiel likely recorded these prophecies over a period of about twenty years following his initial calling. The prophet's central message was to warn the people of Israel about the consequences of their disobedience to God. These particular passages emphasize themes of judgment and the inevitability that God's plans will unfold.

Lesson Outline

I. Ezekiel's Message (Ezekiel 3:10–11)
II. Ezekiel's Personal Loss (Ezekiel 24:15–19)
III. Ezekiel's Prophecy (Ezekiel 24:20–24, 27)

UNIFYING PRINCIPLE

Some people are willing to bear huge sacrifices when they believe it serves a higher purpose. What is the greatest sacrifice one could make? God took Ezekiel's beloved wife and instructed him not to mourn her death. This action would be a visual symbol of God's message to the exiles, who were not to mourn the calamities that were about to befall their families in Jerusalem.

INTRODUCTION

The book of Ezekiel was written during the Babylonian exile. It presents a vivid portrayal of the prophet's calling, his struggles, and the messages that he delivered to his fellow Israelites in exile. Ezekiel had been a priest, but was commissioned as a prophet to warn the Israelites of God's impending judgment due to their ongoing disobedience. In Ezekiel 3:10–11, God commanded the prophet to deliver a message to the people, even though they were unlikely to listen. This passage emphasizes the weight of God's word and Ezekiel's responsibility to speak, regardless of the people's response.

Later, in Ezekiel 24:15–24, 27, the prophet learned about a distressing experience that would be an object lesson for the Israelites. God told Ezekiel that while his wife would soon die, he was to remain silent and not mourn. This symbolic act would be a message about the Israelites' devastation when they learned about the Temple's destruction and the loss of their beloved city.

Together, these verses present Ezekiel's difficult calling to speak God's truth to God's obstinate and rebellious people, who continued to believe false prophets rather than trusting the Lord's word.

EXPOSITION

I. Ezekiel's Message (Ezekiel 3:10–11)

God called Ezekiel to speak His message to the people of Judah whom Nebuchadnezzar had exiled to Babylon. While God said that His people were hard-headed, the Lord promised to give Ezekiel an even harder head. This refers to the boldness, power, and protection God would provide Ezekiel so that he could faithfully relay God's word.

God first instructed Ezekiel to listen carefully to His words. The prophet's task was not merely to be a mouthpiece but to internalize and fully comprehend the messages God called him to deliver. This went beyond mere hearing. The phrase "receive in your heart" (v. 10) emphasizes a level of emotional and intellectual investment. Before he could speak, Ezekiel had to absorb God's words so that they became a part of him. He would have to do this again and again as God gave him new messages. In this verse, "heart" represents the core of a person's being—the place where conviction, understanding, and decision-making happen.

In calling Ezekiel to internalize the message, God was preparing him for his difficult assignment. Ezekiel would be speaking warnings and judgment to God's people who had turned away from Him. To faithfully convey such serious words, Ezekiel could not be detached from them. He had to grasp the gravity of the situation, recognize the significance of God's words, and allow them to influence and direct his own life.

The call to internalize God's words served as both spiritual and emotional preparation for the prophet. This was a common theme for prophets in Scripture. To effectively speak God's truth, they first had to let it shape their lives. Only afterward could their words genuinely reflect God's heart.

Furthermore, internalizing the message emphasized both authenticity and authority. If Ezekiel failed to comprehend the seriousness of God's judgment, or if he merely conveyed God's words without accepting them, his message would lack conviction and urgency. Ezekiel's demeanor, readiness to endure hardships, and obedience to God's call hinged on his profound understanding of the message he received from God.

Verse 10 also alludes to the personal cost of Ezekiel's prophetic role. By internalizing God's words, Ezekiel would accept the weight of his calling and the emotional burden it carried. This emotional and intellectual investment makes Ezekiel's ministry authentic and powerful, underscoring the deep connection between God's spokesman and the message he bears.

In verse 11, God instructed the prophet to go to the exiled Israelites—to his own people—and "speak to them." The people's response was not Ezekiel's concern or responsibility. His duty was simply to speak God's message: "Thus says the Lord GOD." The phrase, "whether they hear or refuse to hear" means more than mere listening. Rather, it emphasizes responding to what one hears. God instructed Ezekiel to faithfully deliver the message regardless of the people's receptiveness or obedience to it.

II. Ezekiel's Personal Loss (Ezekiel 24:15-19)

This passage begins with an oft-repeated phrase (forty-nine times) in the book of Ezekiel: "The word of the Lord came to me" (v. 15). The prophet learned that God would take away "the delight of [his] eyes" with "one blow" (v. 16). This refers to the sudden death of Ezekiel's wife. God's words emphasized the deep love and attachment that Ezekiel had for his wife, which would only intensify his loss. Yet despite the depth of grief that Ezekiel would experience, God commanded him not to "mourn or weep." Unlike the typical reactions of Jewish mourners at that time, Ezekiel was to suppress any outward expressions of sorrow.

Instead, God instructed Ezekiel to "groan quietly" (v. 17) and to maintain his usual demeanor. This included tying his turban—a symbol of his prophetic role—and putting on his sandals, which indicated that he was ready to continue his mission. Ezekiel could not cover his upper lip like someone who was ashamed (Mic. 3:7). Nor could he eat the "bread of mourners" (v. 17; see Jer. 16:7), which was a common food for those mourning a loved one's death.

As God had commanded, Ezekiel "spoke to the people in the morning" (v. 18), perhaps telling them what God had told him. That evening, his wife died, just as God had said. Then the next day, Ezekiel behaved as God commanded—maintaining his composure without mourning. This act of obedience was both a personal sacrifice for Ezekiel and a powerful symbol to the people. His actions served as a visual representation of God's message to Israel—that they would face a devastating loss. Even so, they would not have the opportunity to mourn in accordance with their tradition.

Verse 19 records that the people observed Ezekiel's strange behavior and asked him to explain it. They realized that his actions were not typical for someone who had just experienced a devastating loss, and they want to know what it meant for them. Ezekiel's response to tragedy became a teachable moment for his fellow Israelites who would soon hear another one of God's messages.

III. Ezekiel's Prophecy (Ezekiel 24:20-24, 27)

After the people inquired about Ezekiel's behavior, he first explained that he had received a direct message from God (v. 20).

In verse 21, Ezekiel spoke God's words to the people about the coming destruction of the Temple and the loss of the city of Jerusalem. God's "sanctuary"—which He referred to as "the pride of your power"—was the Temple. As the heart of Israel's worship, the Temple was the most sacred place—the very dwelling of God on earth. Because there was no place like their Temple, God's people had become spiritually arrogant. They considered the Temple to be a type of good-luck charm that would protect them as God's people, despite their disobedience to the Lord (see Jer. 7:4).

The "delight of your eyes" and "your heart's desire" refer to the Temple and the city of Jerusalem, which the people cherished. However, God declared that He would "profane" the sanctuary, which means that He would allow it to be destroyed by a foreign power (Babylon). Just as Ezekiel suddenly lost his wife who was the "delight of his eyes" (v. 16), so the people would likewise experience the sudden loss of that which they held most dear.

Even more devastating was God's additional word: "your sons and your daughters whom you left behind shall fall by the sword" (v. 21). This reveals the death that would befall the Israelites who remained in Jerusalem during the Babylonian onslaught.

While the people's lives had been upended by their exile, the destruction of Jerusalem would obliterate the way of life that they had known. Just as Ezekiel refrained from the typical mourning rituals after his wife's death, so the Israelites would be prohibited from mourning in their customary manner after their city was destroyed. God commanded the people of Israel to behave as Ezekiel did—no mourning or weeping, no signs of grief. Verses 22–23 serve as a stark reminder of the gravity of their situation—there would be no time or chance to grieve the loss of Jerusalem because the consequences would be overwhelming.

Following Ezekiel's example, the people would wear their turbans and sandals as if nothing had happened. The phrase "you shall not mourn nor weep, but you shall pine away in your iniquities" (v. 23) emphasizes that the people would inwardly mourn their fate because of their disobedience. To "pine away" suggests their internal anguish and regret that stems from an awareness of the consequences of their sin. Despite the people's recognition of their sin and their inward sorrow, this would not reverse God's judgment; it was inevitable.

In verse 24, God affirmed that Ezekiel's actions were "a sign" for the people. The prophet's behavior was a living parable to demonstrate the people's conduct after the judgment on Jerusalem. It was a shock for Ezekiel to hear that his beloved wife would be dead within a day. Still, he was forbidden to mourn outwardly. In contrast, God had been warning His people for many years about the judgment coming on their beloved Jerusalem. They were forbidden to mourn because they should not have been surprised at its end, especially when their actions partially led to its destruction. When this happened, the people would realize that God had brought about their downfall.

More than seven years earlier (3:26–27), God had partially restricted Ezekiel's ability to speak unless he received a direct message from the Lord to communicate to the people. Ezekiel 24:27 notes the end of the prophet's symbolic silence and marks the moment when his "mouth will be opened." After a messenger ("one who has escaped") arrives from Jerusalem to confirm the destruction of the city and the Temple, Ezekiel would speak again without restriction. In addition to words of God's judgment on the nations, Ezekiel would also speak messages of restoration and hope for Israel. Then, the people would understand that Ezekiel's actions had truly been prophetic as well as symbolic. Through this, the people would recognize God's authority as the sovereign ruler over all. This verse underscores the ultimate purpose of Ezekiel's prophetic ministry—to bring Israel to a deeper awareness of God's justice, sovereignty, and holiness, even in the midst of destruction.

THE LESSON APPLIED

Ezekiel's life provides valuable lessons on obedience, responsibility, and prophetic witness that can be applied to our lives as believers. Initially, the prophet was commanded to internalize God's message and deliver it to a rebellious people, regardless of their response (Ezek. 3:10–11). This teaches us the importance of obeying God's call, even when a task is daunting or when others are unwilling to listen to us.

Likewise, God instructed Ezekiel not to mourn his personal loss to a situation that was difficult and unavoidable (Ezek. 24:15–24). This reminds us that while we may endure personal suffering, sometimes we must persevere and stand firm in our faith during such times of hardship, trusting God and accepting His will even when we don't understand it.

Finally, the opening of Ezekiel's mouth after the judgment on Jerusalem (Ezek. 24:27) points to the people's eventual recognition of God's sovereignty. This serves as a reminder that God will always fulfill His purposes, and in time, people will eventually recognize His authority.

Overall, this lesson encourages us to remain faithful in our mission, speak the truth even when it's difficult, and trust in God's sovereignty, knowing that His plans will ultimately be revealed and fulfilled.

LET'S TALK ABOUT IT...

Discuss the following questions and visit www.rhboyd.com for more information.

How can we remain faithful in delivering God's message, as Ezekiel was called to do, even when we face rejection or indifference from others?

What personal sacrifices or emotional challenges might we face when obeying God's call? How can we cultivate the strength to endure those challenges, as Ezekiel did when he prophesied as an exile in Babylon?

In what ways can we recognize and trust in God's sovereignty when we don't immediately see the purpose behind challenging situations, as demonstrated in Ezekiel 24:27?

Get Social

Share your views and tag us @rhboydco and use #rhboydco

@rhboydco

Home Daily Devotional Readings
November 17–23, 2025

Monday	Tuesday	Wednesday	Thursday	Friday	Saturday	Sunday
Love Others Despite Suffering	Rejoice to Share Christ's Sufferings	Each Will Answer for His or Her Sin	I Confess My Iniquity	Restore One Another in Gentleness	See to Your Own Sins First	Let the Wicked Repent
1 Peter 4:1–11	1 Peter 4:12–19	Ezekiel 18:1–9	Psalm 38:1–2, 10–22	Galatians 6:1–10	Matthew 7:1–6	Ezekiel 33:7–16a

Lesson XII   **November 23, 2025**

Ezekiel Teaches Personal Responsibility

Adult Topic: To Everything Turn, Turn, Turn
Background Scripture: Ezekiel 18:1–32; 33:1–20
Lesson Passage: Ezekiel 33:7–16

EZEKIEL 33:7–16

KJV

SO thou, O son of man, I have set thee a watchman unto the house of Israel; therefore thou shalt hear the word at my mouth, and warn them from me.
8 When I say unto the wicked, O wicked man, thou shalt surely die; if thou dost not speak to warn the wicked from his way, that wicked man shall die in his iniquity; but his blood will I require at thine hand.
9 Nevertheless, if thou warn the wicked of his way to turn from it; if he do not turn from his way, he shall die in his iniquity; but thou hast delivered thy soul.
10 Therefore, O thou son of man, speak unto the house of Israel; Thus ye speak, saying, If our transgressions and our sins be upon us, and we pine away in them, how should we then live?
11 Say unto them, As I live, saith the Lord God, I have no pleasure in the death of the wicked; but that the wicked turn from his way and live: turn ye, turn ye from your evil ways; for why will ye die, O house of Israel?
12 Therefore, thou son of man, say unto the children of thy people, The righteousness of the righteous shall not deliver him in the day of his transgression: as for the wickedness of the wicked, he shall not fall thereby in the day that he turneth from his wickedness; neither shall the righteous be able to live for his righteousness in the day that he sinneth.
13 When I shall say to the righteous, that he shall surely live; if he trust to his own righteous-

NRSVue

SO you, mortal, I have made a sentinel for the house of Israel; whenever you hear a word from my mouth, you shall give them warning from me.
8 If I say to the wicked, "O wicked ones, you shall surely die," and you do not speak to warn the wicked to turn from their ways, the wicked shall die in their iniquity, but their blood I will require at your hand.
9 But if you warn the wicked to turn from their ways and they do not turn from their ways, the wicked shall die in their iniquity, but you will have saved your life.
10 Now you, mortal, say to the house of Israel: Thus you have said: "Our transgressions and our sins weigh upon us, and we waste away because of them; how then can we live?"
11 Say to them: As I live, says the Lord God, I have no pleasure in the death of the wicked but that the wicked turn from their ways and live; turn back, turn back from your evil ways, for why will you die, O house of Israel?
12 And you, mortal, say to your people: The righteousness of the righteous shall not save them when they transgress, and as for the wickedness of the wicked, it shall not make them stumble when they turn from their wickedness, and the righteous shall not be able to live by their righteousness when they sin.

13 Though I say to the righteous that they shall surely live, yet if they trust in their righteousness

MAIN THOUGHT: So you, mortal, I have made a sentinel for the house of Israel; whenever you hear a word from my mouth, you shall give them warning from me. (Ezekiel 33:7, NRSVue)

EZEKIEL 33:7-16

KJV

ness, and commit iniquity, all his righteousnesses shall not be remembered; but for his iniquity that he hath committed, he shall die for it.

14 Again, when I say unto the wicked, Thou shalt surely die; if he turn from his sin, and do that which is lawful and right;

15 If the wicked restore the pledge, give again that he had robbed, walk in the statutes of life, without committing iniquity; he shall surely live, he shall not die.

16 None of his sins that he hath committed shall be mentioned unto him: he hath done that which is lawful and right; he shall surely live.

NRSVue

and commit iniquity, none of their righteous deeds shall be remembered, but in the iniquity that they have committed they shall die.

14 Again, though I say to the wicked, "You shall surely die," yet if they turn from their sin and do what is lawful and right—

15 if the wicked restore the pledge, give back what they have taken by robbery, and walk in the statutes of life, committing no iniquity—they shall surely live; they shall not die.

16 None of the sins that they have committed shall be remembered against them; they have done what is lawful and right; they shall surely live.

LESSON SETTING

Time: During the Babylonian exile in the sixth century BC
Place: Babylon
Setting: Ezekiel served as a prophet among the Israelites who had been taken captive in Babylon around 597 BC. He symbolized and spoke messages not only about God's judgment against Israel and the nations but also about the hope for restoration. The events in Ezekiel Chapter 33 probably occurred after 586 BC. They recall some of Ezekiel's earlier experiences and messages, including his commissioning (3:17-19) to be a "sentinel" (watchman), tasked with delivering God's warning to the people. In Ezekiel 33:7-16, the prophet warned the Israelite people about the repercussions of their sin and their need for genuine repentance. The context is significant as the Israelites were contending with the aftermath of Jerusalem's destruction and the Temple's ruin. Ezekiel's message was designed to hold them accountable for their actions while offering hope for redemption if they would return to God.

LESSON OUTLINE

I. The Role of the Watchman (Ezekiel 33:7-9)
II. Personal Accountability and Choice (Ezekiel 33:10-12)
III. The Opportunity for Repentance and Mercy (Ezekiel 33:13-16)

UNIFYING PRINCIPLE

It is possible that breaking from the mistakes of the past will enable a person to get a fresh start toward a better life. What assists people in getting a fresh start? As God's sentinel, Ezekiel gave the people a clear warning so that they could have an opportunity to turn from their sin, do the right things, and experience life.

INTRODUCTION

Thousands of prominent Judeans had been exiled to Babylon around 597 BC, yet they continued to trust in the words of false prophets rather than in God's word through the prophet Ezekiel. Thus, they persisted in living as they desired rather than repenting and obeying God's word, as Ezekiel had instructed them.

This lesson recalls two of Ezekiel's earlier experiences. One relates to his responsibility as a watchman for Israel, warning the people of the judgment that was coming (see 3:17–19). Likewise, this passage reiterates the people's responsibility to heed Ezekiel's message by repenting and returning to the Lord for restoration (see 18:21–32).

This lesson highlights the balance between God's justice and mercy. While the consequences of sin are grave, God provides a path to redemption through repentance. Throughout his faithful service, Ezekiel emphasized that salvation is available for all who turn to the Lord, but dire consequences await those who persist in their sinful ways.

EXPOSITION

I. The Role of the Watchman (Ezekiel 33:7–9)

God referred to Ezekiel as "mortal" (v. 7) or "son of man" (KJV). This title, used widely in the book of Ezekiel, emphasized the prophet's humanity and his role as God's messenger. The Lord told Ezekiel that He appointed him as a "sentinel" ("watchman," KJV) for the house of Israel.

Historically, a sentinel stood at a high point on the city wall, keeping watch for any threats outside the city. If the sentinel detected danger, it was his responsibility to alert the citizens in the city to take action. If they disregarded the warning, the burden of the consequences would fall on them.

As the sentinel for Israel, Ezekiel had to deliver the Lord's warning to His people. God expected Ezekiel to confront the people about their sin and the impending judgment they would face if they did not repent.

In verse 8, God elaborated on Ezekiel's profound responsibility. If Ezekiel failed to warn the wicked about their sinful ways, they would perish and God would hold him accountable for their blood. The gravity of Ezekiel's calling was clear—it was about more than merely delivering a message. Instead, in speaking truthfully and urgently, he also had to ensure that the people understood the dire consequences of their sinful ways. If Ezekiel neglected his duty to impart the crucial warning, the destruction that followed would not only affect the wicked but also rest on him.

On the other hand, if Ezekiel delivered God's warning as instructed and the people ignored it, they would "die in their iniquity" (v. 9). In other words, their blood would be on their own heads. In such case, Ezekiel would have fulfilled his duty, and the people would be responsible for their own fate. This emphasizes the principle of individual accountability: Each person must respond to God's warning and take the necessary steps to avoid God's judgment.

II. Personal Accountability and Choice (Ezekiel 33:10–12)

In this passage, the Israelites recognized the gravity of their situation and cried out to Ezekiel, expressing a deep awareness of their sin and its consequences. They were burdened by guilt ("Our transgressions and our sins weigh upon us," v. 10), and understood that their sins brought divine judgment that they could not evade ("we waste away … how then can we live?").

In response, God directed Ezekiel to convey a message of hope and redemption.

Note the central theme of God's message: "I have no pleasure in the death of the wicked" (v. 11). Instead, what God truly desires is for people to acknowledge and turn away from their sinful, evil ways, and to live in alignment with His will. This profound verse reveals God's character, underscoring His attributes of goodness, mercy, grace, and patience. Unlike a vengeful deity enjoying the fall of the wicked, the Lord's goal for humans is not punishment; rather, it is restoration and salvation for all who will trust and follow Him.

God emphasized that there was still the opportunity for forgiveness and renewal if the people would turn away from their transgressions ("their ways"). This implied turning toward the Lord and His ways. If the people did this, they would experience a renewed relationship with their Creator and a life filled with hope and purpose.

In verse 12, God said that the righteous person who turns to sin will suffer the consequences. Likewise, a wicked person who turns from sin will be spared from consequences. This highlights personal accountability: God will judge each person based on the person's actions, but past behavior does not guarantee one's future fate.

III. The Opportunity for Repentance and Mercy (Ezekiel 33:13–16)

These verses continue to emphasize the significance of God's justice, the genuine possibility of repentance, and the bountiful opportunity for salvation. Moreover, the passage again highlights the truth that regardless of past actions or current circumstances, every person has the power to change course through genuine repentance and a desire to change. Ultimately, this is an invitation for transformation, underlining the hope that is always available for those willing to turn to God.

The beginning of verse 13 reiterates a truth from verse 12: If a righteous person turns to sin, their past righteousness will not suffice to save them. In other words, previous good deeds do not ensure a favorable future if one does not remain faithful to God. Thus, a person's current relationship with God—determined by obedience or disobedience—shapes their fate. Because God is just, He will not overlook sin, regardless of a person's prior righteousness.

In verse 14, God elaborated on what He said in the last part of verse 12: If a wicked person turns away from their sin and instead does "what is lawful and right" (according to God's standards), they will not be judged based on their past wickedness. Effectively, God promised to forgive the repentant sinner. This underscores the power of repentance and the hope of salvation for anyone who chooses to change their ways and return to God.

Verse 15 offers two concrete examples of repentance. To "restore the pledge" refers to returning collateral that should not be held for a loan (Deut. 24:6, 10–13, 17). Notice also that it wasn't enough simply to turn away from "robbery"; the truly repentant person would "give back" what they had wrongly taken.

God promised that if the wicked person turned from sin and instead obeyed His commands ("the statutes of life"), they would live. Regardless of what they had done, their previous sins would not be held against them (v. 16).

THE LESSON APPLIED

Ezekiel 33:7–16 offers profound lessons about personal responsibility, accountability, and the opportunity for repentance that apply to everyone's life today.

Just as Ezekiel as a sentinel was responsible to warn the people of Israel of impending danger, so we as believers have a duty to speak the truth and to alert others when they are headed down a destructive path.

In addition, this lesson highlights that God holds individuals accountable for their choices. As such, we are responsible not only for how we live, but also for the consequences of our actions if we turn away from God's way. Therefore, rather than trying to excuse or justify sin, we must take responsibility for it and be willing to turn away from our destructive habits.

Furthermore, God's message to the exiles reminds us that our past actions do not determine our future unless we continue walking the wrong path. Every person, no matter how far he or she has strayed, has the opportunity to go in a different direction. Thus, if someone is currently living in sin or making poor choices, Ezekiel's message offers hope: Through repentance and a commitment to change, anyone can receive God's forgiveness, restore their relationship with Him, and walk in the path of life.

Ultimately, this lesson reminds us that we are responsible, not only for our actions, but also for taking the necessary steps to seek forgiveness and live according to God's will.

LET'S TALK ABOUT IT...

Discuss the following questions and visit www.rhboyd.com for more information.

What does the role of the sentinel/watchman in Ezekiel Chapter 33 teach us about the responsibility we have to warn others about the consequences of their actions? How can we balance truth with compassion as we warn others?

How do the principles of individual accountability in Ezekiel 33:10–12 challenge us to examine our own lives, especially when it comes to making decisions that impact our relationship with God?

Ezekiel 33:13–16 emphasizes the possibility of repentance and forgiveness. How does this message of hope and restoration apply to someone who feels their past mistakes are beyond redemption?

Get Social

Share your views and tag us
@rhboydco and use #rhboydco

@rhboydco

Home Daily Devotional Readings
November 24–30, 2025

Monday	Tuesday	Wednesday	Thursday	Friday	Saturday	Sunday
God Breathes New Life	A Resurrection of Hope	The Thirsty Will Be Refreshed	Rivers of Living Water	Hope for God's New Creation	The Tree of Life	The River of Life
Ezekiel 37:1–7	Ezekiel 37:8–14	Isaiah 55:1–9	John 7:2–10, 37–39	Revelation 21:1–7	Revelation 22:1–5	Ezekiel 47:1–9, 12

Lesson XIII   **November 30, 2025**

Ezekiel's Vision of Hope

Adult Topic: Hope Floats
Background Scripture: Ezekiel 47:1-12
Lesson Passage: Ezekiel 47:1-9, 12

EZEKIEL 47:1-9, 12

KJV

AFTERWARD he brought me again unto the door of the house; and, behold, waters issued out from under the threshold of the house eastward: for the forefront of the house stood toward the east, and the waters came down from under from the right side of the house, at the south side of the altar.

2 Then brought he me out of the way of the gate northward, and led me about the way without unto the utter gate by the way that looketh eastward; and, behold, there ran out waters on the right side.

3 And when the man that had the line in his hand went forth eastward, he measured a thousand cubits, and he brought me through the waters; the waters were to the ankles.

4 Again he measured a thousand, and brought me through the waters; the waters were to the knees. Again he measured a thousand, and brought me through; the waters were to the loins.

5 Afterward he measured a thousand; and it was a river that I could not pass over: for the waters were risen, waters to swim in, a river that could not be passed over.

6 And he said unto me, Son of man, hast thou seen this? Then he brought me, and caused me to return to the brink of the river.

7 Now when I had returned, behold, at the bank of the river were very many trees on the one side and on the other.

8 Then said he unto me, These waters issue out

NRSVue

THEN he brought me back to the entrance of the temple; there water was flowing from below the entryway of the temple toward the east (for the temple faced east), and the water was flowing down from below the south side of the temple, south of the altar.

2 Then he brought me out by way of the north gate and led me around on the outside to the outer gate that faces toward the east, and the water was trickling out on the south side.

3 Going on eastward with a cord in his hand, the man measured one thousand cubits and then led me through the water, and it was ankle-deep.

4 Again he measured one thousand and led me through the water, and it was knee-deep. Again he measured one thousand and led me through the water, and it was up to the waist.

5 Again he measured one thousand, and it was a river that I could not cross, for the water had risen; it was deep enough to swim in, a river that could not be crossed.

6 He said to me, "Mortal, have you seen this?" Then he led me back along the bank of the river.

7 As I came back, I saw on the bank of the river a great many trees on the one side and on the other.

8 He said to me, "This water flows toward the

MAIN THOUGHT: On the banks, on both sides of the river, there will grow all kinds of trees for food. Their leaves will not wither nor their fruit fail, but they will bear fresh fruit every month, because the water for them flows from the sanctuary. Their fruit will be for food, and their leaves for healing. (Ezekiel 47:12)

EZEKIEL 47:1-9, 12

KJV

toward the east country, and go down into the desert, and go into the sea: which being brought forth into the sea, the waters shall be healed.
9 And it shall come to pass, that every thing that liveth, which moveth, whithersoever the rivers shall come, shall live: and there shall be a very great multitude of fish, because these waters shall come thither: for they shall be healed; and every thing shall live whither the river cometh.

• • • • • •

12 And by the river upon the bank thereof, on this side and on that side, shall grow all trees for meat, whose leaf shall not fade, neither shall the fruit thereof be consumed: it shall bring forth new fruit according to his months, because their waters they issued out of the sanctuary: and the fruit thereof shall be for meat, and the leaf thereof for medicine.

NRSVue

eastern region and goes down into the Arabah, and when it enters the sea, the sea of stagnant waters, the water will become fresh.
9 Wherever the river goes, every living creature that swarms will live, and there will be very many fish once these waters reach there. It will become fresh, and everything will live where the river goes.

• • • • • •

12 On the banks, on both sides of the river, there will grow all kinds of trees for food. Their leaves will not wither nor their fruit fail, but they will bear fresh fruit every month, because the water for them flows from the sanctuary. Their fruit will be for food and their leaves for healing."

LESSON SETTING

Time: Likely around 570 BC
Place: Babylon
Setting: Ezekiel 47 presents one of the visions of the future that God gave the prophet Ezekiel while he was living as a captive in Babylon. This vision describes a river, flowing from the Temple, which brings life and healing. Ezekiel, along with thousands of other leaders and elites of Judah, had been taken captive to Babylon in 597 BC, after the Babylonians subdued Judah. Several years later (about 593/592 BC), Ezekiel's prophetic ministry began, and it continued until about 571/570 BC. Initially, Ezekiel delivered God's messages of judgment and issued calls for repentance to the exiled people of Israel. His prophecy recorded in chapter 47 was given following the destruction of Jerusalem and the Temple (which happened in 586 BC), after which many more people from Judah were exiled to Babylon. That event marked a turning point in Ezekiel's ministry, in which he primarily spoke messages of hope and renewal for Israel. The message was much-needed in the aftermath of their exile experience. They had been forcibly taken away from the homeland God had given them to dwell there as His people. Ezekiel's vision of the river flowing from the Temple (Ezek. 47:1-12) offered hope for a future return to the land of promise and the restoration of Israel. The river's depth and breadth allude to the abundance of God's grace. It flows freely, indicating that God's blessings are available to all who come to Him. These verses were likely recorded sometime around 571/570 BC, as part of Ezekiel's final visions.

LESSON OUTLINE

I. The Source of the River: God's Presence and Power (Ezekiel 47:1–2)
II. The Growth and Transformation of the River: Abundance and Healing (Ezekiel 47:3–9)
III. The Fruitfulness of the River: Blessings and Life for All (Ezekiel 47:12)

UNIFYING PRINCIPLE

Seeing water flowing from an area that was once in ruins inspires hope for irrigation, agriculture, and prosperity. Is there hope in these dismal times? Ezekiel noticed the water flowing, the trees growing, and land coming to life, all of which represented hope for the future.

INTRODUCTION

One of the most symbolically rich visions in the book of Ezekiel, this passage describes a river flowing from God's Temple, a divine stream that brings life, healing, and restoration. Prophesied during the Babylonian exile—a time of immense despair for the Israelites—this message offered an inspiring vision of hope.

Ezekiel's prophetic words speak to a future time when God will restore His people and the land, bringing them back from exile and rebuilding the Temple. This vision also highlights a deeper spiritual truth: God's life-giving presence has the power to transform even the most desolate and hopeless situations, offering healing and abundance to all who partake in it. Ezekiel 47 details God's faithfulness and the hope that His restoration brings to all creation.

EXPOSITION

I. The Source of the River: God's Presence and Power (Ezekiel 47:1–2)

In verse 1 (and throughout Ezek. 40–47), "he" refers to the divine messenger (40:3) who guided Ezekiel during his remarkable vision of and beyond the Temple. The first thing that Ezekiel observed was a river that flowed from beneath the "entryway" of the Temple. Outside the Temple, the river flowed toward the east.

The imagery in this passage is not merely descriptive; it is deeply symbolic. In this context, the temple is a symbol of God's dwelling place among His people and highlights His intimate relationship with them. The water flowing from the temple signifies that all life and blessings come from the Lord. Thus, the river represents spiritual renewal and vitality, illustrating how God's presence nourishes those who seek Him.

Note a critical moment in verse 2: "Then he brought me out by way of the north gate and led me around on the outside to the outer gate that faces toward the east, and the water was trickling out on the south side." Beyond merely a physical location, this signifies a spiritual journey in which the prophet would discover more about God's restorative power.

Verse 2 reveals that the river started as a trickle. This symbolizes the subtle beginnings of God's transformative power. The gentle flow suggests the quiet yet profound ways that God works in the world ((e.g., Zechariah 4:10); His work may start inconspicuously, but it has the potential for immense growth. The river's origin in the Temple reinforces another truth: God's presence and authority are the sources of life, renewal, and restoration.

Furthermore, the water's movement away from the temple is a reminder that God's grace was not meant to be confined to a temple. Instead, His blessings always flow outward.

II. The Growth and Transformation of the River: Abundance and Healing (Ezekiel 47:3–9)

In verse 3, the "man" is the divine guide who led Ezekiel in his vision. Holding a measuring line, he "measured one thousand cubits and then led me through the water, and it was ankle-deep." The river's shallow start again notes the initial stages of God's restorative power, which may start small but holds potential for much greater things.

The river's expansion is highlighted in verses 4–5. It rose from "knee-deep" to "up to the waist," finally becoming "a river that could not be crossed." This imagery signifies an intensification of God's work and presence among His people. The deeper the water flows, the more profound and widespread the impact of divine intervention becomes in the world around us.

The question in verse 6 ("Mortal, have you seen this?") was a call for Ezekiel to grasp the significance of what he was witnessing. Ezekiel observed "a great many trees" (v. 7) on the banks of the river. Deeply rooted and nourished by the river's life-giving waters, these trees reflect vibrant growth. Strong and resilient, they thrive in harmony with their environment, thus reinforcing the idea of a flourishing ecosystem where life and prosperity abound.

Verse 8 reveals the river's remarkable healing properties, which extend even to the "Arabah" (the wilderness of Judah) and the [Dead] "sea." Historically, these areas were desolate and lifeless. Yet in Ezekiel's vision, the river turned them into sources of vitality. This transformation emphasizes the radical restoration that God accomplishes in the world, impacting even the most seemingly hopeless places.

Continuing the renewal theme, verse 9 notes the large amount of aquatic life that thrive in the formerly desolate waters, because "everything will live where the river goes." This verse again highlights the vitality and abundance brought by the river.

Through these verses, the river serves as a metaphor for God's restorative power. It is a dynamic force that grows progressively and is far-reaching, bringing healing, rejuvenation, and abundance wherever it flows.

III. The Fruitfulness of the River: Blessings and Life for All (Ezekiel 47:12)

In verse 12, Ezekiel continued to describe the abundant life that came from the river. The thriving fruit trees on both banks of the river highlight the continuous, abundant life that the river provides. These trees, nourished by the water flowing from the Temple, produce fruit every month, consistently providing sustenance. This ongoing cycle of growth and fruit-bearing symbolizes the enduring nature of God's provision—both physical and spiritual—for His people.

The verse concludes with a promise: "Their fruit will be for food and their leaves for healing." This emphasizes the practical and spiritual benefits that comes from the trees. The fruit, which serves for food, symbolizes the sustenance of God's presence. Just as physical fruit sustains the body, the spiritual fruit that comes from God nourishes the soul, providing the strength needed for life and growth. The leaves, which promote healing, indicate that the restoration brought by God also provides physical and emotional healing to His people. In ancient times, certain leaves had medicinal properties. Here, they symbolize the therapeutic and restorative power of God's presence. The leaves also reflect God's work of reconciliation and redemption, healing not only physical bodies but also the brokenness in human spirits and relationships.

THE LESSON APPLIED

The river flowing from the Temple is a metaphor for spiritual renewal and transformation. Just as the river began as a trickle and grew into a mighty force, so God's grace gradually works within people, resulting in spiritual growth. The gradual deepening of the water reflects how a person's spiritual journey often unfolds—in small steps that lead to major changes, deepening one's relationship with God and fostering increased peace, understanding, and purpose.

Likewise, just as the river brought healing to barren areas, so God's presence restores even the most desolate parts of human life.

Finally, the trees along the riverbanks signify that when we stay rooted in God's presence, we grow and produce fruit that benefits others. The continuous cycle of fruit-bearing symbolizes how God's blessings are ongoing, providing nourishment throughout all seasons of life. In addition, the healing leaves signify that God not only provides for us but also empowers us to help restore others.

Just as the river brings life, a person rooted in God's presence will experience a fruitful life characterized by spiritual vitality, healing, and an ever-deepening connection with God's transformative power.

LET'S TALK ABOUT IT...

Discuss the following questions and visit www.rhboyd.com for more information.

How does the imagery of the river in Ezekiel 47:1-9, 12 challenge or inspire your understanding of God's role in bringing transformation and healing to your life?

What areas of your life need spiritual restoration, and how can you open yourself more fully to God's presence to experience that renewal?

How can we, as individuals and communities, act as "trees" along the riverbanks, offering healing and nourishment to others through our actions and faith?

Get Social

Share your views and tag us
@rhboydco and use #rhboydco

@rhboydco

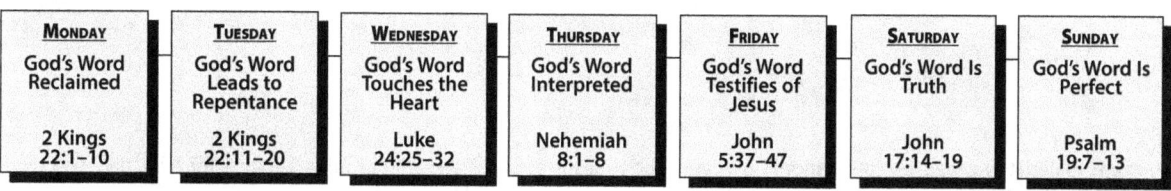

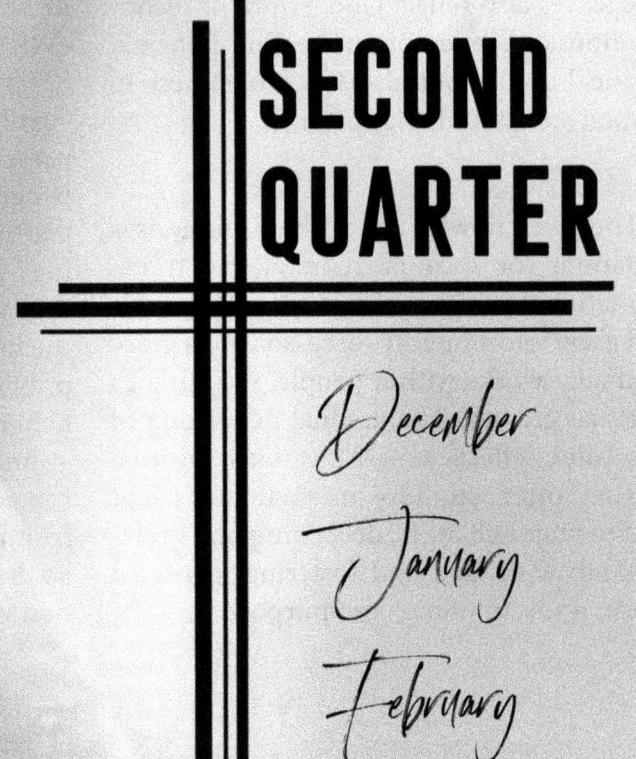

SECOND QUARTER

December
January
February

Lesson material is based on International Sunday School Lessons and International Bible Lessons for Christian Teaching, copyrighted by the International Council of Religious Education, and is used by its permission.

Lesson I   **December 7, 2025**

The Holy Scriptures

Adult Topic: A Life Map
Background Scripture: Deut. 6:4–9; Josh. 1:8–9; 2 Kings 22:8–20; Neh. 8:1–8; Ps. 19:7–14; Luke 24:25–32; Acts 17:10–12; 2 Tim. 3:14–17
Lesson Passage: Psalm 19:7–13; 2 Timothy 3:14–15

PSALM 19:7–13; 2 TIMOTHY 3:14–15

KJV

THE law of the Lord is perfect, converting the soul: the testimony of the Lord is sure, making wise the simple.
8 The statutes of the Lord are right, rejoicing the heart: the commandment of the Lord is pure, enlightening the eyes.

9 The fear of the Lord is clean, enduring for ever: the judgments of the Lord are true and righteous altogether.
10 More to be desired are they than gold, yea, than much fine gold: sweeter also than honey and the honeycomb.

11 Moreover by them is thy servant warned: and in keeping of them there is great reward.
12 Who can understand his errors? cleanse thou me from secret faults.
13 Keep back thy servant also from presumptuous sins; let them not have dominion over me: then shall I be upright, and I shall be innocent from the great transgression.

••• 2 Timothy 3:14–15 •••
14 But continue thou in the things which thou hast learned and hast been assured of, knowing of whom thou hast learned them;
15 And that from a child thou hast known the holy scriptures, which are able to make thee wise unto salvation through faith which is in Christ Jesus.

NRSVue

The law of the Lord is perfect, reviving the soul; the decrees of the Lord are sure, making wise the simple;
8 the precepts of the Lord are right, rejoicing the heart;
the commandment of the Lord is clear, enlightening the eyes;
9 the fear of the Lord is pure, enduring forever; the ordinances of the Lord are true and righteous altogether.
10 More to be desired are they than gold, even much fine gold;
sweeter also than honey and drippings of the honeycomb.
11 Moreover, by them is your servant warned; in keeping them there is great reward.
12 But who can detect one's own errors? Clear me from hidden faults.
13 Keep back your servant also from the insolent; do not let them have dominion over me. Then I shall be blameless and innocent of great transgression.

••• 2 Timothy 3:14–15 •••
14 But as for you, continue in what you have learned and firmly believed, knowing from whom you learned it
15 and how from childhood you have known sacred writings that are able to instruct you for salvation through faith in Christ Jesus.

MAIN THOUGHT: "All scripture is inspired by God and is useful for teaching, for reproof, for correction, and for training in righteousness, so that the person of God may be proficient, equipped for every good work." (2 Timothy 3:16–17, NRSVue)

LESSON SETTING

Time: The exact date unknown but traditionally attributed to David, likely composed during his reign: sometime between 1000 and 960 BC.

Place: The Psalms have no special location; they were written in and around ancient Israel and Jerusalem near David's palace.

Setting: The Bible reveals a comprehensive narrative of God's interactions with humanity, from Genesis to Revelation. The inseparable connection between the Bible and the Spirit of God stems from the Bible's divine inspiration—God-breathed and authoritative. The book of Psalms, also called the Psalter, contains 150 psalms that some traditions say mimic the five books of the Torah in structure and doxological focus. Known as the songbook of Israel, it reveals Christ to believers through themes of praise, lament, thanksgiving, and petition. Divine inspiration is beautifully encapsulated in Psalm 19, which serves as a reflection on God's revelation. The psalm is majestic and contemplative in its setting and presents the natural world as silently proclaiming God's glory. The psalmist sings of creation as an ongoing testimony to God's greatness, with its beauty and order inviting meditation on the Creator's work and awesomeness. While creation itself speaks to God's existence and power, its message is obscured by the sinfulness of humanity (see Rom. 1:18–20). This is where the Torah, or the Law of God, provides clarity. The Torah includes the first five books of the Tanakh, the Jewish Hebrew Bible or Christian Old Testament. It offers a precise, personal, and intimate guide to truth, complementing the general revelation found in creation. The Torah leads readers to understand God's will, purpose, and plan more fully and serves as a light that dispels the darkness of misunderstanding. In 2 Timothy 3:14–15, Apostle Paul emphasizes the usefulness of God's Word, imparting wisdom to the young pastor. Here, the setting transitions from the grandeur of creation and the precision of the Torah to the practical and pastoral guidance found in the New Testament. Jointly, these passages demonstrate the thorough and transformative power of Scripture. They invite believers to recognize the ways God reveals Himself—through the natural world and His written Word.

LESSON OUTLINE

I. The Perfect and Flawless Guide for Life (Psalm 19:7)
II. The Perfect, Enlightening, and Useful Word (Psalm 19:8–9; 2 Timothy; 3:14–15)
III. The Perfect and Priceless Word (Psalm 19:10–13)

UNIFYING PRINCIPLE

People are searching for a framework by which to shape lives rich in meaning and purpose. What is the basis of a purpose-driven life? Psalm 19 lifts up the Law as a trustworthy conduit to knowing God, while Paul's letter to Timothy highlights the usefulness of Scripture for framing our lifelong response to God.

INTRODUCTION

The written laws of humanity have proven to be unjust for some; unreliable, unethical, and frequently misinterpreted for others. On August 1, 2024, the United States and Russia conducted the largest prison swap since the end of the Cold War. The prisoners represent numerous American citizens detained abroad, convicted, and sentenced to lengthy prison terms for crimes the United States claims they did not commit. This underscores the vast disparities and inequities between justice systems worldwide, as there is no universal legal standard to ensure fairness and consistency. This is true even within the United States. A growing number of laws have undergone significant changes, often driven by contentious issues within an increasing multicultural society. These laws demonstrate inequalities and injustices in areas such as voting rights, healthcare, immigration, gun control, and various social justice issues. Furthermore, whether international or domestic, laws tend to evolve with each new generation and change of leadership.

In contrast, our lesson focuses on the inspired writings of the Bible that constitute the only infallible practice and rule of faith. After Jesus' resurrection, He speaks with His followers and reminds them of His teachings. Jesus pointed them to God's Word, teaching followers that He could be found in the writings of Moses, the prophets, and the book of Psalms (Luke 24:44). Seven verses in Psalm 19 describe the supernatural revelation of God's word and the benefits it offers to every believer who uses it as their primary source of wisdom and guidance. In addition, we will explore the life of a New Testament character, Timothy, who gained considerably from adhering to God's word.

EXPOSITION

I. The Perfect and Flawless Guide for Life (Psalm 19:7)

The first six verses of Psalm 19 speak of the revelation of God in nature. Though having no voice, the sun, moon, stars and all of creation are the first sermon heard and seen all over the world. God's handiwork in creation clearly reveals His sovereignty. In the Apostle Paul's longest, weightiest, and most influential letter—written to the church in Rome—his opening chapter speaks of how humanity has denied the knowledge of God, even though it is clearly visible in His creation. Paul professes that while the beauty and order of creation speak volumes about God's existence and character, humanity proves unable to acknowledge this truth (Rom. 1:18–20).

In contrast to the divine revelation in nature, human societies frequently rely on laws and policies that, though intended to govern justly, often fall short. When we talk of the many laws within our governmental life, we often think of them as abstract codes or arid legal rules to follow. Not so with the Psalter. Nor is it merely a collection of devotional articles. The governing principles throughout all the Bible, and particular in Psalm 19, are the unveiling truth of the character, will, and glory of God.

David is the presumed author of Psalm 19. A glimpse into his early life under King Saul may help us understand his love and devotion to God's Law and how Psalm 19 is birthed in his heart. Saul did everything he could to make life miserable for David, who, after defeating the Philistine giant Goliath, becomes more popular than Saul. On one hand, we can imagine that, under these circumstances, David's view of justice might have been severely damaged. Yet, on the other hand, it's evidenced that David considers God's protection, calling God his shepherd, rock, fortress, and deliverer (Psalm 18:2–3; Psalm 23). David's situation reminds us that, although laws are meant to apply to all under their authority, they are not always enforced equally in society. Laws often fail the poor and less powerful, leading to disillusionment and a loss of trust in the very systems designed to protect and guide. This reveals a troubling reality about those responsible for creating and administering laws; it suggests a lack of love and understanding, or commitment to justice and equity. This disparity highlights the limitations and fallibility of human laws.

While humans—and their laws and policies—are flawed, God and His Law stands in direct contrast. God's Law, being perfect, emphasizes the importance of keeping His commandments at the center of daily life (Deut. 6:4–9). Psalm 19 moves beyond the natural revelation of God to God's special revelation of His will and purpose for all creation: His Law. God's Law, as described in verse 7, provides a flawless guide for our lives, offering a "life map" comparable to none other. If one were to ask, "What comes to mind when you think of God's Law?" Many of us might immediately think of the Ten Commandments given to Moses on Mount Sinai. But let's dig deeper; God's Law encompasses so much more. It's a perfect pathway and faithful guide. It is special revelation that lights our way in life. It is a trustworthy gift that will never let us down.

II. The Perfect, Enlightening, and Useful Word
(Psalm 19:8–9; 2 Timothy 3:14–15)

Laws of our natural world are ever-changing and unequal in practice. Not so with God's word. The sixty-six books of the Old and New Testaments, which provide literature, songs, poetry, and practical teaching, have not been altered or updated since their original writings. (This is different from how we understand various Bible translations. These are efforts to re/interpret God's Word to suit contemporary languages or culture toward enhanced and accessible understanding.) Expressing the Word's unchanging nature, Jesus insisted that nothing said or done by Him is done to abolish any part of what was written and that "not one letter or one stroke of a letter" of God's word would pass away until all its content were fulfilled (Matt. 5:17–18). Not bound by human limitations, God's Law remains morally and ethically correct across all generations.

Instructions or user manuals come with nearly everything we use or take to task. God's Word remains true and reliable because it is divinely inspired. This is also what makes it useful (2 Tim. 3:16–17). Bible readers who continue in what is learned can expect to receive correction and training in righteousness (2 Tim. 3:14–15). God's Word serves as a means of revealing errors and helping followers align their lives with God's divine principles. Just as Jesus opened the eyes of His disciples to the truth of Scripture on the road to Emmaus, Paul urges Timothy to hold fast to what Timothy has learned. When Ezra the scribe, in Nehemiah 8, read the Law to the people, their minds and commitment to God became renewed and enlightened—much like the enlightening and corrective power of Scripture described in Psalm 19 and 2 Timothy. This contrasts with the flaws of human laws that typically focus on maintaining order and justice in society through rules and regulations. The Bible's reproof and correction reach the inner soul, fostering transformation and spiritual growth to draw us closer to God and His will.

The inner working of God and His will enlightens us to truth that counters the lies of the world. This also brings inner peace and a sense of satisfaction. The nature of God's word is not to condemn or only to tear down and destroy our character, but to guide and rebuild new character. Once David erred from God's pathway by taking a census of Israel (see 2 Sam. 24). This resulted in God's anger being turned toward David and Israel. David was offered three options for his punishment. Essentially, David could be punished by his enemies or by God. David placed his life and whatever punishment he was to receive in God's hand, believing more in the justice and grace of God than of humans.

To say God's Word is pure is to pronounce it without fault; it is clean and not obstructed or tainted with the sins of the world. In recent years, there has been significant debate over whether certain political leaders should be held accountable to the same laws as ordinary citizens. Such thinking highlights how human laws can be manipulated by power, unlike God's Law, which applies equally to all, without favoritism or bias. Additionally, many laws meant to protect the vulnerable have instead contributed to systemic injustice. In contrast, Psalm 19:7 describes God's Law as perfect, offering true justice for all. This is the omnipresence and omnipotence of the Word. In turn, the godly are asked to respond to God with love, faith, obedience, and devotion.

III. The Perfect and Priceless Word (Psalm 19:10–13)

God told Moses He would take the children of Israel to a land flowing with milk and honey, the Promised Land (Exod. 3:8). The description of the land symbolizes God's abundant provisions. Similarly, David uses the terms "honey" and "gold" to convey God's Word as a source of abundant spiritual wealth and blessing. The word "honey" highlights the supreme desirability of God's word. In Ancient Israel, near Tel Rehov, Israel had a thriving honey beekeeping industry. At the time, honey was highly desired as one of the sweetest substances available. It was often used as a sweetener and a treat. Honey engaged the senses with its rich flavor and smooth texture, making it a powerful metaphor for David's description of God's Word. In like manner, to compare God's Word to gold, which was the most valuable thing on earth, emphasizes the Word's supreme worth.

God's word is not just a source of blessing and rewards; it also serves as a warning system. Just as road signs help drivers avoid hazards, Scripture guides us away from spiritual danger. For example, consider how the wisdom in the book of Proverbs might warn you against dishonest practices at work or in relationships. God laid out to Israel a plan of blessing for obedience and curses for disobedience to His commands (see Deut. 28). In verses 11–13, the psalmist acknowledges the weakness of humanity and the need for God's forgiveness. Forgiveness is paramount for hidden sins and is protective against willful sins. David knew this firsthand. (Consider David's sin with Bathsheba in 2 Samuel 11–12.) Just as a loving parent warns a child about dangers they cannot fully understand, God, in His infinite wisdom, provides us with clear instructions and cautions to steer us away from paths that lead to harm and destruction. In following God's wisdom, we can also find spiritual and emotional healing from our failings. As we conclude, let's remember that while human laws may falter, God's Word does not. It remains a steadfast guide, offering wisdom, correction, and peace.

THE LESSON APPLIED

For the believers of Christ, Psalm 19 reminds us that God's word is not only flawless but able to restore and revive saddened, depressed, and confused souls. We learn that the Word of God is supreme in its value—more supreme than gold and silver. Because of the Word, revival and reform was brought to all of Judah under King Josiah from the discovery of the Book of the Law (see 2 Kings 22). The Word is to be elevated above human laws and policies that so often fail us. Life priorities must reflect the reading of Scripture and the guidance we find in the unfolding wisdom of God. It is our best warning system, protecting us from sin and enlightening us to better pathways.

There is also great cause for joy, in knowing that vigilant application of God's Word renders God's blessings. This takes place following a regular self-examination to uncover and understand one's hidden and deliberate sins. Every effort must be made in the confession of sin and a commitment to walk in God's ways. What we learn from Scripture must be not only practiced in the moment, but held firmly with perseverance. This is especially so in life challenges.

In a world filled with false teachings and shifting moral standards, being rooted in the teachings of Scripture is necessary. Daily reflection of the believer's spiritual journey helps to motivate us to continue walking in God's truth. This lesson encourages us to be diligent in our study of Scripture, to continue to grow in our understanding and application of God's Word with the expectation of a growing faith that is useful in life.

LET'S TALK ABOUT IT...

Discuss the following questions and visit www.rhboyd.com for more information.

This week, as you face decisions at work or home, reflect on Psalm 19:7–13. How does the clarity of God's word bring peace and direction?

Get Social

Share your views and tag us
@rhboydco and use #rhboydco

@rhboydco

Home Daily Devotional Readings
December 8–14, 2025

Monday	Tuesday	Wednesday	Thursday	Friday	Saturday	Sunday
The Father's Motherly Compassion	The Father Seeks Authentic Worshippers	The Father Strengthens the Powerless	The Father Exacts Discipline	The Father Blesses and Forgives	The Father Gives Perfect Gifts	The Father Cares for Our Needs
Isaiah 49:13–17	John 4:20–24	Isaiah 40:27–31	Isaiah 64:1–8	Psalm 103:1–5, 10–14	James 1:13–18	Matthew 6:24–34

Lesson II   **December 14, 2025**

Our Heavenly Father

Adult Topic: Letting Go of Worry
Background Scripture: Ex. 34:4–7; Ps. 103:1–5, 10–14; Isa. 40:27–31; Matt. 6:24–34; John 3:3–6; 4:20–24; 8:40–47; Rom. 2:2–11; 8:14–17; 1 John 4:7–16
Lesson Passage: Matthew 6:24–34

MATTHEW 6:24-34

KJV

NO man can serve two masters: for either he will hate the one, and love the other; or else he will hold to the one, and despise the other. Ye cannot serve God and mammon.
25 Therefore I say unto you, Take no thought for your life, what ye shall eat, or what ye shall drink; nor yet for your body, what ye shall put on. Is not the life more than meat, and the body than raiment?
26 Behold the fowls of the air: for they sow not, neither do they reap, nor gather into barns; yet your heavenly Father feedeth them. Are ye not much better than they?
27 Which of you by taking thought can add one cubit unto his stature?
28 And why take ye thought for raiment? Consider the lilies of the field, how they grow; they toil not, neither do they spin:
29 And yet I say unto you, That even Solomon in all his glory was not arrayed like one of these.
30 Wherefore, if God so clothe the grass of the field, which to day is, and to morrow is cast into the oven, shall he not much more clothe you, O ye of little faith?
31 Therefore take no thought, saying, What shall we eat? or, What shall we drink? or, Wherewithal shall we be clothed?
32 (For after all these things do the Gentiles seek:) for your heavenly Father knoweth that ye have need of all these things.

NRSVue

"NO one can serve two masters, for a slave will either hate the one and love the other or be devoted to the one and despise the other. You cannot serve God and wealth.
25 "Therefore I tell you, do not worry about your life, what you will eat or what you will drink, or about your body, what you will wear. Is not life more than food and the body more than clothing?
26 Look at the birds of the air: they neither sow nor reap nor gather into barns, and yet your heavenly Father feeds them. Are you not of more value than they?
27 And which of you by worrying can add a single hour to your span of life?
28 And why do you worry about clothing? Consider the lilies of the field, how they grow; they neither toil nor spin,
29 yet I tell you, even Solomon in all his glory was not clothed like one of these.
30 But if God so clothes the grass of the field, which is alive today and tomorrow is thrown into the oven, will he not much more clothe you—you of little faith?
31 Therefore do not worry, saying, 'What will we eat?' or 'What will we drink?' or 'What will we wear?'
32 For it is the gentiles who seek all these things, and indeed your heavenly Father knows that you need all these things.

MAIN THOUGHT: Take therefore no thought for the morrow: for the morrow shall take thought for the things of. Sufficient unto the day is the evil thereof.
(Matthew 6:34, KJV)

MATTHEW 6:24-34

KJV

33 But seek ye first the kingdom of God, and his righteousness; and all these things shall be added unto you.

34 Take therefore no thought for the morrow: for the morrow shall take thought for the things of itself. Sufficient unto the day is the evil thereof.

NRSVue

33 But seek first the kingdom of God and his righteousness, and all these things will be given to you as well.

34 "So do not worry about tomorrow, for tomorrow will bring worries of its own. Today's trouble is enough for today.

LESSON SETTING

Time: AD 60–65
Place: Capernaum hillside

Setting: Jesus' Sermon on the Mount is set within the larger context of the Gospel of Matthew. The book was written by Matthew, a Jewish man whom Jesus called away from the duties of working for the Roman Empire as a tax collector. Before his calling, fellow Jews viewed Matthew as a traitor of their faith and culture. Yet, scholars believe the meticulous skills Matthew gained and used in the collection of taxes are seen in the structure of the Matthew's Gospel. He writes primarily to a Jewish audience, frequently connecting Jesus' life of and His teachings to Old Testament scriptures. All this was done with the goal of emphasizing that Jesus of Nazareth is the long-awaited Messiah and King. Our lesson passage of a foundational teaching in Jesus' ministry. The location along the hillside of Capernaum, some ninety miles north of Jerusalem, was an ideal location away from the priest and Pharisees to avoid conflict. Jesus' early teachings often critiqued their approach to righteousness and the Law. His standard of righteousness surpassed the external piety some priests and Pharisees often used as a weapon against ordinary Jewish citizens. Additionally, Jesus' teachings to shift the focus from a legalistic adherence to the Law to a deeper moral and spiritual integrity provided fodder for confrontation in His ministry. Jesus' message on worry—one of the longest teachings on that subject in the Bible—conveys a profound spiritual truth in a relatable and revelatory way.

LESSON OUTLINE

I. The Danger of Divided Loyalty (Matthew 6:24)
II. Overcoming Worry (Matthew 6:25–30)
III. Prioritizing God Above All (Matthew 6:31–34)

UNIFYING PRINCIPLE

Some people are never satisfied with what they have and spend their lives striving for great wealth. What is more important than great wealth? In the Sermon on the Mount, Jesus says that because His heavenly Father will provide for our needs, we can let go of worry and strive for the righteousness of God.

INTRODUCTION

In 1992, the *Journal of Consumer Research* found that there is a direct correlation between materialism, life satisfaction, and psychological well-being, noting that higher levels of materialism are associated with lower life satisfaction and increased anxiety. The desire for and willingness to pursue materialism in American culture have reached record levels. It's no surprise that seeking after the most up-to-date smartphones, designer clothing, or trendiest home decors has created a culture where one's worth is defined by one's possessions. Consequently, the inability to obtain these items has created widespread worry in society.

There is peer pressure on teens for "must-have" items and on parents to stretch their budgets or borrow money they don't have to accommodate. In fact, a 2022 study by the *American Psychological Association* indicated financial pressure as a highly prevalent stressor among adults. Sadly, worry about money and the race to accumulate wealth and possessions escapes no age. Obsession with materialism has deepened societal divisions and fostered a culture where even people of faith are valued more for what they have than for who they are in Christ.

Many believers worry because of a lack of trust in the One who provides. Monetary pressures often blind us to the truth that Jesus alone transforms hearts and lives from discontentment to contentment. Our second lesson in this quarter teaches us that there is no need to worry in the Kingdom of God because of our Father and His sovereign will. God's presence will always be accessible. Therefore, His provisions will always be available for those who place their complete trust in Him.

EXPOSITION

I. The Danger of Divided Loyalty (Matthew 6:24)

Divided loyalty occurs when a person tries to commit to two conflicting authorities, interest, or values. This often leads to inner conflict, inconsistency in actions, and a lack of true devotion to either side. Divided loyalty can manifest anywhere—in relationships, workplaces, or spiritual commitments. Money often demands allegiance through the pursuit of wealth, security, or luxury. Like God, the gain of money promises provision, control, and comfort. While money itself is not evil, money becomes a rival when it takes the place of trust in God's provision. Money as our total pursuit serves self-interest, material gain, and worldly success and is often at the expense of spiritual growth, generosity, and obedience to God. God and God's Word call for selflessness, faith, and a life of contentment—all of which are contrary to greed or obsession with wealth. Loyalty to the Father, first and foremost, is a key teaching of Jesus' ministry to those He taught and those who read and hear His voice today.

Jesus, the Son of God, no doubt was quite aware of Israel's long history of divided loyalty to His Father. They grappled with being torn between trusting God for their livelihood and submitting to the pressures of foreign rule and occupation. It seems the issue of *mammon* and *master* has always been present with Israel, with some choosing wisely at times and others failing miserably. This tension was evident throughout the Old Testament, beginning with the period of the judges and continuing into the New Testament under Roman occupation.

In the book of Judges, Gideon is one example of this struggle. Oppressed by the Midianites who invaded their harvest year after year and unable to escape their constant attacks, the young man Gideon was the one whom God used to deliver them (Judges 6–7). Gideon's thoughts were that of a young adult who had given up on any of the faith-talk of his parents and ancestors. His goal in life was simply trying to grow a decent amount of crops to live on. He had no interest in optimistic faith-talk until God brought an angel into his life. Gideon was used by God to deliver Israel with only the use of 300 men, ensuring that victory was attributed to the divine intervention of God rather than human strength. The victory was a reminder that Israel's true strength rests in the hands of God. However, their victory with Gideon and other judges were short-lived, as their divided loyalty persisted and led to further cycles of disobedience.

During Israel's monarchy period (the period when kings ruled), prophets like Samuel, Elijah, and Isaiah continued to call Israel to trust in God alone, warning that failure to do so by entering into alliances with foreign power would place Israel in danger of God's wrath. At an all-time low was their loyalty to God in the Northern Kingdom during the reign of King Ahab and wife Jezebel. The prophet Elijah confronted them with warnings and astonishing interventions filled with miracles, yet Israel's repentance was once again short-lived, as they promoted Baal worship along with worship of God (1 Kings 18).

II. Overcoming Worry (Matthew 6:25–30)

It is often said that God knows what we need before we even pray for it. This is true not only of our physical needs but also of the wisdom and guidance we require in difficult times. Jesus' teaching on worry in Matthew's Gospel is one of the most comprehensive discussions of the subject in the Bible. The length and depth of this teaching emphasizes God's intentionality in addressing a universal human struggle. Jesus, fully understanding our anxieties, offers a path to trust and peace in God's provision.

Worry refers to an anxious obsession with one's material needs and/or future security. It often stems from a lack of trust in God's provision and care. In today's world, believers face constant pressure to secure their future—whether it's financial stability, career success, or health concerns. Social media, economic uncertainties, and the relentless pace of life can amplify these worries. Jesus' words, "Do not worry about your life" (v. 25), speak directly to these modern anxieties. When we talk and think about God, we often forget that He is the Creator of the heavens and the earth and is fully capable of sustaining what He has created. This truth, also woven into Matthew 6:25–30, reminds us of God's infinite power, care, and provision.

The same God who speaks the universe into existence (Gen. 1:1) is the One who sustains it. Birds do not have storehouses or savings accounts, yet their needs are met daily (v. 26). If God is faithful to provide for them, how much more will He care for us, His most valued creation who are made in His image? When the prophet Elijah was in hiding, God commanded ravens to bring him bread and meat twice a day, showing His ability to use even nature to meet human needs (1 Kings 17:2–6). Our lesson's author, Matthew, was a firsthand witness of Jesus feeding thousands of followers who were unable to get to food on their own. Similarly, God doesn't simply help the flowers of the field survive but lavishes them with beauty. If He clothes grass, which is temporary in its presence, how much more will He clothe and care for us?

In the context of His time, Jesus addressed a Jewish audience deeply concerned about their basic needs and the oppressive realities of Roman occupation as well as religious pressure from temple leaders who enforced purity laws. Today, believers face different challenges but share the same underlining struggle: the fear of not having enough and the pressure to secure our futures. However, Jesus teaches that by choosing to serve God alone, a person can free themselves from the burden of anxiety about material concerns. Trust is placed fully on God's provision and in God's timing and ways to provide. Putting trust in God is resisting to succumb to anxiety; living in contentment and gratitude is the result of trust in God (Rom. 8:14–17). There is also peace and freedom from constant striving for more through self-efforts and personal means. Jesus is calling for faith in Him as the foundation upon which we build our lives and fidelity.

III. Prioritizing God Above All (Matthew 6:31–34)

The people of Jesus' day lived under Roman occupation, which prioritized Roman rule over the Jewish people in all areas of life, regardless of their concerns. Daily survival often took precedence over spiritual focus. This is evident in the decisions, practices, and rules set by temple leaders, which prioritized power over people rather than reflecting God's heart and His call for His people. At the core of God's Kingdom is God's kingship—His authority and dominion over all things. There is no defining location of the Kingdom of God: it refers to the realm where God's will is done. When we prioritize God above all, we trust in His provision, seek first His Kingdom (His will and reign over and in all), and focus on today's opportunities convinced that God will take care of our future. Farmers plant seeds, trusting that the soil, rain, and sun will do their part. No farmer anxiously digs his crops up daily to check on their progress; instead, the farmer trusts in God's natural process, just as each believer must trust in God's provisions. To prioritize God and seek His Kingdom is to actively align our lives with His purposes, trusting that He will take care of our needs as we do. The mission of the Church stems directly from the Kingdom of God.

Jesus commissioned His disciples to "seek first His kingdom and His righteousness" (Matt. 6:33). In so doing, however, it can sometimes be difficult to discern the difference between planning ahead for the future or worry about tomorrow. The worrier fails to see how anxiety and fear-driven motivations disturb well-intended plans. Matthew warns us that there are plenty of trouble-filled days. However, the person who consciously looks and listens to God for planning ahead will have pleasing God as their primary motivation. This is time well spent, whereas worrying—no matter how long it lasts—is time wasted. When we prioritize God above all, we move from the futility of worry to the peace of purposeful planning. We operate in the knowledge that our future is secure in His hands.

Physical, emotional, or spiritual troubles of the world arise daily—and for some, even hourly. Time and technological advances have not shielded us from troubles but have instead carried them forward, passing the burdens of humanity from one generation to the next. However, believers throughout time understand that each new day with God brings new mercies and fresh opportunities to trust in God's provision, grace, and peace. Each new days gives us opportunity to lean into God as eternal and unchanging.

THE LESSON APPLIED

Applying Jesus' teaching on worry involves trusting God's provision, prioritizing God's Kingdom, and cultivating a heart of contentment and gratitude. As Jesus teaches in Matthew 6, the first step to overcome worry is to place our confidence entirely in God's provision. In a world where financial security, career success, and health concerns often dominate our thoughts, Jesus' reminder that God cares for the birds and the lilies reassures us He will certainly provide for us. This trust is active; it means choosing to rely on God's faithfulness rather than our own limited resources. Just as Israel wrestled with divided loyalties, often torn between trusting in God and relying on worldly systems, so too will we. Believers must resist the urge to seek security apart from God. Instead of worrying about tomorrow, we can live with the assurance that our Heavenly Father is in control and will meet our needs at the perfect time.

Jesus' call to seek first the Kingdom and His righteousness challenges us to align our lives with God's priorities, moving away from material concerns that can dominate our minds. This shift requires careful evaluation of how we invest our time, energy, and resources, ensuring that we focus on eternal values rather than temporary gains. When we prioritize God's Kingdom, we reflect the faithfulness that Israel often struggled to maintain under pressure. Trusting God's rule frees us from the "rule" of anxiety, fear, and discontentment.

LET'S TALK ABOUT IT...

Discuss the following questions and visit www.rhboyd.com for more information.

How does trusting in God's provision help us overcome the anxieties of daily life?

In what ways can prioritizing God's Kingdom shift our perspective on what truly matters?

How can practicing contentment and gratitude change our response to life's challenges and uncertainties?

Get Social

Share your views and tag us
@rhboydco and use #rhboydco

@rhboydco

Home Daily Devotional Readings
December 15–21, 2025

Monday	Tuesday	Wednesday	Thursday	Friday	Saturday	Sunday
The Messiah Sits at God's Side	Christ Died for the Ungodly	Christ Offers Eternal Life	Christ Cares for the Sheep	Welcome the Davidic Heir	The Messiah Reigns Victoriously	Christ Rejoices when Sinners Repent
Psalm 110	Romans 5:1–11	John 3:14–21	John 10:9–16	Isaiah 9:3–7	Psalm 2	Luke 15:1–7

Lesson III   December 21, 2025

Christ the Savior

Adult Topic: Safe and Secure
Background Scripture: Luke 2:11, 30–32; 15:3–7; John 3:14–17; 10:9–11, 14–16, 27–28; Acts 3:1–18; Rom. 5:1–11; Phil. 2:5–11; 2 Tim. 1:9–10
Lesson Passage: Luke 15:3–7; Romans 5:6–10

LUKE 15:3-7; ROMANS 5:6-10

KJV

AND he spake this parable unto them, saying,
4 What man of you, having an hundred sheep, if he lose one of them, doth not leave the ninety and nine in the wilderness, and go after that which is lost, until he find it?
5 And when he hath found it, he layeth it on his shoulders, rejoicing.
6 And when he cometh home, he calleth together his friends and neighbours, saying unto them, Rejoice with me; for I have found my sheep which was lost.
7 I say unto you, that likewise joy shall be in heaven over one sinner that repenteth, more than over ninety and nine just persons, which need no repentance.

••• Romans 5:6-10 •••

6 For when we were yet without strength, in due time Christ died for the ungodly.
7 For scarcely for a righteous man will one die: yet peradventure for a good man some would even dare to die.
8 But God commendeth his love toward us, in that, while we were yet sinners, Christ died for us.
9 Much more then, being now justified by his blood, we shall be saved from wrath through him.
10 For if, when we were enemies, we were reconciled to God by the death of his Son, much more, being reconciled, we shall be saved by his life.

NRSVue

SO he told them this parable:
4 "Which one of you, having a hundred sheep and losing one of them, does not leave the ninety-nine in the wilderness and go after the one that is lost until he finds it?
5 And when he has found it, he lays it on his shoulders and rejoices.
6 And when he comes home, he calls together his friends and neighbors, saying to them, 'Rejoice with me, for I have found my lost sheep.'
7 Just so, I tell you, there will be more joy in heaven over one sinner who repents than over ninety-nine righteous persons who need no repentance.

••• Romans 5:6-10 •••

6 For while we were still weak, at the right time Christ died for the ungodly.
7 Indeed, rarely will anyone die for a righteous person—though perhaps for a good person someone might actually dare to die.
8 But God proves his love for us in that while we still were sinners Christ died for us.
9 Much more surely, therefore, since we have now been justified by his blood, will we be saved through him from the wrath of God.
10 For if while we were enemies we were reconciled to God through the death of his Son, much more surely, having been reconciled, will we be saved by his life.

MAIN THOUGHT: For if while we were enemies we were reconciled to God through the death of his Son, much more surely, having been reconciled, will we be saved by his life. (Romans 5:10, NRSVue)

LESSON SETTING

Time: Between AD 50–60

Place: Traveling from Galilee toward Jerusalem, probably Perea (Luke 15); City of Corinth (Romans 5)

Setting: In first-century Judea, shepherds tended their flocks in the rugged countryside and villagers worked the land to provide for their families. The land itself was a mix of a busy city, like Jerusalem and rural areas like the rolling hills of Galilee. This peaceful landscape is in direct contrast to life once it was heavily influenced by occupation of the Roman Empire. Jewish communities' daily lives were disrupted by the oppressive presence of Roman authority, which demanded rule over every sphere of their lives. The Romans enforced their rule over Jewish and Gentile citizens with strict control. Roman soldiers patrolled the roads day and night. Taxes were steep, placing a heavy burden on the people. Local Jewish leaders, such as Pharisees and scribes, were caught between maintaining their strict faith and complying with Roman demands. The sense of oppression was ever-present, as Roman officials brought foreign customs and laws that often clashed with Jewish traditions deeply rooted in the culture. Dissent was not tolerated, and those who defied the empire faced harsh consequences. In the cities, the contrast between Roman wealth and local poverty was striking. Roman buildings and monuments showcased the empire's power, while many local people lived modestly, struggling under the weight of taxes and the limitations imposed on their freedom. Yet, even in this environment, many of those in Jewish communities who held onto their faith and traditions, hoping for deliverance from foreign rule by their Messiah and His Kingdom. This setting of Roman occupation is strikingly similar to the backdrop of last week's lesson from the Gospel of Matthew, particularly the Sermon on the Mount. There, too, we saw the tension between the Jewish peoples' faith and oppressive Roman rule. The constant pressure from the empire shaped daily life and religious practice, creating a backdrop of longing for justice, freedom, and peace in both settings. People lived with the weight of oppressive world powers but clung to the hope of something greater.

LESSON OUTLINE

I. God's Deep Concern for the Lost (Luke 15:3–5)
II. The Joy in Heaven Over One Sinner Who Repents (Luke 15:6–7)
III. Saved by Love: From Sin to Reconciliation (Romans 5:6–10)

UNIFYING PRINCIPLE

People without a sense of belonging can wander through life feeling lost, alone, and without sure foundation. Who can rescue those who feel this way? The same extravagant love that sends the Shepherd to rescue the lost lamb (Luke 15) sent the Lamb of God, Christ, to die so that sinners might be reconciled to God and restored to Him (Romans 5).

INTRODUCTION

When something precious is lost, our first instinct is to search desperately until it's found. Many parents of little children have experienced the fear and urgency of losing sight of a child in a crowded place like a park or grocery store. Parents would hold the child's hand tightly, knowing how quickly he or she could slip away. These places and environments are often prepared for such events and equipped with systems like intercoms to announce a child is missing and Amber Alerts—urgent notifications that grab our attention and signal that a child is missing and must be found immediately. This same urgency is reflected in Luke 15:3–7, where Jesus tells the parable of the lost sheep. Just as an Amber Alert triggers action, the shepherd in the story is driven by love and concern to leave the sheepfold in search of the one that has gone astray.

Jesus possibly chose the number of sheep to be one hundred because it was often interpreted as representing completeness; the absence of even one sheep signified incompleteness. The parable illustrates God's deep concern for the lost and reveals that every one of us matters to Him. The story does not end with the recovery of the lost sheep; it culminates in the shepherd gathering friends and neighbors to celebrate. This communal joy reflects God's heart when the lost are restored to Him. Paul expands on this theme in Romans 5:6–11. While we were still sinners, Christ died for us. Like the jarring sound of an Amber Alert, Christ's death on the cross broke through the barrier of sin, offering reconciliation. God's love is relentless, joyful, and saving. This lesson will explore three key truths: God's deep concern for the lost, the joy in heaven over one sinner who repents, and how we are saved by love.

EXPOSITION

I. God's Deep Concern for the Lost (Luke 15:3–5)

Jesus presents a moving illustration of God's heart for those who are lost. He is the "true shepherd," while the Pharisees and scribes, standing by waiting for Jesus to do something they could criticize, are shepherds with no concern for the lost (Ezek. 34:1–6). The story depicts a shepherd who, upon realizing that one of his one hundred sheep is missing, leaves the ninety-nine in the open field to seek out the one. This parable, though brief, is rich in meaning, highlighting God's deep concern for the lost and His active pursuit of reconciliation. It reveals God's loving character, His desire for every soul, and the lengths to which He goes to bring them back.

The shepherd in this parable is a vivid representation of God's deep love and concern for those who have strayed. The image of the shepherd, common in Jewish culture, evokes care, guidance, and protection. In Luke 2:11 and 30–32, Jesus is announced as the Savior, not just for the righteous but for the lost and marginalized. The lost sheep is a symbol of those who are far from God, and the shepherd's actions underscore God's relentless pursuit of the lost. This theme is echoed in John 3:14–17, where we see the profound depth of God's love.

The shepherd does not delegate the task of finding the lost sheep. He goes after it personally, which points to Jesus' mission. As the Good Shepherd, Jesus is willing to lay down His life for His sheep (see John 10:9–11). This underscores the personal nature of God's concern. His love is not passive or indifferent; it is active and sacrificial. Each lost soul matters deeply to Him. The same urgency that the shepherd feels to find His lost sheep is reflected in God's desire for sinners to return, just as Peter articulates when he calls for repentance and speaks of God's readiness to restore (Acts 3:1–18).

Jesus employed several key teaching methods to communicate, including parables. A parable is a simple story used to convey spiritual or moral lessons. The story of the lost sheep was familiar to His listeners, many of whom lived in farming societies and understood the relationship between shepherds and their flock.

The role of the shepherd in the parable mirrors the pastoral care that Jesus provides as the ultimate Shepherd of His people. In the New Testament, pastors are often referred to as shepherds, entrusted with the care of God's flock. This care, however, comes from the Chief Shepherd, Jesus, who owns and leads His flock. When the shepherd in the parable calls the sheep "My sheep," it highlights God's deep personal investment and ownership over His people.

Ultimately, this parable foreshadows Jesus' own mission. God did not send an angel to seek the lost; He sent His own Son. Jesus came into the world to bring the lost back to God. As Philippians 2:5–11 describes, Christ humbled Himself, even to the point of death on the cross, to reconcile humanity with God. This act of love illustrates God's deep concern for every lost soul, just as the shepherd's pursuit of the one lost sheep illustrates God's personal and sacrificial pursuit of us all.

II. The Joy in Heaven Over One Sinner Who Repents (Luke 15:6–7)

Throughout Scripture, God's love is demonstrated in His relentless pursuit of the lost, calling them back into relationship with Him. In Luke 15, Jesus shares three parables—the lost sheep, the lost coin, and the prodigal son—to illustrate this divine pursuit and the joy that follows when the lost are found. Each parable highlights the immeasurable value God places on every individual and the rejoicing that takes place in heaven when even one sinner repents. This theme is central to Luke 15:6–7, where we are given a glimpse of divine celebration.

The shepherd, having found his lost sheep, calls his friends and neighbors to rejoice with him. This scene echoes the deep joy that fills heaven when one sinner turns back to God. The significance of this joy is magnified by the contrast: ninety-nine righteous persons who need no repentance, and yet the heavens erupt in celebration over the one who was lost but is now found. Those who will be in heaven are not those who were already deemed worthy. They are those who, like the lost sheep, were unworthy until their encounter with the Good Shepherd who laid down His life for them. It is not our worthiness that secures us a place in heaven, but God's sacrificial love. Here, Jesus also affirms the reality of heaven—a place where those who follow and obey Him will one day rest.

This heavenly rejoicing aligns with the essence of "amazing grace"—something given to a soul once lost but now found, once blind but now seeing. This theme of rejoicing evokes the rich traditions of the African American church, particularly the Homecoming Services of the South. Families, once scattered by the Great Migration northward, returned home for these joyful celebrations. Old friends and family would embrace, share memories, and worship together in a spirit of unity and gratitude. Greater than Homecoming gatherings where love and joy overflowed is heaven's joy when one lost soul returns to the fold of God. It is a homecoming of the spirit—a return to the place where one truly belongs and where eternal rest is promised.

III. Saved by Love: From Sin to Reconciliation (Romans 5:6–10)

In Romans 5:6–10, Paul presents the core of the Gospel, highlighting God's love for humanity despite our sin. Christ's sacrifice wasn't a response to our righteousness but an act of love for the weak, ungodly, and lost. His death accomplished what the Law could not—reconciling us to God. This passage underscores the radical, self-giving nature of divine love, which leads us from estrangement to reconciliation through Christ's sacrifice. Paul expresses the human condition and how, despite being estranged from God, Christ dies for us.

Paul begins by emphasizing the remarkable nature of Christ's sacrifice. He states that it occurred "while we were still weak" (v. 6). This weakness was not merely physical but spiritual—our complete inability to save ourselves or attain righteousness apart from God's grace. Humanity, in its sinfulness, was utterly helpless, yet at the appointed time, Christ died for the ungodly. His death was not for the righteous or deserving but for those who had no merit of their own.

In verse 7, Paul underscores how rare such an act of love truly is. It is uncommon for someone to willingly die even for a righteous person—one who follows the Law and does what is morally right. It is slightly more conceivable that someone might lay down their life for a "good" person, meaning one who is noble, kind, and selfless. Yet Christ's sacrifice transcends human reasoning; He did not die for the righteous or the morally upright, but for sinners. His love defies the conditional nature of human love, offering redemption to those who least deserved it.

This passage prepares the reader for Paul's powerful declaration in Romans 5:8–10, where he reveals that Christ's death was the ultimate demonstration of God's love. While human justice and sacrifice operate on principles of merit, God's grace is entirely unmerited. The cross stands as the greatest testament to a love that reaches the powerless, the sinful, and the lost—bringing reconciliation where only condemnation once stood.

We were sinners, yet God demonstrated His love for us. God's love is proven not in response to our goodness but in the face of our sin (v. 8). This act of love was not just for a select few, but for the entire world, just as John 3:16–17 affirms: "For God so loved the world, that he gave his only begotten Son... that the world through him might be saved." God's love is not contingent on human effort but is an unmerited gift, offered to all who believe.

Because of Christ's sacrifice, we are justified by His blood, saved from the wrath that our sins rightly deserve (v. 9). This justification marks a turning point from judgment to mercy. Paul's words here echo the declaration of the angels in Luke 2:11, "For unto you is born this day in the city of David a Savior, which is Christ the Lord." From His birth, Christ's mission was to save the lost—a mission He fulfilled on the cross when He laid down His life for all sinners.

In verse 10, Paul describes the pre-salvation condition of humanity to the church in Rome as not only ungodly but also enemies of God. This is connected to the spiritual weakness referenced in verse 6. We were weak, useless, destitute, and powerless—making us completely unable to save ourselves from sin and, thereby, completely removed from God as enemies of God. The Law, while holy, could not save us from this state (see Rom. 3:20). Christ's death, however, brought the salvation that the Law could never provide.

THE LESSON APPLIED

Human effort and the Law alone have no strength to deliver or free anyone from sin. Without God's intervention, we remain powerless, much like the lost sheep in Jesus' parable. Yet, the Gospel is the story of divine pursuit—God actively seeking and rescuing the lost. For Paul, love is the core message of Christ and is powerfully declared in Romans 5:6–10. God, like the shepherd in Luke 15:3–7, did not leave us wandering in our lostness. In love, He pursued us even in our state of rebellion.

These passages remind us that no one is beyond God's reach, no matter how far they have strayed from God's pathway. Praying for those absent from church and outside of fellowship is always needed. Like the shepherd who leaves the ninety-nine to seek the one, we are called to care for those who feel disconnected, rejected, or unworthy. This can be applied in our daily interactions by extending grace and compassion to those who may not seem to fit into societal norms, offering them a chance for restoration rather than judgment. The parable also encourages us to reflect on our own spiritual journeys. We may experience seasons of wandering, yet the Good Shepherd, Jesus, never ceases to seek us out, ready to bring us back into His fold. His love is not contingent on our worthiness but is eternally rooted in His mercy and grace.

Finally, the parable challenges us to celebrate repentance and reconciliation whenever we witness it. It's a call to share in the joy of salvation and to participate in God's mission of seeking the lost. No matter the size of our church membership, we should view it as incomplete and seek out the one.

LET'S TALK ABOUT IT...

Discuss the following questions and visit www.rhboyd.com for more information.

In the parable of the lost sheep, who and what do the key fictional characters represent in the real world to you?

What do we learn abut the character and attributes of God the Father?

Get Social

Share your views and tag us
@rhboydco and use #rhboydco

@rhboydco

Home Daily Devotional Readings
December 22–28, 2025

Monday	Tuesday	Wednesday	Thursday	Friday	Saturday	Sunday
The Spirit Accomplishes God's Will	The Spirit Bestows Gifts	The Spirit Gives Wisdom and Understanding	The Spirit Works in Jesus's Birth	The Spirit Reveals God's Glory	The Spirit Creates and Renews	The Spirit Affirms Our Adoption
Zechariah 4:1–7	1 Corinthians 12:1–13	Isaiah 11:1–9	Matthew 1:18–25	Acts 7:51–60	Psalm 104:24, 29–35	Romans 8:12–17, 26–27

Lesson IV **December 28, 2025**

The Holy Spirit

Adult Topic: How Three Make One
Background Scripture: Joel 2:28–29; Luke 11:9–13; John 3:5–8; 14:16–17, 26; 15:26–27; 16:7–15; Acts 2:1–21, 32–33; Rom. 8:1–17, 26–27; 1 Cor. 12:1–13; Eph. 1:13–14; 3:14–21; 4:1–6, 30
Lesson Passage: Romans 8:12–17, 26–27

ROMANS 8:12–17, 26–27

KJV

THEREFORE, brethren, we are debtors, not to the flesh, to live after the flesh.
13 For if ye live after the flesh, ye shall die: but if ye through the Spirit do mortify the deeds of the body, ye shall live.
14 For as many as are led by the Spirit of God, they are the sons of God.
15 For ye have not received the spirit of bondage again to fear; but ye have received the Spirit of adoption, whereby we cry, Abba, Father.
16 The Spirit itself beareth witness with our spirit, that we are the children of God:
17 And if children, then heirs; heirs of God, and joint-heirs with Christ; if so be that we suffer with him, that we may be also glorified together.

• • • • • •

26 Likewise the Spirit also helpeth our infirmities: for we know not what we should pray for as we ought: but the Spirit itself maketh intercession for us with groanings which cannot be uttered.
27 And he that searcheth the hearts knoweth what is the mind of the Spirit, because he maketh intercession for the saints according to the will of God.

NRSVue

SO then, brothers and sisters, we are obligated, not to the flesh, to live according to the flesh—
13 for if you live according to the flesh, you will die, but if by the Spirit you put to death the deeds of the body, you will live.
14 For all who are led by the Spirit of God are children of God.
15 For you did not receive a spirit of slavery to fall back into fear, but you received a spirit of adoption. When we cry, "Abba! Father!"
16 it is that very Spirit bearing witness with our spirit that we are children of God,
17 and if children, then heirs: heirs of God and joint heirs with Christ, if we in fact suffer with him so that we may also be glorified with him.

• • • • • •

26 Likewise the Spirit helps us in our weakness, for we do not know how to pray as we ought, but that very Spirit intercedes with groanings too deep for words.

27 And God, who searches hearts, knows what is the mind of the Spirit, because the Spirit intercedes for the saints according to the will of God.

LESSON SETTING

Time: Around ad 57
Place: Corinth, Third Missionary Journey
Setting: The Apostle Paul wrote the book of Romans while living in Corinth and staying with Gaius—a Corinthian convert (Rom. 16:23). Corinth was a major

MAIN THOUGHT: The Spirit itself beareth witness with our spirit, that we are the children of God: (Romans 8:16, KJV)

city in Greece that was part of the ancient Roman world. The city was heavily influenced by Greek philosophy. A wide variety of religious practices ensued, including adherence to and worship of various gods representing different aspects of life and Greek mythology. Paul had spent considerable time in Corinth establishing and strengthening its church. This made his Gospel message and its implications for Law and grace especially relevant to the church at Rome. Though it was his long desire to travel there, Paul had not yet visited Roman congregation (Rom. 1:11–13). While in Corinth, Paul was directly under Roman control. There, Paul would have gained a deeper awareness of Roman dominance over citizens, occupied Jews, and slaves. Because Rome was the center of the Roman Empire and the seat of its greatest influence, to be born and reared there left no escape from its political, cultural, and psychological impact. Roman laws created a highly structured society backed up and supported by its mass military power. The rights, privileges, and social class system in Roman society severely affected one's identity and life choices. Fate and the gods of Rome shaped thinking on human destiny. The political atmosphere rested in the hands of one man—Caesar—who demanded loyalty as one would give to a god. Taken together, what was most important in Rome were the values of hierarchy, duty to the state, reverence for the emperor, and participation in a system of worship where multiple gods or deities are recognized. The accumulation of Roman power, both politically and militarily, had a tremendous psychological and spiritual effect throughout the Empire, but especially for those living in Rome.

LESSON OUTLINE

I. Freedom from the Flesh (Romans 8:12–13)
II. New Children and New Heirs of God (Romans 8:14–17)
III. Prayers That Align with God's Will (Romans 8:26–27)

UNIFYING PRINCIPLE

People find their greatest fulfillment when their actions are consistent with their true selves, values, and character. What shapes one's core identity? Romans tells us that the Holy Spirit is an agent of advocacy and adoption, whereby believers are assured that they belong to God.

INTRODUCTION

The church in Rome was unique in its formation. The exact founder of the church in Rome is not explicitly mentioned in the New Testament. However, some traditions believe it was founded by the Apostle Peter with help from the Apostle Paul. Yet other scholars say the Church grew organically through the spread of the Gospel by Jewish and Gentile converts who had encountered the message of Christ, possibly as early as Pentecost. As such, the Roman church was a diverse community, made up of both Jews and Gentiles, navigating the tension between their distinct cultural backgrounds and their shared faith in Jesus. This mixed congregation faced the daily challenge of reconciling Jewish traditions with the newfound freedom of the Gentiles under the Gospel, all while living under the shadow of Roman rule.

Paul's epistle to this church addresses not only theological issues but also the social and cultural realities of their time. In it is introduced the concept of a new kind of kingdom—one not built on Roman military power, law, or the emperor's control, but on the reign of Jesus Christ. For Jews who awaited a Messiah to free them from Rome, and for Gentiles who lived under the influence of Roman paganism and power, this new kingdom offered a completely different vision of life. It was a kingdom in which both Jew and Gentile were united by one faith and baptism in Christ, no longer separated by the Law or by cultural identities.

Paul's message to this integrated congregation is clear: there is a new King, and His rule is not like Caesar's. This new power, the Holy Spirit, transforms lives, breaks the chains of sin and death, and unites Jews and Gentiles into one family. The mixed and culturally diverse church in Rome was living proof of the power of this new kingdom.

As Paul explains in Romans 8:12-27, the new power—the Holy Spirit—is the key to living in the freedom of God's Kingdom. No longer bound by the flesh, whether in the form of Jewish legalism or Gentile paganism, believers are now children of God, empowered by the Spirit to live in a way that transcends oppressive systems. The Holy Spirit, working in tandem with the Father and the Son, guides believers into this new kingdom, empowering us to live according to God's will and purpose. This is not merely a spiritual message; it is a declaration that God's Kingdom has come, and it is far greater than any earthly empire.

EXPOSITION

I. Freedom from the Flesh (Romans 8:12-13)

The Apostle Paul's teaching on freedom revolves around liberation from sin and the Law through faith in Jesus Christ; a freedom that results in a new life of righteousness, service, and spiritual renewal throughout one's life span. Followers of Christ are no longer enslaved to sin which brings about death, because we have been crucified with Christ and risen in Him.

The Apostle Paul brings forth one of the most compelling spiritual truths in Romans 8:12-13: believers are called to a life of freedom from the flesh. In this context, "flesh" refers not to the physical body but to the sinful nature that dominates human existence before the transformative work of Christ. Paul is concerned with the distinction between living according to the flesh versus living by the Spirit. In these verses, he makes known that while believers were once enslaved to the flesh, they are now free to live by the Spirit.

Paul's assertion in Romans 8:12 emphasizes a noteworthy shift in the believer's identity and responsibility: a change from being enslaved to the flesh, with its corrupt desires, to being committed to the Spirit. Paul came to the defense of the runaway slave Onesimus under the concept of being free in Christ and transformed into a new person. Onesimus is no longer bound by the expectations and limitations of his former life. Onesimus returned to his former master Philemon not as a slave but as a brother in Christ, reflecting his new spiritual obligation (Phil. 1:8-16). Similar, Nicodemus, initially bound by his role and reputation as a Pharisee, approached Jesus secretly by night, seeking understanding. Learning from Jesus about being "born again," his perspective shifted from the legalistic obligations of the flesh to the transformative work of the Spirit (see John 3:1–19).

The use of the word "obligation" in v. 12 refers to moral and spiritual debt. In the flesh, humans are subject to the sinful inclinations that lead to separation from God. The desires of the flesh—selfishness, pride, and worldly ambition—once held sway over the hearts and minds of people. But through Christ's death and resurrection, believers are no longer obligated to these desires. We owe nothing to the sinful nature, which can only bring condemnation.

In Romans 8:13, Paul presents a clear distinction between two paths: the path of the flesh and the path of the Spirit. Living according to the flesh leads to death—both spiritual and physical. Sin, when fully grown, brings forth death (James 1:15). This death is not merely the end of physical life, but it refers to the separation from God, a condition of spiritual death that ultimately leads to eternal judgment. Paul is not only warning against the dangers of sinful living but also highlighting the complete inability of the flesh to bring about any lasting good. No amount of self-effort or human striving in the flesh can bring true life or righteousness. The flesh only breeds decay, guilt, and separation from God.

Conversely, those who live by the Spirit, who actively "put to death the misdeeds of the body," experience true life. This phrase, "put to death the misdeeds of the body," refers to a continual process of mortifying sinful desires and behaviors. All believers, through the power of the Holy Spirit, can overcome the sinful tendencies that once ruled life. It is not a passive process but an active and repetitive one, where the Spirit enables us to resist temptation, seek holiness, and live in righteousness.

II. New Children and New Heirs of God (Romans 8:14–17)

In verses 14–17, Paul continues his emphasis on the believer's transformation through the Spirit. He begins by stating, "For all who are led by the Spirit of God are children of God." This statement not only defines the Christian's identity but also our new relationship with God. To be led by the Spirit means to be guided, directed, and empowered by God in one's daily life. The Spirit is not an impersonal force, but the very presence of God within believers, marking us His own. The Holy Spirit seals believers until the God appointed time of full redemption (Eph. 4:30).

Paul introduces the concept of adoption, a deeply powerful and comforting metaphor, especially to the Roman audience, who were familiar with the legal significance of adoption in their society. Adoption in the Roman world was a formal and legal process, granting the adoptee all the rights and privileges of a biological child, including inheritance. In this light, Paul's message takes on a profound significance. Believers, once estranged from God due to sin, are now adopted into His family through the Holy Spirit. This adoption is not a temporary arrangement, but a permanent, eternal bond that signifies a new status as children of God.

Paul contrasts the spirit of slavery with the spirit of adoption, emphasizing that believers no longer live in fear. In the ancient world, the spirit of slavery symbolized fear, oppression, and powerlessness. However, through Christ, believers are liberated from this bondage and fear. The phrase "Abba! Father!" expresses the intimate relationship believers now have with God. "Abba" is an Aramaic term that conveys deep affection and familiarity, akin to the English "Daddy" or "Papa." This intimate cry reflects the confidence believers have in their relationship with God—a relationship rooted not in fear, but in love and trust.

Furthermore, Paul emphasizes that the Spirit confirms this adoption by bearing witness with the believer's spirit that they are indeed children of God. This divine assurance brings comfort and confidence, as it affirms identity and inheritance in Christ. As children of God, believers are also heirs—heirs of God and co-heirs with Christ. This means that just as Christ is glorified, so too will believers share in that glory, provided we share in His sufferings.

This new identity calls believers into a life of hope, knowing that despite trials and sufferings, we are bound for eternal glory in Christ. Thus, these verses point not only to a believer's present freedom from sin and fear but also to a future hope and inheritance as part of God's family.

And just as the Holy Spirit transforms these Roman Christians by guiding them into a new identity as children of God, so too did the Spirit empower countless African American leaders of faith to revolt against the bondage of slavery and oppression, leading their people toward freedom and justice. Harriet Tubman, often called "Moses" by those she led to freedom, attributed her success in the Underground Railroad to divine guidance and the promptings from God. Fredrick Douglas was a fervent Christan who spoke of God as his source of strength, and he fought spiritual battles against slavery. Sojourner Truth, another prominent figure, based her abolitionist activism on her deep Christian convictions. In the same way, the Spirit that empowered these leaders and those in the church at Rome calls believers today to trust in the Spirit that indwells them, guiding them with courage and conviction to stand for justice, freedom, and the transformative power of God's love.

III. Prayers That Align with God's Will (Romans 8:26–27)

Believers are without excuse when it comes to prayer. God has not only commanded us to pray but has equipped us for it, ensuring that no barrier gets in our way—whether weakness, uncertainty, or fear. Prayer is not an optional activity or a luxury reserved for moments of crisis; it is an expectation, a lifeline, and a privilege for every believer. It is how we commune with the Creator, intercede for others, and line up our hearts with His will. Prayer is most needed in this world filled with distractions and challenges. Most Christians can relate to the idea of not fully knowing what to pray for and, in some cases, how to pray.

In 1 Samuel 1:9–18, Hannah, deeply distressed by her inability to bear children, goes to the Temple and prays. In her anguish, she weeps and prays silently to the point where Eli the priest mistakes her for being drunk. She is so overwhelmed by emotion that her words are unclear, but God hears her heart. This demonstrates how, in moments of deep pain or uncertainty, we may not have the right words to pray, yet God still understands our needs. In Romans 8:26-27, Paul addresses this common struggle, highlighting the crucial role of the Holy Spirit in helping believers pray. Likewise, many former Christian slaves did not have the proper English words to speak out in prayer, but their hearts still cried out to God in deep faith. We learn from Paul's teachings that the Spirit comes alongside us in our weakness, interceding when words fail or when our understanding falls short. This is especially vital because our human limitations often prevent us from praying in alignment with God's will.

In verse 26, Paul describes the Spirit's intercession as "groanings too deep for words." These groanings are not mere expressions of human frustration but are the Spirit's way of translating our deepest needs into prayers that resonate with God's purposes. Even when we are unsure of how to articulate our prayers, the Spirit ensures that what is communicated is perfectly aligned with God's will. God, who searches our hearts, knows the mind of the Spirit, making this intercession not only effective but precise. This relationship between the Father and the Spirit guides us into a deeper spiritual connection with Him.

THE LESSON APPLIED

Applying this lesson involves living by the guidance of the Holy Spirit, just as many African American leaders did during the struggle for freedom. Like Harriet Tubman, Frederick Douglass, and Sojourner Truth, who trusted the Holy Spirit to guide their paths, we too must rely on the Spirit in our daily lives. These leaders sought divine direction in their fight against slavery and injustice, demonstrating how the Spirit indwells and empowers us to stand for what is right and courageously live life according to God's good desires.

As adopted children of God, we can confidently turn to the Holy Spirit for strength and guidance, knowing we are part of God's family. When faced with challenges, we should draw from the Spirit's power to help us live in alignment with God's will. Just as the Spirit helped those before us pray and act with courage, it helps us today to pursue justice, freedom, and transformation in our individual lives and communities.

LET'S TALK ABOUT IT...

Discuss the following questions and visit www.rhboyd.com for more information.

To whom are we obligated?

What is the choice God puts before us?

Who is a Child of God and what does this mean in daily life?

Get Social

Share your views and tag us
@rhboydco and use #rhboydco

@rhboydco

Home Daily Devotional Readings
December 29– January 4, 2026

Monday	Tuesday	Wednesday	Thursday	Friday	Saturday	Sunday
The Man and the Woman Sin	God Pronounces Judgment	God's Wrath Is Revealed	Jesus Warns against Defilement	A Prayer for God's Mercy	God Demands Right Living	Jesus Atones for Our Sins
Genesis 3:1–13	Genesis 3:14–24	Romans 1:18–25	Mark 7:14–23	Psalm 51:1–12	Micah 6:1–8	1 John 1:5–2:6

Lesson V — Sin

January 4, 2026

Adult Topic: The Wrong Path
Background Scripture: Genesis 3:1–24; 6:5–8; Mark 7:14–23; Romans 1:18–32; 3:10–18; 1 John 1:5–2:6
Lesson Passage: 1 John 1:5–2:6

1 JOHN 1:5–2:6

KJV

THIS then is the message which we have heard of him, and declare unto you, that God is light, and in him is no darkness at all.

6 If we say that we have fellowship with him, and walk in darkness, we lie, and do not the truth:

7 But if we walk in the light, as he is in the light, we have fellowship one with another, and the blood of Jesus Christ his Son cleanseth us from all sin.

8 If we say that we have no sin, we deceive ourselves, and the truth is not in us.

9 If we confess our sins, he is faithful and just to forgive us our sins, and to cleanse us from all unrighteousness.

10 If we say that we have not sinned, we make him a liar, and his word is not in us.

• • • • • •

1 My little children, these things write I unto you, that ye sin not. And if any man sin, we have an advocate with the Father, Jesus Christ the righteous:

2 And he is the propitiation for our sins: and not for ours only, but also for the sins of the whole world.

3 And hereby we do know that we know him, if we keep his commandments.

4 He that saith, I know him, and keepeth not his commandments, is a liar, and the truth is not in him.

5 But whoso keepeth his word, in him verily is the love of God perfected: hereby know we that we are in him.

NRSVue

THIS is the message we have heard from him and proclaim to you, that God is light and in him there is no darkness at all.

6 If we say that we have fellowship with him while we are walking in darkness, we lie and do not do what is true;

7 but if we walk in the light as he himself is in the light, we have fellowship with one another, and the blood of Jesus his Son cleanses us from all sin.

8 If we say that we have no sin, we deceive ourselves, and the truth is not in us.

9 If we confess our sins, he who is faithful and just will forgive us our sins and cleanse us from all unrighteousness.

10 If we say that we have not sinned, we make him a liar, and his word is not in us.

• • • • • •

1 My little children, I am writing these things to you so that you may not sin. But if anyone does sin, we have an advocate with the Father, Jesus Christ the righteous,

2 and he is the atoning sacrifice for our sins, and not for ours only but also for the sins of the whole world.

3 Now by this we know that we have come to know him, if we obey his commandments.

4 Whoever says, "I have come to know him," but does not obey his commandments is a liar, and in such a person the truth does not exist;

5 but whoever obeys his word, truly in this person the love of God has reached perfection. By this we know that we are in him:

MAIN THOUGHT: If we say that we have no sin, we deceive ourselves, and the truth is not in us. If we confess our sins, he who is faithful and just will forgive us our sins and cleanse us from all unrighteousness. (1 John 1:8–9, NRSVue)

1 JOHN 1:5–2:6

KJV
6 He that saith he abideth in him ought himself also so to walk, even as he walked.

NRSVue
6 whoever says, "I abide in him," ought to walk in the same way as he walked.

LESSON SETTING

Time: Uncertain: Latter part of 1st century AD, probably between AD 85–90
Place: In or near Ephesus
Setting: First John takes place during a time when Christianity was spreading across the Roman Empire. This was a period of both growth and tension within the Christian community. The epistle has no references to reveal its recipients, indicating the letter could freely circulate throughout the early churches in Asia Minor. First John addresses both theological and practical issues confronting early Christians. The Roman Empire was steeped in Hellenistic culture, which gained traction in the lives of believers. This influence can be seen in the early church's struggle with a belief system that emphasized a sharp division between the spiritual and material worlds. Gnostics—a religious group that rejected the material world and believed in spiritual enlightenment through higher knowledge (or gnosis)—rejected the full humanity of Christ. This context helps explain John's repeated emphasis on Jesus coming in the flesh, countering Gnostic-like heresies that threatened the core Christian message. John's letter, while not primarily focused on a doctrinal point of view, did combat false teaching and doctrinal errors. Following the destruction of the Jerusalem Temple in AD 70, Christianity was emerging as distinct from Judaism. Debates about Jesus' identity of as the Messiah became more pronounced, and John's letter reflects the divide between Christians and those who rejected Jesus as the Messiah. John emphasized that Jesus Christ is the Messiah who gave His life for humanity's sins. Additionally, the growing Christian communities were often supported by wealthy patrons, but there were stark economic disparities between rich and poor. The Roman business system influenced social and economic interactions, and Christians often faced marginalization for refusing to participate in the imperial cult, which required citizens to worship the Roman emperor.

LESSON OUTLINE

I. The True Light of the World (1 John 1: 5)
II. The Consequences of Our Walk (1 John 1:6–10)
III. Christ—Our Advocate for Every Sin (1 John 2:1–6)

UNIFYING PRINCIPLE

We all need an advocate to intercede for us when we do wrong, face trouble, or need help. Who can we trust to intercede justly on our behalf? John reaffirms the Gospel's promise that Jesus Christ, our Advocate, offers us grace and forgiveness.

INTRODUCTION

Have you ever watched the sunrise while on vacation at the Gulf of Mexico beaches or out west near the Rocky Mountains? It is one of nature's most striking displays. As dawn approaches, the darkness of night slowly gives way to light. The sky, once black with only reflecting light from the moon, begins to fill with shades of pink, orange, and gold as the sun's first rays appear. The ocean, once dark and endless, starts to reflect the early light, while mountains, once hidden in shadow, become visible as the sun rises. The light spreads, revealing the landscape, allowing us to see clearly and move with confidence.

In the dark, there is no 20/20 vision; our vision is limited, and we hesitate, unsure of what lies ahead. But when the sun rises, it reveals what and who was hidden. This natural cycle of night and day, created by God, parallels the spiritual truth found in 1 John 1:5–2:2, where we learn that God is light and in Him there is no darkness. Just as the sunrise dispels physical darkness, the light of Christ exposes sin and leads us toward righteousness. However, the light of the sun is but a temporary help. As surely as the sun rises, it will set, and darkness will return along with its limitations. This teaches us to value light when it is present, and to prepare for times of difficulty, when life feels dark.

The connection between the sun and God is found in their immense power. We cannot look directly at the sun because its brightness is too intense for our eyes. Similarly, God's glory is so overwhelming that no sinful human can bear to see it directly (Exod. 33:20, 1 Tim. 6:16). However, just as the atmosphere filters the sun's rays for our benefit, Christ's atoning work enables us to approach God despite His overwhelming holiness. Christ is the only way to God.

EXPOSITION

I. The True Light of the World (1 John 1: 5)

Darkness is not merely an abstract concept; it finds its ultimate embodiment in Satan, the adversary of God and the enemy of humanity. From the very beginning, Satan has operated as the deceiver and destroyer, opposing God's light and truth. Jesus described him as a murderer from the beginning and the father of lies, highlighting the enemy's inherent nature as darkness (John 8:44). The nature of Satan is diametrically opposed to the light of God.

John begins his epistle by establishing a foundational truth about the nature of God: He is not like a light, He is light; that is His nature. Light is the essence of God, and there is no darkness in Him at all—no ignorance, error, untruthfulness, sin, or death. This statement is not just a theological declaration; it's a profound revelation about the moral and spiritual purity of God. By declaring that God is light and devoid of darkness, John paints a picture of God's absolute holiness and righteousness.

Light as an expression of God's nature is prevalent in Scripture. In the Old Testament, God's presence is often represented by light, as seen when Moses encounters God in the burning bush (Exod. 3:2), or when the Israelites are guided by a pillar of fire (Exod. 13:21). In the New Testament, Jesus declares, "I am the light of the world" (John 8:12), and the prophet Isaiah speaks of the light of God coming forth to shine in the darkness of this world (Isa. 9:2).

Darkness is both spiritual and moral, representing far more than just the absence of light; it is a force with tangible presence and power. Throughout Scripture, darkness is associated with sin, ignorance, and rebellion against God. It is the realm where evil thrives and where deception, fear, and destruction flourish. The danger of darkness lies in its ability to obscure truth and lead individuals astray. Those who walk in darkness, as the Bible frequently warns, are blind to the path that leads to life (2 Cor. 4:3–6). This blindness is not merely intellectual ignorance but a moral disorientation. Darkness distorts reality, allowing evil to masquerade as good and lies to seem like truth.

Yet, despite its power, darkness is not invincible. John's Gospel reminds us that "the light shines in the darkness, and the darkness has not overcome it" (John 1:5). Darkness may be present and real, but it is ultimately defeated by the light of Christ. While darkness poses significant danger, the hope and promise of God's light are stronger, offering deliverance and redemption to all who turn to Him.

II. The Consequences of Our Walk (1 John 1:6–10)

According to John, there are two ways of living: walking in darkness and walking in light—each having its own consequences. To "walk in darkness" refers to living a life of sin, hidden from the light of God's truth. Sin that remains unconfessed becomes a barrier between us and God. A pattern of unconfessed sin can become a stronghold. When sin is not confessed and repented of over time, this foothold becomes the stronghold where sin dominates and spiritual growth is hindered.

When we freely yield to sin and walk in darkness, we deceive ourselves (v. 6) and fail to practice living in God's truth. In this state, we are spiritually barren, incapable of producing the fruits of righteousness that God desires. Practicing truth is essential because it aligns our lives with God's light, keeping us from self-deception and allowing His transformative grace to work within us. Light is the product of remaining in the vine of Christ (John 15:4–5), which is essential to daily life.

John's warning in verse 6 is clear: if we claim to have fellowship with God but continue in sin, we are living a lie. This is not just a matter of outward behavior; it reflects the heart. A person who walks in darkness not only hides their sin from others but may even deceive themselves into thinking their actions are acceptable. This is how lies become so strong they become a form of "truth" to us.

Ananias and Sapphira died because they attempted to deceive the apostles by lying about the amount they gave (Acts 5:1–10). In doing so, they ultimately lied to the Holy Spirit, resulting in sudden judgment for their dishonesty and hypocrisy (Acts 5:1–10). Deception leads to spiritual blindness and distance from God. Unconfessed sin festers and hardens the heart. There is no benefit that comes of this; it only prevents us from experiencing the transformative power of God's grace and forgiveness.

Spiritual barrenness is a natural consequence of this way of living. Just as a tree without sunlight cannot bear fruit, a soul living in unconfessed sin cannot bear the spiritual fruits of love, joy, peace, and righteousness. The life of King Saul offers a vivid portrayal of self-deception, unconfessed sin, and a hardened heart that leads to spiritual blindness and distance from God (see 1 Sam. 15). The longer we remain in darkness, the more distant we become from God's presence, and the more difficult it becomes to return to Him.

On the other hand, walking in the light brings transformation. John assures us in verse 7 that if we walk in the light as God is in the light, we will have fellowship with one another, and the blood of Jesus will cleanse us from all sin. This promise of cleansing is one of the greatest comforts in Scripture. No matter how deep or persistent our sin may be, God's light has the power to purify and restore us. Confession is the key to walking in the light. To confess our sins is to bring them into the open, allowing God's light to expose them and cleanse us.

In contrast to the self-deception of walking in darkness, confession is an act of truth-telling before God. It acknowledges that we have sinned, but it also trusts in God's willingness and ability to forgive. John's words in 1:9 provide assurance: "If we confess our sins, he is faithful and just to forgive us our sins and to cleanse us from all unrighteousness." After committing adultery with Bathsheba and arranging the death of her husband, Uriah, David's confession is captured in Psalm 51, where he cries out to God for mercy, acknowledging his sin and asking for cleansing and restoration. The use of the present tense in Greek, particularly in this passage (1 John 1:9), indicates that God's forgiveness is available repeatedly—every time we confess our sins. However, confession must be from a sincere heart.

When we are cleansed, we become spiritually fruitful. Just as light causes plants to grow and flourish, walking in God's light allows our souls to produce the fruits of righteousness. These fruits manifest in our relationships, our service to others, and our personal growth in holiness. The choice is clear: walking in darkness leads to spiritual barrenness, while walking in the light leads to cleansing and fruitfulness.

III. Christ—Our Advocate for Every Sin (1 John 2:1–6)

First John 2 opens with a pastoral tone, as John addresses his audience as "my little children." Children often struggle to express themselves effectively when they need help. God's concern is that believers avoid sin, but God recognizes the reality that we will all fall short at times. When we do, He reminds us that we are not left without hope. We have an advocate in Jesus Christ.

Jesus Christ, described as "the righteous" in verse 1, stands as our advocate before God the Father. In the context of a courtroom, an advocate is someone who pleads on behalf of another. Jesus takes on this role by interceding for us even when we sin, and He never grows weary. His advocacy is not based on a believer's good works or innocence but on His righteousness. Because He is perfectly righteous, Jesus is able to represent us before God and secure our forgiveness. Scripture depicts Jesus, after the resurrection, as ascended and at the right hand of the Father, fully able to advocate on behalf of all believers (Rom. 8:34).

John also adds that Jesus is "the propitiation for our sins: and not for ours only, but also for the sins of the whole world" (v. 2). The term "propitiation" refers to a sacrifice that turns away wrath. Jesus' death on the cross satisfied the demands of God's justice, absorbing the punishment for sin that humanity deserved. This act of love and sacrifice makes forgiveness available not just to a select "good" few, but to the entire world. Turning away wrath is the central mission of the cross.

The scope of Jesus' forgiveness is all-encompassing. No sin is too great for His atoning sacrifice. Whether we commit sins in ignorance or willfully disobey, Jesus' blood is sufficient to cover all. No amount of time spent in sin can disqualify someone from receiving forgiveness. No place is beyond the reach of God's grace, no matter where sin occurs. This forgiveness is a gift of grace, and it highlights the ongoing nature of Jesus' work in our lives. Even after we are saved, His role as advocate continues, ensuring that we remain in right standing with God.

This truth should bring comfort and assurance to every believer. While we strive to live in the light and avoid sin, we will inevitably fall short. In those moments, we can take heart in knowing that Jesus is on our side, advocating for our forgiveness. His sacrifice is final and complete, providing the means for us to be cleansed from every sin and restored to fellowship with the Father.

THE LESSON APPLIED

John's message is deeply practical, calling us to examine our daily walk and relationship with God. To apply this lesson, we must first acknowledge our need for the light of God that is available in every area of life. Dr. Martin Luther King, Jr., exemplifying this message, said, "Darkness cannot drive out darkness; only light can do that."

Walking in the light means living as an open book, recognizing our sins, and continually seeking God's truth. This requires a daily habit of self-reflection, confession, and repentance. We must remember that anyone who claims to be without sin is living in self-deception. True spiritual growth comes from admitting our failings and turning to Christ. This lesson encourages us to let go of pride and self-justification, humbling ourselves before God and others. When we walk in God's light, we are not only forgiven but transformed, leading to healthy relationships, service to others, and spiritual maturity.

LET'S TALK ABOUT IT...

Discuss the following questions and visit www.rhboyd.com for more information.

What areas of your life remain in spiritual darkness, and how can you allow God's light to expose and heal them through confession and repentance?

How does knowing Jesus as your advocate shape the way you respond to your own failures and the failures of others in your daily walk with God?

Get Social

Share your views and tag us
@rhboydco and use #rhboydco

@rhboydco

Home Daily Devotional Readings
January 5–11, 2026

Monday	Tuesday	Wednesday	Thursday	Friday	Saturday	Sunday
Turn Away from Sin	Turn Toward Righteousness	Jesus Has Power to Forgive Sins	Draw Near to God by Faith	Repent and Seek God's Face	Repent and Be Baptized	The Prodigal Returns
Ezekiel 18:20–23, 27–32	Isaiah 1:10–21	Mark 2:1–12	Hebrews 11:1–10	2 Chronicles 7:12–16	Acts 2:32–39	Luke 1 5:11–24

Lesson VI   **January 11, 2026**

Repentance and Faith

Adult Topic: A Generous and Forgiving Parent
Background Scripture: Isa. 1:10–21; Ezek. 18:20–23, 27–32; Mark 2:1–12; Luke 3:1–14; 15:11–24; Acts 2:32–39; Heb. 11:1–10
Lesson Passage: Luke 15:11–24; Acts 2:32–39

LUKE 15:11-24; ACTS 2:38-39

KJV	NRSVue
AND he said, A certain man had two sons:	THEN Jesus said, "There was a man who had two sons.
12 And the younger of them said to his father, Father, give me the portion of goods that falleth to me. And he divided unto them his living.	12 The younger of them said to his father, 'Father, give me the share of the wealth that will belong to me.' So he divided his assets between them.
13 And not many days after the younger son gathered all together, and took his journey into a far country, and there wasted his substance with riotous living.	13 A few days later the younger son gathered all he had and traveled to a distant region, and there he squandered his wealth in dissolute living.
14 And when he had spent all, there arose a mighty famine in that land; and he began to be in want.	14 When he had spent everything, a severe famine took place throughout that region, and he began to be in need.
15 And he went and joined himself to a citizen of that country; and he sent him into his fields to feed swine.	15 So he went and hired himself out to one of the citizens of that region, who sent him to his fields to feed the pigs.
16 And he would fain have filled his belly with the husks that the swine did eat: and no man gave unto him.	16 He would gladly have filled his stomach with the pods that the pigs were eating, and no one gave him anything.
17 And when he came to himself, he said, How many hired servants of my father's have bread enough and to spare, and I perish with hunger!	17 But when he came to his senses he said, 'How many of my father's hired hands have bread enough and to spare, but here I am dying of hunger!
18 I will arise and go to my father, and will say unto him, Father, I have sinned against heaven, and before thee,	18 I will get up and go to my father, and I will say to him, "Father, I have sinned against heaven and before you;
19 And am no more worthy to be called thy son: make me as one of thy hired servants.	19 I am no longer worthy to be called your son; treat me like one of your hired hands."'
20 And he arose, and came to his father. But when he was yet a great way off, his father saw him, and had compassion, and ran, and fell on his neck, and kissed him.	20 So he set off and went to his father. But while he was still far off, his father saw him and was filled with compassion; he ran and put his arms around him and kissed him.

MAIN THOUGHT: For this my son was dead, and is alive again; he was lost, and is found. And they began to be merry. (Luke 15:24, KJV)

LUKE 15:11-24; ACTS 2:38-39

KJV

21 And the son said unto him, Father, I have sinned against heaven, and in thy sight, and am no more worthy to be called thy son.

22 But the father said to his servants, Bring forth the best robe, and put it on him; and put a ring on his hand, and shoes on his feet:

23 And bring hither the fatted calf, and kill it; and let us eat, and be merry:

24 For this my son was dead, and is alive again; he was lost, and is found. And they began to be merry.

••••••

38 Then Peter said unto them, Repent, and be baptized every one of you in the name of Jesus Christ for the remission of sins, and ye shall receive the gift of the Holy Ghost.

39 For the promise is unto you, and to your children, and to all that are afar off, even as many as the Lord our God shall call.

NRSVue

21 Then the son said to him, 'Father, I have sinned against heaven and before you; I am no longer worthy to be called your son.'

22 But the father said to his slaves, 'Quickly, bring out a robe—the best one—and put it on him; put a ring on his finger and sandals on his feet.

23 And get the fatted calf and kill it, and let us eat and celebrate,

24 for this son of mine was dead and is alive again; he was lost and is found!' And they began to celebrate.

••••••

38 Peter said to them, "Repent and be baptized every one of you in the name of Jesus Christ so that your sins may be forgiven, and you will receive the gift of the Holy Spirit.

39 For the promise is for you, for your children, and for all who are far away, everyone whom the Lord our God calls to him."

LESSON SETTING

Time: AD 30–33

Place: Jesus' journey in regions of Judea and Galilee

Setting: Luke, a physician and historian, likely interacted with many Jewish families, deepening his understanding of their life and customs. Though his Gospel doesn't detail the family in the parable, context suggests the brothers were born into a devout Jewish home, circumcised on the eighth day, and raised in the Torah. Their Bar Mitzvah marked their transition into adulthood, guided by their father, a landowner ensuring they lived by Jewish traditions. While Matthew traces Jesus' genealogy to Abraham, Luke traces it to Adam, emphasizing that Jesus came for all—an idea central to both the parable and Peter's sermon at Pentecost (Acts 2:14-36).

LESSON OUTLINE

I. Generosity and Welcome Mat for the Lost (Luke 15:11-20)

II. God's Forgiving and Generous Heart (Luke 15:21-24; Acts 2:38-39)

UNIFYING PRINCIPLE

We can sometimes have problems apologizing or making amends for our wrongdoing. What is an appropriate way to admit our wrongful acts and restore healthy relationships? Luke and Acts affirm that repentance from sin and turning to God in Christ are the only

INTRODUCTION

Life is full of pivotal moments—those unexpected instances that change the course of our lives. These moments catch us "in and out of season" and aren't reserved for the spiritually devout or extraordinary. Think about a parent who, after years of distance, decides to reconnect with their children. Maybe they realize the effects of their absence or the length of time. This decision—this pivotal moment—reshapes the family. With the parent now engaged, love and wisdom is poured into their children's lives.

Consider a teacher, burned out from overcrowded classrooms, who chooses to reignite their passion by viewing each student as untapped potential. Or picture a coach who, after a disappointing season, decides to focus not just on winning but on building character in the team. These moments, though not grand headlines, carry extraordinary power to change our paths. They cause us to come to ourselves, see life differently, and to act in ways that leave a lasting impact.

The parable of the lost son tells the story of such a moment—a turning point in the life of a young man who, after hitting rock bottom, comes to a realization that alters his future. This decision impacts not only him but everyone around him.

But Jesus is pointing to something broader than just familial relationships. He is speaking to Israel as a nation—lost and far from the Father—and to believers today. Just as the lost son came home and Israel is called back, we too are invited to return to the Father. The parable reveals God's heart for all who are distant, whether a wayward son, a nation, or believers who have drifted.

EXPOSITION

I. Generosity and Welcome Mat for the Lost (Luke 15:11–20)

The parable of the prodigal son offers a profound message about personal transformation and God's grace. Central to this story is the son's decision to return, marked by three key words: *I*, *will*, and *arise*. These words highlight his turning point and reflect a believer's necessary steps of repentance and renewal in our journey with God.

The word "I" signals the moment when the prodigal son realizes his own responsibility. In verse 17, he "came to himself" and acknowledged, "I perish with hunger." This confession of his personal condition is the first step toward repentance. He admits where he is. This is foundational in our spiritual lives. Repentance begins with the realization of where we are in our spiritual and natural lives. This echoes teachings in Isaiah 1:18, where God invites the sinner to reason together with Him, recognizing their sinful state and the need for cleansing.

Next comes the word "will." It is not enough to recognize one's condition; there must be a resolve to act. The prodigal son says, "I will arise and go to my father" (v. 18). This reflects his decision to change direction, to leave behind his mistakes, and to seek reconciliation. The word "will" is the turning point in any repentance process. It speaks to our freedom of choice, something we also see emphasized in Ezekiel 18:27–32, where God calls the wicked to turn from their ways and live. The son's moment of willful action mirrors our own need to resolve in our hearts to return to God, recognizing that faith without action is incomplete.

Finally, "arise" marks the beginning of the journey. The prodigal son does not just think about returning or plan it indefinitely;

he gets up and moves. He returns to his father (v. 20). This action is the culmination of his internal transformation, a physical response to his decision to repent. The significance of this word is seen in how God responds. The father, seeing his son from afar, runs to him. The son's act of arising is met with immediate grace. In this, we see the same message reflected in Mark 1:14–20, where Jesus calls disciples to follow Him, and they immediately leave their nets and follow. Their decision to arise initiates a new life direction, one filled with purpose and reconciliation.

In Ezekiel 18:23, God declares, "Do I take any pleasure in the death of the wicked? Rather, am I not pleased when they turn from their ways and live?" The prodigal son's decision to arise reverberates this divine call to life and reconciliation. Similarly, Acts 2:38–39 emphasizes repentance and the promise of the Holy Spirit for those who turn back to God, reinforcing the idea that God's grace is immediate and abundant for those who choose to return.

II. God's Forgiving and Generous Heart (Luke 15:21–24; Acts 2:38–39)

In Luke 15:21–24 and Acts 2:38–39, we find a powerful illustration of God's forgiving and generous heart. Many people in both crowds would likely identify with the prodigal son's story on a personal level. They may have experienced moments in their own lives when they made poor choices, faced the consequences, and longed for a second chance. These passages reveal not only the nature of God's forgiveness but also the fullness of His generosity, offering not just pardon for sin but full restoration to a place of honor and purpose in His family.

The prodigal son's confession is deeply significant, as it encapsulates the essence of repentance. He acknowledges the full weight of his sin, not only against his father but against heaven, indicating he understands that his wrongdoing is both personal and spiritual. This moment of confession, triggered by the son's reflection on his life choices, is essential for receiving the father's forgiveness, just as confession is essential for receiving God's forgiveness in our spiritual lives. Confession is more than an acknowledgment of mistakes; it is recognition of sin's depth and its destructive impact on our relationship with God and others. The prodigal son's confession reflects the act of repentance that believers are called to make in our own lives.

This is a theme resounded in Peter's sermon at Pentecost in Acts 2:38, where he calls the people to "repent and be baptized, every one of you, in the name of Jesus Christ for the forgiveness of your sins." Peter's call for repentance in Acts 2:38–39 is directly linked to the promise of forgiveness. This connection between repentance and forgiveness is a central theme of the Christian faith, underscoring the truth that God is always ready to forgive those who come to Him with a contrite heart. But God's response to repentance does not stop at forgiveness; it extends into generous restoration, as seen in both the parable and Peter's message.

After the son confesses his sins, the father's response is immediate and overwhelming (Luke 15: 22). He orders his servants to bring the best robe, a ring, and sandals for his son—each holding deep symbolic meaning. The robe represents honor and dignity, restoring the son's status within the family. The ring symbolizes authority, signifying that the son has been fully reinstated as a member of the household with all its rights and privileges. The sandals are significant because, in that culture, only free men wore sandals; slaves did not. By giving his son sandals, the father is making it clear that the son has been restored to his position as a free member of the family, not a servant or hired hand.

The father's generous restoration of his son is a picture of how God's generous heart restores those who come to Him in repentance. It is not a partial or begrudging restoration but a full and generous embrace, restoring us to the fullness of our identity in Christ. This theme is mentioned in Acts 2:38–39, when Peter promises that those who repent will not only receive the forgiveness of sins but also the gift of the Holy Spirit. The Holy Spirit is the ultimate expression of God's generosity, as He empowers us to live new, transformed lives in Christ.

The father's response to the prodigal son also highlights the joy that comes with forgiveness and restoration (Luke 15:23–24). The father's call for a celebration is not merely a private family affair but a public declaration of the father's joy in his son's return. It symbolizes the joy in heaven over one sinner who repents, as Jesus emphasizes earlier in Luke 15:7 and 10. This theme of joy is further reflected in Peter's message, when he extends the promise of forgiveness and the gift of the Holy Spirit to "you and your children and for all who are far off" (Acts 2:39). The phrase "all who are far off" is particularly significant, as it underscores the inclusiveness of God's grace. No one is too far gone to receive God's forgiveness and restoration.

We find a different example of sons leaving their father in Mark 1:18–20. James and John, alongside Simon and Andrew, are called by Jesus to leave their earthly father and follow a higher calling. Unlike the prodigal son, who leaves his father in rebellion, seeking the darkness of self-indulgence, these sons are not running from their father's house. Instead, they are being drawn away from their earthly ties to answer the call of the Son of God. Their departure from their father, Zebedee, represents a movement toward light and purpose, in contrast to the prodigal's descent into darkness.

While the prodigal son abandons his father for a life of excess that leads to brokenness, the sons in Mark leave their father not for personal gain but to respond to Jesus' invitation. They exemplify a different kind of separation—one driven by divine calling, not rebellion. The prodigal son, in his distance from his father, seeks only self-gratification. He eventually realizes the emptiness of that path. In contrast, the sons called by Jesus willingly leave behind their earthly obligations to embrace the light of a higher mission, demonstrating that not all separations from family or parental figures lead to destruction—some lead to greater purpose and divine fulfillment.

This contrast illuminates two paths: the prodigal son's journey away from his father to experience the darkness of life, and the calling of James and John to leave their father for the light of Christ. In both cases, the earthly father plays a role, but while one son returns after realizing his failure, the others step forward into something greater from the start. This highlights the dual nature of God's calling. God does not merely call believers *away* from something; He also calls us *toward* something. God's call always invites us into something higher and more meaningful. Whether we are returning from the far country like the prodigal son or stepping into the calling like James and John, God's response is one of grace, generosity, and restoration.

THE LESSON APPLIED

This lesson invites us to explore the themes of repentance, forgiveness, and God's generous heart in ways deeply relevant to modern life. Adults today face many challenges—personal failures, broken relationships, and the constant pull of culture and societal expectations. At all times, we must discern whether our choices and direction are prompted by God's call or the world's demands. The parable of the prodigal son offers a roadmap for those of us who have drifted away from our faith, family, or values. It reminds us that God is always waiting to restore and renew us. In applying this lesson, we are encouraged to take ownership of our spiritual journeys by recognizing where we have strayed, much like the prodigal son's "I will arise" moment.

Repentance involves not just feeling regret but making an active decision to return to God. This can mean engaging in spiritual disciplines like prayer, Bible study, or seeking reconciliation with others. Additionally, God's generous forgiveness challenges us to extend grace to others. Whether it's within families, workplaces, or friendships, we are called to embody forgiveness and restoration in interactions, reflecting God's heart for healing and reconciliation.

LET'S TALK ABOUT IT...

Discuss the following questions and visit www.rhboyd.com for more information.

Think about a pivotal moment in your life when you had to make a significant decision, much like the prodigal son deciding to return to his father.

How did that moment shape your future?

How can the Church actively support and encourage individuals experiencing their own "I will arise" moments to take steps toward repentance, healing, and restoration?

What specific actions or ministries can the Church offer to assist people in returning to God and rebuilding their lives?

Get Social

Share your views and tag us
@rhboydco and use #rhboydco

@rhboydco

Home Daily Devotional Readings
January 12–18, 2026

Monday	Tuesday	Wednesday	Thursday	Friday	Saturday	Sunday
Praying for Wisdom	Praying and Seeking God	Praying with Thanksgiving	Praying for Protection	Praying as Jesus Taught	Praying for Others	Praying for Mercy
James 1:2-8	Jeremiah 29:10-14	Philippians 4:4-9	Psalm 61	Matthew 6:5-15	Genesis 18:23-33	Luke 18:9-14

Lesson VII — January 18, 2026

Prayer

Adult Topic: A Time to Be Bold; A Time to Be Humble
Background Scripture: Gen. 18:23–33; Exod. 32:31–32; Neh. 1:4–11; Dan. 6:10; Matt. 6:5–15; Luke 18:1–14; John 17:1–26; 1 Thess. 5:17; 1 John 5:14–15
Lesson Passage: Genesis 18:25–27; Luke 18:9–14; 1 John 5:14–15

GENESIS 18:25–27; LUKE 18:9–14; 1 JOHN 5:14–15

KJV

THAT be far from thee to do after this manner, to slay the righteous with the wicked: and that the righteous should be as the wicked, that be far from thee: Shall not the Judge of all the earth do right?

26 And the Lord said, If I find in Sodom fifty righteous within the city, then I will spare all the place for their sakes.

27 And Abraham answered and said, Behold now, I have taken upon me to speak unto the Lord, which am but dust and ashes:

••• Luke 18:9–14 •••

9 And he spake this parable unto certain which trusted in themselves that they were righteous, and despised others:

10 Two men went up into the temple to pray; the one a Pharisee, and the other a publican.

11 The Pharisee stood and prayed thus with himself, God, I thank thee, that I am not as other men are, extortioners, unjust, adulterers, or even as this publican.

12 I fast twice in the week, I give tithes of all that I possess.

13 And the publican, standing afar off, would not lift up so much as his eyes unto heaven, but smote upon his breast, saying, God be merciful to me a sinner.

14 I tell you, this man went down to his house justified rather than the other: for every one that exalteth himself shall be abased; and he that humbleth himself shall be exalted.

NRSVue

FAR be it from you to do such a thing, to slay the righteous with the wicked, so that the righteous fare as the wicked! Far be that from you! Shall not the Judge of all the earth do what is just?"

26 And the Lord said, "If I find at Sodom fifty righteous in the city, I will forgive the whole place for their sake."

27 Abraham answered, "Let me take it upon myself to speak to my lord, I who am but dust and ashes.

••• Luke 18:9–14 •••

9 He also told this parable to some who trusted in themselves that they were righteous and regarded others with contempt:

10 "Two men went up to the temple to pray, one a Pharisee and the other a tax collector.

11 The Pharisee, standing by himself, was praying thus, 'God, I thank you that I am not like other people: thieves, rogues, adulterers, or even like this tax collector.

12 I fast twice a week; I give a tenth of all my income.'

13 But the tax collector, standing far off, would not even lift up his eyes to heaven but was beating his breast and saying, 'God, be merciful to me, a sinner!'

14 I tell you, this man went down to his home justified rather than the other, for all who exalt themselves will be humbled, but all who humble themselves will be exalted."

MAIN THOUGHT: "I tell you, this man went down to his home justified rather than the other, for all who exalt themselves will be humbled, but all who humble themselves will be exalted." (Luke 18:14, NRSVue)

GENESIS 18:25–27; LUKE 18:9–14; 1 JOHN 5:14–15

KJV

••• 1 John 5:14–15 •••

14 And this is the confidence that we have in him, that, if we ask any thing according to his will, he heareth us:

15 And if we know that he hear us, whatsoever we ask, we know that we have the petitions that we desired of him.

NRSVue

••• 1 John 5:14–15 •••

14 And this is the boldness we have in him, that if we ask anything according to his will, he hears us.

15 And if we know that he hears us in whatever we ask, we know that we have obtained the requests made of him.

LESSON SETTING

Time: 2000 years BC (Gen. 18); First Century AD (Luke 18); AD 85–95 (1 John 5)

Place: Near Hebron (Gen. 18); Temple in Jerusalem (Luke 18); Ephesus (1 John 5)

Setting: Genesis 18:25–27 takes place around 2,000 years before Christ, during the time of Abraham, who lived a nomadic lifestyle. Abraham is conversing with God about the fate of the cities of Sodom and Gomorrah, near which his nephew Lot, who once lived with him, has pitched his tent with his wife and family. God had just visited Abraham to confirm His promise that Abraham's wife, Sarah, would have a son. The setting shows Abraham's close relationship with God and his willingness to speak up for others. In Luke 18:9–14, Jesus is teaching a lesson through a parable set in the Temple, the central place of worship and prayer for Jewish people in Jerusalem. It takes place during the time of the Roman Empire and when Jewish life is strongly influenced by religious practice and social division. Jesus tells this parable to a mixed audience of religious leaders and everyday people. The story compares two men praying in the Temple: a Pharisee, who was a respected religious leader, and a tax collector, who was often seen as a sinner because of his job. First John 5:14–15 is set in the early Christian church—a time when Christians are facing the challenge of false teachings. The letter, likely written by the Apostle John, encourages believers by reminding them that they can confidently pray to God, knowing He hears them when they ask according to His will. This passage shows a shift in how prayer is understood—from the Old Testament focus on priests interceding for the people to the new way of praying directly to God through faith in Jesus.

LESSON OUTLINE

I. Praying with Boldness (Genesis 18: 25–27)
II. Praying with Humility (Luke 18: 9–14)
III. Praying with Confidence (1 John 5: 14–15)

UNIFYING PRINCIPLE

Becoming complacent in society and comparing ourselves to others can lead to pride and devastation. How can we guard ourselves against self-righteousness and pride?

INTRODUCTION

Prayer is a practice that bridges the gap between the divine and the human, providing a way to bring our deepest concerns, praises, and requests before a God who listens. The first recorded prayer in the Bible occurs in Genesis 4:26, where it is noted that people began to "call upon the name of the Lord." From this moment, the practice of prayer weaves its way throughout Scripture, revealing the development of a relationship between God and His people. The patriarchs, prophets, and apostles all modeled lives of prayer, not as a ritualistic duty but as an essential part of their faith journey.

From Abraham's bold negotiation with God over Sodom's fate to Hannah's heartfelt plea for a child and from David's cries for help in the Psalms to Jesus' prayers in Gethsemane, these prayers reveal that God is not distant or disinterested but is engaged with the personal and collective cries of humanity. The last prayer in the Bible, found in Revelation 22:20, reveals the heart of the Apostle John's prayer life: "Come, Lord Jesus." This cry points to the longing for God's presence and the ultimate fulfillment of His promises.

Throughout the Bible, prayer is a vehicle that not only presents requests to God but also transforms the believer's heart to reflect His will. It serves as an avenue for boldness in our intercessions, humility in our confessions, and confidence in our hope. As we explore these dimensions of prayer—boldness, humility, and confidence—each brings us into a deeper understanding of how prayer is meant to shape us. We are invited to approach God, not as distant spectators but as participants in His divine will, knowing that our prayers matter.

EXPOSITION

I. Praying with Boldness (Genesis 18:25–27)

Abraham engages in a bold, reverent conversation with God, interceding for the city of Sodom. This moment is particularly profound because Abraham is not merely speaking with God but negotiating with Him. The scene unfolds as Abraham stands before three divine visitors—often understood as a theophany, or a manifestation of God, accompanied by two angels. Abraham, recognizing their divine nature, speaks with both reverence and boldness, pleading for the righteous in Sodom. He dares to ask, "Shall not the Judge of all the earth do right?" (v. 25). His boldness is not rooted in arrogance, but in confidence in God's character, appealing to God's sense of justice and mercy.

Abraham's negotiation, in which he appeals to God six times, challenges modern myths that suggest we cannot question God or speak to Him boldly. Far from timid or distant, Abraham's prayer shows that God invites persistent, courageous intercession. His boldness reflects deep trust in God's righteousness as he advocates for the city. This deep engagement with God models how we, too, can approach Him in bold prayer—aligned with His heart for justice yet tempered by humility.

This kind of boldness is beautifully illustrated in Psalm 141, where the psalmist offers his prayers as incense before God. The image of prayer rising like incense emphasizes that bold prayers are offerings, not demands. Abraham's prayer reflects this same posture: though he speaks boldly, he remains mindful of his position before God, humbling himself with the words, "I am but dust and ashes" (v. 27).

Bold prayer requires persistence, as seen in Nehemiah 1:4–11 and Daniel 6:10. Nehemiah wept, fasted, and prayed for the restoration of Jerusalem, and Daniel continued to pray even in the face of death. Their boldness came from a deep faith in God's sovereignty and a heart aligned with His purposes. Abraham's persistent negotiation with God, asking six times, underscores that boldness in prayer is not for selfish gain but for the sake of others, even those who we feel may not deserve it.

Nevertheless, boldness and persistence in prayer must always be balanced with humility. Jesus Himself exemplified this in His prayer in Gethsemane, when He asked for the cup of suffering to pass from Him, yet submitted fully to God's will, saying, "Nevertheless not my will, but thine, be done" (Luke 22:42). Abraham's prayer for Sodom shows that boldness in prayer invites us to engage deeply with God, trust in His character, and bring our most profound concerns before Him.

II. Praying with Humility (Luke 18:9–14)

Jesus' parable of the Pharisee and the tax collector offers a vivid example of the heart's posture in prayer. The Pharisee, confident in his own righteousness, prays with pride—boasting of his religious accomplishments, fasting, and tithing—while comparing himself to others, especially the tax collector. His prayer, centered on himself rather than God, reveals a lack of humility. As someone educated in the Law, the Pharisee had been given much, and thus much was required of him (Luke 12:48), particularly in how he approached God. Despite his knowledge, he exalts himself before the Almighty rather than humbling himself, speaking of his own deeds while belittling others. He uses his position to take on a harmful posture.

In contrast, the tax collector, aware of his own sinfulness, stands at a distance, unable to lift his eyes toward heaven. He beats his chest and pleads, "God, be merciful to me, a sinner" (v. 13). His prayer is simple but filled with humility and dependence on God's grace. Jesus concludes the parable by affirming that the tax collector, not the Pharisee, went home justified. Saying he was "justified" means that the tax collector was declared "righteous" or "made right" before God. In biblical terms, to be "justified" means being accepted by God, forgiven of sin, and brought into a right relationship with Him.

This reversal of expectations points to a central truth: God responds to humility and repentance, not self-righteousness. The contrast between the two men highlights that it is not outward appearances or accomplishments that please God but a heart fully aware of its need for Him (see Eph. 2:8–9). The tax collector's attitude echoes Abraham's humble plea for Sodom—not based on merit, but on God's mercy. In both cases, prayer comes from a place of dependence on God's goodness, rather than a sense of entitlement or comparison with others.

This principle of humble yet bold prayer is reflected in the lives of Nelson Mandela and Mahatma Gandhi, whose leadership was deeply marked by spiritual reliance and intercession for their people. Though coming from different faith traditions, both demonstrated how humility in prayer can become a force for justice and transformation, aligning with the biblical teaching that "God opposes the proud but gives grace to the humble" (James 4:6).

Nelson Mandela endured twenty-seven years of imprisonment, yet his prayers were not centered on personal deliverance.

Instead, his focus was on the liberation and reconciliation of South Africa. Like the tax collector in Jesus' parable, Mandela acknowledged the brokenness of humanity and the need for divine intervention. After his release, his humility before God deepened his resolve to pursue justice through peace rather than revenge.

Though not a Christian, Mahatma Gandhi's fasting and prayer for India's independence echoed the persistence of Nehemiah, who prayed and acted on behalf of his people (Neh. 1:4–11). Gandhi's reliance on spiritual strength over military might reflected his trust in a higher power, appealing to divine justice while embracing personal sacrifice. The lives of Mandela and Gandhi remind us that the most powerful prayers arise from humble hearts surrendered to God's will, empowered by trust in His righteousness and mercy.

III. Praying with Confidence (1 John 5:14–15)

In 1 John 5:14–15, the Apostle John assures believers that they can approach God boldly in prayer, knowing that He hears them. This confidence is not based on personal merit but on God's faithfulness to His promises. John emphasizes that when we pray according to God's will, we can trust that He not only listens but also responds. This challenges believers to align their desires with God's purposes, seeking His guidance rather than simply presenting personal requests. True confidence in prayer comes from a deep relationship with God, cultivated through faith and obedience.

Confidence in prayer comes from knowing that God's plans are always good and that His power is limitless. As we grow in our faith and understanding of God's will, we learn to pray prayers that reflect His Kingdom's values—justice, love, and mercy.

Throughout history, the power of praying with confidence has been evident, especially during times of great adversity. The Civil Rights Movement offers powerful examples of leaders who not only prayed with boldness but with unwavering confidence in God's will for justice.

Figures like Rev. Dr. Martin Luther King, Jr., Rosa Parks, and Rep. John Lewis knelt in prayer, believing that God would bring about change despite the overwhelming challenges they faced. Their prayers were deeply rooted in the biblical vision of justice and equality, trusting that the God of heaven cared for the oppressed and would bring deliverance in His timing. Dr. King's famous prayer before the Montgomery bus boycott was a plea for divine guidance, but it was also a confident declaration that the struggle for equality aligned with God's will for all people to live in freedom and dignity.

Similarly, in the face of violent resistance and systemic oppression, civil rights leaders and ordinary believers alike prayed with assurance, knowing that they were part of a greater spiritual battle for the soul of a nation. They believed that God heard their prayers, even when the answers seemed delayed, trusting that justice would ultimately prevail.

Just as those who fought for civil rights trusted God's perfect timing, we too are called to pray with confidence, knowing that when our prayers align with His will, they are powerful and effective. This confidence is a gift from God. It fuels perseverance in the face of setbacks and gives believers the strength to hold on to faith even when the answers seem far off. This passage reminds us that prayer is not a passive exercise but an active engagement with God's will, trusting His wisdom and sovereignty.

THE LESSON APPLIED

Boldness, humility, and confidence in prayer are qualities that stem from a deep conviction rooted in truth, guided by wisdom, and directed by God's Spirit. Boldness and confidence without knowledge can be reckless, causing more harm than good. Romans 10:2 warns of those who have "a zeal for God, but not according to knowledge." It's possible to be passionate yet misguided, fervent but misinformed.

Consider Peter's transformation. Before Pentecost, his zeal led him to cut off a soldier's ear, acting impulsively and without understanding. After being filled with the Holy Spirit, Peter's boldness became purposeful as he preached the Gospel with power and clarity. His knowledge of Christ reshaped his zeal into courageous, Spirit-led action. In our walk with Christ, let us pray for wisdom to accompany our passion. A believer must not rush ahead without divine direction or lag behind in fear. When we approach God's throne, we are invited to ask the Holy Spirit to align our prayers with God's will, temper them with humility, and shape them according to Scripture—so that our actions beyond prayer follow suit.

As you pray today, consider what areas of need you've been afraid to ask God to handle. Trust that He can meet those needs. Challenge yourself to come before Him with humility, knowing that He is both able and willing to respond. Let your prayers be marked by bold faith and deep trust in the God who hears you.

LET'S TALK ABOUT IT...

Discuss the following questions and visit www.rhboyd.com for more information.

What areas in your life require bold prayers that you've hesitated to bring before God?

In what ways can humility shape your approach to prayer, especially in admitting your limitations and need for God's help?

How does trusting God to handle your bold requests change your perspective on situations that seem overwhelming?

Get Social

Share your views and tag us
@rhboydco and use #rhboydco

@rhboydco

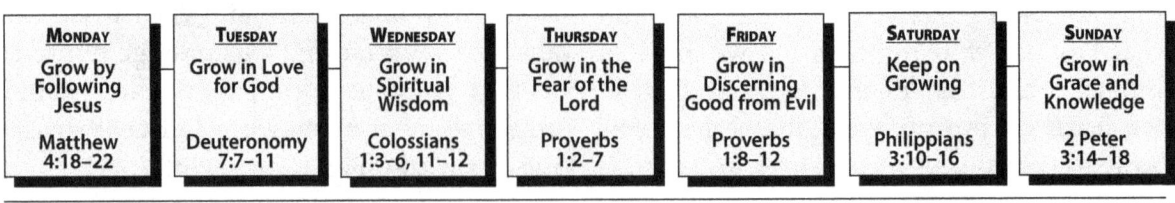

Home Daily Devotional Readings
January 19– 25, 2026

MONDAY	TUESDAY	WEDNESDAY	THURSDAY	FRIDAY	SATURDAY	SUNDAY
Grow by Following Jesus	Grow in Love for God	Grow in Spiritual Wisdom	Grow in the Fear of the Lord	Grow in Discerning Good from Evil	Keep on Growing	Grow in Grace and Knowledge
Matthew 4:18–22	Deuteronomy 7:7–11	Colossians 1:3–6, 11–12	Proverbs 1:2–7	Proverbs 1:8–12	Philippians 3:10–16	2 Peter 3:14–18

Lesson VIII   **January 25, 2026**

Christian Growth

Adult Topic: If at First You Don't Succeed, You're Probably Human

Background Scripture: Matt. 4:18–20; 16:15–18; Luke 2:40, 52; John 1:40–42; 21:15–19; Eph. 4:11–16; Phil. 1:6, 9–11; 3:12–16; Col. 1:9–11; Heb. 6:1–3; 2 Pet. 3:14–18

Lesson Passage: Matt. 4:18–20; 16:16–18; John 21:15–18; 2 Peter 3:14–15, 18

MATTHEW 4:18–20; 16:16–18; JOHN 21:15–18; 2 PETER 3:14–15, 18

KJV

AND Jesus, walking by the sea of Galilee, saw two brethren, Simon called Peter, and Andrew his brother, casting a net into the sea: for they were fishers.

19 And he saith unto them, Follow me, and I will make you fishers of men.

20 And they straightway left their nets, and followed him.

••• Matthew 16:16–18 •••

16 And Simon Peter answered and said, Thou art the Christ, the Son of the living God.

17 And Jesus answered and said unto him, Blessed art thou, Simon Barjona: for flesh and blood hath not revealed it unto thee, but my Father which is in heaven.

18 And I say also unto thee, That thou art Peter, and upon this rock I will build my church; and the gates of hell shall not prevail against it.

••• John 21:15–18 •••

15 So when they had dined, Jesus saith to Simon Peter, Simon, son of Jonas, lovest thou me more than these? He saith unto him, Yea, Lord; thou knowest that I love thee. He saith unto him, Feed my lambs.

16 He saith to him again the second time, Simon, son of Jonas, lovest thou me? He saith unto him, Yea, Lord; thou knowest that I love thee. He saith unto him, Feed my sheep.

17 He saith unto him the third time, Simon, son of Jonas, lovest thou me? Peter was grieved because he said unto him the third time, Lovest thou me? And he said unto him, Lord, thou

NRSVue

AS he walked by the Sea of Galilee, he saw two brothers, Simon, who is called Peter, and Andrew his brother, casting a net into the sea—for they were fishers.

19 And he said to them, "Follow me, and I will make you fishers of people."

20 Immediately they left their nets and followed him.

••• Matthew 16:16–18 •••

16 Simon Peter answered, "You are the Messiah, the Son of the living God."

17 And Jesus answered him, "Blessed are you, Simon son of Jonah! For flesh and blood has not revealed this to you but my Father in heaven.

18 And I tell you, you are Peter, and on this rock I will build my church, and the gates of Hades will not prevail against it.

••• John 21:15–18 •••

15 When they had finished breakfast, Jesus said to Simon Peter, "Simon son of John, do you love me more than these?" He said to him, "Yes, Lord; you know that I love you." Jesus said to him, "Feed my lambs."

16 A second time he said to him, "Simon son of John, do you love me?" He said to him, "Yes, Lord; you know that I love you." Jesus said to him, "Tend my sheep."

17 He said to him the third time, "Simon son of John, do you love me?" Peter felt hurt because he said to him the third time, "Do you love me?" And he said to him, "Lord, you know every-

MAIN THOUGHT: He saith unto him the third time, Simon, son of Jonas, lovest thou me? Peter was grieved because he said unto him the third time, Lovest thou me? And he said unto him, Lord, thou knowest all things; thou knowest that I love thee. Jesus saith unto him, Feed my sheep. (John 21:17, KJV)

MATTHEW 4:18-20; 16:16-18; JOHN 21:15-18; 2 PETER 3:14-15, 18

KJV

knowest all things; thou knowest that I love thee. Jesus saith unto him, Feed my sheep.

18 Verily, verily, I say unto thee, When thou wast young, thou girdest thyself, and walkedst whither thou wouldest: but when thou shalt be old, thou shalt stretch forth thy hands, and another shall gird thee, and carry thee whither thou wouldest not.

••• 2 Peter 3:14-15 •••

14 Wherefore, beloved, seeing that ye look for such things, be diligent that ye may be found of him in peace, without spot, and blameless.

15 And account that the longsuffering of our Lord is salvation; even as our beloved brother Paul also according to the wisdom given unto him hath written unto you;

••• 2 Peter 3:18 •••

18 But grow in grace, and in the knowledge of our Lord and Saviour Jesus Christ. To him be glory both now and for ever. Amen.

NRSVue

thing; you know that I love you." Jesus said to him, "Feed my sheep.

18 Very truly, I tell you, when you were younger, you used to fasten your own belt and to go wherever you wished. But when you grow old, you will stretch out your hands, and someone else will fasten a belt around you and take you where you do not wish to go."

••• 2 Peter 3:14-15 •••

14 Therefore, beloved, while you are waiting for these things, strive to be found by him at peace, without spot or blemish,

15 and regard the patience of our Lord as salvation. So also our beloved brother Paul wrote to you according to the wisdom given him,

••• 2 Peter 3:18 •••

18 But grow in the grace and knowledge of our Lord and Savior Jesus Christ. To him be the glory both now and to the day of eternity. Amen.

LESSON SETTING

Time: AD 64-68, near the end of Peter's life
Place: Near the Sea of Galilee
Setting: The people of Judea, including Peter, lived under the strain of Roman taxation and the anticipation of the promised Messiah. The synagogue and the teachings of the Law of Moses were central to daily life. Yet, despite being a community pillar, the synagogue often left many spiritually disconnected due to the flawed administration of the Torah. The writings of Matthew and John reflect the tensions of the time, addressing the social, political, and religious dynamics that shaped Jesus' ministry. Matthew, once a tax collector, uniquely portrays life under Roman rule, while John, a fellow Galilean, offers a personal and spiritual dimension to the struggles of their environment.

LESSON OUTLINE

I. The Call to Follow Jesus (Matthew 4:18-20)
II. Restoration and Commission through Love (John 21:15-18)
III. Maturing in Grace and Knowledge (2 Peter 3:14-15, 18)

UNIFYING PRINCIPLE

Even those trying to emulate a trusted mentor may stumble. How can we learn and grow through mistakes? The ups and downs of Peter's life as Christ's disciple are a model of perseverance for all who desire to grow in the grace and knowledge of Jesus Christ.

INTRODUCTION

Biblical character studies offer enormous value, revealing timeless lessons through the lives of individuals which with God worked. The stories of these faithful yet flawed figures reveal that God's purpose often shines through human imperfections, offering wisdom, hope, and warnings to guide our spiritual walk today. Peter, one of the most prominent disciples, stands out among these biblical figures as someone whose story resonates deeply with Christians.

Peter's journey shows that faith is not linear—even those closest to Jesus can falter. From his call as a fisherman to his restoration after denying Christ and his mature leadership in the early church, Peter's life highlights the process of spiritual growth. His journey begins in Matthew 4:18–20, where he is called by Jesus while working alongside his brother Andrew. This call represents more than a simple career change; it was an invitation into a mission that would transform Peter and countless others. Much like other figures in the Bible, Peter's journey begins with an act of faith.

One important aspect of Peter's story is his humanity. Like all of us, Peter faced moments of doubt and failure. In Matthew 16:16–18, Peter confesses Jesus as the Messiah, but later, he famously denies Jesus three times (John 18:15–27). Yet, these moments of weakness were not the end of Peter's story. His restoration, found in John 21:15–18, reveals that failure is part of the journey toward growth and maturity. The same Jesus who called Peter at the shores of Galilee seeks to restore him with a renewed purpose, commissioning him to "feed my sheep." Just as Peter was transformed by Jesus' love, so too are believers today called into a lifelong process of spiritual growth.

EXPOSITION

I. The Call to Follow Jesus (Matthew 4:18–20)

God consistently takes the initiative in calling individuals into a relationship with Him. In Genesis 12:1, Abram was not searching for God; God sought Abram, directing him toward an unknown future with the promise of becoming a great nation. In Exodus 3:4, Moses encountered God in the burning bush while tending sheep, unaware that he was about to be called into divine service. In John 6:44, Jesus declares, "No man can come to me, except the Father which hath sent me draw him," underlining that even faith itself begins with God's initiative.

Peter's journey of spiritual growth begins in a way he likely doesn't fully understand. The narrative begins with Peter and his brother Andrew being called by a rabbi named Jesus as they work as fishermen. When Jesus says, "Follow me, and I will make you fishers of men" (v. 19), Peter likely understands this call in practical terms—as a new opportunity to use his skills differently. However, Jesus isn't just offering a new way of life; He is inviting Peter into a mission that will shape the foundations of the early church. Though Peter could not have known the full scope of this call, his willingness to follow sets him on a path of deep spiritual growth.

What is remarkable is how quickly Peter and Andrew responds. They "straightway left their nets, and followed him" (v. 20). This is an act of faith, even if it is not yet fully informed. They leave behind their jobs and their way of life—without hesitation. This immediate obedience, despite not knowing what will come next, is a crucial part of spiritual growth. New believers today take similar steps of faith without fully understanding all that Christian life will require. We, too, trust that we will be taught, shaped, and led by Christ as we grow in faith.

Peter's transformation is not immediate. His decision to follow Jesus marks the beginning of a long journey of growth, filled with both faith and failure. Over time, Peter will come to understand that Jesus is not just a rabbi, but the Messiah. He witnesses miracles, hears teachings that challenge everything he knows, and eventually becomes a leading figure in the early church. But all of this begins with a simple call from Jesus and Peter's decision to respond.

In today's world, the journey of faith often begins the same way. Many believers respond to Jesus without fully grasping the depth of the Christian faith or our future role in it. Like Peter, we need to be taught and shaped by the Word of God, prayer, community, and learning. Just as Jesus transforms Peter into the leader He needs, He works to transform modern believers into disciples who can live out their faith fully. Ultimately, Peter's call to follow Jesus in Matthew 4:18–20 reminds us that spiritual growth doesn't require us to meet a preapproved standard. Jesus calls us as we are, knowing He will guide us into the people He desires us to be.

II. Restoration and Commission Through Love (John 21:15–18)

In John 21:15–18, we witness the powerful restoration of Peter following his denial of Jesus. After the Resurrection, Jesus seeks out Peter—not to condemn him, but to restore and commission him for further service. This moment is crucial because it underscores the nature of Christ's love and grace—it is restorative, not punitive. Peter, who denies knowing Jesus three times, is now given the opportunity to reaffirm his love for Jesus three times. This act of restoration highlights that failure does not disqualify us from service in God's Kingdom.

Peter's restoration is not only personal but missional. Jesus asks him to "feed my lambs," "tend my sheep," and "feed my sheep" (NRSVue). These commands are a clear call to pastoral care and leadership. Despite Peter's earlier failure, Jesus entrusts him with a renewed mission. This teaches us that restoration is not just about healing past wounds, but also about preparing us for future service. Peter's experience mirrors the truth found in Philippians 1:6: that the one who began a good work in you will continue to complete it until the day of Jesus Christ. Restoration equips us to fulfill our calling with renewed purpose and focus.

The threefold restoration of Peter also speaks to the depth of God's grace. Colossians 1:9–11 encourages believers to be filled with the knowledge of God's will and to live lives worthy of the Lord. Peter's life, restored and recommissioned, reflects this transformation. His leadership in the early church is not a result of his own strength but a testimony to God's grace working through his weakness.

For believers today, Peter's restoration serves as a reminder that no matter how far we may stray, Christ is always willing to restore us and bring us back into fellowship with Him. The restoration process is not about our failures but about God's ability to redeem those failures for His glory. In Ephesians 4:11–16, Paul emphasizes the importance of spiritual leadership within the church. Peter's story illustrates how restored individuals can play a critical role in building up the Body of Christ.

Just as Peter was restored to a position of leadership, believers who experience restoration are often called to serve in ways that reflect renewed commitment to Christ. This process of restoration and recommissioning is ongoing, as seen in Philippians 3:12–16, where Paul urges believers to press on toward the goal despite their past. Peter's story offers hope and encouragement to those of us who may feel disqualified by past mistakes. In Christ, restoration is always possible, and with it comes the opportunity to serve again with renewed purpose.

III. Maturing in Grace and Knowledge (2 Peter 3:14–15, 18)

In 2 Peter 3:14–15 and 18, the Apostle Peter emphasizes the importance of growth in both grace and knowledge. This call to spiritual maturity reflects his understanding that the Christian life is a journey that requires both an increasing awareness of God's grace and a deeper knowledge of Christ. Peter, now writing as a mature leader in the church, knows firsthand the value of continual growth in the Christian faith. His exhortation to "grow in the grace and knowledge of our Lord and Savior Jesus Christ" (v. 18) speaks to the dynamic, ongoing nature of spiritual formation.

Peter's journey from fisherman to leader was one marked by moments of both failure and restoration. But through it all, he grew in his understanding of who Jesus was and what it meant to follow Him. The grace Peter experienced, particularly in his restoration after denying Jesus, shaped his view of spiritual growth. Grace is not just God's favor toward us; it is His active work in our lives, transforming us from the inside out. This growth is not instantaneous but progressive, inviting us to learn how to live out our faith daily.

However, Peter also highlights the necessity of growing in knowledge. This is not merely intellectual knowledge; it is an experiential and relational understanding of who Christ is. Peter's emphasis on knowledge is particularly important because it safeguards believers from being led astray by false teachings—a concern he addresses earlier in the same chapter (see 2 Pet. 3:3–7). Knowledge of Christ anchors us in God's truth, helping us to discern and live out God's will more faithfully.

Peter's call to grow in grace and knowledge also has a communal dimension. His leadership in the early church demonstrated the importance of helping others mature in their faith, and his exhortation to believers in this epistle is a continuation of that mission. Growth is not an individual pursuit but one that happens in community. This is the God-designed space where we encourage and support one another in our walk with Christ. Furthermore, Peter's final exhortation to "be diligent to be found by Him in peace, without spot or blemish" (v. 14), reflects the urgency of spiritual growth.

Spiritual growth, according to Peter, is not optional; it is essential for those who await Christ's return. The delay of His return, as Peter notes in verse 15, is a demonstration of God's patience, giving us time to grow, repent, and bring others into the knowledge of Christ. Ultimately, Peter's message is one of hope and perseverance. Growth in grace and knowledge is a lifelong process—one that requires diligence, patience, and a deep reliance on God's power working within us. Here, we are reminded of the saints mentioned in Hebrews 11, whose faith grew over time. We, too, are called to continually mature in our faith, trusting that the same grace that restored Peter will also guide and sustain us in our journey of becoming more like Christ.

THE LESSON APPLIED

Believers can apply the lessons from Peter's journey by embracing spiritual growth and recognizing it as a continuous process. First, we should recognize that we don't need to have everything figured out to follow Christ. We can start where we are and as we are, trusting that God's call will provide us with the guidance that leads to transformation over time.

This calls for a willingness to take steps of faith in our everyday lives, even when we don't fully understand the process or outcomes. It is inevitable that, sometimes, we might respond to the Gospel without fully grasping the depth of what it is saying. Whether through hearing a sermon, attending Bible study, or being baptized, we, like Peter, must be taught and guided by Christ in our faith journey. We can trust the God of the process.

Next, when we experience failure or fall short in our spiritual walk, we should remember that God's grace offers complete restoration. Rather than dwelling on mistakes, we can turn to God for forgiveness and seek to renew our commitment to His service. God's grace is sufficient, His forgiveness is eternal, and His love is everlasting. Finally, believers can apply this lesson by being intentional about growing in both grace and knowledge. This means living out our faith through acts of love, compassion, and service, allowing God's grace to transform both our character and our relationships with others.

LET'S TALK ABOUT IT...

Discuss the following questions and visit www.rhboyd.com for more information.

How does Peter's response to Jesus' call inspire you to take steps of faith in your own life?

What lessons can you draw from Peter's restoration?

In what practical ways can you grow in both grace and knowledge, as Peter exhorts in 2 Peter 3:14–18?

Get Social

Share your views and tag us
@rhboydco and use #rhboydco

@rhboydco

Home Daily Devotional Readings
January 26–February 1, 2026

Monday	Tuesday	Wednesday	Thursday	Friday	Saturday	Sunday
A Community of Testimony and Praise	A Community of Hope-Filled Heirs	A Community with Divine Authority	A Community Made Strong Together	A Community United in Worship	A Community Silently Growing	A Community of Oneness
Psalm 22:22-28	Ephesians 1:15-23	Matthew 16:13-20	Ecclesiastes 4:7-12	Psalm 150	Mark 4:26-32	Ephesians 4:4-16

Lesson IX   **February 1, 2026**

Working Together Makes Us Better

Adult Topic: The Christian Church
Background Scripture: Matt. 16:13–20; Mark 4:26–32; Rom. 12:4–8; Eph. 1:15–23; 2:13–22; 4:4–6, 11–18; 5:22–27; 1 Tim. 3:15
Lesson Passage: Mark 4:26–32; Ephesians 4:4–6, 11–18

MARK 4:26–32; EPHESIANS 4:4–6, 11–18

KJV

AND he said, So is the kingdom of God, as if a man should cast seed into the ground;

27 And should sleep, and rise night and day, and the seed should spring and grow up, he knoweth not how.

28 For the earth bringeth forth fruit of herself; first the blade, then the ear, after that the full corn in the ear.

29 But when the fruit is brought forth, immediately he putteth in the sickle, because the harvest is come.

30 And he said, Whereunto shall we liken the kingdom of God? or with what comparison shall we compare it?

31 It is like a grain of mustard seed, which, when it is sown in the earth, is less than all the seeds that be in the earth:

32 But when it is sown, it groweth up, and becometh greater than all herbs, and shooteth out great branches; so that the fowls of the air may lodge under the shadow of it.

••• Ephesians 4:4–6 •••
4 There is one body, and one Spirit, even as ye are called in one hope of your calling;
5 One Lord, one faith, one baptism,
6 One God and Father of all, who is above all, and through all, and in you all.

••• Ephesians 4:11–18 •••
11 And he gave some, apostles; and some, prophets; and some, evangelists; and some, pastors and teachers;
12 For the perfecting of the saints, for the work

NRSVue

HE also said, "The kingdom of God is as if someone would scatter seed on the ground

27 and would sleep and rise night and day, and the seed would sprout and grow, he does not know how.

28 The earth produces of itself first the stalk, then the head, then the full grain in the head.

29 But when the grain is ripe, at once he goes in with his sickle because the harvest has come."

30 He also said, "With what can we compare the kingdom of God, or what parable will we use for it?

31 It is like a mustard seed, which, when sown upon the ground, is the smallest of all the seeds on earth,

32 yet when it is sown it grows up and becomes the greatest of all shrubs and puts forth large branches, so that the birds of the air can make nests in its shade.

••• Ephesians 4:4–6 •••
4 there is one body and one Spirit, just as you were called to the one hope of your calling,
5 one Lord, one faith, one baptism,
6 one God and Father of all, who is above all and through all and in all

••• Ephesians 4:11–18 •••
11 He himself granted that some are apostles, prophets, evangelists, pastors and teachers
12 to equip the saints for the work of ministry,

MAIN THOUGHT: "[B]ut speaking the truth in love, we must grow up in every way into him who is the head, into Christ, from whom the whole body, joined and knit together by every ligament with which it is equipped, as each part is working properly, promotes the body's growth in building itself up in love." (Ephesians 4:15–16, NRSVue)

MARK 4:26-32; EPHESIANS 4:4-6, 11-18

KJV	NRSVue
of the ministry, for the edifying of the body of Christ:	for building up the body of Christ,
13 Till we all come in the unity of the faith, and of the knowledge of the Son of God, unto a perfect man, unto the measure of the stature of the fulness of Christ:	13 until all of us come to the unity of the faith and of the knowledge of the Son of God, to maturity, to the measure of the full stature of Christ.
14 That we henceforth be no more children, tossed to and fro, and carried about with every wind of doctrine, by the sleight of men, and cunning craftiness, whereby they lie in wait to deceive;	14 We must no longer be children, tossed to and fro and blown about by every wind of doctrine by people's trickery, by their craftiness in deceitful scheming;
15 But speaking the truth in love, may grow up into him in all things, which is the head, even Christ:	15 but speaking the truth in love, we must grow up in every way into him who is the head, into Christ,
16 From whom the whole body fitly joined together and compacted by that which every joint supplieth, according to the effectual working in the measure of every part, maketh increase of the body unto the edifying of itself in love.	16 from whom the whole body, joined and knit together by every ligament with which it is equipped, as each part is working properly, promotes the body's growth in building itself up in love.
17 This I say therefore, and testify in the Lord, that ye henceforth walk not as other Gentiles walk, in the vanity of their mind,	17 Now this I affirm and insist on in the Lord: you must no longer walk as the gentiles walk, in the futility of their minds;
18 Having the understanding darkened, being alienated from the life of God through the ignorance that is in them, because of the blindness of their heart:	18 they are darkened in their understanding, alienated from the life of God because of their ignorance and hardness of heart.

LESSON SETTING

Time: Around AD 27–30 (Mark 4); around AD 60–62 (Eph. 4)
Place: Region of Galilee (Mark 4); while Paul was in Rome (Eph. 4)
Setting: In this period of the church's development, the Gospel's expansion beyond Judaism to diverse audiences created growing tensions. This serves as the backdrop for the writings of Mark, traditionally seen as the author of his Gospel, and Paul, author of Ephesians.

LESSON SETTING

I. The Kingdom Grows in Stages (Mark 4:26–32)
II. Unity in the Body of Christ (Ephesians 4:4–6)
III. Building Together with Spiritual Gifts (Ephesians 4:11–18)

UNIFYING PRINCIPLE

An infinite number of issues threaten the unity of families, communities, and nations. How will we resist what threatens to divide us? When we use the unique gifts Christ gave the Church, we can grow together and experience spiritual unity.

INTRODUCTION

Throughout history, deception has caused division and harm to communities. Paul's warning against being carried away by false doctrines remains relevant today, as falsehood continues to plague society with serious consequences. From the beginning, deception has been a destructive force. In Eden, the serpent's cunning led Adam and Eve to question God's command, breaking their relationship with Him. Similarly, false prophets in Israel's history misled the people, causing division and rebellion.

Today, falsehood seems even more overwhelming with social media and digital information spreading misinformation rapidly. People are "tossed to and fro" by various doctrines and conspiracy theories on platforms where anyone can claim their version of the truth. The multicultural makeup of the U.S. faces unique challenges as misinformation worsens racial tensions. The damage caused by deception runs deep. Social and political divides grow, relationships strain, and community unity unravels. Paul saw these patterns in the early church, where false teachings disrupted unity. Even Jude, Jesus' brother, warned the early church about false teachings that had "crept in unnoticed," deceiving many (see Jude 1).

Falsehood can harm both church and society, pulling people from truth and fostering division. Despite these challenges, the church is called to practice unity by rising above them, as working together makes us stronger. In light of Paul's broader teaching, the church's unity and growth remain central, as seen in his words to the Ephesians and in Mark's Gospel, where the mysterious but steady growth of God's Kingdom is emphasized.

EXPOSITION

I. The Kingdom Grows in Stages (Mark 4:26–32)

Jesus shares a parable about God's Kingdom, revealing how it grows in hidden, gradual ways until it reaches profound impact. This highlights both the nature of the Kingdom's growth and the quiet, steady development of unity among its people. Unlike worldly kingdoms relying on visible power, the Kingdom of Heaven grows differently—beginning with small, unseen efforts that transform over time. Through imagery of seeds, planting, and growth, Jesus illustrates how God's Kingdom often starts unassumingly but ultimately becomes powerful and expansive. This was transformative for Jesus' audience, who expected God's Kingdom to arrive with undeniable power.

Jesus compares the Kingdom to a man scattering seed, which grows independently of the sower's effort or understanding. As the man goes about his life, the seed sprouts in stages, from blade to full grain. This illustrates that God's Kingdom grows gradually, often beyond our control or awareness. The seed represents God's Word, which, when received by a willing heart, begins a journey of spiritual growth that cannot be rushed or controlled. Just as the sower waits for each stage to unfold, believers are reminded that spiritual growth takes time and must be entrusted to God's timing and power.

Even when progress is unseen, God's Kingdom advances within and around us. Just as a seed matures step by step, the Kingdom advances quietly, drawing believers together in unity and purpose as they mature in faith. This process is both comforting and challenging, reminding us to surrender impatience and control, trusting that God's work unfolds perfectly.

To deepen this lesson, Jesus offers a second parable: the mustard seed. Though the smallest of seeds, it grows into a large plant providing shelter for birds. Jesus shows how God's Kingdom often begins with small acts of faith, expanding into something far more profound than its humble origins suggest. This pattern—small beginnings leading to great impact—is echoed in stories of Old Testament figures like Gideon, who began as a reluctant leader. His growth from timidity to strength reflects the Kingdom's power to turn hesitant beginnings into impactful service (see Judg. 6–8). Today's believers experience this hidden growth as God uses everyday experiences—interactions, challenges, and opposition—to shape our hearts.

II. Unity in the Body of Christ (Ephesians 4:4–6)

Disunity poses a serious danger to any organization, especially the church. It disrupts harmony, hinders progress, and invites conflict. An Old Testament example of disunity is found in Numbers 16, where Korah, Dathan, and Abiram led a rebellion against Moses and Aaron. Driven by jealousy and a thirst for power, they rejected God's appointed leadership, causing division among the Israelites and bringing His judgment upon them. This tragic episode highlights how disunity fractures communities, breeding distrust and chaos.

Disunity is not merely a breakdown of relationships. It threatens the very purpose of a group. When people refuse to work together, even God-ordained missions can be delayed or derailed. The rebellion in the wilderness reminds us that no mission, however sacred, is immune to the consequences of division. Whether in the church, family, or any organization, unity is essential for success. Disunity weakens influence, hinders productivity, and invites destruction from within. The call to work together, embracing diverse roles with humility, remains critical to fulfilling any shared purpose. Without unity, even the strongest structure crumbles under its own divided weight.

Paul emphasizes unity as a core part of the church, where all believers are "one body" joined by "one Spirit." This message was vital for the early church, which included people from diverse backgrounds: Jews, Gentiles, slaves, and free. Even with their differences, Paul urges believers to see themselves as one family in Christ, united by the Holy Spirit. This unity connects people who might not otherwise come together, enabling them to share a common purpose and identity as the Body of Christ.

The Spirit's presence within each believer strengthens this sense of belonging, making them part of something greater than themselves. Paul uses the image of a "body" to show how each member has a role within the church. This idea, echoed in Romans 12:4–8, reminds us that although believers have unique gifts, we all serve together for God's mission. Instead of focusing on personal goals, believers align with Christ's mission, which centers on love, service, and unity. Paul highlights core beliefs all Christians share—"one Lord, one faith, one baptism"—to strengthen this unity.

These foundational beliefs are like building blocks, helping Christians find common ground. The "one Lord" is Jesus, who unites believers and calls each into a relationship with God and each other. Similarly, baptism acts as a symbol of shared commitment, marking each person as part of the same spiritual journey. Through unity, the

Church becomes a family able to overcome differences and live as one. This vision reflects the work of Jesus, who "broke down the wall of hostility" (Eph. 2:14). This is exemplified in the relationship between Paul and the disciples. Former rivals became partners for God's Kingdom.

By working together as "one body," the Church displays God's love in a divided world. This unity equips believers to carry out God's plan, becoming a powerful example of what it means to live as God's people. In this way, the Church reflects the Kingdom of Heaven, drawing others into a life-changing community centered on Christ.

III. Building Together with Spiritual Gifts (Ephesians 4:11–18)

Paul emphasizes the essential role of spiritual gifts in forming a unified, mature church. While these gifts are crucial for equipping believers, they can also become sources of tension. When gifts are misused for self-promotion or placed above others, they risk undermining the Church's purpose of love and unity. Instead, Paul insists that spiritual gifts strengthen the Body of Christ, equipping the Church to carry out its mission through growth and community. Paul's vision extends beyond a functional unity—where members work together toward a common goal—to a discerning, spiritually mature Church that withstands doctrinal challenges.

Later in Ephesians 6, Paul provides a metaphor for the Church's defense against spiritual adversaries by way of the "armor of God" (vv. 11–18). Each piece of armor represents an aspect of defense and strength. The "belt of truth" signifies God's truth as essential for holding everything together, just as a belt secures a soldier's armor. The "breastplate of righteousness" reflects moral integrity, shielding the heart against temptations that might weaken unity. "Laced up sandals in preparation for the gospel of peace" help us stand in integrity as we share God's Word, ensuring we are always ready, "in and out of season" (2 Tim. 4:2). The "shield of faith" guards against subtle yet destructive forces—doubts, fears, and pride—that destabilize the community.

The "helmet of salvation" guards the mind and the "sword of the Spirit" is the Word of God, which defends against errors threatening faith. Scripture is a powerful weapon that repels falsehood, strengthening believers' commitment to truth, as seen in Christ's responses to temptation (see Matt. 4:1–11). Prayer underpins this armor, keeping each piece in place and enabling reliance on God's wisdom. By "praying at all times in the Spirit," the church remains aligned with God's guidance, standing firm not only in doctrine but in love and unity. Together, these elements form a protective layer, enabling believers to remain steadfast in faith and mission.

Beyond armor, humbly embracing gifts prevents division and fortifies the community against teachings that erode its foundation. Spiritual maturity allows believers to value each gift, fostering respect among members and reducing divisions based on perceived superiority. A mature Church values every role within the Body of Christ, reinforcing resilience against harmful teachings and pressures, both internal and external. This unity isn't just practical but represents a spiritual strength that bolsters the Church's witness to the world. With discernment, believers form a community capable of withstanding challenges, reflecting God's peace and stability.

Ultimately, the purpose of spiritual gifts and the armor of God is to manifest God's Kingdom within His Church—a community grounded in love, service, and faith—and within His world. Paul's message is clear: rather than letting differences divide, believers are called to embody a unity that reflects God's intention for us

THE LESSON APPLIED

This lesson challenges today's Church to pursue unity intentionally—even when faced with differences in background, opinions, or social concerns. In a time when social media and political divisions can easily pull us apart, God's Church has an essential role in demonstrating that unity is possible through Christ. We are called to be examples of harmony by addressing conflicts with love, using spiritual gifts to serve others, and embodying Christ's compassion and patience.

Rather than being drawn into divisive conversations or adopting the world's standards of judgment, we are called to focus on the Kingdom values of love, forgiveness, and humility. Prayer, as emphasized by Paul, must be central to maintaining this unity. Prayer keeps us aligned with God's purpose and reminds us that our ultimate mission is to reflect Christ to the world—not to win arguments or assert our personal preferences.

Finally, embracing our spiritual gifts is crucial for strengthening the Body. Instead of competing or comparing, the Church grows strongest when members use gifts to build others up. By focusing on cooperation over competition, we demonstrate a unique community that stands apart from worldly divisions. When believers work together in love, we offer a true reflection of God's Kingdom, inviting others to experience genuine peace and belonging.

LET'S TALK ABOUT IT...

Discuss the following questions and visit www.rhboyd.com for more information.

How can we address disagreements within our church in a way that builds understanding and unity?

How can each member's spiritual gifts be used to create a stronger, more welcoming church community?

Get Social
Share your views and tag us
@rhboydco and use #rhboydco

@rhboydco

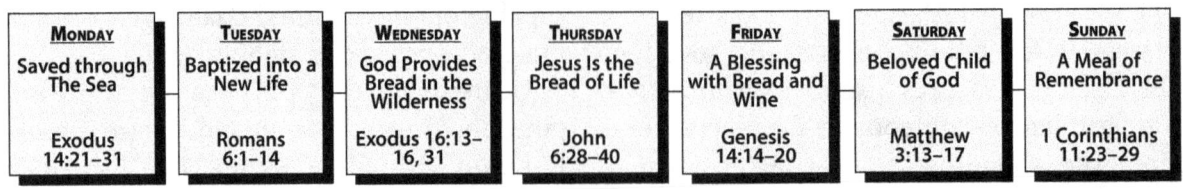

Home Daily Devotional Readings
February 2–8, 2026

Monday	Tuesday	Wednesday	Thursday	Friday	Saturday	Sunday
Saved through The Sea	Baptized into a New Life	God Provides Bread in the Wilderness	Jesus Is the Bread of Life	A Blessing with Bread and Wine	Beloved Child of God	A Meal of Remembrance
Exodus 14:21–31	Romans 6:1–14	Exodus 16:13–16, 31	John 6:28–40	Genesis 14:14–20	Matthew 3:13–17	1 Corinthians 11:23–29

Lesson X   **February 8, 2026**

Baptism and the Lord's Supper

Adult Topic: Outer Expressions of Inner Truths
Background Scripture: Matt. 3:13–17; 28:19–20; Acts 2:38, 41; Rom. 6:1–14; 1 Cor. 11:23–29
Lesson Passage: Matthew 3:13–17; 28:19–20; 1 Corinthians 11:23–29

MATTHEW 3:13–17; 28:19–20; 1 CORINTHIANS 11:23–29

KJV

THEN cometh Jesus from Galilee to Jordan unto John, to be baptized of him.
14 But John forbad him, saying, I have need to be baptized of thee, and comest thou to me?

15 And Jesus answering said unto him, Suffer it to be so now: for thus it becometh us to fulfil all righteousness. Then he suffered him.
16 And Jesus, when he was baptized, went up straightway out of the water: and, lo, the heavens were opened unto him, and he saw the Spirit of God descending like a dove, and lighting upon him:
17 And lo a voice from heaven, saying, This is my beloved Son, in whom I am well pleased.

••• Matthew 28:19–20 •••
19 Go ye therefore, and teach all nations, baptizing them in the name of the Father, and of the Son, and of the Holy Ghost:
20 Teaching them to observe all things whatsoever I have commanded you: and, lo, I am with you always, even unto the end of the world. Amen.

••• 1 Corinthians 11:23–29 •••
23 For I have received of the Lord that which also I delivered unto you, that the Lord Jesus the same night in which he was betrayed took bread:
24 And when he had given thanks, he brake it, and said, Take, eat: this is my body, which is broken for you: this do in remembrance of me.

NRSVue

THEN Jesus came from Galilee to John at the Jordan, to be baptized by him.
14 John would have prevented him, saying, "I need to be baptized by you, and do you come to me?"
15 But Jesus answered him, "Let it be so now, for it is proper for us in this way to fulfill all righteousness." Then he consented.
16 And when Jesus had been baptized, just as he came up from the water, suddenly the heavens were opened to him and he saw God's Spirit descending like a dove and alighting on him.

17 And a voice from the heavens said, "This is my Son, the Beloved, with whom I am well pleased."

••• Matthew 28:19–20•••
19 Go therefore and make disciples of all nations, baptizing them in the name of the Father and of the Son and of the Holy Spirit
20 and teaching them to obey everything that I have commanded you. And remember, I am with you always, to the end of the age.

••• 1 Corinthians 11:23–29 •••
23 For I received from the Lord what I also handed on to you, that the Lord Jesus on the night when he was betrayed took a loaf of bread, 24 and when he had given thanks, he broke it and said, "This is my body that is for you. Do this in remembrance of me."

MAIN THOUGHT: Go ye therefore, and teach all nations, baptizing them in the name of the Father, and of the Son, and of the Holy Ghost: Teaching them to observe all things whatsoever I have commanded you: and, lo, I am with you always, even unto the end of the world. Amen. (Matthew 28:19–20, KJV)

MATTHEW 3:13-17; 28:19-20; 1 CORINTHIANS 11:23-29

KJV	NRSVue
25 After the same manner also he took the cup, when he had supped, saying, this cup is the new testament in my blood: this do ye, as oft as ye drink it, in remembrance of me.	25 In the same way he took the cup also, after supper, saying, "This cup is the new covenant in my blood. Do this, as often as you drink it, in remembrance of me."
26 For as often as ye eat this bread, and drink this cup, ye do shew the Lord's death till he come.	26 For as often as you eat this bread and drink the cup, you proclaim the Lord's death until he comes.
27 Wherefore whosoever shall eat this bread, and drink this cup of the Lord, unworthily, shall be guilty of the body and blood of the Lord.	27 Whoever, therefore, eats the bread or drinks the cup of the Lord in an unworthy manner will be answerable for the body and blood of the Lord.
28 But let a man examine himself, and so let him eat of that bread, and drink of that cup.	28 Examine yourselves, and only then eat of the bread and drink of the cup.
29 For he that eateth and drinketh unworthily, eateth and drinketh damnation to himself, not discerning the Lord's body.	29 For all who eat and drink without discerning the body eat and drink judgment against themselves.

LESSON SETTING

Time: AD 1st century, during Jesus' ministry, around AD 27–30 (Matt.); Around AD 53–54 (1 Cor. 11)

Place: Likely Galilee or Judea, Israel (Matt.); Ephesus (1 Cor. 11

Setting: As Jesus approaches His crucifixion, He prepares His disciples for what lay ahead, telling them three times that He would suffer, die, and rise again. Yet despite His clear words, the disciples struggle to understand. Their minds were fixed on hopes of a Messianic deliverer who would restore Israel's earthly kingdom. The Gospels of Matthew, Mark, and Luke, each recounting Jesus' predictions, show the disciples' reactions ranging from denial to confusion and fear. These repeated misunderstandings culminate in Jesus leading them to the Upper Room, where He shares one final moment before His death. Jesus' last lesson reframes their expectations and binds them to His mission in a way they cannot not yet fully comprehend. Here, Jesus institutes the Lord's Supper and opens their hearts to a deeper truth.

LESSON OUTLINE

I. A King's Humble Submission (Matthew 3:13–17)
II. Expressing the Heart of the Kingdom (Matthew 28:19–20)
III. Table of Remembrance and Unity (1 Corinthians 11:23–29)

UNIFYING PRINCIPLE

People seek a strengthening and steadying force for life's journey. What gives vitality to our life and work? Christ gave baptism and the Lord's Supper to the Church as vital to its mission and witness of God's saving work.

INTRODUCTION

God's call for inner righteousness resonates from the earliest passages of the Old Testament to the teachings of Jesus. In Genesis, the story of Cain and Abel shows that God's interactions with humanity are based not only on actions but also on the heart's posture (Gen. 4:3–7). The Law given to Israel emphasizes that their outward actions alone could never make them truly righteous. In the prophets, Isaiah chastises the people for empty sacrifices and offerings, declaring that their outward forms of worship is meaningless without a heart that seeks justice, mercy, and humility before God (Isa. 1:11–17).

In the New Testament, Jesus builds on these truths, teaching that the purity God desires extends beyond the external to the heart's inner condition. In His Sermon on the Mount, Jesus confronts the superficial righteousness of the Pharisees, who focused on outward obedience to the Law yet neglected the weightier matters of the heart. He also emphasizes that sins like murder and adultery begin in the heart, teaching that true righteousness requires addressing these inner sins before they manifest outwardly (Matt. 5:21–28).

The continuity of God's desire for inner righteousness culminates in the practices and teachings established by Jesus, where outward expressions flow from a transformed heart. As we explore the journey from His baptism to His call for discipleship and the shared table of communion, we witness how these outward acts reflect the inner truths of God's Kingdom. Jesus' ministry models for us the call to embody inner transformation, inviting us to examine how our actions bear witness to the righteousness God has always desired.

EXPOSITION

I. A King's Humble Submission (Matthew 3:13–17)

Jesus' baptism marks the beginning of His public ministry and affirms His connection to humanity. At the Jordan River, He stands face to face with John, His cousin, their lives intertwined by prophecy. This meeting of cousins is no ordinary reunion; it is a significant theological encounter. John, the forerunner, has been calling others to repent in preparation for the Kingdom of heaven.

As Jesus joins those in need of repentance, John is understandably taken aback—he knows Jesus as the sinless One, greater than he, and initially resists. Jesus' decision to undergo a baptism of repentance, despite His sinlessness, underscores His solidarity with humanity. In this act, He embraces His mission to fulfill God's righteous plan, foreshadowing the sin He will bear on the cross. As Jesus rises from the water, divine affirmation follows; the heavens open to speak (Matt. 3:16). This anointing reflects the consecration of prophets and kings, marking Jesus as God's chosen servant, empowered for His mission.

In Matthew's narrative, the Spirit's descent aligns Jesus with Israel's anointed kings of old, establishing His divine authority as the coming King. The Father's voice affirms Jesus' identity and mission, declaring, "This is my Son, the Beloved, with whom I am well pleased" (Matt. 3:17). This statement weaves together themes from Psalm 2:7, celebrating the King as God's Son, and Isaiah 42:1, where the Suffering Servant is chosen by God. This divine approval reveals Jesus as both the anticipated Messiah and the servant who will bear the weight of humanity's sin.

II. Expressing the Heart of the Kingdom (Matthew 28:19-20)

In the Old Testament, God's call to His people foreshadowed the Great Commission. Through promises to Abraham (Gen. 12:1-3) and the mission of Israel as a "light to the nations" (Isa. 49:6), God's plan for global redemption was already unfolding. This divine purpose finds its full expression in Jesus' command to make disciples of all nations, connecting the Old Testament's mission to the Great Commission's fulfillment.

The Great Commission's call to "make disciples of all nations" resonates across time and culture, reaching into the hearts of those who lived under the oppressive yoke of slavery. For slaves and former slaves, baptism was not just a sacrament of salvation but also a gateway to the hope and liberation that comes through belonging to Christ. When Jesus commands His followers to "baptize them in the name of the Father, Son, and Holy Spirit," He invites believers into a shared identity that transcends earthly divisions and human suffering. More than a personal milestone, baptism declares one's worth and agency.

Jesus' command to "teach them to obey everything I have commanded you" offers a vision that not only transforms individuals but empowers entire communities. Jesus' promise, "I am with you always, to the very end of the age," offers enduring hope. For those oppressed by slavery, this assurance of divine presence affirmed they were not abandoned in their struggle. Christ's presence sustained them, granting courage to live faithfully and envision spiritual and societal freedom. The Great Commission empowers believers—then and now—to embrace our role as disciples in God's kingdom, where justice will ultimately prevail.

III. Table of Remembrance and Unity (1 Corinthians 11:23-29)

The Lord's Supper holds unique meaning as a sacred ritual of communion and remembrance, drawing Christians into deeper reflection on Christ's sacrificial death, the new covenant it established, and their continued communion with Him. When believers partake in the bread, they recall the agony and humility Christ endured on the cross, accepting the ultimate sacrifice for humanity's redemption. The bread serves as a powerful symbol that brings Christ's sacrifice into present experience, uniting believers with that key moment in history.

The cup in the Lord's Supper signifies Jesus' blood, poured out to establish the new covenant—unlike the old covenant, which relied on animal sacrifices that could not fully reconcile humanity to God. The cup thus becomes a symbol of divine grace and mercy extended to all who believe. Drinking from the cup is more than a ritualistic act; it is a symbolic reaffirmation of believers' acceptance of God's grace and forgiveness made possible through Christ's blood.

The Lord's Supper also embodies an opportunity for unity. In his article, "Racial Reconciliation and the Opportunity of the Lord's Supper," Dr. James C. Black notes that this sacrament calls us to "build community, to 're-member' the 'dismembered' body of Christ, to unlearn racial prejudices through the thankful practice of seeing God's face in one another." In partaking of the Lord's Supper, Christians participate in an act that reaffirms their union not only with Christ but with each other, regardless of race, background, or status. This sacrament becomes a space for believers to confess sin, receive forgiveness, and anticipate a future marked by unity, echoing the "hopeful expectation of the eschaton."

Thus, the Lord's Supper looks back, works in the present, and anticipates a future. It is a memorial of Christ's sacrifice and a call for believers to intentionally embrace unity and practice reconciliation. It binds us to one another as we partake of one loaf and one cup, fostering a community rooted in grace and love, a reflection of the eternal fellowship awaiting all believers in God's Kingdom.

THE LESSON APPLIED

Having studied the meaning and significance of the Lord's Supper, believers are called to approach this sacrament with renewed intentionality, humility, and reverence. Paul's teaching encourages self-examination. This means we must take time to reflect on our relationship with God and others. The Lord's Supper is a sacred reminder of Christ's sacrifice, and preparing ourselves spiritually honors His love and forgiveness. Seek reconciliation where necessary; we are called to approach the table with a sincere desire to align our hearts with God's will.

Additionally, remember that the Lord's Supper is an act of unity within the Church. It's not just an individual experience; it's a community proclamation of faith in Jesus. As we participate, each member should consider ways we can strengthen the bonds within our church family. Perhaps this means forgiving an offense, reaching out to someone who feels isolated, or serving within our community. The Lord's Supper should inspire actions that reflect Christ's love, reminding us that we are one body under His leadership.

LET'S TALK ABOUT IT...

Discuss the following questions and visit www.rhboyd.com for more information.

How can you actively prepare your heart before partaking in the Lord's Supper to approach it with reverence and humility?

In what specific ways can you live out the sacrificial love of Christ, as reflected in the Lord's Supper, in your daily life?

Get Social

Share your views and tag us
@rhboydco and use #rhboydco

@rhboydco

Home Daily Devotional Readings
February 9–15, 2026

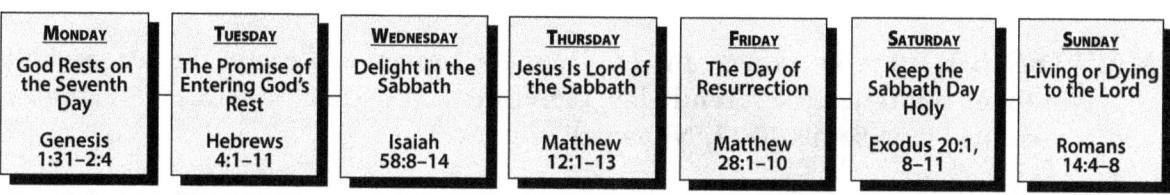

Monday	Tuesday	Wednesday	Thursday	Friday	Saturday	Sunday
God Rests on the Seventh Day	The Promise of Entering God's Rest	Delight in the Sabbath	Jesus Is Lord of the Sabbath	The Day of Resurrection	Keep the Sabbath Day Holy	Living or Dying to the Lord
Genesis 1:31–2:4	Hebrews 4:1–11	Isaiah 58:8–14	Matthew 12:1–13	Matthew 28:1–10	Exodus 20:1, 8–11	Romans 14:4–8

Lesson XI   **February 15, 2026**

The Lord's Day

Adult Topic: Rhythms of Rest and Work
Background Scripture: Gen. 2:2–3; Exod. 20:8–11; Matt. 12:1–14; 28:1–10; John 20:19; Acts 20:7; Rom. 14:4–6; Rev. 1:10
Lesson Passage: Exodus 20:8–11; Romans 14:4–6; Revelation 1:10

EXODUS 20:8-11; ROMANS 14:4-6; REVELATION 1:10

KJV

REMEMBER the sabbath day, to keep it holy.
9 Six days shalt thou labour, and do all thy work:
10 But the seventh day is the sabbath of the Lord thy God: in it thou shalt not do any work, thou, nor thy son, nor thy daughter, thy manservant, nor thy maidservant, nor thy cattle, nor thy stranger that is within thy gates:
11 For in six days the Lord made heaven and earth, the sea, and all that in them is, and rested the seventh day: wherefore the Lord blessed the sabbath day, and hallowed it.

•••Romans 14:4-6•••
4 Who art thou that judgest another man's servant? to his own master he standeth or falleth. Yea, he shall be holden up: for God is able to make him stand.
5 One man esteemeth one day above another: another esteemeth every day alike. Let every man be fully persuaded in his own mind.
6 He that regardeth the day, regardeth it unto the Lord; and he that regardeth not the day, to the Lord he doth not regard it. He that eateth, eateth to the Lord, for he giveth God thanks; and he that eateth not, to the Lord he eateth not, and giveth God thanks.

•••Revelation 1:10•••
10 I was in the Spirit on the Lord's day, and heard behind me a great voice, as of a trumpet,

NRSVue

"REMEMBER the Sabbath day and keep it holy.
9 Six days you shall labor and do all your work.
10 But the seventh day is a Sabbath to the Lord your God; you shall not do any work—you, your son or your daughter, your male or female slave, your livestock, or the alien resident in your towns.
11 For in six days the Lord made heaven and earth, the sea, and all that is in them, but rested the seventh day; therefore the Lord blessed the Sabbath day and consecrated it.

•••Romans 14:4-6•••
4 Who are you to pass judgment on slaves of another? It is before their own lord that they stand or fall. And they will be upheld, for the Lord is able to make them stand.
5 Some judge one day to be better than another, while others judge all days to be alike. Let all be fully convinced in their own minds.
6 Those who observe the day, observe it for the Lord. Also those who eat, eat for the Lord, since they give thanks to God, while those who abstain, abstain for the Lord and give thanks to God.

•••Revelation 1:10•••
10 I was in the spirit on the Lord's day, and I heard behind me a loud voice like a trumpet

MAIN THOUGHT: For in six days the LORD made heaven and earth, the sea, and all that is in them, but rested the seventh day; therefore the LORD blessed the Sabbath day and consecrated it. (Exodus 20:11, NRSVue)

LESSON SETTING

Time: 13th century, around 1290 BC (Exod. 20); Paul's third missionary journey, around AD mid-50s (Rom. 14); Around AD 95 (Rev. 1)

Place: Exodus from Egypt (Exod. 20); Corinth, Greece (Rom. 14); John's exile on the island of Patmos (Rev. 1)

Setting: In ancient Egypt, the Israelites toiled under the crushing demands of slavery, where every moment of their lives was dictated by Pharaoh's relentless drive for productivity. Pharaoh's decrees left no room for reprieve; their labor served his kingdom alone, building cities, monuments, and storage houses that would glorify his name and power. At one point, to tighten his grip and make their labor even more grueling, Pharaoh ordered the Israelites to make bricks without providing straw—an essential material. This command was both punishment and assertion of his control, adding yet another layer of hardship to an already brutal existence. Moses, a Hebrew raised with the privileges and power of the royal family, witnessed both the luxury of Pharaoh's court and the brutality of Egyptian rule over his people. This perspective set him apart and ultimately prepared him for the unique role he would later assume. After years away from Egypt because of an act of defiance, Moses returned as a messenger of God's deliverance, confronting Pharaoh and leading the Israelites out of slavery. In freeing His people, God not only broke the chains of their physical bondage but also sought to reorient their understanding of work and life. He introduced a new rhythm that included rest—a radical departure from the relentless demands of Pharaoh. And how amazing that Moses, once a part of Pharaoh's household, would now be the very messenger of this new way. In this divine pattern, work would be meaningful and balanced with a dedicated time for renewal. This rest was a gift, affirming their dignity and humanity, marking a stark contrast from the unceasing labor that had defined their years in Egypt. Just as the Sabbath in the Old Testament signaled liberation and divine rhythm, the Lord's Day in the New Testament emerged as a new expression of freedom and rest—one rooted in the resurrection of Christ, which brought a deeper meaning and purpose to the lives of His followers.

LESSON OUTLINE

I. Honoring God through Creation and Rest (Exodus 20:8–11)
II. Living in Grace and Freedom (Romans 14:4–6)
III. Celebrating the Lord's Victory (Revelation 1:10)

UNIFYING PRINCIPLE

We carve out time to do the things that are important to us. How do we prioritize our daily activities? The biblical witness shows that just as the Jews kept the Sabbath to honor God's creative and liberating acts, the early Christians set apart the Lord's Day as a testimony to the Resurrection and God's gift of rest.

INTRODUCTION

Burnout is a state of emotional, physical, and mental exhaustion resulting from prolonged and excessive stress. It leaves one feeling overwhelmed, drained, and unable to keep up with unrelenting demands. In the Bible, King Saul is a striking example of a leader who fell into burnout because he failed to value rest and dependence on God. This was especially evident when he faced threats like the Philistines. Instead of seeking reassurance in God's timing and guidance, Saul grew impatient. Overwhelmed by fear of losing control, he took matters into his own hands by performing a sacrificial ritual that only Samuel, the prophet, was authorized to conduct (1 Sam. 13:8–14).

Saul's act wasn't merely disobedient; it showed a restless heart that lacked trust in God's provision. His failure to pause, rest, and seek God's direction ultimately cost him God's favor and support. The prophet Elijah also experienced burnout. Elijah showed remarkable courage and faith on Mount Carmel, confronting the prophets of Baal (1 Kings 18). But after this victory, his strength reached its limit. Elijah's weariness stemmed from his isolation and belief that he alone bore God's mission. This reveals that even the most faithful need rest to regain strength and perspective.

Saul's and Elijah's stories illustrate the risks of ignoring the need for rest and renewal. When we push too far without pause, we risk burnout, which can lead to poor choices, despair, and a lost sense of purpose. As former Facebook/META COO Sheryl Sandberg wisely said, "Burnout is what happens when you try to avoid being human for too long." As we reflect on the Lord's Day, consider how the rhythms of rest and work offer a sacred opportunity for renewal and reconnection with God.

EXPOSITION

I. Honoring God through Creation and Rest (Exodus 20:8–11)

God's command to "remember the sabbath day and keep it holy" is not an arbitrary rule but a divine invitation to align life with the example set by the Creator. Through the Sabbath, believers acknowledge God's authority, recognize His provision, and affirm their dependence on Him. This truth was particularly needed for the Israelites, whose lives in Egypt had been defined by unrelenting labor under Pharaoh's oppressive rule. Their work was devoid of personal benefit or acknowledgment, serving only to build monuments to Pharaoh's glory.

Yet, in their deliverance, God redefined the purpose of their labor. The Sabbath became a revolutionary concept for a people whose identity had been reduced to endless productivity. It was an opportunity to rest and reflect on their Creator, affirming their humanity and worth in a way that Pharaoh's demands never allowed. Yet, the Sabbath is not automatic; it requires a conscious decision to honor God's command. The Israelites had to choose to yield to God's authority, even as they faced consequences for disobedience.

Today, believers face a similar choice. Neglecting rest can erode family relationships, strain marriages, and disrupt spiritual vitality. It is an act of faith to trust God by embracing rest. The Sabbath invites believers to find restoration in God's presence, equipping them to serve Him more effectively. The call to Sabbath rest ultimately points to Jesus Christ, who embodies perfect rest for the weary soul. In Christ, believers cease striving and find lasting rest in His grace, knowing that He is sufficient for every need (Matt. 11:28).

II. Living in Grace and Freedom (Romans 14:4–6)

Judging others assumes a position that no one has the right to hold. It suggests moral superiority, disregards one's own role as a servant, and reflects a lack of trust in God's ability to guide His people. Human understanding is inherently limited, often shaped by incomplete information and personal bias. In contrast, God sees the heart clearly and comprehensively (1 Sam. 16:7). Paul reminds us that rather than focusing on others' perceived shortcomings, we should prioritize our own faithfulness to God.

Beyond individual relationships, Paul addresses the broader impact of judgment on the Church. Criticism rooted in personal preference fosters division, undermining the unity Christ calls believers to uphold. Instead, Christians are to affirm one another, appreciating the diverse ways people respond to God's grace. Paul's exhortation to the Roman church remains relevant today, challenging us to resist allowing minor differences to disrupt harmony. In verses 5–6, Paul shifts to specific examples of disagreement, such as the observance of sacred days and dietary practices. His guidance highlights the significance of personal conviction. Whether one esteems certain days or considers all days equal, what matters is the intent to honor God.

This freedom allows believers to express their faith in diverse ways without imposing their views on others. When believers refrain from judgment and honor one another's convictions, the diversity of worship and practice becomes a testament to God's creativity and generosity. Through mutual respect and shared commitment to glorifying God, the Church becomes a unified witness to the world, showcasing the transformative power of the Gospel.

III. Celebrating the Lord's Victory (Revelation 1:10)

Throughout Christian history, the question of which day to worship has sparked passionate discussions among believers. Some Christian denominations continue to observe Saturday as the Sabbath, honoring the original command found in the Old Testament. They view Saturday as the seventh day, designated by God as holy after His work of creation. However, the majority of Christians worship on Sunday, the "Lord's Day," seeing it as the fulfillment of the Sabbath through Jesus Christ's resurrection. John's description of being "in the Spirit on the Lord's Day" highlights Sunday as the day of Resurrection, a celebration of Jesus' victory over sin and death.

While the Sabbath focused on God's rest after creation, the Lord's Day celebrates Christ's fulfillment of God's promises and the beginning of new life. The early church chose Sunday for worship, not to disregard the Sabbath, but to reflect the importance of Jesus' resurrection. The Lord's Day points to the eternal rest found in Him (see Heb. 4:9–10). This rest is no longer about strict observance but about living in the reality of what Christ has accomplished. The focus moves from a day commemorating creation to one proclaiming redemption.

John's experience on the Lord's Day reminds believers of the personal communion available through worship. His phrase "in the Spirit" signifies a deeply connected relationship with God, offering encouragement and renewal. For John, exiled on Patmos, worship became a lifeline of faith, anchoring him in the assurance of Christ's triumph. Worship on the Lord's Day is not simply a practice. Observing the Lord's Day reminds us that our hope is in Christ, who has already completed the work of salvation.

THE LESSON APPLIED

The transition from the Sabbath to the Lord's Day reflects the movement from the shadows of the Old Covenant to the fulfillment found in the New Covenant. The Sabbath, while meaningful, was a sign pointing to Christ. The Lord's Day fulfills this, celebrating Jesus' victory and foreshadowing eternal rest in Him. It offers believers a time to honor God, find renewal, and live with the confidence that our ultimate rest is secure in Christ. This understanding transforms worship from obligation to joyful anticipation of all that God has prepared for His people.

The call to balance work and rest remains urgent in our overworked world. Observing the Lord's Day challenges believers to step back from constant activity and acknowledge that true peace and fulfillment come from God. Taking intentional time to pause is an act of faith, allowing God to restore and realign our hearts. Observing the Lord's Day also encourages us to embrace kindness and understanding within the church. We learn to respect different ways people express their devotion.

In today's divided culture, fostering harmony within the Body of Christ becomes a powerful testimony. We are reminded to focus on what unites us rather than allowing small differences to divide us. Finally, the Lord's Day serves as a reminder of hope and victory. In a world filled with worry and uncertainty, worship anchors us in Christ's triumph. Worship shifts our focus from life's pressures to the renewal and rest God offers through Jesus.

LET'S TALK ABOUT IT...

Discuss the following questions and visit www.rhboyd.com for more information.

How can you intentionally set aside time to rest and reconnect with God in a way that honors Him and strengthens your faith?

In what ways can you show grace and understanding toward others who express their devotion to God differently than you do?

Get Social

Share your views and tag us
@rhboydco and use #rhboydco

@rhboydco

Home Daily Devotional Readings
February 16–22, 2026

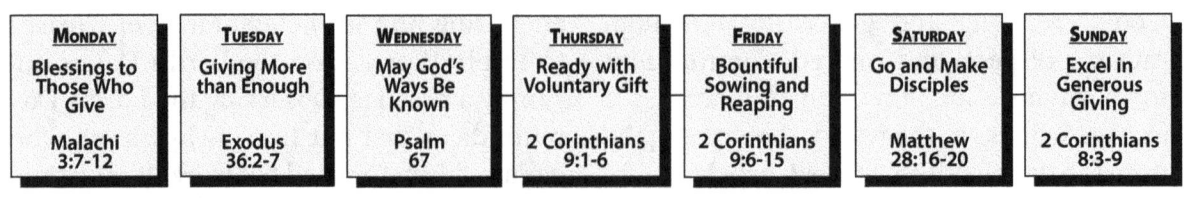

Monday	Tuesday	Wednesday	Thursday	Friday	Saturday	Sunday
Blessings to Those Who Give	Giving More than Enough	May God's Ways Be Known	Ready with Voluntary Gift	Bountiful Sowing and Reaping	Go and Make Disciples	Excel in Generous Giving
Malachi 3:7-12	Exodus 36:2-7	Psalm 67	2 Corinthians 9:1-6	2 Corinthians 9:6-15	Matthew 28:16-20	2 Corinthians 8:3-9

Lesson XII February 22, 2026

Stewardship and Mission

Adult Topic: Values, Money, and Experiences
Background Scripture: Gen. 12:1–3; Deut. 8:17–18; Jonah 3:1–10; Mal. 3:7–12; Matt. 28:18–20; Acts 1:6–8; 13:1–3; 26:12–20; Rom. 1:14–16; 1 Cor. 16:2; 2 Cor. 8:1–15; 9:1–15
Lesson Passage: Acts 1:6–8; 2 Corinthians 8:3–9

ACTS 1:6–8; 2 CORINTHIANS 8:3–9

KJV

WHEN they therefore were come together, they asked of him, saying, Lord, wilt thou at this time restore again the kingdom to Israel?

7 And he said unto them, It is not for you to know the times or the seasons, which the Father hath put in his own power.

8 But ye shall receive power, after that the Holy Ghost is come upon you: and ye shall be witnesses unto me both in Jerusalem, and in all Judaea, and in Samaria, and unto the uttermost part of the earth.

••• 2 Corinthians 8:3–9 •••

3 For to their power, I bear record, yea, and beyond their power they were willing of themselves;

4 Praying us with much intreaty that we would receive the gift, and take upon us the fellowship of the ministering to the saints.

5 And this they did, not as we hoped, but first gave their own selves to the Lord, and unto us by the will of God.

6 Insomuch that we desired Titus, that as he had begun, so he would also finish in you the same grace also.

7 Therefore, as ye abound in every thing, in faith, and utterance, and knowledge, and in all diligence, and in your love to us, see that ye abound in this grace also.

NRSVue

SO when they had come together, they asked him, "Lord, is this the time when you will restore the kingdom to Israel?"

7 He replied, "It is not for you to know the times or periods that the Father has set by his own authority.

8 But you will receive power when the Holy Spirit has come upon you, and you will be my witnesses in Jerusalem, in all Judea and Samaria, and to the ends of the earth."

••• 2 Corinthians 8:3–9 •••

3 For, as I can testify, they voluntarily gave according to their means and even beyond their means,

4 begging us earnestly for the favor of partnering in this ministry to the saints,

5 and not as we expected. Instead, they gave themselves first to the Lord and, by the will of God, to us,

6 so that we might urge Titus that, as he had already made a beginning, so he should also complete this generous undertaking among you.

7 Now as you excel in everything—in faith, in speech, in knowledge, in utmost eagerness, and in our love for you—so we want you to excel also in this generous undertaking.

MAIN THOUGHT: "For ye know the grace of our Lord Jesus Christ, that, though he was rich, yet for your sakes he became poor, that ye through his poverty might be rich." (2 Corinthians 8:9, KJV)

ACTS 1:6–8; 2 CORINTHIANS 8:3–9

KJV

8 I speak not by commandment, but by occasion of the forwardness of others, and to prove the sincerity of your love.

9 For ye know the grace of our Lord Jesus Christ, that, though he was rich, yet for your sakes he became poor, that ye through his poverty might be rich.

NRSVue

8 I do not say this as a command, but I am, by mentioning the eagerness of others, testing the genuineness of your love.

9 For you know the generous act of our Lord Jesus Christ, that though he was rich, yet for your sakes he became poor, so that by his poverty you might become rich.

LESSON SETTING

Time: AD 33 (Acts 1); AD 55–56 (2 Cor. 8)

Place: Jerusalem, on the Mount of Olives (Acts 1); Region of Greece, in a prominent city of Macedonia (2 Cor. 8)

Setting: The Acts of the Apostles is unique in the New Testament for its intent to record the events and growth of the early church. It is considered the second part of a two-volume collection, with the first book being the Gospel of Luke. The book of Acts marks the beginning of a transformative era in God's redemptive plan. No longer confined to the shadows of Old Testament rituals and laws, the people of God are introduced to a new covenant through Jesus Christ. Acts serves as the bridge between the promises made to Israel and their fulfillment in Christ, ushering in the age of the Holy Spirit and the global mission of the church. At this pivotal moment, the emerging church is learning to walk in the way of Christ. Jesus' ascension and His command in Acts 1:6–8 redefine the mission of God's people. The focus shifts from national restoration to spiritual renewal, a universal Kingdom no longer tied to Israel's political aspirations but open to all humanity. The early believers, initially uncertain and hesitant, are being taught to rely on the Holy Spirit for guidance, power, and boldness to witness. The Church is not merely an extension of Judaism but a new spiritual family practicing the teachings of Christ. Communities are gathering for prayer, worship, and acts of selfless giving, as seen in Paul's letters. Leaders such as Titus are emerging to encourage faithfulness and unity, ensuring the church's mission remains Christ-centered. This is a time of transformation as God's people step into their role as light and witnesses to the world.

LESSON OUTLINE

I. Christ-Centered Mission (Acts 1:6–8)

II. The Paradox of Generosity (2 Corinthians 8:3–9)

UNIFYING PRINCIPLE

We are deeply concerned with living the most fulfilling life possible. How can we live this life in a happy and gratifying way? Acts and 1 Corinthians describe principles for stewardship and mission that prioritize heaven's gains over earthly gains.

INTRODUCTION

Winning souls is not merely about persuasion but about embodying God's love through action and truth. It requires wisdom, patience, and a heart aligned with God's mission. With this understanding of the Bible's guiding principles, the accounts of Barabbas and certain temple leaders remind us that misdirected zeal and authority can lead to ruin rather than redemption. Their failures prompt us to ask: Are we pursuing the right mission with the right heart and methods?

Barabbas was a man of great zeal, committed to a mission he believed would free Israel from Roman occupation. His energy was boundless, and his actions demonstrated his willingness to sacrifice anything—except himself—for the cause. However, his methods, rooted in violence and rebellion, were ultimately misguided. He sought liberation through destruction and force, failing to see that true freedom comes not through the sword but through the cross (Luke 23:19).

Temple leaders, entrusted with Israel's spiritual well-being, were stewards of the Law and mediators of God's Word. Yet, as the Gospels reveal, some lost sight of God's mission. In their zeal to protect power and tradition, they rejected Jesus' authority and plotted His death (see e.g. Matt. 26:3–5; John 11:47–53). Scripture does not record what became of Barabbas after his release and there is no biblical record of whether the temple leaders ever repented of their actions. But we know what became of Jesus. He fulfilled His mission, not through insurrection or political maneuvering, but through sacrificial love. Through today's lesson, we learn God's Kingdom is not built on rebellion or manipulation but on surrender, generosity, and faithful stewardship.

EXPOSITION

I. Christ-Centered Mission (Acts 1:6–8)

The mission of the church, as outlined in Acts 1:6–8, is a call to line up with Christ's vision for the Kingdom of God as a mission marked by inclusivity, empowerment, and global outreach. In this passage, the apostles ask about restoring Israel's political kingdom, revealing their lingering misunderstanding of Jesus's purpose. In response, Jesus redirects their focus to a spiritual mission, empowered by the Holy Spirit and intended to reach the ends of the earth. This mission requires a shift from self-centered ambitions to a Christ-centered purpose, emphasizing service and stewardship.

The Laodicean church, described as "lukewarm" in Revelation 3:16, serves as a cautionary tale. Their material wealth gave them a false sense of security, but Jesus exposed their spiritual poverty. This complacency contrasts with the Macedonian churches, who, despite their poverty, gave sacrificially to advance the Gospel (2 Cor. 8:1–5). A Christ-centered mission is fueled by generosity and spiritual devotion, not material abundance. Additionally, a Christ-centered stewardship flows from a deep relationship with God.

Pastor and author Rick Warren's vision of a purpose-driven church closely reflects the mandate of Acts 1:8. He emphasizes the need to balance worship, fellowship, discipleship, ministry, and evangelism, warning that "A church that exists only for itself is a contradiction." This perspective underscores the need for churches to focus outwardly, engaging communities and extending the Gospel's reach to all people and nations. As Pastor Warren aptly states, "A great commitment to the Great

Commandment and the Great Commission will grow a great church." Similarly, Minister Oswald Chambers insightfully observed, "The church ceases to be a spiritual society when it is on the lookout for the development of its own organization."

These reflections challenge the Church to prioritize spiritual transformation over institutional preservation and to lean on a source beyond ourselves. The Church's mission relies on divine enablement rather than human effort or organizational power. Empowered by the Holy Spirit, we are called to witness boldly, give sacrificially, and serve humbly. By embracing the principles of Acts 1:6–8, the Church can embody the transformative power of the Gospel and faithfully advance God's Kingdom.

II. The Paradox of Generosity (2 Corinthians 8:3–9)

A paradox is a statement or concept that appears contradictory at first but reveals a deeper truth upon reflection. In the Christian faith, the paradox of generosity challenges conventional wisdom. While the world often equates gaining with keeping and hoarding, the teachings of Christ show that true abundance comes through giving. The more we pour out our time, resources, and love, the more we experience spiritual fulfillment, joy, and a deeper connection with God. This contrast between genuine and superficial giving sets the stage for understanding the deeper spiritual truth behind generosity.

In verse 9, Paul describes Jesus as the model of selflessness, who "though He was rich, yet for your sakes He became poor, so that by His poverty you might become rich." Jesus, in leaving the glory of heaven, took on the limitations and struggles of humanity to bring salvation to a broken world. His incarnation was not an act of necessity but one of grace and generosity, as He gave Himself completely for the sake of others. This act redefined richness, shifting it from material possession to spiritual abundance and eternal life.

The Corinthians are urged to reflect on this example as they participate in a collection for the believers in Jerusalem. Paul highlights the transformative power of grace within the Macedonians, whose actions demonstrate the essence of generosity despite their own trials. He explains that their giving is not motivated by external pressure but by their deep devotion to Christ. They give beyond their means because they have first offered themselves to the Lord, aligning their hearts with His mission. Their lives exemplify the truth that generosity flows naturally from a life fully surrendered to God.

Generosity, however, is not limited to financial contributions. It is a way of life that encompasses time, talents, and resources dedicated to God's purposes. This aspect of generosity was exemplified by Titus, for example. Titus, a key figure in guiding and inspiring the church of Corinth's giving efforts, was more than a facilitator—he embodied the grace he inspired, bridging the church to its mission. As Paul's trusted emissary, Titus helped ensure accountability while encouraging believers to embrace the spirit of giving. His role reminds us of the importance of leadership that fosters unity and spiritual growth within the church.

For Paul, the Corinthians' giving was not simply about meeting a need. It was an act of worship that reflected their gratitude for God's grace. Generosity aligns believers with God's mission, enabling us to participate in the advancement of His Kingdom. By setting aside resources for God's work, as Paul instructs in 1 Corinthians 16:2, believers demonstrate a heart reshaped by grace and a desire to serve others as Christ did. The paradox of generosity becomes a lens through which we view our role in God's mission. By giving of ourselves—whether through time, resources, or service—we align our hearts with God's will and become active participants in His work. In this way, we honor Christ's sacrifice.

THE LESSON APPLIED

Believers today are called to examine how our lives reflect Christ's mission and generosity in practical ways. Are we actively aligning our resources—time, talents, and finances—with God's purposes? For instance, stewardship begins in our local church, where we can invest in ministries that spread the Gospel, provide for the needy, and nurture spiritual growth. This lesson calls us to consider evaluating our personal spending and giving habits: Are they guided by a desire to advance God's Kingdom or are they driven by personal comfort and security?

Jesus' example calls us to sacrificial living—not by compulsion, but gratitude. Modern believers can follow this by embracing simplicity to create margin for generosity. For example, volunteering at a food bank, mentoring youth, or donating to missions are tangible ways to reflect God's heart for the world. Additionally, we can influence others by cultivating a culture of generosity in our families. Parents can teach children to set aside a portion of their allowance for giving, demonstrating that generosity is a response to God's grace.

LET'S TALK ABOUT IT...

Discuss the following questions and visit www.rhboyd.com for more information.

How does Jesus' example of becoming poor for our sake challenge our view of wealth and generosity?

What steps can you take to ensure that your generosity—whether in time, talents, or finances—aligns with God's mission?

Get Social

Share your views and tag us
@rhboydco and use #rhboydco

@rhboydco

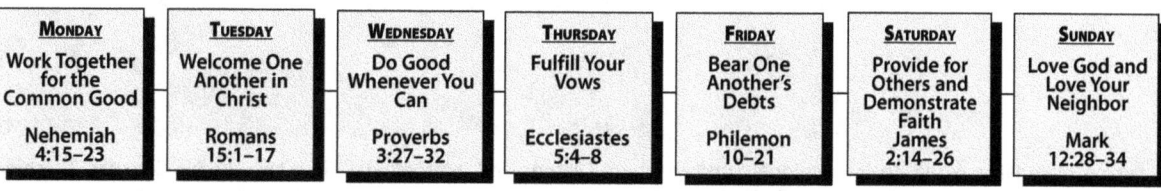

THIRD QUARTER

March
April
May

Lesson material is based on International Sunday School Lessons and International Bible Lessons for Christian Teaching, copyrighted by the International Council of Religious Education, and is used by its permission.

Lesson I March 1, 2026

Recognizing Our Debt to Others

Adult Topic: Love Acts
Background Scripture: Neh. 4:15–23; Mark 12:28–34; Rom. 15:1–7; Phil. 2:1–8; Col. 3:12; 4:1; James 2:14–17
Lesson Passage: Mark 12:28–34; James 2:14–17

MARK 12:28-34; JAMES 2:14-17

KJV

AND one of the scribes came, and having heard them reasoning together, and perceiving that he had answered them well, asked him, Which is the first commandment of all?

29 And Jesus answered him, The first of all the commandments is, Hear, O Israel; The Lord our God is one Lord:

30 And thou shalt love the Lord thy God with all thy heart, and with all thy soul, and with all thy mind, and with all thy strength: this is the first commandment.

31 And the second is like, namely this, Thou shalt love thy neighbour as thyself. There is none other commandment greater than these.

32 And the scribe said unto him, Well, Master, thou hast said the truth: for there is one God; and there is none other but he:

33 And to love him with all the heart, and with all the understanding, and with all the soul, and with all the strength, and to love his neighbour as himself, is more than all whole burnt offerings and sacrifices.

34 And when Jesus saw that he answered discreetly, he said unto him, Thou art not far from the kingdom of God. And no man after that durst ask him any question.

••• James 2:14–17 •••

14 What doth it profit, my brethren, though a man say he hath faith, and have not works? can faith save him?

15 If a brother or sister be naked, and destitute of daily food,

NRSVue

ONE of the scribes came near and heard them disputing with one another, and seeing that he answered them well he asked him, "Which commandment is the first of all?"

29 Jesus answered, "The first is, 'Hear, O Israel: the Lord our God, the Lord is one;

30 you shall love the Lord your God with all your heart and with all your soul and with all your mind and with all your strength.'

31 The second is this, 'You shall love your neighbor as yourself.' There is no other commandment greater than these."

32 Then the scribe said to him, "You are right, Teacher; you have truly said that 'he is one, and besides him there is no other';

33 and 'to love him with all the heart and with all the understanding and with all the strength' and 'to love one's neighbor as oneself'—this is much more important than all whole burnt offerings and sacrifices."

34 When Jesus saw that he answered wisely, he said to him, "You are not far from the kingdom of God." After that no one dared to ask him any question.

••• James 2:14–17 •••

14 What good is it, my brothers and sisters, if someone claims to have faith but does not have works? Surely that faith cannot save, can it?

15 If a brother or sister is naked and lacks daily food

MAIN THOUGHT: [The scribe said to Jesus,] ". . . 'to love [God] with all the heart, and with all the understanding, and with all the strength,' and 'to love one's neighbor as oneself,'—this is much more important than all whole burnt offerings and sacrifices." (Mark 12:33, NRSVue)

MARK 12:28-34; JAMES 2:14-17

KJV

16 And one of you say unto them, Depart in peace, be ye warmed and filled; notwithstanding ye give them not those things which are needful to the body; what doth it profit?
17 Even so faith, if it hath not works, is dead, being alone.

NRSVue

16 and one of you says to them, "Go in peace; keep warm and eat your fill," and yet you do not supply their bodily needs, what is the good of that?
17 So faith by itself, if it has no works, is dead.

LESSON SETTING

Time: AD 33
Place: Jerusalem, within the Temple courts
Setting: Mark 12:28-34 reveals a private conversation between Jesus and a scribe who, after witnessing Jesus' interaction with the religious leaders, was impressed with Him and genuinely wanted to talk (unlike the other religious leaders) about what he thought was the only thing that mattered in the faith.

LESSON OUTLINE

I. Which Commandment is the Greatest? (Mark 12:28-31)
II. Commendation for Commitment to the Command (Mark 12:32-34)
III. The Great Commandment and Works of Faith (James 2:14-17)

UNIFYING PRINCIPLE

We often have difficulties developing and maintaining healthy, wholesome relationships with one another. How can we build strong social bonds that sustain healthy relationships? Mark's Gospel points to Jesus' commands, which stress the love of God and neighbor, while James stresses how works are essential to healthy relationship.

INTRODUCTION

To devout Jews living in Jerusalem at the time of Jesus, the Law of Moses was as sacred as the Bible is to Christians today. Integral to their religious life, the Torah (another word for "law") consisted of a body of rules, regulations, and guidelines given by God to the Israelites through the mouth of Moses. These laws governed the moral conduct and social structure by which the Jewish people were to live their lives. For the Jewish leaders, who were the supposed "experts" in its interpretation and proper application, the Law was often the subject of great discussion, sharp disagreement, and intense debate. The question of the Law and its greatest precept sets the stage for our lesson.

It entails a chance encounter between a certain scribe and Jesus during the Passover festivals. The Gospel of Mark is the only Gospel that records this interaction (at least in this way). Its uniqueness suggests that such an encounter has a deeper significance that the author of the Gospel intended his readers to receive. Perhaps the writer wanted to contrast his actions with those of the Pharisees, Sadducees, and Herodians to show that not all religious leaders were opposed to Jesus and His teachings.

EXPOSITION

I. Which Commandment Is the Greatest? (Mark 12:28–31)

After Jesus challenges the Sadducees' ignorance of the Law and instead uses it to remind them that the Lord is the God of the living (v. 27), His response catches the attention of a certain scribe.

A "scribe" or lawyer was a member of the Jewish religious leadership, specifically trained in the interpretation and teaching of the Torah. Scribes were highly respected for their knowledge of the Scriptures and their ability to understand Jewish law. They often served as teachers, legal experts, and advisors within the community of believers.

Verse 28 begins with an unnamed scribe coming to Jesus and asking for His insight into what is believed to be a controversial issue among the leaders. "Which is the first commandment of all?" the scribe asks. In other words, "Which of the commandments is the most important?"

Because of the abundance of laws to be followed (613 to be exact: 248 requirements and 365 prohibitions), the religious leaders would rank them according to importance. They divided the commandments into "weightier" categories, which referred to those laws that required greater commitment, and "lighter" categories, those that required less. The scribe's question to Jesus was his attempt to solicit Jesus' opinion on the matter.

While it could be argued that he was sent by the other leaders to ask Jesus this question, the scribe was ultimately prompted to think and observe beyond any effort to "test" Jesus. But there is no indication that he was trying to do this in a way that would trap Jesus into saying something that could later be used against Him. The assumption is that he is asking Jesus in earnest and with a sincere approach to engage Him in theological discourse.

In response to the scribe's question in verse 28, Jesus quotes the Shema (pronounced SHE-MA) from Deuteronomy 6:4-5 in verse 29. His recitation of the Law includes a notable addition to the original wording of Deuteronomy 6. Along with the command to love God with all one's heart, soul, and strength, Jesus adds the phrase "... with all your mind..." to the list. This addition means believers should hold nothing back from devotion to the Lord God.

In Old Testament thought, the heart was analogous to the seat of human judgment. But by the time of Jesus, and with the influence of Greek culture, this idea evolved philosophically to more accurately reflect the complex factors involved in making appropriate decisions. Instead of "heart," the term "mind" was used to refer to our ability to exercise free will, and the term "heart" was designated to reflect one's deepest convictions and moral center.

To love God with all one's heart and mind, according to Jesus, is a choice that involves one's entire being. It is the choice to love God with all of our heart, through our faith; with all of our mind, through our understanding, which will ultimately be demonstrated with all of our strength, through our actions.

Unlike the heart and mind, loving God with one's whole soul is demonstrated by devotional exercises that honor Him. In addition to the heart and mind, 1st century thought considered the soul to be the emotional center of the self. This perspective emphasizes that the soul includes our deepest feelings, desires, and passions.

Loving God with our whole soul means that our emotional life is deeply intertwined with both the intellectual and spiritual life. It involves a heartfelt commitment that goes beyond logical reasoning or emotional affection; it is a deep, all-encompassing devotion.

Notice that the lawyer did not ask Jesus what the second greatest commandment was, but He gave it anyway in verse 30. Quoting from Leviticus 19:18, Jesus says, "...and the second...great commandment, like the first, is that...you shall love your neighbor as yourself.

This addition of Jesus may have caught the scribe's attention because it would have echoed the popular Talmudic statement made by the well-known Jewish sage and scholar of the time, Hillel the Elder.

It was said that when Hillel was challenged to teach the entire Torah while his listeners stood on one foot, he famously replied, "Whatever is hateful to you, do not do to your fellow man. This is the entire Torah, and the rest is commentary. Now go and study." From this statement alone, he has been credited with inventing the famous "Golden Rule" of doing unto others as you would have them do unto you.

While Jesus' interpretation of Leviticus is similar to Hillel's, it's not the same. Hillel exhorts his listeners to avoid doing to others what they would not want done to them. His wisdom stops short, however, at the negative implication of the statement (don't do what you don't want done to you). In contrast, Jesus' interpretation implicitly adds the imperative to do for others what one would want done for oneself. For Jesus, actively seeking the good of and for others elevates the moral standard and encourages compassion in the believer. His interpretation inspires followers to go beyond mere avoidance of harm and engage in acts of love and service.

In Leviticus 19:18, the term "neighbor" refers to fellow Israelites, but Jesus' definition of neighbor, according to Luke 10:25–27, extends the love command to all resident immigrants, including Gentiles, Samaritans, and even one's enemy.

Redefining the scope of "neighbor" to include everyone and how we should treat them is an essential factor in the second great commandment and how it links to the first. Our love for God is most evident in how we love our neighbor. We cannot separate the two.

Jesus concludes His answer in verse 31 by saying, "there is no greater commandment than these," reinforcing His opening statement in verse 29." Love for God and others requires whatever is necessary to show devotion. Of all the commands and prohibitions in the Mosaic Law, the only two that matter are love of the Lord and love of your neighbor. Love for God results in obeying the primary part of the Law that describes obligations to Him. Love for God resists idolatry and reserve heartfelt devotion solely for Him.

II. Commendation for Commitment to the Command (Mark 12:32–34)

Instead of resisting Jesus' explanation of the Law, the scribe affirms it with a response that indicates an appreciation for Jesus' theological insight. Like Jesus, the scribe understands the difference between the letter and spirit of the Law. The heart, not any rituals, is the center of God's will.

The scribe responds in three distinct parts (vv. 32–33). The first "...well said, Teacher..." should be taken at face value. Jesus previously answers the religious leaders "well" in verses 14, and 24. He also answers the scribe "well" which he (the scribe) deeply appreciates. Although he does not address Jesus as

"Teacher" at the beginning, he does in the end, which contrasts with the attitudes and actions of the other leaders.

The second part of the scribe's response "...You have spoken the truth, for there is one God and no other besides Him..." underscores his knowledge and conviction as an expert in the Law. This scribe already knew the answer to the question; his inquiry sought information instead of an exploration. However, Jesus' provides the scribe with inspiration, as evidenced by the third part of his response.

The scribe demonstrates his deepest insight by adding his own interpretation, He confirms for readers of this gospel that Jesus' teaching transcends the most entrenched prejudices and preconceptions of the religious leaders. To love God and to love one's neighbor "...is more than whole burnt offerings and sacrifices..."

The scribe recognizes that one pleases God by keeping these two all-encompassing commandments instead of offering sacrifices; and by using "all," he strongly emphasizes obedience.

For any religious leader who relies mainly upon traditions of his faith that focus on rules, regulations and rituals, it is striking that this scribe accepts this interpretation of the Law. It is possible that more leaders of Judaism in Jesus' day shared this view.

Moved by the scribe's discerning response, Jesus looks at him keenly and decides...that he answered wisely...in verse 34. He commends the scribe for his words and the conviction behind them.

This man favorably receives Jesus' teaching and character. In turn, Jesus says, "...you are not far from the kingdom of God." His commendation provokes the scribe to reflect further; while he was close to the kingdom of God, following and obeying Jesus would bring the scribe into it. He understands that it is readily available to him.

III. The Great Commandment and Works of Faith (James 2:14-17)

In addition to his admonition against showing partiality (2:1-13), the author of this letter warns believers against those who fail to put their faith into practice by caring for others. Rhetorically, he asks, "What good is it...if someone says he has faith...but does not have works?"

In the years of early Christianity, a contradiction between Paul, who says that one is saved by faith without works, and James, who says faith without works cannot save, existed. Interestingly, there is not a contradiction. Each belief asserts that one is saved by grace through faith; one evidences faith with corresponding actions.

James has a different purpose in writing about faith and works than Paul does. James' purpose is pastoral. He wants to admonish Christians that half-hearted faith is incomplete; that kind of faith is merely theoretical, It is not practical and cannot save.

James condemns such "faith" as useless intellectual assent to doctrines. He refutes the idea that salvation by faith is purely self-serving. Genuine faith requires commitment to others and leads to compassion for those in need.

In the early history of the Church, there were disengaged disciples who considered themselves religious (James 1:26). They lived like others in society but confessed Christ. James views this approach as a false faith.

In verse 15, the writer hypothetically illustrates the inadequacy of false faith. He asks, "what does it profit...a brother or sister...who...is naked and has no daily food...and is only offered well wishes and peaceful greetings?" This is analogous to faith without action, which the author describes as dead. Faith is a verb, not simply a feeling.

THE LESSON APPLIED

God wants disciples to love Him with their whole being. No matter how much each of us loves God, every believer has the ability to love Him better. Loving God better is a lifelong pursuit and the essence of Christian discipleship.

Church traditions maintain that going to church, reading the Bible, and saying prayers demonstrate our love for God. Sincerely practicing these disciplines, disciples discover myriad ways to show love for God, not the least of which is meeting the needs of others. Living to love God means love for our neighbor.

While our love for God is how we demonstrate our faithfulness to Him, it is also how we express our faith. Faith, like love, is a verb. These traits are displayed through our actions. As the saying goes, "Don't just talk about it. Be about it!" According to the book of James, faith without works is useless (James 2:17). This requirement inspires our loving works for God's Kingdom and our kindness toward others. Therefore, our commitment to God and our neighbor is the evidence of a living faith and the ultimate description of how true love manifests itself.

LET'S TALK ABOUT IT...

Discuss the following questions and visit www.rhboyd.com for more information.

Which command from God is most important for believers to follow... (hint: it's a 'trick' question) "...love God with all of our heart, mind, soul and strength?" or "...love our neighbor as ourselves?"

How does loving God, loving our neighbor, and practicing our faith complement each other?

Why is the great commandment to love God and our neighbor as ourselves the most difficult to practice?

How does religious tradition interfere with our commitment to demonstrating love for God and our neighbor?

Get Social

Share your views and tag us
@rhboydco and use #rhboydco

@rhboydco

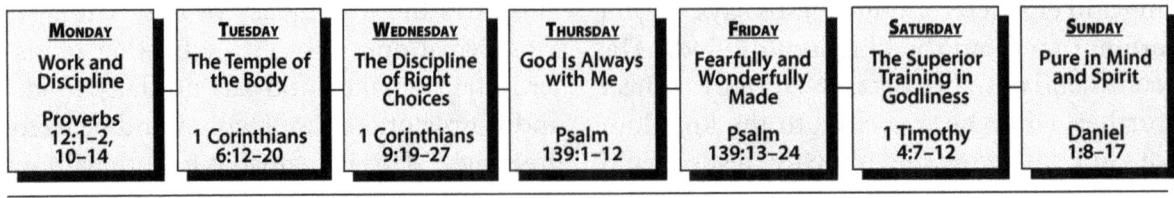

Lesson II — March 8, 2026

Keeping Fit for the Sake of Others

Adult Topic: Physical and Spiritual Fitness
Background Scripture: Daniel 1:8–20; 1 Corinthians 9:19–27; 1 Timothy 4:7–12; 2 Timothy 2:1–5
Lesson Passage: Daniel 1:8–17; 1 Timothy 4:7–8

DANIEL 1:8–17; 1 TIMOTHY 4:7–8

KJV

BUT Daniel purposed in his heart that he would not defile himself with the portion of the king's meat, nor with the wine which he drank: therefore he requested of the prince of the eunuchs that he might not defile himself.

9 Now God had brought Daniel into favour and tender love with the prince of the eunuchs.

10 And the prince of the eunuchs said unto Daniel, I fear my lord the king, who hath appointed your meat and your drink: for why should he see your faces worse liking than the children which are of your sort? then shall ye make me endanger my head to the king.

11 Then said Daniel to Melzar, whom the prince of the eunuchs had set over Daniel, Hananiah, Mishael, and Azariah,

12 Prove thy servants, I beseech thee, ten days; and let them give us pulse to eat, and water to drink.

13 Then let our countenances be looked upon before thee, and the countenance of the children that eat of the portion of the king's meat: and as thou seest, deal with thy servants.

14 So he consented to them in this matter, and proved them ten days.

15 And at the end of ten days their countenances appeared fairer and fatter in flesh than all the children which did eat the portion of the king's meat.

16 Thus Melzar took away the portion of their meat, and the wine that they should drink; and gave them pulse.

NRSVue

BUT Daniel resolved that he would not defile himself with the royal rations of food and wine, so he asked the palace master to allow him not to defile himself.

9 Now God granted Daniel favor and compassion from the palace master.

10 The palace master said to Daniel, "I am afraid of my lord the king; he has appointed your food and your drink. If he should see you in poorer condition than the other young men of your age, you would endanger my head with the king."

11 Then Daniel asked the guard whom the palace master had appointed over Daniel, Hananiah, Mishael, and Azariah:

12 "Please test your servants for ten days. Let us be given vegetables to eat and water to drink.

13 You can then compare our appearance with the appearance of the young men who eat the royal rations and deal with your servants according to what you observe."

14 So he agreed to this proposal and tested them for ten days.

15 At the end of ten days it was observed that they appeared better and fatter than all the young men who had been eating the royal rations.

16 So the guard continued to withdraw their royal rations and the wine they were to drink and gave them vegetables.

MAIN THOUGHT: Train yourself in godliness, for, while physical training is of some value, godliness is valuable in every way, holding promise for both the present life and the life to come. (1 Timothy 4:7–8, NRSVue)

DANIEL 1:8–17; 1 TIMOTHY 4:7–8

KJV

17 As for these four children, God gave them knowledge and skill in all learning and wisdom: and Daniel had understanding in all visions and dreams.

••• 1 Timothy 4:7–8 •••

7 But refuse profane and old wives' fables, and exercise thyself rather unto godliness.

8 For bodily exercise profiteth little: but godliness is profitable unto all things, having promise of the life that now is, and of that which is to come.

NRSVue

17 To these four young men God gave knowledge and skill in every aspect of literature and wisdom; Daniel also had insight into all visions and dreams.

••• 1 Timothy 4:7–8 •••

7 Have nothing to do with profane and foolish tales. Train yourself in godliness,

8 for, while physical training is of some value, godliness is valuable in every way, holding promise for both the present life and the life to come.

LESSON SETTING

Time: Spring (May–June) 605 BC
Place: Babylon
Setting: In 587 BC, Nebuchadnezzar, king of the Babylonian Empire, destroyed the Kingdom of Judah and its capital, Jerusalem. The Jews subsequently referred to him not only as the greatest enemy they had ever faced, but also as the "destroyer of nations." The destruction of Jerusalem led to the infamous "Babylonian Captivity," as the populations of the conquered cities and people from the surrounding areas were deported to Babylon. Upon arrival, the Jewish captives were treated with extreme cruelty; some were used as spectacles of humiliation, while others were slaughtered for entertainment. A few, however, were culturally indoctrinated to assimilate and serve the conquering king and kingdom. Daniel, Mishael, Hananiah, and Azariah, also known, respectively, as Belteshazzar, Shadrach, Meshach, and Abed-Nego, respectively, were some of the young captive Jewish men chosen by the king for this purpose. These three young men exemplify the biblical principle of prioritizing obedience to God over human authority. Their stories encourage believers to stand firm in their convictions, demonstrate courage in the face of opposition, and trust in God's sovereignty and deliverance.

LESSON OUTLINE

I. Rejecting the King's Delicacies for "The King's" Delight (Daniel 1:8–14)
II. Spiritual Sustenance Over Physical Food (Daniel 1:15–17)
III. The Key to Spiritual Fitness (1 Timothy 4:7–8

UNIFYING PRINCIPLE

We desire good health in mind, body, and spirit. What enables us to keep physically and spiritually fit? The Book of Daniel and Paul's First Letter to Timothy stress the significance of striving for physical and spiritual fitness; they please God and benefit others.

INTRODUCTION

During the Neo–Babylonian Era (605–562 BC), the conqueror went to great lengths to assimilate any conquered people into his kingdom. Victory resulted in relocating them to different regions, imposing the conqueror's language, culture and religious practices and integrating them into governmental and military systems. The king hoped to minimize resistance, gain loyalty, and strengthen the social cohesion of the empire. This strategy facilitated control over vast territories and promoted cultural exchange and economic integration thereby contributing to the empire's prosperity and stability. Babylon's invasion of Judah and subsequent destruction of Jerusalem occurred in this way.

The king specially chose Daniel and his three teenage companions, Hananiah, Mishael, and Azariah, out of the captives of Judah. Their families enjoyed high social standing. They were physically fit and highly intelligent, thus meeting the criteria that Nebuchadnezzar wanted in people who would serve in his kingdom.

The king appointed Ashpenaz, the chief officer of the eunuchs, to ensure their indoctrination progressed smoothly. He oversaw their education Babylonian language and literature. Ashpenaz, responsible for their training and welfare, provided them with royal food and wine for three years. This rigorous process sought to fully integrate them as loyal and capable servants of the Babylonian Empire.

EXPOSITION

I. Rejecting the King's Delicacies for "The King's" Delight (Daniel 1:8–14)

The eighth verse shows Daniel and his friends' determination that they would not defile themselves with any of the king's food, delicacies or wine. Their resistance to this carefully curated dietary plan undermined the Babylonian acculturation process.

There is no record of the young men protesting compliance with the assimilation program. They did not reject the Babylonian names they were given. Daniel was renamed "Belteshazzar," Hananiah was renamed Shadrach, Mishael was renamed Meshach, and Azariah was renamed Abed–Nego.

Also, they did not refuse the formal training they received. They studied mathematics, astronomy and government besides languages and literature. What compels them to draw a line in the sand of their conscience with dietary concerns?

Consider two factors in answering this question. First, because of improper preparation including failure to drain blood, the Law of Moses made many of the foods eaten at the Babylonian court (e.g., pork and horse meat) unclean. Eating such foods would have been a sin for a practicing Jew. It would have made an individual ceremonially unclean.

Second, occasionally, the meat and wine would have been sacrificed to Babylonian gods with idolatrous worship, making them undesirable. Although Jewish law allowed wine, Daniel's reluctance to drink it may be explained by its use as a libation in pagan rituals.

To partake of this food would have been an indirect act of worship of Babylonian deities. Daniel, Mishael, Hananiah, and Azariah's refusal to eat the king's food was based on their deep religious conviction to remain faithful to their God.

To avoid defilement, Daniel asked Ashpenaz if he could receive a substitute diet. This simple request required Daniel to be courteous, tactful, and courageous. Asking for a different meal could have been seen as an insult to the king and an act of direct defiance of Nebuchadnezzar's orders. Refusing to eat could provoke social pressure from Daniel's peers. Everyone else complied, but Daniel and his friends set themselves apart.

Judah was nine hundred miles away; their people would never know if they were keeping God's laws. Naturally, they could argue that since God had not protected them from captivity, they did not need to obey His commands. They may have become bitter against God. While these factors might have caused others to compromise, Daniel and his friends remained faithful to their God.

What may have sustained Daniel's and the three other young men's faithful resolve is their assurance that His faithfulness yielded the favor and goodwill of the chief of the eunuchs. Ashpenaz did not believe in Yahweh but Daniel's commitment to his God impressed him. Ashpenaz genuinely admired these Jewish captives which assured their survival and advancement.

Ashpenaz liked and respected the young men yet he feared the king more. The king specifically determined the food and drink for his special captives. Ashpenaz realized granting Daniel's request for an alternative meal plan could cost his job and also his head. He feared that if Daniel and his friends rebuffed the king's fine food, they would become unhealthy. Their malnourished condition would evidence their defiance and set them apart from other captives.

Recognizing Ashpenaz's dilemma regarding his food request, Daniel turns his proposal to the steward directly responsible for meals. He asks simply for vegetables to eat and water to drink in place of the king's food. After ten days, he adds, "let our appearance be examined before you in comparison with the appearance of the young men who ate the portion of the king's delicacies. If, after the trial, their appearance is healthy, they will be allowed to continue their diet." Ten days sufficed to see the effects. The steward agreed and conducted the experiment.

The substitute meal plan consisted of a food called "pulse" with water. Pulse was any kind of food that grows from seed. It included any mixture of vegetables, fruits, grains, peas, lentils, beans, and non-grain bread.

II. Spiritual Sustenance Over Physical Food (Daniel 1:15–17)

After the ten-day trial, Daniel and his friends looked better and healthier than any of the young men who ate the rich food and drink from the king's delicacies. Their appearance proved the superiority of their diet but also reflected God's favor upon them and their faithfulness to Him. Vindicated by God's grace, these young men continued to receive the food they requested from the steward.

God rewarded the young men's faithful discipline. In time, God gave them knowledge and skill in literature and wisdom. Each of them received the gift of keen intellectual ability. Additionally, Daniel acquired gifts that the others did not have. He received understanding of visions and dreams. That divine gift would greatly benefit King Nebuchadnezzar. Dreams and their interpretation were a very important part of Babylonian wisdom. They firmly believed that God spoke to people through them. Daniel's gifts, as detailed in the seventeenth verse, prepares the reader for visions and dreams to follow and hints towards his eventual elevation in Babylon.

II. The Key to Spiritual Fitness (1 Timothy 4:7–8)

The mentor–mentee relationship between the Apostle Paul and Timothy surpassed mere instruction and guidance. It was deeply personal, loving, and nurturing, similar to that of a father and son. Paul valued Timothy's potential and provided spiritual guidance, emotional support and encouragement. He describes Timothy as his "true son in the faith" underscoring the loving and familial bond they shared.

Filled with fatherly advice, Paul's letters to Timothy urge him to remain steadfast in his faith, to preach the Word with boldness and to live with integrity and godliness. He encourages Timothy to resist anyone who looks down on him because of his youth; instead set an example for other believers in speech, conduct, love, faith, and purity.

Paul's mentoring program for Timothy includes entrusting him with important responsibilities, sending him to various churches to represent Paul and resolving important issues within the faith community.

The fourth chapter establishes the methodology Timothy uses to instruct the brethren in righteousness; through the faith and good doctrine he received previously.

In order for Timothy to maintain integrity while teaching the faith, Paul warns him to reject profane and old wives' fables. Paul describes popular heretical teachings in the Greco–Roman world of religious thought this way. They consisted of mythological stories that included gods and goddesses with human–like flaws and immoral behavior; superstitions based on fear and ignorance such as omens, charms and rituals to minimize evil. Paul also warned Timothy to avoid false doctrines. These teachings included Gnosticism which mixed Christian ideas with speculative thinking that suggested salvation comes through the acquisition of hidden and exclusive knowledge and Docetism, the belief that Jesus Christ did not have a real physical body but only appeared to have one, implying that the divine Christ could not have truly become flesh.

Entertaining these false teachings would distract Timothy from his primary goal of spreading the gospel of truth. Paul's command to "reject" was intentionally strong; "have nothing to do with" these ungodly ideas" is a more accurate translation. Paul does not want Timothy to occupy his time and thoughts with profane and irrational gossip that creates confusion.

To protect Timothy from the methods and manipulation of false teachers, Paul urges him to pursue godliness.

Borrowing a metaphor from athletics, he exhorts Timothy not to waste time on empty ideas but to focus on vigorous training as he prepares for God's highest purpose.

As in 1 Corinthians 9:19–27, Paul, in the eighth verse, compares the discipline of believers to the athletic contests of the Isthmian Games. The faithful believer and the athlete need practice and training to be effective. However, bodily exercise profits very little while godliness is profitable for all things. Paul recommends that Timothy and his readers focus and train for a godly life rather than emphasize bodily exercise.

Godliness builds a strong resolve within all components of human consciousness including the body.

Godliness involves living under the Lordship of Christ. Its benefits far surpass those of physical training. Bodily exercise offers temporary advantages that one can only experience in this life. Godliness impacts every aspect of life, earthly and eternally. Paul emphasizes spiritual discipline yields lasting rewards and shapes one's character and relationship with God. By prioritizing godliness, believers invest in their spiritual well-being which holds promise in this life and the one to come.

Timothy had demonstrated a tendency toward outward self-discipline, which is why Paul encourages him to cultivate a life of faith and devotion. The lifelong pursuit of godliness brings extensive and lasting benefits. These benefits are not earned solely by living a godly lifestyle. They are already provided by God's grace through Christ.

THE LESSON APPLIED

Physical fitness and spiritual strength are different measures of health. As we age, our physical bodies decline regardless of our level of physical activity and the nutritious content of our diet. Conversely, constant practice of spiritual disciplines only serve to strengthen our minds, hearts and characters over a lifetime. They do not diminish over time.

The human spirit is not subject to the same limitations as the human body. Spiritual practices build resilience, wisdom, and inner peace that sustain us through life's challenges. Through prayer, Bible study and consistent practice of our faith, we continually deepen our relationship with God.

Unlike physical fitness, which peaks at a certain stage of life and then slowly declines as human beings age, spiritual growth continues throughout our lives. It gives us a sense of purpose that transcends the physical realm.

LET'S TALK ABOUT IT...

Discuss the following questions and visit www.rhboyd.com for more information.

What guarantees Daniel, Mishael, Hananiah, and Azariah's good health while being held captive in Babylon?

Should physical fitness matter in comparison to spiritual strength?

What does spiritual fitness involve?

How does Paul encourage Timothy to become spiritually fit?

Get Social

Share your views and tag us
@rhboydco and use #rhboydco

@rhboydco

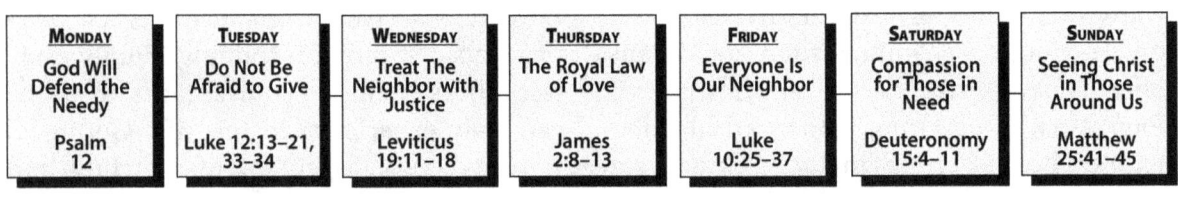

Lesson III   **March 15, 2026**

Helping Neighbors in Need

Adult Topic: Giving Generously
Background Scripture: Deut. 15:1–11; Matthew 25:31–46; Luke 10:25–37; James 1:27; 2:14–17
Lesson Passage: Deut. 15:4–11; Matt. 25:42–45

DEUTERONOMY 15:4–11; MATTHEW 25:42–45

KJV

SAVE when there shall be no poor among you; for the Lord shall greatly bless thee in the land which the Lord thy God giveth thee for an inheritance to possess it:

5 Only if thou carefully hearken unto the voice of the Lord thy God, to observe to do all these commandments which I command thee this day.

6 For the Lord thy God blesseth thee, as he promised thee: and thou shalt lend unto many nations, but thou shalt not borrow; and thou shalt reign over many nations, but they shall not reign over thee.

7 If there be among you a poor man of one of thy brethren within any of thy gates in thy land which the Lord thy God giveth thee, thou shalt not harden thine heart, nor shut thine hand from thy poor brother:

8 But thou shalt open thine hand wide unto him, and shalt surely lend him sufficient for his need, in that which he wanteth.

9 Beware that there be not a thought in thy wicked heart, saying, The seventh year, the year of release, is at hand; and thine eye be evil against thy poor brother, and thou givest him nought; and he cry unto the Lord against thee, and it be sin unto thee.

10 Thou shalt surely give him, and thine heart shall not be grieved when thou givest unto him: because that for this thing the Lord thy God shall bless thee in all thy works, and in all that thou puttest thine hand unto.

NRSVue

THERE will, however, be no one in need among you, because the Lord is sure to bless you in the land that the Lord your God is giving you as a possession to occupy,

5 if only you will obey the Lord your God by diligently observing this entire commandment that I command you today.

6 When the Lord your God has blessed you, as he promised you, you will lend to many nations, but you will not borrow; you will rule over many nations, but they will not rule over you.

7 "If there is among you anyone in need, a member of your community in any of your towns within the land that the Lord your God is giving you, do not be hard-hearted or tight-fisted toward your needy neighbor.

8 You should rather open your hand, willingly lending enough to meet the need, whatever it may be.

9 Be careful that you do not entertain a mean thought, thinking, 'The seventh year, the year of remission, is near,' and therefore view your needy neighbor with hostility and give nothing; your neighbor might cry to the Lord against you, and you would incur guilt.

10 Give liberally and be ungrudging when you do so, for on this account the Lord your God will bless you in all your work and in all that you undertake.

MAIN THOUGHT: Since there will never cease to be some in need on the earth, I therefore command you, "Open your hand to the poor and needy neighbor in your land." (Deuteronomy 15:11, NRSVue)

DEUTERONOMY 15:4–11; MATTHEW 25:42–45

KJV

11 For the poor shall never cease out of the land: therefore I command thee, saying, Thou shalt open thine hand wide unto thy brother, to thy poor, and to thy needy, in thy land.

••• Matthew 25:42–45 •••

42 For I was an hungred, and ye gave me no meat: I was thirsty, and ye gave me no drink:
43 I was a stranger, and ye took me not in: naked, and ye clothed me not: sick, and in prison, and ye visited me not.
44 Then shall they also answer him, saying, Lord, when saw we thee an hungred, or athirst, or a stranger, or naked, or sick, or in prison, and did not minister unto thee?
45 Then shall he answer them, saying, Verily I say unto you, Inasmuch as ye did it not to one of the least of these, ye did it not to me.

NRSVue

11 Since there will never cease to be some in need on the earth, I therefore command you, 'Open your hand to the poor and needy neighbor in your land.'

••• Matthew 25:42–45 •••

42 for I was hungry and you gave me no food, I was thirsty and you gave me nothing to drink,
43 I was a stranger and you did not welcome me, naked and you did not give me clothing, sick and in prison and you did not visit me.'
44 Then they also will answer, 'Lord, when was it that we saw you hungry or thirsty or a stranger or naked or sick or in prison and did not take care of you?'
45 Then he will answer them, 'Truly I tell you, just as you did not do it to one of the least of these, you did not do it to me.'

LESSON SETTING

Time: Late 13th Century BC
Place: Plains of Moab
Setting: Deuteronomy 15:4–11 is part of Moses' final discourses to the Israelites in preparation for entering the Promised Land. The plains of Moab, east of the Jordan River, near the northeastern edge of the Dead Sea, served as a staging area after their forty-year journey in the wilderness. The occasion is Moses' reiteration of the Laws and Commandments given by God to guide the Israelites in their new life in Canaan. Matthew 25:42–45 is from the Sermon on the Mount (Olivet Discourse), which takes place just before Jesus' arrest and Crucifixion.

LESSON OUTLINE

I. The Blessings of an Obedient Nation (Deuteronomy 15:4–6)
II. The Blessings of a Generous People (Deuteronomy 15:7–11)
III. The Judgment of the Goats (Matthew 25:42–45)

UNIFYING PRINCIPLE

We sometimes have doubts about helping those who turn to us for assistance. What determines our willingness and standards for helping others? The Deuteronomy passage and verses from Matthew 25 reveal God's command to give generously to needy people.

INTRODUCTION

Deuteronomy 15:4–11 and Matthew 25:42–45 emphasize the necessity of giving generously and caring for people in need. These passages highlight ethical and moral responsibilities for believers as they uplift marginalized and vulnerable communities.

Deuteronomy 15:4–11 addresses the Year of Release, a practice of forgiving debts every seven years to prevent long-term poverty and economic disparity. Moses declares that there should be no poor among the Israelites if they obey God's commands. He exhorts them to be gracious and generous especially towards their fellow Israelites who are in need. This practice reflects God's concern for social justice and economic fairness.

As Jesus speaks about the final judgment in Matthew 25:42–45, He condemns people who fail to show compassion toward needy persons. He underscores the importance of compassionate action as well as social justice advocacy.

Together, these passages call believers to a life of generosity and compassion, emphasizing that giving generously is a fundamental aspect of faith and a reflection of God's love and justice.

EXPOSITION

I. The Blessings of an Obedient Nation (Deuteronomy 15:4–6)

Deuteronomy 15 begins with the introduction of the Year of Release. Moses instituted this event to occur every seven years wherein debts were to be forgiven and those who had fallen into economic distress were given a fresh start.

This practice promoted social justice and economic fairness by preventing accumulation of burdensome debt and ensuring poverty did not persist among the Israelites.

Moses posits that there should not be any poverty in a land as rich as the one the Lord was giving them. God's covenant with His people enables them to live under His blessing which includes generous provision for daily necessities. Ideally, because poverty is non-existent, the need to borrow does not exist. Simply, Moses says, "The Lord will bless to the end, so that there will be no poor among you."

The total lack of poverty was an ideal and not the reality. Arguably, failure to obey God's commands creates a tension that allows two different economic states: poverty or abundance. Obedience is indicative of what could be a reality if the people carried out God's commands and receive His abundance.

Full compliance with covenant requirements was prerequisite for Israel's prosperity in the land. "They are to carefully obey the voice of the LORD."

This demand recurs throughout the book of Deuteronomy. Only when Israel fully obeys God will they receive His blessing. This call to obedience is the grateful response of a saved people whose greatest desire is to please their covenant God. Their strict observance of His commandments is the key to securing and maintaining God's promises. Obedience results in general economic well-being.

The sixth verse focuses on God's blessings as a result of obedience. Moses announces, "For the LORD your God will bless you just as He promised." The prevailing concept of blessing includes material prosperity, fertility, and success in various endeavors. These ancient patriarchal promises would become the means of blessing the whole world.

An additional result of obedience to God would lead to international prominence.

Israel will lend to many nations and not borrow; she will reign over many nations but none will reign over her.

II. The Blessings of a Generous People (Deuteronomy 15:7-11)

Having considered the theoretical possibility of avoiding poverty, Moses shifts to its practical reality. In these verses, he acknowledges realistic conditions and instructs more affluent persons in society in dealing with poor people.

How does Israel demonstrate gratitude for God's generosity? How do they express thanksgiving for His grace in the land where they will live? They repay that grace by helping the poor among them. Moses warns them against a hardened heart that shuts their hands to poor people.

A "hard heart" and a "closed hand" indicate apathy and insensitivity toward the plight of persons in need. Moses' commandment primarily addresses this common attitude of wealthy Israelites. It seems incongruent that those who have much would be so dismissive of those who have very little. However, the disregard for those living in poverty persists to this day.

The eighth verse reflects they were to open their hands wide and willingly to lend sufficiently to the needy, whatever he needs. The presence of poor people demands an attitude toward them of gentleness of heart and openness of hand. Moses exhorts the people to adopt a spirit of compassionate generosity.

A hypothetical scenario of a brother who needs a loan as the Sabbatical year (year of release) is near tests commitment to this principle. Fearing failure to receive full repayment, people might rebuff loans as the Sabbatical year approaches. Moses characterizes this act as evil because it leaves the needy unsatisfied. Thus, he must cry out to the Lord against his transgressor. The purpose of the loan to a fellow Israelite was not a return on investment but to provide generously for people in need.

If Israel gave generously, she would be generously blessed and equally experience success in everything. The loans were more like gifts of charity. Senseless from an economic perspective, this practice was fundamental from a covenantal perspective. Essentially, Israel trusts and relies upon God's provision.

The eleventh verse seems to contradict the whole passage. The poor never cease though eradicating poverty is possible through God's desire and Israel's obedience. Israel's inability to obey the Law explains this contradiction. Therefore, they would always have the poor among them.

In Deuteronomy, the writer often classifies the poor as widows and orphans (14:29, etc.). These people, through no fault of their own, lost provision and protection of a husband or father resulting from disease, accident or war. The dispossessed, people without landed property, live in similar social situations as widows and orphans.

Because the poor will be with Israel always, Moses tells them, "You shall open your hand wide to your brother, to your poor and your needy."

This passage references human anatomy especially eyes, hands, and the heart. Israel's response to poverty was to be holistic, encompassing her intentions and actions. Open-handed generosity could only come from a compassionate heart. Selflessness can only come from a willing and obedient heart committed to loving God. Of course, reluctant obedience could provide for the poor but an unwilling heart would ultimately degrade the recipient.

III. The Judgment of the Goats (Matthew 25:42–45)

In Matthew 25:31–40 Jesus teaches on the final judgment. Set within the Olivet Discourse which Jesus delivers on the Mount of Olives shortly before His arrest and crucifixion, He emphasizes the importance of compassionate action and ethical responsibility for believers.

In the final judgment, the Son of Man will come in His glory with all the angels and sit on a throne where all nations of the earth gather before Him. He will separate people into two groups like a shepherd separates sheep from goats. Sheep and goats intermingled freely and often looked quite similar, at least from a distance.

The wool of the sheep made them more valuable than the goats. Naturally, Jesus chooses the sheep to represent the righteous who are blessed by God and will inherit His Kingdom. He places them on His right side, the place of honor. He puts the goats who represent the unrighteous on His left side, the place of disgrace.

Jesus blesses the sheep for their good behavior. They care for Christ by feeding the hungry, giving drink to the thirsty, clothing the naked, showing hospitality to the stranger, and visiting the sick and imprisoned. They did these acts of kindness without seeking reward or acknowledgment for their deeds. As they perform these acts of kindness for their brothers and sisters, they give this service to Jesus Himself.

The focus then shifts to the judgment of the unrighteous. Jesus condemns them to eternal punishment for their lack of regard for the poor and vulnerable among them. The goats live as the symmetrical antithesis to the character of the sheep. The sheep are invited to come inherit the Kingdom that had been prepared for them. Conversely, the goats are banished from the King's presence and favor. The sheep receive eternal life while the goats descend to eternal damnation.

The sin of neglect explains their judgment. Jesus accuses the unrighteous of failing to act with compassion when He was in need. The list of needy conditions they failed to meet is not exhaustive but representative of numerous needs the poor have. Each need is central to survival and quality of life.

The unrighteous goats feel surprised at the King's accusation of neglecting to care for Him. To resolve their confusion, they ask, "Lord, when did we see You hungry or thirsty or a stranger or naked or sick or in prison, and did not minister to You?"

The goats' surprise suggests that they were focused on their own concerns rather than the needs of others. Their self–centeredness prevented them from seeing opportunities to serve marginalized and vulnerable people.

They may have misunderstood what it means to be righteous. They may have believed that righteousness equated with religious rituals and personal piety instead of compassion and social justice.

Regardless of the reason for their neglect, Jesus still condemns it. In the solemn language of the fortieth verse, He declares, "inasmuch as you did not do it to one of the least of these, you did not do it to Me." Their neglect of needy disciples equals neglecting Him.

By identifying Himself with the "least of these," Jesus stresses that caring for people in need partially defines His person and mission. It emphasizes the intrinsic worth and dignity of every person, especially those whom society marginalizes. With a broader perspective, it calls for a universal ethic of compassion and justice; urging believers to see Christ in vulnerable people and to respond with love and service.

Jesus offers the illustration of the Judgment Day to inspire believers to prepare. They properly prepare living in compassion and service. Embodying these values, believers not only prepare for the final judgment but also create a more just and compassionate world, reflecting the love and grace of God in their daily lives.

THE LESSON APPLIED

It is unfortunate that many Christians limit acts of generosity to monetary gifts. While recipients respect and appreciate such kindness, the giver must be careful about underlying motives for acts of generosity. There are people who give money to avoid dirtying their hands and having to do anything else.

More is needed by those who have resources to give. God gives all of us abilities, endowments and graces that can only emerge through a willingness to give.

As followers of Christ, we must consider the call from God to give generously of our time, talents, presence, and even our money.

LET'S TALK ABOUT IT...

Discuss the following questions and visit www.rhboyd.com for more information.

How does Deuteronomy 15:4-11 emphasize the importance of being open-handed and generous towards those in need within a community?

In what ways does the Year of Release reflect God's concern for social justice and economic fairness? How does it compare to our current economic practices?

How does Jesus identify Himself with the marginalized and vulnerable, and what does this imply about our responsibility to give generously?

How does the failure to care for the needy, impact our relationship with Christ and our standing in the final judgment?

How can we cultivate a heart of generosity and compassion in our daily lives and communities?

Get Social
Share your views and tag us
@rhboydco and use #rhboydco

@rhboydco

Home Daily Devotional Readings
March 16–22, 2026

Monday	Tuesday	Wednesday	Thursday	Friday	Saturday	Sunday
Souls Bound Together	Abide in God's Love	Loving God and Each Other	All Peoples Will Worship God	Living Together in Unity	Children of God through Faith	God Accepts Us All
1 Samuel 18:1-5	1 John 4:7-16	1 John 4:17-21	Isaiah 56:3-8	Psalm 133-134	Galatians 3:25-29	Acts 10:9-15, 30-35

Lesson IV | March 22, 2026

All Are One in Christ

Adult Topic: Putting an End to Prejudice and Discrimination
Background Scripture: Ruth 1:1–18; John 4:5–10; Acts 10:1–11:18; Rom. 1:14; Gal. 3:28–29
Lesson Passage: Acts 10:9–15, 30–35; Gal. 3:28–29

ACTS 10:9-15, 30-35; GALATIANS 3:28-29

KJV

ON the morrow, as they went on their journey, and drew nigh unto the city, Peter went up upon the housetop to pray about the sixth hour:
10 And he became very hungry, and would have eaten: but while they made ready, he fell into a trance,
11 And saw heaven opened, and a certain vessel descending upon him, as it had been a great sheet knit at the four corners, and let down to the earth:
12 Wherein were all manner of fourfooted beasts of the earth, and wild beasts, and creeping things, and fowls of the air.
13 And there came a voice to him, Rise, Peter; kill, and eat.
14 But Peter said, Not so, Lord; for I have never eaten any thing that is common or unclean.
15 And the voice spake unto him again the second time, What God hath cleansed, that call not thou common.

••• 30-35 •••

30 And Cornelius said, Four days ago I was fasting until this hour; and at the ninth hour I prayed in my house, and, behold, a man stood before me in bright clothing,
31 And said, Cornelius, thy prayer is heard, and thine alms are had in remembrance in the sight of God.
32 Send therefore to Joppa, and call hither Simon, whose surname is Peter; he is lodged in the house of one Simon a tanner by the sea side: who, when he cometh, shall speak unto thee.

NRSVue

ABOUT noon the next day, as they were on their journey and approaching the city, Peter went up on the roof to pray.
10 He became hungry and wanted something to eat, and while it was being prepared he fell into a trance.
11 He saw the heaven opened and something like a large sheet coming down, being lowered to the ground by its four corners.
12 In it were all kinds of four-footed creatures and reptiles and birds of the air.
13 Then he heard a voice saying, "Get up, Peter; kill and eat."
14 But Peter said, "By no means, Lord, for I have never eaten anything that is profane or unclean."
15 The voice said to him again, a second time, "What God has made clean, you must not call profane."

••• 30-35 •••

30 Cornelius replied, "Four days ago at this very hour, at three o'clock, I was praying in my house when suddenly a man in dazzling clothes stood before me.
31 He said, 'Cornelius, your prayer has been heard, and your alms have been remembered before God.
32 Send therefore to Joppa and ask for Simon, who is called Peter; he is staying in the home of Simon, a tanner, by the sea.'

MAIN THOUGHT: There is no longer Jew or Greek, there is no longer slave or free, there is no longer male and female; for all of you are one in Christ Jesus. (Galatians 3:28, NRSVue)

ACTS 10:9-15, 30-35; GALATIANS 3:28-29

KJV

33 Immediately therefore I sent to thee; and thou hast well done that thou art come. Now therefore are we all here present before God, to hear all things that are commanded thee of God.
34 Then Peter opened his mouth, and said, Of a truth I perceive that God is no respecter of persons:
35 But in every nation he that feareth him, and worketh righteousness, is accepted with him.

••• Galatians 3:28-29 •••

28 There is neither Jew nor Greek, there is neither bond nor free, there is neither male nor female: for ye are all one in Christ Jesus.
29 And if ye be Christ's, then are ye Abraham's seed, and heirs according to the promise.

NRSVue

33 Therefore I sent for you immediately, and you have been kind enough to come. So now all of us are here in the presence of God to listen to all that the Lord has commanded you to say."
34 Then Peter began to speak to them: "I truly understand that God shows no partiality,
35 but in every people anyone who fears him and practices righteousness is acceptable to him.

••• Galatians 3:28-29 •••

28 There is no longer Jew or Greek; there is no longer slave or free; there is no longer male and female, for all of you are one in Christ Jesus.
29 And if you belong to Christ, then you are Abraham's offspring, heirs according to the promise.

LESSON SETTING

Time: From AD 30-62
Place: Joppa and Caesarea
Setting: As the Gospel spread into a wider missionary outreach, and as the Christian message was increasingly shared by Hellenistic Jewish converts such as Stephen (who was later martyred) and Philip, the theological question of the legitimacy of Gentile acceptance arose. This question involved two major issues: First, must Gentiles become Jews as a prerequisite to becoming Christians (i.e., Should they undergo the Jewish proselytizing procedure upon conversion to Christianity)? This would have required circumcision for male converts and the adoption of such Jewish legal distinctives as kosher food laws. The second major issue was the question of table fellowship between Jewish and Gentile Christians, since Gentiles did not follow kosher practices. Because God gave the gift of the Spirit to the Gentiles in Cornelius' house without their going through the proselytizing process, Peter became convinced that such Jewish conversion procedures were not necessary for the Christian mission to the Gentiles.

LESSON OUTLINE

I. Between Vision and the Trance (Acts 10:9-15)
II. The Purpose for the Encounter (Acts 10:30-35)
III. All are One in Christ (Galatians: 3:28-29)

UNIFYING PRINCIPLE

Racial and social biases disrupt relationships among people. How can we learn to accept and respect one another's uniqueness and differences? Peter's vision in Acts and Paul's spiritual revelations in Galatians indicate God's impartiality and acceptance of all persons in Christ Jesus.

INTRODUCTION

The tenth chapter of Acts begins with a man named Cornelius, a Roman centurion of the Italian regiment who lived in Caesarea. A devout and godly man, he was well known and respected in the early Judeo-Christian communities to whom Luke wrote.

It is important to know about Cornelius for two reasons. First, he receives a vision from God that instructs him to send men to Joppa to find Simon Peter. At Cornelius' house, Peter will introduce him to the faith. This encounter in turn becomes the catalysts that officially opens the Gospel of Christ to the Gentile world.

Second, Jewish-Christian converts would have thought this Gentile to be unworthy to receive the grace of adoption and not even to be in fellowship with other Jews.

On the day Cornelius sends his delegation to find and retrieve Peter, God speaks to Peter and prepares him for the encounter. Today's lesson details the events in which God uses Peter to introduce the Christian faith to Cornelius, a Gentile, whom God also uses.

EXPOSITION

I. Between Vision and the Trance (Acts 10:9–15)

Approximately thirty miles from Caesarea, Joppa was a significant port city on the Mediterranean coast. It was crucial in trade and transportation, serving as a gateway for goods and merchants traveling into the region.

Cornelius' men and accompanying neighbors arrive in Joppa around noon the next day. When they get to the city, Peter is already there. He came earlier to attend Tabitha's funeral, a believer who had just died. God uses Peter to miraculously bring her back to life.

Peter was staying with Simon the Tanner who is also a believer. Known for his profession of turning animal hides into leather, Simon's trade was considered unclean by observant Jews due to constant contact with dead animals.

Peter was perched on the roof of Simon's house praying to God. Observant Jews usually did not pray at noon. They prayed three different times during the day: sunrise, three in the afternoon and sunset. Luke's description of Peter praying at noon emphasizes his faithful commitment and regular fellowship with God.

Noon was not the usual time for weekday meals. People ate a light meal in the morning and a more substantial one in late afternoon. It is likely Peter missed his mid-morning meal. Being famished and weary, he was most susceptible to the trance in which he fell.

Unlike a vision in which one is fully conscious, a trance occurs in a semi-conscious state. God gives Cornelius a vision to summon Peter to receive Cornelius into the Christian faith and experience transformation by God's grace. Peter's trance prepares him for his meeting with Cornelius. In that trance, God addresses Peter's attitude toward Gentiles and corrects his devotion to the Law over God's grace.

First-century Jews tolerated Gentiles but did not accept them as equals within their religious and social communities. Gentiles were considered impure people who lived outside covenant relationship with God. Jewish laws and customs created clear boundaries with Gentiles. Religious leaders and texts reinforced this separation and distinctiveness of Jewish people. Prior to Peter's encounter with God through the trance, he discriminated against Gentiles.

Peter's trance is a spiritual experience that opens his mind and his spirit to a greater understanding of God's plans. Peter sees heaven open and a large sheet descends to Earth. The sheet contains a picnic spread of live animals, wild beasts, creeping things, and birds. A voice from God instructs Peter to "rise, kill, and eat."

This divine command puzzles Peter because the Law does not permit observant Jews to eat unclean animals. Leviticus 11 specifies dietary restrictions. Ezekiel 4:14 deals with eating forbidden foods among Gentiles. Characteristically, Peter is argumentative and boldly declares to the "voice" that "he has never eaten anything unclean or common."

God rebukes Peter for his resistance by reminding him that nothing He has made is common. This exhortation reinforces God's sovereign prerogative, which entitles Him to change or abolish the Law.

Luke emphasizes Peter's stubbornness as his exchange with God occurs three times in exact repetition. Peter vigorously refuses to eat food that is legally unclean. God ignores his protest and reissues the command adding, do not call anything that God has made impure.

II. The Purpose of the Encounter (Acts 10:30–35)

Peter's encounter with God ends at the moment when Cornelius' men arrive at Simon's house. The Spirit guides Peter to return with them to Caesarea. They arrive on the third day after the original vision.

Upon entering Cornelius' house, Peter is met with a reverent greeting. It indicates that the host understands the divine significance of Peter's arrival, that there is a greater purpose to his being there. He relates the visit to the vision he received just four days prior.

Peter marvels at the large group of "relatives and close friends" who assemble at the house. He recalls the lesson from his vision in Joppa. He remembers the animals on the sheet. Peter realizes what God means when He says, "do not call anything He has made common." God invites him to apply the truth from the trance.

Cornelius recounts the vision he received from God. He speaks of the appearance of a man in bright clothing who told him that God heard his prayer and thought favorably of his alms of service. This representative of God instructed him to seek Peter and bring him to Caesarea and listen to his words.

Luke includes this account for a third time. The repetition underscores the importance of divine guidance which orchestrates this holy moment.

Peter overcomes his initial uncertainty about the reasons and purpose of the visit to Cornelius. As he listens to the details of Cornelius' vision, Peter accepts that God plans this encounter. Cornelius shares Peter's perspective and gathers his family and friends.

As Peter reflects upon his encounter with God, it becomes clear to him that he is to share the Gospel with this gathering of Gentiles.

The audience waits to hear the Lord's message from Peter. He contextualizes his sermon, "I have now had it demonstrated before my eyes that God divinely orchestrated these events with precision." Peter then admits that he is truly convinced that God does not show any partiality.

In Peter's trance, the animals represented all of God's people. They hail from every nation, fear Him and pursue works righteousness. Both Jew and Gentile are welcome to experience His grace; God does not show favoritism.

The encounter between Peter and Cornelius is as significant to the Christian mission as the outpouring of the Holy Spirit at Pentecost. Peter's acceptance of Cornelius opens the door all people to receive the grace of Christ's salvation.

The Gospel of Matthew 16:16-19 foretells Peter's introduction of Gentiles into the faith. Because of his true confession of Christ as the true Messiah, the Lord gives Peter the keys of the Kingdom. God chooses Peter to open the door for all nations to enter.

III. All are One in Christ (Galatians 3:28-29)

The Apostle Paul writes to the early Christian community in Galatia to address the influence of the Judaizers. They taught that Gentile converts had to follow Jewish law to be fully accepted as Christians. Paul vehemently opposes this teaching and insists faith in Christ alone suffices for salvation.

Galatia was a melting pot of ethnic, cultural, and social backgrounds. This diversity presents opportunities and challenges for new believers. Paul's strives to unite these diverse disciples in faith in Christ thereby in shaping identity and theology in early Christian community.

Galatia's population included Greeks and Romans. A significant Jewish community also resided there; they were influential in defining early Christian communities.

People from various social classes including enslaved persons, freedmen, and free citizens comprised the Church. In addition, former pagans and Jewish converts brought knowledge of the Hebrew Scripture and Jewish traditions.

Paul offers a vertical image of change between individuals and God that grace accomplishes. He also refers to its horizontal effect, between individuals and society. He states, "you are all one in Christ Jesus." Paul declares that unity must exist among believers in Christ. He lists three significant pairs of distinctions in the ancient world: Jew and Gentile, slave and free, male and female. These attributes often determined social status, rights, and religious privileges.

Gentiles, slaves, and women could not ordinarily inherit any land owned by Israelites. In the new covenant, Christ considers them "sons of God" and "heirs of salvation".

Paul eliminates false distinctions between the enslaved and the free in Christ. While the ancient world accepted human enslavement, the church did not. Secular world roles did not matter in Christ because disciples were equal. Slaves and free citizens stand before God as unworthy. Christ's grace accepts and forgives both of them.

There was also no distinction between male and female in this community of believers. Ancient society disparaged women while Christ openly embraced them. Like Gentiles and the enslaved, women came to faith, baptism, and salvation on the same terms; equally acceptable to God and equally loved by Him. A prime example of His accept toward women can be found Luke 8:1-3, which illustrates how Jesus included women in His ministry, acknowledging their contributions and allowing them to be active participants in His mission

In Christ, human distinctions lose their significance.

THE LESSON APPLIED

The maturity of a believer's faith can be measured by the inclusiveness of his or her personal theology. One's love and devotion to God extends to all of His creation, regardless of differences. Few argue against this conceptualization of God's grace but many, if not most, Christians fail to apply it in their own lives. All human beings have biases or even prejudices; however, our goal should be to grow toward embracing all of God's creation rather than seeking to confine ourselves and our associations to those who live and believe solely as we do.

Peter and Paul teach us that we should not focus solely on becoming a Christian but rather on living "in Christ," which is the greater challenge to our faithfulness.

To be "in Christ" means to have unity with Him and others who have chosen Him as Savior. Our identity in Christ intersects with all other identities, including gender, race, ethnicity, and culture. We are challenged to love and accept one another, breaking down barriers rather than creating deeper divisions. Often we forget that Jesus expressed condemnation for religious authorities, not those who were regarded as sinners. Through our interactions, we personify Christian compassion, humility, and grace, reflecting Christ's love. Disciples, as Christ's representatives, are obligated to strive toward eliminating divisions.

LET'S TALK ABOUT IT...

Discuss the following questions and visit www.rhboyd.com for more information.

How does Peter's resistance to God's command (during his trance) relate to any resistance to God you experienced since your salvation?

How can the Church better accept, love, and include disciples who believe contrasting philosophies?

Do you believe current Black Baptist churches function as unified members in Christ? If not, what do you think causes disunity?

What are the characteristics of a unified church community? List and explain them.

What beliefs and actions are necessary for a church to practice unity in Christ?

Get Social

Share your views and tag us
@rhboydco and use #rhboydco

@rhboydco

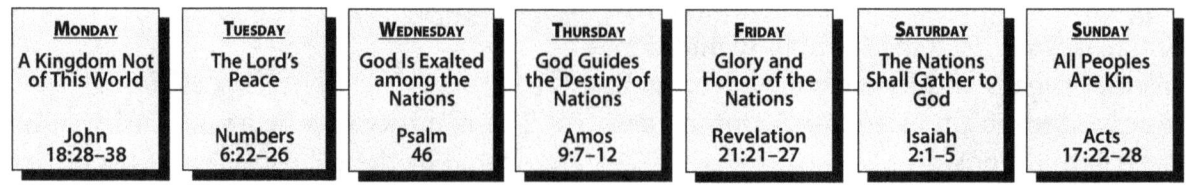

Lesson V — March 29, 2026

World Peace through Mutual Understanding

Adult Topic: Understanding Leads to Peace
Background Scripture: Isa. 2:2–22; 11:6–10; John 18:28–38; Acts 17:22–28; Eph. 4:4–6, 13–19
Lesson Passage: Isaiah 2:2–4; Acts 17:26–28

ISAIAH 2:2-4; ACTS 17:26-28

KJV

AND it shall come to pass in the last days, that the mountain of the Lord's house shall be established in the top of the mountains, and shall be exalted above the hills; and all nations shall flow unto it.
3 And many people shall go and say, Come ye, and let us go up to the mountain of the Lord, to the house of the God of Jacob; and he will teach us of his ways, and we will walk in his paths: for out of Zion shall go forth the law, and the word of the Lord from Jerusalem.
4 And he shall judge among the nations, and shall rebuke many people: and they shall beat their swords into plowshares, and their spears into pruninghooks: nation shall not lift up sword against nation, neither shall they learn war any more.

••• Acts 17:26–28 •••

26 And hath made of one blood all nations of men for to dwell on all the face of the earth, and hath determined the times before appointed, and the bounds of their habitation;
27 That they should seek the Lord, if haply they might feel after him, and find him, though he be not far from every one of us:
28 For in him we live, and move, and have our being; as certain also of your own poets have said, For we are also his offspring.

NRSVue

IN days to come the mountain of the Lord's house shall be established as the highest of the mountains and shall be raised above the hills; all the nations shall stream to it.
3 Many peoples shall come and say, "Come, let us go up to the mountain of the Lord, to the house of the God of Jacob, that he may teach us his ways and that we may walk in his paths." For out of Zion shall go forth instruction and the word of the Lord from Jerusalem.
4 He shall judge between the nations and shall arbitrate for many peoples; they shall beat their swords into plowshares and their spears into pruning hooks; nation shall not lift up sword against nation; neither shall they learn war any more.

••• Acts 17:26–28 •••

26 From one ancestor he made all peoples to inhabit the whole earth, and he allotted the times of their existence and the boundaries of the places where they would live,
27 so that they would search for God and perhaps fumble about for him and find him—though indeed he is not far from each one of us.
28 For 'In him we live and move and have our being'; as even some of your own poets have said, 'For we, too, are his offspring.'

MAIN THOUGHT: Many peoples shall come and say, "Come, let us go up to the mountain of the Lord, to the house of the God of Jacob; that he may teach us his ways that we may walk in his paths." For out of Zion shall go forth instruction, and the word of the LORD from Jerusalem. (Isaiah 2:3, NRSVue)

LESSON SETTING

Time: 8th Century BC
Place: Jerusalem
Setting: Isaiah was a counselor to kings from 740 to 680 BC during a critical time of crisis in Israel. They were at war on two fronts, one with Syria in 734 and Assyria from 734 to 701 BC. By 605 BC, Babylon had overtaken Assyria to become the dominant power in the ancient Near East. Nebuchadnezzar, one of Babylon's rulers, conquered Judah and sent the people into exile (BC 587) as Isaiah had prophesied. After a series of progressively weaker successors to Nebuchadnezzar, the Medo-Persian Empire under Cyrus the Great gained control of the region in 539 BC. Cyrus is named by Isaiah as God's agent to bring the exiles of Judah back to the land of promise. Isaiah bases his message of a glorious future on God's ability to accomplish this remarkable first step.

LESSON OUTLINE

I. A Future Hope (Isaiah 2:2-4)
II. Paul in Athens Greece (A Historical Perspective)
III. The Sovereignty of God (Acts 17:26-18)

UNIFYING PRINCIPLE

Attainment of knowledge causes some people to arrogantly share opinions and ostracize others. How do people in a learning community search for wisdom in a mutually respectful manner? Isaiah centers knowledge and peace within a "fully realized" relationship with God. Paul understands Christ as the revelation of God's wisdom.

INTRODUCTION

Many scholars consider Isaiah 2:1-5 a late addition, written after the exile of Judah and Jerusalem in 587 BC and 150 years after the prophet's lifetime. It reflects an evolving understanding of God's plan for His people. It foretells a messianic age when God's establishes His Kingdom peace reigns. It depicts a future in which God's justice and righteousness prevail.

During Ahaz's reign, the nation resembled a wounded soldier. Except for Zion, enemies captured all of its territory. Murder became normal; vulnerable people were left undefended. Some people assumed their sacrifices were pleasing to God (1:10-15, 29). God, however, rejected them and their sacrifices.

Referencing a covenant process, Isaiah appeals to the nation to embrace new values and transform their temple worship. God desires pure hearts, righteous actions, and covenantal faithfulness.

Isaiah establishes a general theological direction for his listeners and readers in the first chapter. The second through the sixth chapters consist of early sermons collected during Uzziah's reign. The first sermon contrasts future exultation of God with humiliation of proud people.

EXPOSITION

I. A Future Hope (Isaiah 2:2–4)

Isaiah encourages his audience to look beyond their current situation so they do not become mired in hopelessness and despair. In using the phrase, "in the latter days," he suggests a very different life at a future time. "The future" does not necessarily mean the end of time itself.

The Hebrew community interestingly saw the future as they looked to their past. They faced the past and looked back to a future time of restoration. Ironically, they held the past before them and the future behind them as they looked backed.

The Hebrew community greatly valued its history and traditions. They constantly reflected upon foundational events, such as the Exodus and events leading to it, the giving of the Law at Mount Sinai, and the Covenant with Abraham. Beyond being historical facts, these events were living realities that shaped the identity and faith of the Hebrew people. The past yielded lessons, guidance and hope for the future.

Isaiah defines this future hope of the "latter days" in four stages. First, he describes exaltation of the mountain of the Lord's house which refers to Mount Zion in Jerusalem where the Temple stood. High places were often sites of worship where priests performed rituals in honor of a prescribed deity.

As Israel worshiped only one God, they observed only one central place of worship, the place where God chose for His name to dwell (see Deuteronomy 12).

Still, Israel worshiped at high places and amongst idolatrous gods. This practice was inconsistent with their monotheism; it risked corrupting Israel's worship with pagan elements. God, however, promises to raise His mountain on top of the other mountains. Exalted above places for the worship of pagan gods, His mountain shows He alone is to be worshiped.

The phrase, "and all nations shall flow to it," introduces the second phase of Israel's future hope. It foreshadows a time when all nations will flow to the mountain of God, like rivers flowing into the oceans. They will go to Jerusalem for instruction in His ways. The metaphor of rivers suggests God will draw the people to Him.

The idea that all nations will come to know God is a prominent theme in Isaiah. Its roots stem from the original promise to Abraham, "all the nations of the earth shall be blessed through you" (Gen 12:3).

The universal knowledge of the Law is the third future prophecy, "for out of Zion will go forth the law." Although Judah turned away from God's teaching, Isaiah sees a time when all nations will eagerly seek it. People from many nations will come to God to learn "His ways and walk in His paths." They will go into the world and share divine decrees, enabling adoption into the holy family to everyone.

The final phase of Isaiah's prophecy will be a state of peace that results when previously warring nations "beat their swords into plowshares and their spears into pruning hooks." These words are prominently inscribed on a statue—a blacksmith beats swords into plowshares—outside the United Nations headquarters. The sculpture was a gift from the then Soviet Union presented in 1959. The bronze statue symbolizing the desire to put an end to war and convert means of destruction into creative tools for the benefit of humanity.

God's peace leads to disarmament. Weapons of war are no longer needed. All that is necessary are the tools of agriculture that nourish life. God's direct intervention as "Judge between the nations" achieves this majestic peace.

II. Paul in Athens Greece (A Historical Perspective)

In Acts 17:26, Paul awaits the arrival of Silas and Timothy in Athens. While waiting, Paul regularly visits the "marketplace" to discuss the Gospel with anyone who happened to be there.

Athens had been reduced to a dim reflection of her glorious light of politics and culture that flourished 500 years earlier. Its population numbered approximately 5,000 voting citizens. The Romans controlled her political power to maintain Athens as a free city. Nevertheless, Athens historically remained a center of education and the arts.

Paul has a disdain for many monuments and artistic symbols though he appreciates the culture. He objects to these artistic works because they were presented for worship to idol gods.

Statues depicting exploits of myriad gods were plentiful in Athens. Everywhere, he sees columns with the head of Hermes, temples erected in tribute to other gods and altars open to pagan sacrifices. These artifacts greatly trouble and enrage Paul. His daily defense of the Gospel in the marketplace captures the attention of a philosophical society. This group met regularly to discuss life, liberty, meaning, and existence. Two classical schools of thought, Epicureans and Stoics, greatly influenced them.

The Epicureans (340–270 BC) believed the universe and all beings were composed of atoms that were only temporarily active. They therefore rejected any thought of life beyond this world. Although they did not deny the existence of gods, they did not believe any gods were involved in this world. The greatest good emerges in happiness, pleasure and freedom from pain including superstitious fears of death.

Zeno (340–265 BC) founded the Stoics. Their belief in logos (universal reason) as the divine force that holds the universe together gave them confidence that life could be lived in harmony with nature. They were pantheistic, believing that a spark of divinity lives in all creation. Also, self-sufficiency and acceptance of fate were essential to their belief system. The Stoics advocated a high standard of ethics. Their belief that everyone had a spark of divinity in turn led to universal brotherhood even for the enslaved.

The local philosophical group disputed with Paul and labeled him a "babbler." They accused him of behaving like a bird picking up and scattering seeds of information without any critical thinking.

Other listeners interpreted his emphasis on "Jesus" and "The Resurrection" to be the names of new gods. They relegated Paul's preaching as a promotion of a new god and goddess. They considered him to be a polytheist like themselves.

To settle any dispute, the group summons Paul to speak before the Areopagus. They gathered at the Acropolis, a prominent meeting place for the highest governmental council and later a judicial court. The Areopagus also exercised jurisdiction of religious and moral questions.

They offered Paul an opportunity to explain in detail this new teaching. Their request reflected their role as the guardians of new doctrines about gods and religion.

Paul begins his address with foundational themes of Old Testament theology. His concentrates upon God as Creator and proper worship of the Creator God.

Speaking directly to his audience, the language of Paul's speech references Greek philosophy, as Paul appeals to Athenian intellectuals. He describes their sense of religion. He notes that on his arrival in the city he observed an altar with the inscription "TO AN UNKNOWN GOD." The society recognized and honored any gods whom they knew but also any gods whom they did not know.

Paul utilizes this presentation to introduce the Athenians to this "unknown God," proclaiming that He is the God of Israel, the Creator and Sustainer of life.

III. The Sovereignty of God (Acts 17:26–28)

An affirmation of the unity of humanity begins this brief passage. "God made from one blood every nation of men to dwell." Paul emphasizes the common origin and equality of all people. This idea was a radical one for the Greeks to hear. They considered themselves superior to other nations. Paul's assertion challenges any concept of individual or group superiority; rather it promotes a vision of universal brotherhood under one Creator.

God created humankind and determined times and boundaries for their dwelling, says Paul. This fact expresses God's sovereignty over human history and geography. He is not a distant deity but One who intervenes in the affairs of nations, determining their rise and fall and the extent of their territories. Paul's claim demonstrates God's omnipotence and excellence above other deities.

Paul explains the reason for God's cosmic order is to encourage humankind to seek Him. Seeking God is a common theme in the Old Testament. The call to "seek God" was always made to those within the covenant community, to Israel to whom God revealed Himself. In Athens, it is a call to Gentiles for whom the true God is "unknown."

The diversity and dispersion of humanity leads people to seek God which is the purpose of their existence. Despite the vastness of the world and differences amongst people, God is accessible to anyone who seeks Him. In His presence everyone is equal. For Paul, seeking God equates with groping for Him in the darkness of ignorance. Although God is near and accessible, many people do not see Him because of their spiritual blindness.

Paul reassures his audience in the twenty-eighth verse that they can reach God. "He is not far from each one of us." God is omnipresent and intimately involved in His creation. He is close enough to touch, and in Him we live and move and have our being. Paul adds words reminiscent of Greek poets, "we are his offspring." These words are actual quotations from poets who were often quoted in the ancient world.

Paul uses these quotations to affirm the fact that even Greek poets, who were considered to be inspired themselves, testified to the fact that humans are made like the gods. Thus, there was no need to construct objects of worship out of "gold or silver or stone." Paul reiterates the Old Testament's strong opposition to pagan worship and idolatry. Simultaneously, he offers the Athenians an appropriate means of calling upon the living God.

Paul's use of Greek poetry demonstrates the importance of engaging culture to effectively communicate the Gospel. It shows that the Gospel does not oppose any culture, but rather interacts with it and transforms residents.

THE LESSON APPLIED

Regrettably, our national culture has slowly nurtured hate until its poisonous effects have damaged our social contract and relationships. As the fundamental basis for our deep and seemingly irreconcilable divisions, hate is the pure expression of evil. Disciples cannot deny this is our fight.

From a spiritual perspective, the conflict between good and evil is a battle between love and hate. God's love is the greatest instrument believers have to combat hatred. Through His selfless sacrifice, Christ demonstrates the transformative power of love. He calls us to love to improve the lives of everyone whom we encounter.

Intentionality about bridging relational gaps between groups and individuals is one of the ways we best reflect Christ's love. Infusing Christian principles, ideas and practices into society is a practical means. Creating forums and platforms that invite different opinions, foster critical thinking, and encourage spiritual development is an additional means of sharing love. It invites a deeper sense of God's presence.

Being open to others causes them to be open to you. Open-mindedness allows one's true self to emerge and experience God through authentic worship of Him and within intimate fellowship with Him. The relationships we build flow from a common context of knowing who God is. Our mutual understanding creates conditions for love, justice, truth, and peace in society.

LET'S TALK ABOUT IT...

Discuss the following questions and visit www.rhboyd.com for more information.

What primary issue between groups fuels hostility towards each other?

What is the primary method to combat the issue in the first question?

What is the difference between equity, equality, and justice?

Discuss and explain how God demonstrates His attributes in your life: omnipresence, omnipotence, omniscience, and omni-benevolence.

What are the challenges to unifying people under one God?

How do we address those challenges?

Get Social

Share your views and tag us
@rhboydco and use #rhboydco

@rhboydco

Home Daily Devotional Readings
April March 30–5, 2026

Monday	Tuesday	Wednesday	Thursday	Friday	Saturday	Sunday
Many Dwellings in the Father's House	Encouraging Words of Hope	I Know that My Redeemer Lives	Awake and Sing for Joy	Give Thanks to the Lord	Christ Is Risen from the Dead	Death Is Swallowed Up in Victory
John 14:1–4	1 Thessalonians 4:13–18	Job 19:23–27	Isaiah 26:12–19	Psalm 118:15–24	1 Corinthians 15:13–20	1 Corinthians 15:50–58

Lesson VI   **April 5, 2026 (Easter)**

The Future Life

Adult Topic: Thoughts on Life and Death
Background Scripture: Matt. 25:31–46; Mark 12:26–27; Luke 24:1–12; John 14:1–6; 1 Cor. 15:3–20, 50–58; 1 Thess. 4:13–18; Rev. 22:1–5
Lesson Passage: 1 Corinthians 15:13–20, 51–58

1 CORINTHIANS 15:13-20, 51-58

KJV

BUT if there be no resurrection of the dead, then is Christ not risen:
14 And if Christ be not risen, then is our preaching vain, and your faith is also vain.
15 Yea, and we are found false witnesses of God; because we have testified of God that he raised up Christ: whom he raised not up, if so be that the dead rise not.
16 For if the dead rise not, then is not Christ raised:
17 And if Christ be not raised, your faith is vain; ye are yet in your sins.
18 Then they also which are fallen asleep in Christ are perished.
19 If in this life only we have hope in Christ, we are of all men most miserable.
20 But now is Christ risen from the dead, and become the firstfruits of them that slept.

••• 15:51-58 •••

51 Behold, I shew you a mystery; We shall not all sleep, but we shall all be changed,
52 In a moment, in the twinkling of an eye, at the last trump: for the trumpet shall sound, and the dead shall be raised incorruptible, and we shall be changed.
53 For this corruptible must put on incorruption, and this mortal must put on immortality.

54 So when this corruptible shall have put on incorruption, and this mortal shall have put on immortality, then shall be brought to pass the saying that is written, Death is swallowed up in victory.

NRSVue

IF there is no resurrection of the dead, then Christ has not been raised,
14 and if Christ has not been raised, then our proclamation is in vain and your faith is in vain.
15 We are even found to be misrepresenting God, because we testified of God that he raised Christ—whom he did not raise if it is true that the dead are not raised.
16 For if the dead are not raised, then Christ has not been raised.
17 If Christ has not been raised, your faith is futile, and you are still in your sins.
18 Then those also who have died in Christ have perished.
19 If for this life only we have hoped in Christ, we are of all people most to be pitied.
20 But in fact Christ has been raised from the dead, the first fruits of those who have died

••• 15:51-58 •••

51 Look, I will tell you a mystery! We will not all die, but we will all be changed,
52 in a moment, in the twinkling of an eye, at the last trumpet. For the trumpet will sound, and the dead will be raised imperishable, and we will be changed.
53 For this perishable body must put on imperishability, and this mortal body must put on immortality.
54 When this perishable body puts on imperishability and this mortal body puts on immortality, then the saying that is written will be fulfilled: "Death has been swallowed up in victory."

MAIN THOUGHT: In fact Christ has been raised from the dead, the first fruits of those who have died. (1 Corinthians 15:20, NRSVue)

1 CORINTHIANS 15:13-20, 51-58

KJV

55 O death, where is thy sting? O grave, where is thy victory?
56 The sting of death is sin; and the strength of sin is the law.
57 But thanks be to God, which giveth us the victory through our Lord Jesus Christ.
58 Therefore, my beloved brethren, be ye stedfast, unmoveable, always abounding in the work of the Lord, forasmuch as ye know that your labour is not in vain in the Lord.

NRSVue

55 "Where, O death, is your victory? Where, O death, is your sting?"
56 The sting of death is sin, and the power of sin is the law.
57 But thanks be to God, who gives us the victory through our Lord Jesus Christ.
58 Therefore, my beloved brothers and sisters, be steadfast, immovable, always excelling in the work of the Lord because you know that in the Lord your labor is not in vain.

LESSON SETTING

Time: AD 55
Place: Roman Corinth
Setting: In Paul's day, Corinth was a place of commercial importance. Located on an isthmus between northern Greece and the Peloponnesian peninsula, it boasted in having two harbors, Lechaeum on the Ionian Sea to the west and Cenchrea on the Aegean Sea to the east, which together contributed to the economic stability of the city. As a result of its economic strength a large majority of Corinth's population was transient and cosmopolitan. The city attracted many whose purpose for visiting was illicit pleasure, so much so that it eventually became known to all that to be a Corinthian was to live a debauched lifestyle. Immorality has always been a hallmark of the city, and with it, its influence and impact on the newly formed Christian church there. While in Ephesus at that time, Paul wrote this letter to the church in Corinth out of concern that they might become influenced by the culture of the city. His intent for the letter was to encourage members in the faith community to be the contrast to the culture by maintaining Christian unity.

LESSON OUTLINE

I. Resistance to the Resurrection (1 Corinthians 15:13–19)
II. Christ IS Risen from the Dead (1 Corinthians 15:20)
III. The Reward of the Resurrection (1 Corinthians 15:51–58)

UNIFYING PRINCIPLE

Disciples and non-disciples alike wonder what happens after death. What reasonable expectations can we have for life after death? Jesus' resurrection is foundational to Paul's expectation for anyone who believes in Christ and will share in a future resurrection.

INTRODUCTION

The final chapter of 1 Corinthians focuses the resurrection of Jesus. To his chagrin, Paul learns there were some in the community of faith who doubted its validity. Considering Paul's argument in 15:35–49, it appears the problem was not a question of life after death but the bodily nature of a physical resurrection. Possibly, the people who denied the resurrection were a minority of the upper class who would have held such philosophical leanings.

Paul treats the Corinthians as students in need of further instruction. He does not seek harsh discipline for anyone who doubts. Instead, Paul educates them about the significance of the resurrection as it relates to the believer's future hope.

EXPOSITION

I. Resistance to the Resurrection (1 Corinthians 15:13–19)

Paul poses a dilemma to his audience to further validate his opening argument. Speaking specifically to disciples who believe in the resurrection of Christ but not in general resurrection of the dead, Paul insists both concepts are inextricably linked. They logically stand or fall together.

The church in Corinth had individually and collectively accepted Jesus Christ as the true Messiah and the One who died for their sins and was raised from the dead. However, a sector in the church could not accept the illogical notion of a general resurrection from the dead of people who had died in Christ.

This resistance to belief in a universal resurrection indicates residual and strong influences of earlier religious and philosophical views. The Sadducees were aristocratic priestly leaders. They did not believe in life after death. Instead, they maintained the soul perished with the body. For any Jewish believer who once belonged to this tradition, belief in the resurrection would have been difficult.

Believers in Corinth, who were former pagans and influenced by Greek philosophy, thought resurrection of the dead inconceivable. They believed in an afterlife but not in a bodily resurrection. Whereas the soul is immortal and immaterial, the body, being made of matter, is evil. Unsurprisingly, they scoffed at Paul's proclamation in Athens (Acts 17:32).

Greek philosophy rejected the idea of bodily resurrection; and taught that the true "self" continues as an immaterial, noncorporeal body made of spirit. The body was merely a temporary receptacle for the soul. According to their belief, upon death, the soul would leave the body to begin its journey to the underworld.

Paul attempts to disabuse them of their misinformed assumptions. He maintains the connection between the resurrection of the body and the Resurrection of Christ. He uses a rhetorical question and a direct statement. He offers a dilemma: "If there is no resurrection of the dead, then Christ is not risen either." If God lacks power to raise Christ from the dead, He equally lacks power to raise anyone else.

Another way to phrase the dilemma is, "Since Christ is preached to have been raised from the dead, how can some of you (logically) say that there is no resurrection of the dead?" The answer is, "You cannot."

Paul continues the logical "if" and "then" sequence. If the dead cannot be raised, then Jesus could not have been raised. If Jesus was not raised from the dead, then preaching and faith are pointless. Without the Resurrection of Christ, the Gospel is false. Preaching it is therefore useless. Anyone proclaiming the Gospel would be complicit as false witnesses of God. In short, these denials of the bodily resurrection make Christ's sacrifice and Christianity meaningless.

Paul emphasizes the necessity of believing in the resurrection of the dead. If the dead do not rise, then Christ is not risen. If Christ has not risen from the grave, Jesus remains buried in an unknown tomb. Even after twenty centuries, these denials would crush the Jesus Movement's faith in their risen Lord.

Paul lists the consequences of disbelieving the resurrection of the dead. If Christ has not been raised, personal faith is futile. Anyone who died believing in Christ has perished forever.

Furthermore, anyone who does not believe in the resurrection is still living in their sins. Such persons have not been delivered from punishment. They continue living in sin and will experience punishment while they live and after they die.

Those who have fallen asleep in Christ are the Christian dead. "Sleep" was a common euphemism for death. It was especially appropriate for Christians as death was non-threatening sleep from which they expect to awake in peace. Without Christ's resurrection, the Christian dead would have perished. Those perished are lost to God forever. This is the fate of those disciples who died trusting in Christ, if He has not been raised from the dead.

What is the ultimate consequence of living if Christ has not been raised from the dead? If our hope in Christ is only good for this life, we deserve pity. All believers will lose their future hope which is the reward promised to those who have died in Christ. Paul recognizes there are present benefits for Christian disciples in this life. However, the Christian community have integrity only if it is grounded in the truth of the resurrection, the ultimate fulfillment of God's promises. If the resurrection did not occur, then God fails to fulfill His covenantal promise and believers do not have any future hope.

II. Christ IS Risen from the Dead (1 Corinthians 15:20)

Paul turns his attention to the positive testimony that reinforces the belief in Christ's resurrection from the dead. For Paul, the resurrection was a historical fact that directly impacts the lives of believers. His declaration, "Christ has indeed been raised from the dead," is the hallmark of the Christian faith. He directs his impassioned argument specifically to those who denied the resurrection from the dead.

Paul symbolizes Christ's resurrection as the "firstfruits." This Old Testament concept (Lev. 23:9–14) describes a consecrated portion of the harvest offered to God, ostensibly the best of the crops. Christ is the first to be raised from the dead and He represents more resurrection bodies to come.

This metaphor means Jesus' resurrection guarantees the resurrection of believers. Jesus' resurrection is the firstfruit because His resurrection decisively overthrew death itself. Previous resurrections did nothing to abolish death itself.

Paul's claim that Jesus is the "first fruit of those who have fallen asleep" suggests three things: First, Christ triumphs over death. Second, His resurrection certifies the resurrection of all persons who believe in Him. His resurrection is the first installment of many more to come. Third, Christ's resurrection foreshadows the resurrection of His people. As He died and was raised in power, believers who die in Him will also be raised in power.

III. The Reward of the Resurrection (1 Corinthians 15:51–58)

Paul addresses the question, "What happens to the living when the Lord returns?" It is unclear whether believers in Corinth specifically ask Paul about the "rapture" of any living saints as mentioned in 1 Thessalonians 4:13–18. Nonetheless, Paul wants them to understand the significance of his teachings on the spiritual body and Christ's return for those believers who are still alive when He comes again.

Paul assures believers some of them may never taste death before Christ returns. The lack of physical death will not affect their eternal destination.

The secret mystery that Paul reveals in verse 51 is Christ's return initiates a transformation for all people in Christ, those who have already died in Christ and those who are still living for Him. This necessary transformation, contrary to Greek philosophy, fuses body and spirit into another perfect and holy form.

Paul's use of the inclusive pronoun "we" suggests he counts himself among those who will be alive at the time of Christ's return. He too will be changed into a spiritual body ready to receive Him, though knowledge of Christ's return was as unknown then as it still is today.

He employs a series of illustrations in the next verse. He demonstrates the abruptness of the bodily change that will take place when Christ returns. It will be sudden, in a moment, and in the twinkling of an eye. The change will be a transformation from mortality to immortality; that which is corruptible will become incorruptible. Death will be swallowed up in the victory of Christ's resurrection.

He taunts death as if it were a person; asking it, "Where is your sting and where is your victory?" Sin reinforces the inevitability of death which is why Paul refers to it as the "sting" of death. Through Christ's resurrection, which brings forgiveness of sin, Christ permanently and irreversibly defeats the sting of death.

Paul concludes his argument by exhorting the church to be steadfast and immovable in the faith. They were to maintain their conviction in the Gospel and resurrection regardless of how convincing opposing arguments were. Those who denied the resurrection undermined the Gospel. If the community yielded to false teaching, they would deny their only hope for salvation. They were to affirm the truth of Christ's resurrection, their union with Christ, and their future resurrection because of Christ.

To strengthen their belief in the resurrection, Paul encourages them to maintain regular participation in the work of the Lord. It encompasses a major requirement of the life and lifestyle of every believer. Their commitment to the Lord's work makes every experience and encounter meaningful. With this admonition, the apostle's argument completes a full circle. It affirms the Corinthians' salvation provided that they steadfastly believe the Gospel and Resurrection of Christ which assures their resurrection.

THE LESSON APPLIED

Existential questions about life, death, and an afterlife are natural for humankind to ask. Disciples address these questions through the assurance we have in the resurrection of Christ. Paul admonishes his listeners and readers to conceptualize life through the prism of belief in Christ. For the believer, honoring the resurrection of Christ demands more than a superficial annual observance of a religious tradition for a few days. Rather, it is an opportunity for disciples to reflect on His great sacrifice, His victory over death, and in consequence, our victory over the daily challenges that we inevitably face.

The Resurrection of Christ is the cornerstone of the Christian faith. It empowers us with profound hope and meaning. It turns death into a transition to new and eternal life. This belief permeates our daily lives and influences how we handle trials and tribulations. Reflecting on Christ's triumph over death reminds us of God's love and power to overcome our struggles. Even when our circumstances and options appear to be 'dead,' God still has the power to resurrect them so that we may be overcomers, even those things that seem impossible.

This reflection increases faith, courage, and compassion; knowing Christ secures our ultimate victory. Accordingly, the Resurrection is not just a historical event. It is a living reality that shapes our identity and defines our destiny as Christian disciples. This reflection increases faith, courage, and compassion, knowing has already Christ secured our ultimate victory.

LET'S TALK ABOUT IT...

Discuss the following questions and visit www.rhboyd.com for more information.

What do you think about the idea that believers who have died in Christ, regardless of how long they have been dead, will be resurrected when Christ returns?

How does Christ's resurrection inspire you to serve and worship Him?

What are some challenges to belief in the resurrection in the twenty-first century? Does this belief still make sense?

In your words, what does it means to live in the power of the resurrection?

Should disciples fear death? Are you afraid to die? Why or why not? Please explain.

Get Social
Share your views and tag us
@rhboydco and use #rhboydco

@rhboydco

Lesson VII — **April 12, 2026**

Respect for Rightful Authority

Adult Topic: Whose Rules Rule?
Background Scripture: Mark 12:13–17; Romans 13:1–14; 1 Peter 2:13–1
Lesson Passage: Mark 12:17; Romans 13:1, 6–8; 1 Peter 2:13–17

MARK 12:17; ROMANS 13:1, 6–8; 1 PETER 2:13–17

KJV

AND Jesus answering said unto them, Render to Caesar the things that are Caesar's, and to God the things that are God's. And they marvelled at him.

••• Romans 13:1; 6-8 •••

1 Let every soul be subject unto the higher powers. For there is no power but of God: the powers that be are ordained of God.

••••••

6 For for this cause pay ye tribute also: for they are God's ministers, attending continually upon this very thing.
7 Render therefore to all their dues: tribute to whom tribute is due; custom to whom custom; fear to whom fear; honour to whom honour.

8 Owe no man any thing, but to love one another: for he that loveth another hath fulfilled the law.

••• 1 Peter 2:13-17 •••

13 Submit yourselves to every ordinance of man for the Lord's sake: whether it be to the king, as supreme;
14 Or unto governors, as unto them that are sent by him for the punishment of evildoers, and for the praise of them that do well.
15 For so is the will of God, that with well doing ye may put to silence the ignorance of foolish men:
16 As free, and not using your liberty for a cloke of maliciousness, but as the servants of God.
17 Honour all men. Love the brotherhood. Fear God. Honour the king.

NRSVue

JESUS said to them, "Give to Caesar the things that are Caesar's and to God the things that are God's." And they were utterly amazed at him.

••• Romans 13:1; 6-8 •••

1 Let every person be subject to the governing authorities, for there is no authority except from God, and those authorities that exist have been instituted by God.

••••••

6 For the same reason you also pay taxes, for the authorities are God's agents, busy with this very thing.
7 Pay to all what is due them: taxes to whom taxes are due, revenue to whom revenue is due, respect to whom respect is due, honor to whom honor is due.

8 Owe no one anything, except to love one another, for the one who loves another has fulfilled the law.

••• 1 Peter 2:13-17 •••

13 For the Lord's sake be subject to every human authority, whether to the emperor as supreme

14 or to governors as sent by him to punish those who do wrong and to praise those who do right.

15 For it is God's will that by doing right you should silence the ignorance of the foolish.

16 As servants of God, live as free people, yet do not use your freedom as a pretext for evil.
17 Honor everyone. Love the family of believers. Fear God. Honor the emperor.

MAIN THOUGHT: Jesus said to them, "Give to the emperor the things that are the emperor's, and to God the things that are God's." And they were utterly amazed at him. (Mark 12:17, NRSVue)

LESSON SETTING

Time: AD 33–90
Place: Palestine, Asia Minor
Setting: First-century Palestine during the life of Jesus, according to the author of the Gospel of Mark, consisted of a diverse and complex society under Roman occupation. In addition to the relentless desert sun, the region was characterized by political tension, social stratification, and religious fervor. The Jewish population was divided into several sects, including Pharisees, Sadducees, Zealots, and other lesser-known groups, each with its own beliefs and practices. Daily life was influenced by Roman laws and taxes, while the Temple in Jerusalem remained the spiritual center. In this context, Jesus' teachings and miracles challenged both religious authorities and social norms, ultimately leading to His crucifixion.

LESSON OUTLINE

I. Pay Caesar, but Give to God (Mark 12:17)
II. Representing God through Respect for the Government (Romans 13:1)
III. The Believer's Love Debt (Romans 13:6–8)
IV. Compliance Through Conviction (1 Peter 2:13–17)

UNIFYING PRINCIPLE

Generally, people respect and obey those in authority. What establishes a leader's rightful authority? The Gospel of Mark and the books of Romans and 1 Peter affirm God's ultimate authority. They also advocate respect of and obedience to rightful governance of human leaders.

INTRODUCTION

The New Testament addresses the relationship between believers and secular authorities. It details respect and obedience as integral aspects of Christian conduct. In Mark 12:17, Jesus teaches, "Render unto Caesar the things that are Caesar's, and unto God the things that are God's." Believers have a dual responsibility to earthly government and divine authority.

Paul further elaborates upon this principle in Romans 13:1, 6–8 where he instructs believers to submit to governing authorities. He states God ordains governmental authority. He emphasizes paying taxes and performing civic duties are expressions of love and respect for fellow citizens.

Similarly, 1 Peter 2:13–17 calls for submission to every human institution for the Lord's sake. Whether emperors or governors, obedience silences ignorance and honors God. These passages assert a consistent biblical theme of respect and obedience to authority. Beyond being a civic duty, these traits reflect faith and commitment to God's order. Adhering to these teachings, believers demonstrate integrity, promote peace and evidence the Gospel's transformative power in all dimensions of life.

EXPOSITION

I. Pay Caesar, but Give to God (Mark 12:17)

Jesus responds to a question, more accurately, a test, posed by a representative from the Pharisees and Herodians.

The Pharisees were known for their strict adherence to Torah and Jewish traditions. They influenced common people and often clashed with Jesus about the Law and religious practices. The Pharisees deemed Jesus a threat and sought to discredit him.

The Herodians politically supported the dynasty of King Herod and Roman authority. Sympathetic to Roman government, they cooperated with occupying forces. They disagreed with the Pharisees who resented Roman rule and strove to preserve Jewish religious and cultural identity.

Pharisees and Herodians united in their opposition to Jesus. They tried to entrap Him with the question about paying taxes to Caesar. If Jesus opposes taxes, Rome would consider him to be a rebel. His support of taxes jeopardized favor with Jewish people who resented Roman taxation.

Jesus skillfully avoids their trap. He asks for a coin minted by the emperor. Jesus shows it was stamped with Tiberius Caesar's image; indicating that it was his personal property while in circulation.

Jesus' saying acknowledges the legitimacy of secular authority while affirming God's sovereignty. His response conveys a profound message about civic duty and spiritual devotion.

II. Representing God through Respect for the Government (Romans 13:1)

Romans offers a comprehensive exposition of the Gospel, dealing with theological doctrine and practical living. Paul addresses a believer's conduct in relation to governmental authorities. Paul writes to Christians living in Rome, where the political climate was often hostile to their burgeoning community. He recommends respect and obedience to authorities. Such behavior honors their faith and depicts trust in God's sovereignty.

Paul's instruction furthers the belief that God establishes political authority. He asserts, "There is no authority except from God," This idea underscores God's sovereignty. Every form of human government operates within God's overarching permissive will. Then, submission to authorities equates with obedience to God's order.

This call to submission does not imply blind obedience to unjust, immoral and unethical commands. The broader biblical narrative cautions against following human laws that contradict God's laws. Believers must prioritize their allegiance to God.

Paul's teachings continually challenge believers to balance their civic responsibilities with their spiritual convictions. Respect and obedience toward authorities occurs while maintaining primary allegiance to God's authority.

III. The Believer's Love Debt (Romans 13:6–8)

Paul endorses the legitimacy of paying taxes when he describes government officials as God's ministers. God grants their authority to secure and maintain civil order. Paul elevates their function to a divine mandate, a part of God's providential plan.

The authorities partially derived validity from their dedication to their duties which included administration of justice.

Obedience to reasonable laws enables believers to honor the role of God's government and His use of authorities to accomplish His will.

Paul lists four specific areas of the believer's civil duty. First, they must pay taxes to whom taxes are due. Second, he instructs believers to fulfill the financial obligation of giving customs necessary to provide government services.

Paul, third, exhorts Christians to show appropriate reverence toward civic leaders. Finally, Paul instructs believers to show honor and consideration to anyone who deserves them. Showing honor implies a deeper recognition of the dignity and worthiness of political officials.

Interestingly, Paul discusses the only debt that must remain unpaid. "Owe no one anything except to love." There is no limit to the obligation to love. We who belong to the family of God are to love everyone. Just as God's love extends to all, our concern must reach believers and unbelievers alike. Love fulfills all requirements of the Law.

His usage of the "law" exceeds the Law of Moses. It encompasses the sum moral laws.

Since most of these laws regulate interpersonal relationships, Paul focuses upon the second greatest commandment, the one commanding love of neighbor.

The debt of love has transformative potential. As believers approach their civic duties with love, they become agents of positive change. Their actions reflect the character of Christ in the public sphere.

IV. Compliance Through Conviction (1 Peter 2:13–17)

Legend holds that the Apostle Peter wrote this letter to Christians scattered throughout Asia Minor which is modern-day Turkey. Standing firm in the faith and endeavoring to live holy and godly lives are the overarching themes of this epistle. Peter encourages his fellow disciples to persevere despite any hardships they endure.

As it relates to governmental authority, the apostle instructs his readers to submit to every rule of humankind for the Lord's sake. This submission is an act of obedience to God. Christians demonstrate their trust in God's sovereignty and His ultimate control over all earthly powers. This idea is a standard aspect of New Testament ethical exhortation (Romans 13:1, 5; Titus 3:1). Submit means to subordinate to a higher authority. Believers obey unless commanded to sin.

Peter specifically mentions the emperor and his governors. Regional officials appointed by the emperor to maintain order and enforce laws (governors) were procurators, proconsuls and officials who collected taxes. The emperor simply represents the highest level of authority in the Roman Empire.

One purpose of governing authorities is to punish evildoers. Believers are to behave as good and honorable citizens; thereby strengthening the social fabric. Rulers partially preserve order in society by praising good citizens.

Peter does not suggest that rulers always serve this purpose. He was well of the likes of Pharaoh and Nebuchadnezzar who resisted God's will. Moreover, early Christians witnessed Christ's unjust condemnation by Pontius Pilate and Herod Agrippa's equally unjust death sentence for James. However, the most oppressive governments restrain evil and rebuff anarchy.

In verse 15, Peter explains the necessity of submission to authority. Simply stated, it is the will of God. It silences foolish persons. By living uprightly and respecting authority, Christians counter false accusations and negative stereotypes. Their good behavior furthers their faith and disarms critics. Rather than denigrating unbelievers' intellectual abilities, Peter refers to Proverbs which morally degrades foolish people. Their failure to fear the Lord and walk in His ways (Prov 1:7) yields their ignorance and culpability. Good deeds by Christians silence such people.

The apostle also considers any motives behind believers' submission. Three phrases hint toward acceptable motivations and actions when submitting to governing authorities. Disciples submit as free people. Christ ransomed them with His blood and freed them from futile and worldly lifestyles. Believers' submission is never servile or weak.

Second, believers do not use their liberty as a cloak for vice or an excuse to indulge evil. True freedom rebuffs wickedness and any type of slavery. Christians do not respond slavishly to the dictates of government. Their freedom and strength in Christ propel their obedience (Matthew 17:24–27).

Third, believers submit as loyal servants of God. Peter uses the word, "bondservant," which translates into unequivocal fidelity. Believers do not enjoy unconditional freedom. They exercise it under God's authority. Unwavering devotion to God liberates disciples to honor Him in daily living including submission to government to accomplish God's will and purposes.

Peter concludes this passage with a series of admonitions to respect people regardless of social position. He begins with a universal call to honor everyone. Believers treat each person with dignity and respect because God creates humankind in His image, Imago Dei.

Non-believers alike deserve respect and honor. Christians do not distinguish between powerful and preferred people and working and poor persons. Believers reflect God's unfailing love and limitless grace towards all people with their consideration and care.

The author's exhortation to love the brotherhood emphasizes the necessity of mutual love and affirmation within the Christian community. Love is the distinguishing characteristic of Christian disciples (John 13:35 & 1 Peter 4:8). It includes selflessness, compassion, and concern for the welfare of fellow believers.

While believers are to honor people in authority with respect for their offices, they do not worship and fear them. Disciples only fear God. Fear of God is reverence and awe that they have for Him. They recognize God's holiness and unlimited power. Believers' fear of God is the foundation for vocational choices and personal relationships.

THE LESSON APPLIED

How do African-American disciples apply today's lesson? How do we show respect and honor for laws and governmental authorities who have systemically oppressed and systematically exploited us? Someone, who is a social justice advocate, might find it challenging to obey the lesson's instructions and likely to disconnect between rhetoric and reality.

Notwithstanding any reservations, it remains the Christian's duty to submit to the government. This command is hard to accept, especially under certain regimes or political climates. It begs the question, Does God expect us to submit to cruel and inhumane authorities?

But to overcome, focus on Almighty God who is greater than human laws, governments, and social systems. He empowers us to choose wisely, endure hardships, and create a more Christlike society. Our faithfulness in witnessing to God's love through obedience to Christ's teachings opposes hatred and shows the world who truly rules.

Consider the historical examples of Harriet Tubman, Nat Turner, Frederick Douglass, Rosa Parks, Dr. Martin Luther King, Jr., and countless other and anonymous African-American Christians who face daily dilemmas regarding whether to obey unjust laws. How did they reconcile their choices to adhere to higher laws of morality and justice? Beyond the African Diaspora in the United States, these questions also relate to the treatment of Jews in Nazi Germany, the struggle for home rule in Northern Ireland, and tribal conflicts and genocide in the Sudan and Somalia. How should Christians respond to government actions and laws in those situations?

Finally, personalize this lesson. Would you have resisted slavery in the American South? Would you have risked death by aiding Harriet Tubman? Would you have fought to defeat segregation though it was legal? If you lived in Germany during the World War II era, would you have hidden Jews in your house and helped them to escape? What about the crisis in Northern Ireland? Are there any current laws that you would disobey because they violate God's universal laws of justice and equality?

LET'S TALK ABOUT IT...

Discuss the following questions and visit www.rhboyd.com for more information.

What is the difference between respect and honor as it relates to our worship of God?

Explain how the separation of church and state is consistent with Jesus' command to render unto Caesar what is Caesar's and to God what is God's.

How do you determine when a state or government law conflicts with God's will? How would you advise other believers?

How do Christians balance civil disobedience and social justice with their religious obligations?

Get Social
Share your views and tag us
@rhboydco and use #rhboydco

@rhboydco

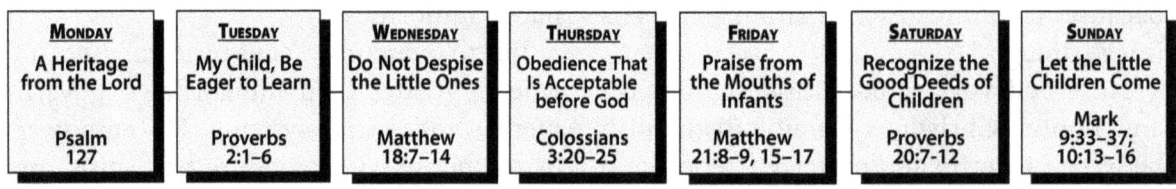

Lesson VIII April 19, 2026

The Child in a Christian World

Adult Topic: The Beauty of Dependence
Background Scripture: Matt. 18:1–6; Mark 9:36–37, 42; 10:13–16; Luke 2:1–20
Lesson Passage: Mark 9:36–37, 42; 10:13–16

MARK 9:36–37, 42; 10:13–16

KJV

AND he took a child, and set him in the midst of them: and when he had taken him in his arms, he said unto them,

37 Whosoever shall receive one of such children in my name, receiveth me: and whosoever shall receive me, receiveth not me, but him that sent me.

• • • • • •

42 And whosoever shall offend one of these little ones that believe in me, it is better for him that a millstone were hanged about his neck, and he were cast into the sea.

• • • • • •

13 And they brought young children to him, that he should touch them: and his disciples rebuked those that brought them.
14 But when Jesus saw it, he was much displeased, and said unto them, Suffer the little children to come unto me, and forbid them not: for of such is the kingdom of God.
15 Verily I say unto you, Whosoever shall not receive the kingdom of God as a little child, he shall not enter therein.
16 And he took them up in his arms, put his hands upon them, and blessed them.

NRSVue

THEN he took a little child and put it among them, and taking it in his arms he said to them,

37 "Whoever welcomes one such child in my name welcomes me, and whoever welcomes me welcomes not me but the one who sent me."

• • • • • •

42 "If any of you cause one of these little ones who believe in me to sin, it would be better for you if a great millstone were hung around your neck and you were thrown into the sea.

• • • • • •

13 People were bringing children to him in order that he might touch them, and the disciples spoke sternly to them.
14 But when Jesus saw this, he was indignant and said to them, "Let the children come to me; do not stop them, for it is to such as these that the kingdom of God belongs.
15 Truly I tell you, whoever does not receive the kingdom of God as a little child will never enter it."
16 And he took them up in his arms, laid his hands on them, and blessed them.

LESSON SETTING

Time: AD 33–90
Place: Capernaum
Setting: The events in the Gospel of Mark 9—10 take place, according to the evangelist, during Jesus' final journey to Jerusalem, where He would be crucified. The cultural context includes Jewish expectations of the Messiah and

MAIN THOUGHT: "Truly I tell you, whoever does not receive the kingdom of God as a little child will never enter it." (Mark 10:15, NRSVue)

the Roman occupation of Israel. Jesus' teachings often challenged both the religious leaders' interpretations of the Law and the social norms of the day. These chapters are crucial for understanding Jesus' mission and the nature of His Kingdom, preparing the disciples for the challenges ahead, and reinforcing the principles of faith, humility, and service. They also emphasize the transformative power of Jesus' message and the radical call to discipleship.

LESSON OUTLINE

I. Receiving a Child is Receiving Jesus (Mark 9:36–37)
II. Don't be a Stumbling Block (Mark 9:42)
III. Receiving Jesus like a Child (Mark 10:13–16)

UNIFYING PRINCIPLE

Accumulating wealth and securing power are standard worldly measures for success. Are there alternative methods and paths to determine success? Jesus teaches us to become "like children" who find riches and esteem in their relationships with the Father. Mere financial gain and self-seeking power are futile in God's economy.

INTRODUCTION

Today's lesson follows Jesus' transfiguration. Jesus takes Peter, James, and John onto a high mountain and reveals His true nature to them. Afterwards, a sharp discussion arose among the disciples relating to who amongst them is the greatest.

Jesus turns this argument into a teachable moment. He uses the example of a child to illustrate humility, service, and seriousness of causing others to stumble. In a broader context, Jesus is preparing His disciples for His impending death and resurrection and emphasizing values of the Kingdom of God.

EXPOSITION

I. Receiving a Child is Receiving Jesus (Mark 9:36–37)

On the road to Capernaum, Jesus addresses the disciples' argument. He takes a little child and places him in front of them. Jesus shocks the disciples by having this child sitting on the Lord's lap while He teaches. These men considered Jesus action to be inappropriate because children were not looked upon favorably in ancient Israel.

Jesus taught with His words and by symbolic actions. He uses the child to dramatize and illustrate this parable. Its significance becomes apparent when considering the lowly place children held. Interestingly, the same Aramaic word meant child and servant.

Children represent innocence, helplessness, and vulnerability. Two passages, Matthew 18:5 and Luke 9:48, depict children as helpless. It is therefore the responsibility of disciples to receive them with care and concern.

Hence, Jesus takes the child into the crook of His arms, thereby developing a picture of reliance, affection, and repose. Securely grasping this child contrasts starkly with the prior debate regarding who among them was greater.

Some scholars posit that the disciples' debate centers upon "what is greatness" instead of "who is the greatest?" Which is preferable, Daniel's Son of Man coming in the clouds or Isaiah's Suffering Servant? Is a Suffering Son of Man greater than a conquering Messiah?

Service and care for the most vulnerable people reveal true greatness. Jesus announces this spiritual principle, "Whoever receives one of these little children in My name receives Me." To respect and assist marginalized people reflect Christ's character and recognizes everyone's inherent worth.

Jesus equates receiving Him with receiving God, the Holy One who sent Him. This divine unity emphasizes one divine essence, purpose and mission. As the perfect representation of God, Jesus embodies His will and Person.

II. Don't be a Stumbling Block (Mark 9:42)

Jesus reprimands His disciples for their intolerance of individuals who invoke the name of the Lord to exorcise demons but do not belong to the Jesus movement. Jesus sternly cautions them against becoming an obstacle to other people's spiritual development. For Jesus, anyone who utilizes the name of Jesus with sincerity is an ally, if not a fellow disciple.

Jesus includes people who are inexperienced, vulnerable and new to the faith in this parabolic teaching. Again, causing these individuals whom society views as insignificant to stumble and preventing them from accessing the truth has severe consequences. It would be better for him that a millstone were hung around his neck and he were thrown into the sea.

This strict warning emphasizes the seriousness of leading others into sin or away from faith. The millstone imagery underscores the weight of the offense. Drowning underneath such a burden reflects the irreversible and devastating consequences of causing spiritual harm to others.

This teaching coheres with Jesus' emphasis on humility, service, and protection of vulnerable persons. Trust, dependence, and openness are essential to entering the Kingdom of God. Jesus challenges societal norms that ignore and devalue marginalized people.

Jesus imposes a higher standard of conduct. He urges disciples to consider their impact on others. Actions and words have significant affects and effects especially on impressionable and neophyte believers. Nurturing and protecting the spiritual well-being of fellow disciples is paramount.

In Mark 9:42, the evangelist issues a powerful call to live the values of the Kingdom of God with integrity and compassion. Believers are to create a community that nurtures vulnerable people with care, compassion, and respect. This teaching remains relevant today. It reminds us of the profound responsibility we have for each other as we share our spiritual journey.

III. Receiving Jesus like a Child (Mark 10:13–16)

Beyond capturing Jesus' love for children, this passage primarily concerns the kind of people who are eligible to enter the Kingdom of God.

The passage lies within a broader narrative in which Jesus teaches about discipleship and the Kingdom of God. Mark places this account after the culmination of a wedding. This order explains the previous discussions about marriage and divorce and the presence of children at the beginning of the chapter. Then as well as now, we naturally associate weddings and children.

We cannot exaggerate Jesus' celebrity status during the last week of His life in Jerusalem. He drew crowds wherever He went. Possibly, the disciples assume they are protecting Jesus from unnecessary interruptions. Generally, they rebuke anyone who approaches Him and specifically people who bring children to Him. They overlook the motives and reasons for which parents bring their children to Jesus. Like the woman with the issue of blood, they want Jesus to touch, heal, and bless them.

Well-intentioned yet misguided in their attempt to guard Jesus, the disciples become a stumbling block for people who need Him. They were preventing people from receiving God's limitless grace and accompanying blessings.

In their defense, the disciples reason that they must prevent any easy access to Jesus because they viewed Him as being too important to bother with unimportant people and their problems.

The disciples' attitude and actions greatly displease Jesus. He rebukes the disciples and then teaches them an important lesson about faith and the Kingdom of God. Jesus subverts social norms in welcoming and blessing the children. He certifies their inherent worth. More than a kind gesture, Jesus' blessing upon children is a profound statement regarding the inclusive nature of God's Kingdom.

Jesus instructs His disciples, "Let the little children come to me, and do not forbid them." He uses children in a teaching metaphor about entrance and composition of the Kingdom of God. Because children were treated indifferently and relegated as lower-class persons, Jesus includes them as representative of all marginalized people whom He welcomes into God's Kingdom.

Instead of rebuffing people, Jesus extends an open invitation to anyone who approaches God's Kingdom like a child, "such is the kingdom of God." The Kingdom of God includes men and women who have an innocent (unvarnished and unstained) faith and desire to live His presence.

Jesus references children to teach His disciples how to receive the blessings of the Kingdom. To please God, disciples cultivate humility and childlike interdependence upon God. His Kingdom surpasses worldly concerns regarding achievements, financial gain and social status. A child's open heart with filled with unwavering faith and trust in Almighty God makes a person receptive to the grace of God.

In the fifteenth verse, Jesus reiterates the fundamental point that unless one receives the Kingdom of God like a little child, he cannot enter. A childlike disposition makes one eligible to receive Jesus and the Kingdom of God.

Easily, children have the ability to believe in the most incredible things. They can imagine a world beyond themselves. Unfortunately, this natural gift fades as one matures into adulthood.

Being eligible for the Kingdom means believing in Him with the freedom of a child. Trust, innocence, and a sense of awe and creativity are the characteristics of this childlike faith. It requires resisting skepticism and relying wholeheartedly upon Christ. Genuine reliance and unconditional trust upon the Divine unfold. Adults can rediscover simplicity and beauty of faith and return to fundamental principles of love, trust, and hope.

Children naturally depend on their parents for everything from basic needs to emotional support. This dependence is not a weakness but beautifully expresses trust and humility. These qualities illustrate how believers should approach their relationship with God.

This dependence recognizes that one cannot accomplish everything on one's own and needs divine guidance. It balances human limitations and divine and infinite power. Believers open themselves to fully experiencing God's grace and provision.

Additionally, faith and this dependency fosters constant communication and reliance on Him. It prioritizes constant prayer and gratitude; recognizing God's handiwork in every aspect of their existence.

Jesus concludes this teaching on the Kingdom by taking the children into His arms. He lays hands on them and blesses them, visually demonstrating that the blessings of the Kingdom are available to anyone who comes like a child.

His actions are a powerful reminder that the Kingdom of God is open to all who approach with humble and trusting hearts.

Finally, the evangelist composes this passage to invite his readers to reflect on their own faith and to strive for a childlike openness and receptivity to God's love. He also challenges disciples to create an environment reflective of the inclusive and loving nature of Jesus' ministry.

THE LESSON APPLIED

There is so much we can learn from children particularly when poisonous dictates of religious idealism taint our perspective.

Children ask questions about God that adults ignore. Their hearts are pure and motives are genuine. Their innocence and openness ideally depict what the Kingdom of God is like. They provide insight into how to approach our relationship with God. Their ability to forgive quickly, love unconditionally, and trust unreservedly are qualities that enrich our spiritual journey.

Observing children reminds us to approach God with a sense of awe and wonder, free from the cynicism and doubt that often accompany adulthood. Children embody the essence of true faith and remind us of simplicity and purity that characterize our walk with God.

Their natural curiosity and unguarded hearts encourage us to seek a more genuine connection with the divine. By emulating their example, we strip away complexities and barriers that hinder our spiritual growth. Consequently, allowing us to experience a more profound and authentic relationship with God.

As we study this lesson, a quarter of the twenty-first century has elapsed. Arguably, "GenZers" and "Alphas" do not question the scientific method as one of the most reliable means to determine truth. The Bible no longer factors significantly as a trustworthy tool to derive certainty. The ascent of higher biblical criticism since the Progressive Era (1880 to 1920) eroded general reliance upon the scriptures as the revelation of the Word of God and it trustworthiness as guide for life. Consequently, cynicism and doubt permeate the pews of each church. Disciples struggle to rely on the Bible. The practical disadvantages of this erosion of faith and practice of spiritual disciplines are an indifference to prayer, worship, fellowship, and reliance upon Christ's teachings. Further, disciples struggle to trust God. Children however remind us of the necessity of believing in God despite the rise of secularism and humanism. They more significantly teach us to genuinely rely upon God regardless of any challenges or crises we face daily.

It is necessary to trust God with a childlike faith which means practically to believe unwaveringly that He is able to do anything that the Word of God says. Prior to the rebellion, arrogance, and unbridled questioning of adolescence, children believe unconditionally in their parents' abilities to resolve any problem. Whether a scraped knee, common cold, playground spat, potty accident, fear of the dark, monsters hiding in the closet or any other colossal childhood problem, children run with open arms, wholehearted faith, and unquestionable trust in their parents to "do something about it." Jaded by life's daily struggles, adult disciples fear that Almighty God may not be able to resolve their challenges. Whether finances, health, employment, relationships and myriad situations, disciples need to apply childlike faith by seeking the will of God as the answer to any challenge that they experience.

Finally, the need to grow personally and develop spiritually by progressing from mental and intellectual faith in God to wholehearted and unswerving trust in Him is of utmost importance. Many people believe in God. They assert that is He is the "Creator of the ends of the Earth and the Maker of all that is seen and unseen." Do they mature spiritually to the point of unconditionally trusting God despite physical circumstances that contradict His character? Trust enables them to rely steadfastly upon Almighty God.

LET'S TALK ABOUT IT...

Discuss the following questions and visit www.rhboyd.com for more information.

How does this lesson affect your views on abortion?

What is the difference, in your words, between having a "childlike" faith verses having faith?

How do Christians today behave like the disciples in this lesson in preventing people from getting close to Jesus?

What is the Kingdom of God, and how is it relevant in the United States of America?

What does it mean to receive the Kingdom of God?

Get Social

Share your views and tag us
@rhboydco and use #rhboydco

@rhboydco

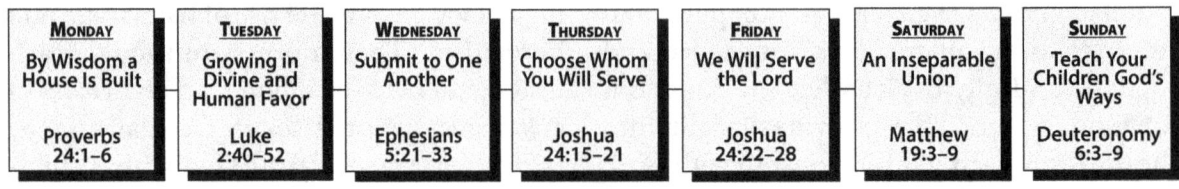

Lesson IX   **April 26, 2026**

The Christian Home in a Modern World

Adult Topic: Love that Shapes Society
Background Scripture: Deut. 6:3-9; Matt. 19:3-9; Luke 2:40-52; 24:28-32; Eph. 6:1-9; 2 Tim. 1:3-5; 3:14-15
Lesson Passage: Deuteronomy 6:3-9; Matthew 19:3-9

DEUTERONOMY 6:3-9; MATTHEW 19:3-9

KJV	NRSVue
HEAR therefore, O Israel, and observe to do it; that it may be well with thee, and that ye may increase mightily, as the Lord God of thy fathers hath promised thee, in the land that floweth with milk and honey.	HEAR therefore, O Israel, and observe them diligently, so that it may go well with you and so that you may multiply greatly in a land flowing with milk and honey, as the Lord, the God of your ancestors, has promised you.
4 Hear, O Israel: The Lord our God is one Lord:	4 "Hear, O Israel: The Lord is our God, the Lord alone.
5 And thou shalt love the Lord thy God with all thine heart, and with all thy soul, and with all thy might.	5 You shall love the Lord your God with all your heart and with all your soul and with all your might.
6 And these words, which I command thee this day, shall be in thine heart:	6 Keep these words that I am commanding you today in your heart.
7 And thou shalt teach them diligently unto thy children, and shalt talk of them when thou sittest in thine house, and when thou walkest by the way, and when thou liest down, and when thou risest up.	7 Recite them to your children and talk about them when you are at home and when you are away, when you lie down and when you rise.
8 And thou shalt bind them for a sign upon thine hand, and they shall be as frontlets between thine eyes.	8 Bind them as a sign on your hand, fix them as an emblem on your forehead,
9 And thou shalt write them upon the posts of thy house, and on thy gates.	9 and write them on the doorposts of your house and on your gates.
••• Matthew 19:3-9 •••	••• Matthew 19:3-9 •••
3 The Pharisees also came unto him, tempting him, and saying unto him, Is it lawful for a man to put away his wife for every cause?	3 Some Pharisees came to him, and to test him they asked, "Is it lawful for a man to divorce his wife for any cause?"
4 And he answered and said unto them, Have ye not read, that he which made them at the beginning made them male and female,	4 He answered, "Have you not read that the one who made them at the beginning 'made them male and female,'
5 And said, For this cause shall a man leave father and mother, and shall cleave to his wife: and they twain shall be one flesh?	5 and said, 'For this reason a man shall leave his father and mother and be joined to his wife, and the two shall become one flesh'?

MAIN THOUGHT: Keep these words that I am commanding you today in your heart. Recite them to your children and talk about them when you are at home and when you are away, when you lie down and when you rise. (Deuteronomy 6:6-7, NRSVue)

DEUTERONOMY 6:3-9; MATTHEW 19:3-9

KJV

6 Wherefore they are no more twain, but one flesh. What therefore God hath joined together, let not man put asunder.

7 They say unto him, Why did Moses then command to give a writing of divorcement, and to put her away?

8 He saith unto them, Moses because of the hardness of your hearts suffered you to put away your wives: but from the beginning it was not so.

9 And I say unto you, Whosoever shall put away his wife, except it be for fornication, and shall marry another, committeth adultery: and whoso marrieth her which is put away doth commit adultery.

NRSVue

6 So they are no longer two but one flesh. Therefore what God has joined together, let no one separate."

7 They said to him, "Why then did Moses command us to give a certificate of dismissal and to divorce her?"

8 He said to them, "It was because you were so hard-hearted that Moses allowed you to divorce your wives, but from the beginning it was not so.

9 And I say to you, whoever divorces his wife, except for sexual immorality, and marries another commits adultery, and he who marries a divorced woman commits adultery."

LESSON SETTING

Time: 1400 BC
Place: Plains of Moab
Setting: The children of Israel are poised in the plains of Moab to launch an attack across the Jordan River in response to God's purpose and command to enter and occupy the land of promise. God had prepared the way in every respect for this transition. The book of Deuteronomy (and most likely much of the rest of the Pentateuch) was written by Moses on the eve of the conquest of Canaan to address two main concerns. First, it was important for the people to understand their identity and what their God intended for them in the years ahead. Deuteronomy reiterates the covenant to a new generation. The Sinai generation of thirty-eight years earlier was largely out of the picture. The new generation was about to embark on the conquest and needed the covenant reiterated and reaffirmed. Second, Moses was about to die, so it was imperative that he write the entire collection of tradition and truth that he understood to be the revelation of God. The composition would serve as the body of law and practice for the covenant community from that day forward.

LESSON OUTLINE

I. The Greatest Commandment of All (Deuteronomy 6:3-4)
II. The Importance of the Greatest Command (Deuteronomy 6:6-9)
III. Love Marriage and Divorce (Matthew 19:3-9)

UNIFYING PRINCIPLE

Some people see a correlation between values learned in the home and the moral compass of the dominant culture in society. What is the role of family in shaping societal values? We learn from Jesus and the Deuteronomic covenant that God demands that we honor the contract of marriage, that we love and respect family members, and that we teach the precepts of faith to our children.

INTRODUCTION

Deuteronomy is largely a collection of repetitive sermons that Moses preaches to the children of Israel shortly before his death. They settled near the plains of Moab adjacent to the Promised Land after forty years of wandering in the wilderness. The sermons direct Israel to faithfully obey the covenant laws.

Deuteronomy primarily addresses Israel's future. Reflecting on the nation's past mistakes, Moses admonishes the nation to avoid repeating them when they live in the Promised Land.

Deuteronomy 6 concerns a pivotal moment for the Israelites. They begin their transition from nomadic living to settling in the land promised to their ancestors. This moment compelled their incorporation of extensive laws governing all aspects of life. The details of the laws expand upon the great commandment of Deuteronomy 6:5; Israel must love the LORD with all their heart, soul, and strength.

EXPOSITION

I. The Greatest Commandment of All (Deuteronomy 6:3–4)

God prescribes the Law through Moses and forms a religious people whose national character would be wholehearted and single-minded devotion to the Lord their God. The people reverence the Lord through acceptable worship and steadfast obedience to His will.

In the third verse, Moses exhorts the children of Israel to hear and carefully obey all laws that he presents to them. He emphasizes hearing and doing to teach a deep-rooted spiritual principle. Understanding God's Word involves putting it into practice.

Obedience by the children of Israel is essential to their well-being and prosperity in the Promised Land. God conditions His promises upon their obedience. God promises to bless them abundantly and multiply those blessings while they live in Canaan.

The writer of Deuteronomy first describes Canaan as a land of milk and honey instead of the "good land" (1:25, 35; 3:25; 4:21, 22). Moses utilizes this favorable expression to entice and persuade the people to obey.

The description of the land indicates its natural bounty inclusive of an abundant supply of food, domesticated animals, and natural resources.

The phrase, "a land flowing with milk and honey," exaggerate the land's bounty and natural resources. Two commodities, the product of human labor and the product of nature, represent the abundance of blessings that God's promises yield. Canaan's bounty and fertility contrast greatly with hardships of the desert and terrain of Egypt, a land whose fields had to be watered by foot.

The reference to "the LORD God of your fathers" connects the wilderness generation to the promises made to their ancestors. It reinforces continuity of God's covenant and faithfulness. The Law Moses imparts to the children of Israel include moral laws to govern ethical behavior, ceremonial laws that prescribe rituals, and judicial laws that render legal judgments. Moses' teachings ensure a holistic approach to living in accordance with God's will.

The Ten Commandments, "The Decalogue," of Deuteronomy 5:6–21 contain great principles of covenant relationship between God and His people. The Law teaches the children of Israel how to relate to a perfectly holy, righteous and infinite God. It reveals God's character and outlines Israel's responsibilities in relationship to

Him. The Ten Commandments summarize the entire Law.

The fourth and fifth verses further refine the Ten Commandments as they distill their essence, the Shema: "Hear, O Israel, The Lord our God, the Lord is one. You shall love the Lord your God with all your heart and with all your soul and with all your strength."

The Decalogue summarizes the Torah and the Shema summarizes the Decalogue. Moreover, the Shema expresses the purpose of the whole person as he relates to God in sixteen words. Daily in Jewish prayers, adherents recite it as a statement of faith.

Meaning "to hear," the Shema, begins with a command and proceeds to a decree. "To hear" in Hebrew equates with "to obey" especially in covenantal contexts. Practically speaking, to listen to God and disobey His command means you did not hear Him.

Obedience to God's commandments and will starts with complete acceptance God's sovereignty. Worshiping God through obedience to His commands and will is a foundational principle of Judaism. Moses admonishes the children of Israel to hear and obey the one and only Yahweh, the God of their fathers. He underscores the uniqueness and exclusivity of God, amongst other known deities, which only Israel has. Moses provides an unmistakable basis for monotheistic faith.

The Lord's unique oneness requires Israel's acknowledgment and holistic obedience. In covenant language, obedience equals love. To obey is to love God; and to love God is to obey with every component of one's being.

II. The Importance of the Greatest Command (Deuteronomy 6:6–9)

The sixth verse exhorts the people to commit the Law to the minds and hearts. Contrary to contemporary conceptualization of "heart" as the seat of emotions, ancient Hebrew thought considered "heart" to refer to reason and rationality. Therefore, the commandment means constant reflection on their obligation to love God through obedience in daily living.

Covenant recipients and beneficiaries were to engrave the Law upon their hearts. Conjure the image of an engraver using a hammer and chisel to painstakingly and meticulously carve text into granite. The labor that this task requires is daunting. It is worthwhile as the message remains indelibly.

Future generations of Israelites must receive and transmit the words of the Lord's everlasting covenant and revelation to their posterity.

With clear hyperbole in the seventh verse, Moses reinforces this message with constant repetition. Whether sitting at home or walking on the road, lying down to sleep or rising for the tasks of a new day, parents and children as teachers and students discuss covenant matters and faithful adherence.

The contrasting places and postures intentionally suggests an all-encompassing concept. Sitting and walking as well as laying down and rising encompasses all human effort. Likewise, retiring at night and rising in the morning allude to the totality of time. The truth of the covenant, according to Moses, must be at the center of work and life.

A metaphor in the eighth verse depicts how thoroughly the people were to incorporate the covenant and Law into their lives. They were to bind the Law to their hands and foreheads. The Law infiltrates the work of their hands. It remains constantly on their minds. Originally interpreted metaphorically, later modern Jewish tradition developed this practice literally.

Known as "tefillin," frontlets are small leather boxes containing scrolls of parchment inscribed with verses from the Shema. Traditionally, Jewish men wore these boxes during weekday morning prayers. Strapped to the arm and forehead, they symbolize commitment to God's commandments in thought and deed.

III. Love Marriage and Divorce (Matthew 19:3-9)

In Matthew 19:3-9, a Pharisee approaches Jesus to test Him with a question about the legality of divorce. This encounter occurs while Jesus teaches in the region of Judea beyond the Jordan where large crowds follow Him. The Pharisee's question is not a genuine inquiry but a test. He and his fellow Pharisees hope to trap Jesus into saying something that could twist against Him.

There were two main schools of thought relating to divorce, a controversial issue in Jewish society. Holding the stricter view, Rabbi Shammai allowed divorce only for serious offenses. Rabbi Hillel held the more lenient view; he allowed divorce for almost any reason.

In responding to the Pharisee's question, Jesus refers to the creation narrative in Genesis. He emphasizes the divine intention for marriage. By asking them "have you not read," Jesus challenges their scholarship of scripture for which the Pharisees were known. Citing Genesis 1:27 and 2:24, Jesus declares that marriage is a creation ordinance intended to last a lifetime between one man and one woman.

The phrase, "one flesh," signifies an inseparable bond that marriage creates and reinforces its sanctity and permanence. Almighty God ordains the union of marriage. People, therefore, should not lightly dissolve it. God means it to be indissoluble.

Dissatisfied with Jesus' answer, the Pharisee asks a follow-up question. "Why then did Moses command a man to give his wife a certificate of divorce and put her away?" They cite Deuteronomy 24:1-4 where Moses allowed divorce under certain circumstances. Their interpretation of the text reveals a misunderstanding of Moses' concession. What they deem to be a command is a reluctant allowance.

Jesus does not challenge their logic. He considers only the permanence of the Law. He explains that Moses allowed divorce because of the hardened condition of the human heart which is a consequence of humanity's fall from the grace of God. God did not create people to divorce. He also does not intend that those who are re-created by faith in Christ to practice divorce.

Jesus' words in the ninth verse fuels ongoing discussion about Christian marriage. The controversy about divorce overshadows his teachings on marriage, covenant and faithfulness. The Pharisees' attempt to exploit a legal loophole to justify adultery by manipulating Jesus into endorsing divorce. Yet, Jesus maintains the integrity of marriage. His reserves his strongest condemnation for persons who initiate divorce to satisfy selfish ambitions. According to Jesus, anyone who divorces his wife and marries another woman, while having a living former wife, commits adultery.

Jesus reaffirms God's intention for marriage as a lifelong, sacred union. He employs the creation narrative and calls His followers to a higher standard of marital fidelity and integrity. Marriage is not merely a human contract but a divine covenant that reflects God's unwavering commitment to His people.

THE LESSON APPLIED

Like everything we need to survive in life: food to eat, air to breathe, water we drink, God's love is essential to our existence. Unfortunately, we take recurring natural and invaluable resources for granted. As we spike our food supply with antibiotics and other chemicals and pollute our air and water, we arrogantly act as if we have an inexhaustible supply.

As it relates to our love for God, believers misguidedly consider it as important only when attending a worship service, Bible study or church gathering. Knowing God's love for us is to know what true love is. He teaches us how to love as we accept His unfailing love for us. God's unwavering and unconditional love empowers us with security and liberates us with confidence to discover our purpose in life.

In understanding and accepting this divine love, we acquire inner peace and fulfillment in who we are. God's love guides us through life's daily challenges. It provides comfort and strength in times of grief, loss, and need. It inspires and equips us to love others selflessly. It fosters communities built on compassion and kindness. Acceptance of God's love results in meaningful lives that reflect His grace and mercy in daily living.

LET'S TALK ABOUT IT...

Discuss the following questions and visit www.rhboyd.com for more information.

How can loving God with all of our heart, soul, and strength influence the way we build and maintain relationships within our communities?

Explain how teaching Shema to children will help the younger generation contribute to developing a more compassionate and cohesive society?

In your opinion, how do the concepts of love and fidelity in marriage serve as a foundation for a stable community?

Both passages in today's lesson highlight the importance of love and commitment. How can these principles be applied to address social issues such as poverty, injustice, and inequality in our communities?

Get Social

Share your views and tag us
@rhboydco and use #rhboydco

@rhboydco

Home Daily Devotional Readings
April 27–May 3, 2026

Monday	Tuesday	Wednesday	Thursday	Friday	Saturday	Sunday
Seek the Welfare of the City	God's Own People	Pray for Those in Authority	God Is Sovereign over the Nations	Our Citizenship Is in Heaven	A Season of National Repentance	God's Compassion for All
Jeremiah 29:3–7	1 Peter 2:4–12	1 Timothy 2:1–8	Psalm 33:10–22	Philippians 3:17–21	Jonah 3:1–5	Jonah 4:6–11

Lesson X — May 3, 2026

The Higher Patriotism

Adult Topic: Grace Beyond Borders
Background Scripture: Jonah 1–4
Lesson Passage: Jonah 1:1-3; 3:1-5; 4:6-11

JONAH 1:1-3; 3:1-5; 4:6-11

KJV

NOW the word of the Lord came unto Jonah the son of Amittai, saying,
2 Arise, go to Nineveh, that great city, and cry against it; for their wickedness is come up before me.
3 But Jonah rose up to flee unto Tarshish from the presence of the Lord, and went down to Joppa; and he found a ship going to Tarshish: so he paid the fare thereof, and went down into it, to go with them unto Tarshish from the presence of the Lord.

••• 3:1-5 •••
1 And the word of the Lord came unto Jonah the second time, saying,
2 Arise, go unto Nineveh, that great city, and preach unto it the preaching that I bid thee.
3 So Jonah arose, and went unto Nineveh, according to the word of the Lord. Now Nineveh was an exceeding great city of three days' journey.
4 And Jonah began to enter into the city a day's journey, and he cried, and said, Yet forty days, and Nineveh shall be overthrown.
5 So the people of Nineveh believed God, and proclaimed a fast, and put on sackcloth, from the greatest of them even to the least of them.

••• 4:6-11 •••
6 And the Lord God prepared a gourd, and made it to come up over Jonah, that it might be a shadow over his head, to deliver him from his grief. So Jonah was exceeding glad of the gourd.

NRSVue

NOW the word of the Lord came to Jonah son of Amittai, saying,
2 "Go at once to Nineveh, that great city, and cry out against it, for their wickedness has come up before me."
3 But Jonah set out to flee to Tarshish from the presence of the Lord. He went down to Joppa and found a ship going to Tarshish; so he paid his fare and went on board, to go with them to Tarshish, away from the presence of the Lord.

••• 3:1-5 •••
1 The word of the Lord came to Jonah a second time, saying,
2 "Get up, go to Nineveh, that great city, and proclaim to it the message that I tell you."
3 So Jonah set out and went to Nineveh, according to the word of the Lord. Now Nineveh was an exceedingly large city, a three days' walk across.
4 Jonah began to go into the city, going a day's walk. And he cried out, "Forty days more, and Nineveh shall be overthrown!"
5 And the people of Nineveh believed God; they proclaimed a fast, and everyone, great and small, put on sackcloth.

••• 4:6-11 •••
6 The Lord God appointed a bush and made it come up over Jonah, to give shade over his head, to save him from his discomfort, so Jonah was very happy about the bush.

MAIN THOUGHT: The LORD said, "You are concerned about the bush, for which you did not labor and which you did not grow; it came into being in a night and perished in a night. And should I not be concerned about Nineveh . . . ?" (Jonah 4:10-11, NRSVue)

JONAH 1:1-3; 3:1-5; 4:6-11

KJV

7 But God prepared a worm when the morning rose the next day, and it smote the gourd that it withered.

8 And it came to pass, when the sun did arise, that God prepared a vehement east wind; and the sun beat upon the head of Jonah, that he fainted, and wished in himself to die, and said, It is better for me to die than to live.

9 And God said to Jonah, Doest thou well to be angry for the gourd? And he said, I do well to be angry, even unto death.

10 Then said the Lord, Thou hast had pity on the gourd, for the which thou hast not laboured, neither madest it grow; which came up in a night, and perished in a night:

11 And should not I spare Nineveh, that great city, wherein are more than sixscore thousand persons that cannot discern between their right hand and their left hand; and also much cattle?

NRSVue

7 But when dawn came up the next day, God appointed a worm that attacked the bush, so that it withered.

8 When the sun rose, God prepared a sultry east wind, and the sun beat down on the head of Jonah so that he was faint and asked that he might die. He said, "It is better for me to die than to live."

9 But God said to Jonah, "Is it right for you to be angry about the bush?" And he said, "Yes, angry enough to die."

10 Then the Lord said, "You are concerned about the bush, for which you did not labor and which you did not grow; it came into being in a night and perished in a night.

11 And should I not be concerned about Nineveh, that great city, in which there are more than a hundred and twenty thousand persons who do not know their right hand from their left and also many animals?"

LESSON SETTING

Time: 810–783 BC
Place: Nineveh
Setting: The historical setting of Jonah is rooted in the eighth century BC during the reign of Jeroboam II in Israel (782–753 BC). This was a time of relative peace and prosperity for Israel, although the dominant empire of Assyria was a looming threat. Jonah, a prophet from Israel, was called by God to go to Nineveh, the capital of Assyria, to pronounce judgment on its wickedness. Nineveh was a major city in the Assyrian empire, known for its grandeur as well as its brutality. Jonah's mission to Nineveh was unusual because prophets usually delivered messages within Israel. This story highlights the tension between Israel and Assyria and sets the stage for Jonah's dramatic journey and the broader themes of mercy and repentance.

LESSON OUTLINE

I. Jonah's Commissioning and Flight (Jonah 1:1-3)
II. Jonah's Re-commission and Compliance (Jonah 3:1-5)
III. Jonah's Lesson about Grace (Jonah 4:6-11)

UNIFYING PRINCIPLE

People tend to make decisions and form allegiances based on loyalty to their country of origin. Can patriotism go too far? Even after God rescued Jonah from death, and yet he hated to see God's grace so freely given to others.

INTRODUCTION

Eighth century BC, prophets including Amos, Hosea, Isaiah, and Micah addressed myriad spiritual and social issues of their era. Known for boldness, they willingly confronted the people and leaders of Israel and Judah with their sins, especially idolatry, social injustice, and neglect of the covenant with God.

These prophets delivered messages of impending judgment because of the nation's unfaithfulness. They also offered hope for repentance and restoration. Their messages exceeded spiritual concerns. They focused upon ethical and moral conduct in society. They sought a community that reflected God's justice and compassion.

Isaiah's prophecies include future visions in which justice and peace prevail. Prophesying in the Northern Kingdom of Israel, Amos and Hosea concentrated upon social justice and sincere worship. Micah, in the Southern Kingdom of Judah, emphasized the importance of justice, mercy, and humility before God.

EXPOSITION

I. Jonah's Commissioning and Flight (Jonah 1:1–3)

The book of Jonah opens with God's self-revelation to the prophet. It begins with a description of the prophet's call. "Arise and go to Nineveh." His commission from God foreshadows his dramatic journey.

Nineveh was a major city of the Assyrian Empire of which Israel was a vassal state. During Jonah's ministry, however, the empire faced internal issues and conflicts with neighboring states. They provided a respite for regions like Israel.

Located on the eastern bank of the Tigris River, Nineveh symbolized Assyrian power and cruelty. God commissions Jonah to travel to the city and condemn its wickedness. This assignment reflects God's mercy and universal concern for all nations. Jonah's mission was unprecedented as God's prophets usually delivered messages within the borders of and only for the people of Israel.

Jonah's responds to God's command with immediate defiance. Instead of obeying God's command to go to Nineveh, he flees to Tarshish in the opposite direction. Lying in a distant place in the western Mediterranean, Tarshish possibly was modern-day Spain. Still, Jonah's flight to Tarshish weaves through the port city of Joppa where he boards a ship.

Jonah's disobedience underscores his fear of the violence in Nineveh and his reluctance to see the Lord spare her His judgment.

II. Jonah's Re-commission and Compliance (Jonah 3:1–5)

The first two verses in the first and third chapters appear redundant; the verses are so similar. The author of the book desires to show his readers the extent of Jonah's change and how much more change he needed resulting from his experience of running from the Lord.

God's presence faithfully engulfs Jonah despite his vain attempt to flee from God. The sea storm and its aftermath evidence God's abiding presence and protection. God sends a storm, calms the sea, influences sailors, uses a large fish and forgives Jonah's insolence. Jonah completes a circle of living and now has a softer heart.

As the third chapter opens, we do not know if Jonah is still on the beach where the fish spat him out or if he returned home in Israel. The author does not mention any reproach for the prophet's previous disobedience. God speaks to the prophet a second time. Throughout Jonah's ordeal, he relies upon God while God remains silent. However, God breaks His silence in this third chapter.

Initially, God permits Jonah to cry out against the city of Nineveh in his own words. Now, the Lord says to him, "Preach the message that I tell you." The message requires Jonah's complete dependence on hearing God's voice and precisely following His command.

Jonah departs his home in Israel and travels five hundred miles northeast to Nineveh. Camels and donkey caravans were the usual means of transportation. That modality necessitated approximately a month of travel time.

The author's intention in recounting Jonah's immediate obedience to God's command in the third verse is to contrast it with the prophet's earlier disobedience. The Jonah of this chapter receives forgiveness for fleeing God's presence, redemption by the fish's regurgitation of him and recommissioning of his prophetic ministry.

An exceedingly great city, Nineveh spans a large geographic area and comprises an important urban center. It also is a significant city for God's purposes. Interestingly, the translation for "exceedingly great" is "great in the sight of God." Although the people of Nineveh were not Israelites, they were important in the eyes of God who was equally concerned about their spiritual wellbeing.

Nineveh's complexity made a one-day stop impractical. Three days of preaching would be necessary to reach the city's population. God's message for Nineveh could not be delivered quickly. So, Jonah traveled to different areas and spoke to as many groups as possible.

Jonah's arrival was undoubtedly dramatic. His clothing, language, and dialect were distinctive. His demeanor and lifestyle differed from an average Ninevite. Combined with an existential message of doom, Jonah's arrival and preaching added spice to local society.

The message from the Lord was succinct. Jonah preached repeatedly, as he went through the city, "Yet forty days, and Nineveh shall be overthrown." He does not provide a reason for the destruction, nor does Jonah describe the manner of the destruction. Remarkably, he does not issue an explicit call to repentance. Was there any possibility of deliverance following repentance?

The fifth verse depicts a whirlwind of activity by the people. Revival breaks out in the city as Jonah's message spreads amongst hearers and those who heard from others thereby reaching the entire populace. En masse, the people accept the divine source of Jonah's message. They believe that the threat could happen.

As a result of this miraculous revival, the people of Nineveh repent of their sins and begin to believe in God. The personal name of the deity, LORD, shifts within the book. Jonah changes to the generic word God (Elohim). This literary move suggests the novice believers had yet to learn about the LORD. Their fear of imminent destruction primarily caused their widespread conversion.

The Ninevites' initial belief in God demonstrates their inward transformation. The proclamation of a citywide fast articulates an inward change has occurred. The uniform observance of wearing sackcloth symbolized outward change. Sackcloth, a coarse cloth most often made of goat's hair, was the customary garment of the poor and the mourning. Prophets often wore sackcloth as a sign of mourning for the sins of the people.

III. Jonah's Lesson about Grace (Jonah 4:6–11)

Hoping God would destroy Nineveh, Jonah goes to a hill on the east side of the city and builds a shelter. The aggressive Assyrian heat overpowers the shelter's effectiveness to shade him from the sun. The Lord God prepares a plant which grows above Jonah. God supplies Jonah with shade and protection from the heat. His unmerited favor toward the prophet becomes a lesson for Jonah as it relates to God's compassion and mercy toward the people of Nineveh.

God miraculously uses a plant to deliver Jonah from natural threats. Deliverance literally translates "deliver him from evil" which expresses the general state of Jonah's mind and mood. Average daily maximum temperatures in Mesopotamia approach 110 degrees Fahrenheit. Heat was a major health and well-being factor. Any shade would have been a gift of relief.

Jonah's gratitude for the plant is both fascinating and tragic. The Hebrew text says, "Jonah rejoiced with great joy over the plant." He is ecstatic. For the first time, he is happy. However, Jonah does not express similar emotions about the mass repentance of the Ninevites. Jonah's expresses great joy over a plant, but reacts to the deliverance of Nineveh in an opposite manner.

Possibly, a twofold reason explains Jonah's happiness. He first experiences relief from oppressive heat. He also sees miraculous growth of a plant that indicates God's favor. That miracle redeems his disappointment because of Nineveh's repentance.

Jonah's disdain regarding the people's deliverance is brief and fleeting. God quickly ends Jonah's happiness and any ill-conceived notions that contributed to it. The lesson of grace continues.

God prepares a worm to chew at the root of the plant which withers. A vehement east wind combines with scorching sun to beat upon Jonah's head. God utilizes these natural elements to teach Jonah important spiritual lessons. They also demonstrate His sovereign power over creation.

In the ninth verse, God asks about Jonah's anger a second time. The inquiry exposes Jonah's inability to discern God's will, his ineffectiveness in determining what is important, his self-centeredness in response to God's calling, and his indifference towards God's grace. "Is it right for you to be angry about the plant?" The prophet misguidedly esteems that plant and the comfort it yields to him above God's salvation of the city. Jonah's desire for death reveals his distorted view of the value of life.

THE LESSON APPLIED

Jonah personifies a regrettable trend and perspective in some sectors of American Christianity that furthers a false notion that disciples can manage God's grace. More specifically, grossly misguided brothers and sisters within the broad swath of the evangelical community are often intolerant of any persons or groups that espouse different beliefs. They can often demand oppressive and draconian laws and rituals to punish and deprive marginalized and vulnerable people of their needs. Meanwhile, they insist they have the love of Christ in their hearts and are doing His will. While they acknowledge God's grace and mercy are sufficient for the forgiveness of human sin, they often lack empathy for others and can set an standard for faith that is impossible to abide.

This distortion and contradiction of God's grace parallels Jonah's challenge. His repulsive sense of entitlement blinded him from understanding God's grace toward anyone other than himself or his people. God places no restrictions on who He will welcome into His embrace. His position as a descendant of God's chosen people had prejudiced Jonah with privileged thinking.

Disciples, who themselves have been saved from sin by grace, must demonstrate the same measure of God's grace toward a sometimes unkind and unloving world filled with judgment and condemnation.

Jesus stood out from the fray of religious leaders because He offered a fresh message of hope and forgiveness. That message has not changed in 2,000 years. Just as God extended Himself to the Ninevites, and Jesus offered Himself to the world, His disciples have no authority to pick and choose whom God is willing to embrace.

Our heavenly Father expects us to engage in intentional acts of Christlike love and random acts of kindness that honor Him and bless His people. As followers of Christ and His ambassadors, we are to be instruments of His grace and mercy.

LET'S TALK ABOUT IT...

Discuss the following questions and visit www.rhboyd.com for more information.

Why did Jonah initially run away from God's command to go to Nineveh? What does this tell us about his understanding of God's grace?

How did Jonah react to God's compassion towards Nineveh? What does his reaction reveal about his understanding of God's grace?

God provided a plant to give Jonah shade and then took it away. What lesson was God teaching Jonah through this experience about His grace and compassion?

How can we apply the lesson of "grace beyond borders" in our own lives? Are there people or groups we find difficult to extend grace to, and how can we overcome these barriers?

Get Social

Share your views and tag us @rhboydco and use #rhboydco

@rhboydco

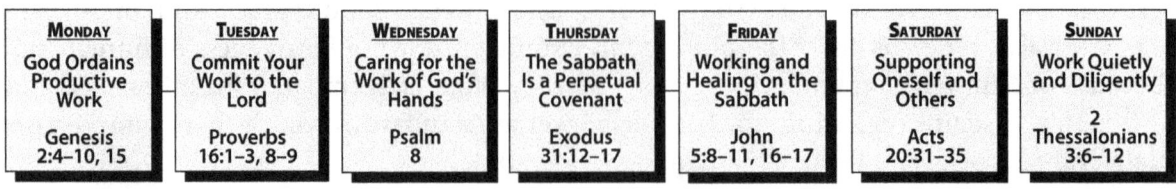

Lesson XI   **May 10, 2026**

Useful Work as Christian Duty

Adult Topic: A Good Day's Work
Background Scripture: Gen. 2:15–25; Exod. 20:9; Neh. 6:3; John 5:17; 9:4; Acts 20:33–35; 2 Thess. 3:6–12; Eph. 4:28
Lesson Passage: Gen. 2:15; Exod. 20:9; John 5:17; 9:4; Acts 20:33–35; 2 Thess. 3:6–12

GENESIS 2:15; EXODUS 20:9; JOHN 5:17; 9:4; ACTS 20:33-35; 2 THESSALONIANS 3:6-12

KJV	NRSVue
AND the Lord God took the man, and put him into the garden of Eden to dress it and to keep it.	THE Lord God took the man and put him in the garden of Eden to till it and keep it.
••• Exodus 20:9 •••	••• Exodus 20:9 •••
9 Six days shalt thou labour, and do all thy work:	9 Six days you shall labor and do all your work.
••• John 5:17; 9:4 •••	••• John 5:17; 9:4 •••
17 But Jesus answered them, My Father worketh hitherto, and I work.	17 But Jesus answered them, "My Father is still working, and I also am working."
••• 9:4 •••	••• 9:4 •••
4 I must work the works of him that sent me, while it is day: the night cometh, when no man can work.	4 We must work the works of him who sent me while it is day; night is coming, when no one can work.
••• Acts 20:33-35 •••	••• Acts 20:33-35 •••
33 I have coveted no man's silver, or gold, or apparel.	33 I coveted no one's silver or gold or clothing.
34 Yea, ye yourselves know, that these hands have ministered unto my necessities, and to them that were with me.	34 You know for yourselves that I worked with my own hands to support myself and my companions.
35 I have shewed you all things, how that so labouring ye ought to support the weak, and to remember the words of the Lord Jesus, how he said, It is more blessed to give than to receive.	35 In all this I have given you an example that by such work we must support the weak, remembering the words of the Lord Jesus, for he himself said, 'It is more blessed to give than to receive.' "
••• 2 Thessalonians 3:6-12 •••	••• 2 Thessalonians 3:6-12 •••
6 Now we command you, brethren, in the name of our Lord Jesus Christ, that ye withdraw yourselves from every brother that walketh disorderly, and not after the tradition which he received of us.	6 Now we command you, brothers and sisters, in the name of our Lord Jesus Christ, to keep away from every brother or sister living irresponsibly and not according to the tradition that they[a] received from us.
7 For yourselves know how ye ought to follow us: for we behaved not ourselves disorderly among you;	7 For you yourselves know how you ought to imitate us; we were not irresponsible when we were with you,

MAIN THOUGHT: "In all this I have given you an example that by such work we must support the weak, remembering the words of the Lord Jesus, for he himself said, 'It is more blessed to give than to receive.'" (Acts 20:35, NRSVue)

GENESIS 2:15; EXODUS 20:9; JOHN 5:17; 9:4; ACTS 20:33-35; 2 THESSALONIANS 3:6-12

KJV	NRSVue
8 Neither did we eat any man's bread for nought; but wrought with labour and travail night and day, that we might not be chargeable to any of you:	8 and we did not eat anyone's bread without paying for it, but with toil and labor we worked night and day so that we might not burden any of you.
9 Not because we have not power, but to make ourselves an ensample unto you to follow us.	9 This was not because we do not have that right but in order to give you an example to imitate.
10 For even when we were with you, this we commanded you, that if any would not work, neither should he eat.	10 For even when we were with you, we gave you this command: anyone unwilling to work should not eat.
11 For we hear that there are some which walk among you disorderly, working not at all, but are busybodies.	11 For we hear that some of you are living irresponsibly, mere busybodies, not doing any work.
12 Now them that are such we command and exhort by our Lord Jesus Christ, that with quietness they work, and eat their own bread.	12 Now such persons we command and exhort in the Lord Jesus Christ to do their work quietly and to earn their own living.

LESSON SETTING

Time: Beginning of Time
Place: All of Creation
Setting: In the beginning, God created the heavens and the earth, formed man from the dust, and breathed life into him. God planted a garden in Eden, a place of beauty and abundance, with every tree that is pleasing to the sight and good for food, including the Tree of Life and the Tree of the Knowledge of Good and Evil. This setting provides a foundational understanding of humanity's role and the relationship with God and creation. With all that God created in the Genesis narratives, what is often overlooked and eclipsed by other features of His creation is the concept of work and labor. Work is part of God's created order for humanity, as we are called to be stewards of His creation and accountable to Him.

LESSON OUTLINE

I. The Foundation of Work (Genesis 2:15, Exodus 20:9)
II. Work from Jesus' and Paul's View (John 5:17, Acts 20:33-35)
III. The Call to Work (2 Thessalonians 3:6-12)

UNIFYING PRINCIPLE

People struggle with idleness. How can we guard against idleness? God ordains work both as a means of self-reliance and self-determination. A source of generosity toward others, work enables us to emulate God's attributes of grace, giving, compassion, and faithfulness.

INTRODUCTION

Deeply rooted in biblical teaching, work has a significant place in the Christian life. God places Adam in the Garden of Eden to work and care for it. The dignity and identity that work bestows are components of God's original plan for humanity. The Ten Commandments (Exodus 20:9) reinforce this idea by emphasizing balance between work and rest.

Jesus endorses this concept in John 5:17, "My Father is always at work to this day, and I too am working." He declares work is a divine activity that reflects God's continual commitment and involvement with His creation.

The Apostle Paul provides practical guidance on work in Acts 20:33–35, where he emphasizes hard work and helping the weak. Quoting Jesus, Paul advises, "It is more blessed to give than to receive." This teaching underscores the importance of diligence and generosity.

Finally, 2 Thessalonians 3:6–12 addresses the necessity of work as foundational to a disciplined life. The author warns against idleness and encourages believers to earn their keep. Together, these passages present work as a divine calling, a means of serving others, and a way to fulfill one's faith responsibly and productively.

EXPOSITION

I. The Foundation of Work (Genesis 2:15, Exodus 20:9)

God places Adam in the garden to be the chief steward of it. The fifteenth verse, depending upon choice of translation, could read, "The Lord God took the man and caused him to rest in the Garden of Eden to tend and keep it." God did not create humanity to live idly. Work is central to discovering purpose in life. Enjoyment of creation is a divine benefit given to humanity. It, however, includes the responsibility of caring for creation.

Working in and maintaining the garden are parts of God's order for humanity. We have an obligation to preserve, protect, and care for God's creation. The Garden of Eden provides humanity with a purposeful existence. Established before the "Fall," the command to work is a God-given assignment, not a cursed condition.

The garden places work and rest side by side. They contrast and complement each other. Moses reinforces this duality in Exodus 20:8–9 with God's command to keep the Sabbath. Literally meaning "to rest" intentionally, the Sabbath occurs on the seventh day following all necessary work in six days.

The Sabbath is an observance unique to Israel. However, the basis for observance of the Sabbath starts with the creation story (Genesis 2:3–4). It is a part of the cosmic order; its significance lies beyond human influence. The Sabbath is a day of rest, blessing, and rejoicing.

II. Work from Jesus' and Paul's View (John 5:17, Acts 20:33–35)

The tradition of the Sabbath becomes a sacred practice among Jewish believers. The practice of Sabbath legitimizes strict compliance of the Law which excludes any work for any reason. For Jesus, the practice of the Sabbath includes work that glorifies God such as works of healing.

In the Gospel of John 5:1–16, Jesus heals a man at the pool of Bethsaida. The healed man reports Jesus to the Jewish authorities who then persecute Him for violating Sabbath traditions. Instead of challenging their interpretation of Sabbath laws, Jesus links His work to the Father. He says, "My Father has worked until now, and I have worked."

The religious leaders supported the concept that if God stopped working, everything would collapse. They falsely thought God must work all the time. They exempted God from the Sabbath. A human being is not God, according to these Jewish elders. If "man" works the whole week without resting, he is trying to be like God.

In the Gospel of John, Jesus equates work with healing which glorifies the Father. In his farewell address to the Ephesian elders, Paul's perspective of work that glorifies the Father occurs within ministry and service to others.

Paul addresses the church leaders in Acts 20:33 regarding their relationship to material goods. He asserts his lack of greed and covetousness to emphasize his commitment to working for God without seeking personal gain. Paul warns Ephesian elders against these traits of many popular figures in the church then and now.

Religious leaders could easily exploit their positions to gain material wealth. This being so, Paul pleads for a standard of selfless service. He rebuffs coveting silver, gold, or clothing, focusing upon spiritual rather than material wealth.

He reminds the elders how he worked with his own hands to support himself and his companions. To avoid financially burdening the fledging Ephesian church, Paul provides his own necessities. He demonstrates the value of hard work and how God blesses hard work.

To resist exploitation of newly converted disciples, Paul worked as a tentmaker. He became notorious for working. The believers in Corinth accused him of refusing their hospitality. His secular work as a tentmaker was as important as his work to spread the Gospel. Therefore, Paul intertwines his work ethic and theology. He personifies industriousness and self-sufficiency. Ministry should never be a means of personal enrichment, but rather, it is service to God and others.

Paul concludes with an emphasis upon helping weak people through hard work. He quotes Jesus as saying, "it is more blessed to give than to receive," a teaching not found in the Gospels but preserved by oral tradition. This principle furthers service and generosity. He admonishes the elders to emulate selflessness and compassion.

III. The Call to Work (2 Thessalonians 3:6–12)

Paul writes 2 Thessalonians to address the Day of the Lord, the need for orderly conduct, the problem of idleness and the importance of diligent work.

Paul strongly instructs believers to withdraw from every brother who walks disorderly. Who were these *ataktoi* or "idle and disorderly" Christians? Because Christ was soon to return, they abandoned pursuit of material gain. They reasoned working for material gain equated with laying up treasures on earth.

These believers were known by their persistence in living in a manner contrary to the "teaching" they had received from Paul.

Paul exhorts the Church in the name of our Lord Jesus Christ to reinforce the command's importance. He suspects believers who call on the name of Jesus will feel be compelled to obey.

Paul reminds the Thessalonians of his ministry companions to emphasize the command. "You yourselves know how you should follow us, for we were not disorderly among you." He and his companions did not refuse to work, nor did they take advantage of the generosity of others.

Through Paul's leadership, believers in Thessalonica were obligated to "imitate" those who established them in the faith. Teachers instructed their students with words (*logos*) and lifestyle (*ethos*). Students incorporated the lessons into their knowledge base and emulated their teacher's behavior.

Paul concentrates upon idleness and its dangers. He and his associates did not eat anyone's bread free of charge. This statement refers to more than food. It includes life's necessities, which require hard work to obtain. Paul also did not accept gifts from the church. He also did not receive any compensation from his ministry.

Paul had critics as an itinerant missionary of the Gospel. Specifically, the passage, 1 Thessalonians 2:3–12, suggests that he had opponents in Thessalonica who had alleged Paul was motivated by greed. Paul answers these accusations with evidence from his life. He has routinely refused church support. Instead, he provides for his own needs to freely share the Gospel. Providing for himself allows him to refute his critics. It also coheres his understanding of the Gospel. God gave it freely and Paul received it freely. Appropriately, Paul shares freely what God gave to him without cost.

He explains that he did not want to burden the Thessalonian disciples. He hopes that they will not draw erroneous conclusions from his actions. Though he and his associates had the right to receive compensation, they willingly forfeit that authority. They illustrate generosity, humility, self-sacrifice and willingness to work hard for the Kingdom. In accepting personal responsibility, the apostle expects believers to demonstrate it.

Paul also reminds the church of his teaching. "If anyone will not work, neither shall he eat." This applied to any able-bodied people who were unwilling to work. This rather harsh-sounding remedy, "he shall not eat," was not punitive, but was an incentive to work. Church discipline in the Pauline letters is always redemptive and constructive. Recommendations are always corrective.

He identifies the offenders as not being busy; they are busybodies. His play on words gives a sharp edge to his description. These people were working in a useless way. Busy with everyone else's problems, they failed to attend to their own affairs.

Followers of Christ must display an outward calm that reflects an inner peace which is quite the opposite of their busy, fussy and excited actions.

THE LESSON APPLIED

As Americans, we distort the means, purposes, and objectives of work. Many citizens worship work. We sacrifice our bodies and physical health on the altar of capitalism. In a twisted reversal during our later years, we spend our accumulated wealth trying to regain the health we squandered, chasing monetary wealth. Rightly, we are known as a country of hard-working people who produce great products. Arguably, greed fuels our relentless drive to work.

For believers, work means more than earning a living. Rather than worshiping at the altar of capitalism and conspicuous consumption, work is an extension of our worship of Almighty God. Our jobs create opportunities to demonstrate attributes of God's character. Simply, we show the transformative difference our faithful actions can make in the lives of other people.

How does a disciple determine what his work should be? For Christians, "doing comes from being." That phrase means practically that Christian values primarily decide how a believer allots his time, talent, treasure, and temperament. Of course, God respects a disciple's gifts, abilities, endowments and personality in guiding him toward meaningful work. Consider listing your four cardinal principles and passions. What job could you do to turn those answers into purpose? Imagine getting up each morning and commuting to purpose instead of routinely going to work. "If you do what you love, you will never work a day in your life." That saying becomes true in every disciple's life who genuinely relies upon God to reveal the answer.

Does Paul's teaching regarding work in 2 Thessalonians have any relevance to employment and unemployment policy in the United States? How would we apply the principle, "If you do not work, then you do not eat," to welfare rules and regulations? Should we retain the social safety net of entitlements that comprise the monthly income of millions of American residents? Discuss what you believe the "Christian" position to be. Which biblical principles support your answers?

LET'S TALK ABOUT IT...

Discuss the following questions and visit www.rhboyd.com for more information.

Explain the importance of responsibility and stewardship in our daily work.

How does the balance between work and rest reflect God's design for human flourishing?

In what ways can our daily work be seen as an act of worship and service to God, according to the principles found in Genesis 2:15 and Exodus 20:9?

In what ways can our work be seen as a means to serve and bless others?

What is the relation between the work we do for a living and the purpose God has assigned to us?

How does 2 Thessalonians 3:6–12 encourage us to view our work as a form of service and obedience to God?

Get Social
Share your views and tag us
@rhboydco and use #rhboydco

@rhboydco

Home Daily Devotional Readings
May 11–17, 2026

Monday	Tuesday	Wednesday	Thursday	Friday	Saturday	Sunday
Work Diligently before God	The Workers and Their Wages	God Demands Justice for All	Wait Patiently for God's Justice	Rendering Service with Enthusiasm	Justice for the Common Worker	Contentment, Humility, and Generosity
Proverbs 10:1–5, 15–16	Matthew 20:1–16	Amos 5:6–15	James 5:1–11	Colossians 3:12–17	Deuteronomy 24:14–21	1 Timothy 6:6–8, 17–19

Lesson XII   May 17, 2026

The Christian Spirit in Industry

Adult Topic: Cultivating Generosity
Background Scripture: Exod. 1:8–14; 20:17; Deut. 24:14–15; Amos 5:6–15; Zech. 8:16–17; Matt. 20:1–16; Mark 12:1–9; Luke 3:14; Eph. 6:1–9; 1 Tim. 6:17–19
Lesson Passage: Deut. 24:14–21; Ephesians 6:5–9; 1 Timothy 6:17–19

DEUTERONOMY 24:14–21; EPHESIANS 6:5–9; 1 TIMOTHY 6:17–19

KJV	NRSVue
THOU shalt not oppress an hired servant that is poor and needy, whether he be of thy brethren, or of thy strangers that are in thy land within thy gates:	"YOU shall not withhold the wages of poor and needy laborers, whether other Israelites or aliens who reside in your land in one of your towns.
15 At his day thou shalt give him his hire, neither shall the sun go down upon it; for he is poor, and setteth his heart upon it: lest he cry against thee unto the Lord, and it be sin unto thee.	15 You shall pay them their wages daily before sunset, because they are poor and their livelihood depends on them; otherwise they might cry to the Lord against you, and you would incur guilt.
16 The fathers shall not be put to death for the children, neither shall the children be put to death for the fathers: every man shall be put to death for his own sin.	16 "Parents shall not be put to death for their children, nor shall children be put to death for their parents; only for their own crimes may persons be put to death.
17 Thou shalt not pervert the judgment of the stranger, nor of the fatherless; nor take a widow's raiment to pledge:	17 "You shall not deprive a resident alien or an orphan of justice; you shall not take a widow's garment in pledge.
18 But thou shalt remember that thou wast a bondman in Egypt, and the Lord thy God redeemed thee thence: therefore I command thee to do this thing.	18 Remember that you were a slave in Egypt and the Lord your God redeemed you from there; therefore I command you to do this.
19 When thou cuttest down thine harvest in thy field, and hast forgot a sheaf in the field, thou shalt not go again to fetch it: it shall be for the stranger, for the fatherless, and for the widow: that the Lord thy God may bless thee in all the work of thine hands.	19 "When you reap your harvest in your field and forget a sheaf in the field, you shall not go back to get it; it shall be left for the alien, the orphan, and the widow, so that the Lord your God may bless you in all your undertakings.
20 When thou beatest thine olive tree, thou shalt not go over the boughs again: it shall be for the stranger, for the fatherless, and for the widow.	20 When you beat your olive trees, do not strip what is left; it shall be for the alien, the orphan, and the widow.
21 When thou gatherest the grapes of thy vineyard, thou shalt not glean it afterward: it shall be for the stranger, for the fatherless, and for the widow.	21 "When you gather the grapes of your vineyard, do not glean what is left; it shall be for the alien, the orphan, and the widow.

MAIN THOUGHT: When you reap your harvest in your field and forget a sheaf in the field, you shall not go back to get it; it shall be left for the alien, the orphan, and the widow, so that the LORD your God may bless you in all your undertakings. (Deuteronomy 24:19, NRSVue)

DEUTERONOMY 24:14-21; EPHESIANS 6:5-9; 1 TIMOTHY 6:17-19

KJV	NRSVue

••• Ephesians 6:5-9 •••

KJV	NRSVue
5 Servants, be obedient to them that are your masters according to the flesh, with fear and trembling, in singleness of your heart, as unto Christ;	5 Slaves, obey your earthly masters with respect and trembling, in singleness of heart, as you obey Christ,
6 Not with eyeservice, as menpleasers; but as the servants of Christ, doing the will of God from the heart;	6 not with a slavery performed merely for looks, to please people, but as slaves of Christ, doing the will of God from the soul.
7 With good will doing service, as to the Lord, and not to men:	7 Render service with enthusiasm, as for the Lord and not for humans,
8 Knowing that whatsoever good thing any man doeth, the same shall he receive of the Lord, whether he be bond or free.	8 knowing that whatever good we do, we will receive the same again from the Lord, whether we are enslaved or free.
9 And, ye masters, do the same things unto them, forbearing threatening: knowing that your Master also is in heaven; neither is there respect of persons with him.	9 And, masters, do the same to them. Stop threatening them, for you know that both of you have the same Lord in heaven, and with him there is no partiality.

••• 1 Timothy 6:17-19 •••

KJV	NRSVue
17 Charge them that are rich in this world, that they be not highminded, nor trust in uncertain riches, but in the living God, who giveth us richly all things to enjoy;	17 As for those who in the present age are rich, command them not to be haughty or to set their hopes on the uncertainty of riches but rather on God, who richly provides us with everything for our enjoyment.
18 That they do good, that they be rich in good works, ready to distribute, willing to communicate;	18 They are to do good, to be rich in good works, generous, and ready to share,
19 Laying up in store for themselves a good foundation against the time to come, that they may lay hold on eternal life.	19 thus storing up for themselves the treasure of a good foundation for the future, so that they may take hold of the life that really is life.

LESSON SETTING

Time: 1406 BC

Place: Plains of Moab east of the Jordan

Setting: The book of Deuteronomy is a book believed to have been written by Moses as final instructions to the children of Israel as they entered the Promised Land. The common theme underlying the commandment was that each Israelite was to practice the discipline of generosity, especially within the socially unbalanced power dynamic. This theme of generosity was echoed more than a thousand years later in the words and works of the Apostle Paul. In his letters to Timothy and the Christians in Ephesus, probably written during his imprisonment in Rome around AD 62, Paul urged the practice of generosity as a means of reflecting the character of Christ.

LESSON OUTLINE

I. Ethical Treatment for those in Need (Deuteronomy 24:14–21)
II. Generosity in Enslavement (Ephesians 6:5–9)
III. The Worth and Wealth of Generosity (1 Timothy 6:17–19)

UNIFYING PRINCIPLE

People hoard resources because they fear scarcity. Are there any inherent motivations to treat people equitably? What motivates people to share with others in need? Scripture directs us to work together and treat others as the Lord teaches. Disciples attain wealth through good works and sharing generously with each other.

INTRODUCTION

As disciples of Christ, we primarily emulate His mind, heart, and character. Generosity is a cardinal characteristic to incorporate into daily living.

Grace should be a natural extension of Christian personality. However, generosity does not flow naturally. To achieve this Christ-like trait, disciples must intentionally practice it until it becomes a part of their personalities.

Cultivating generosity is a central theme in the Bible; it fosters selflessness, justice, and stewardship. These texts, Deuteronomy 24:14–21, Ephesians 6:5–9, and 1 Timothy 6:17–19 offer insight on acquiring and implementing these virtues.

These passages provide a comprehensive biblical framework for cultivating generosity and fostering justice, respect, and selfless giving in building communities that reflects God's love and care towards everyone.

EXPOSITION

I. Ethical Treatment for those in Need (Deuteronomy 24:14–21)

This passage opens with the general command to care for the poor. These individuals had lost family land or other means of independent income. Circumstances reduced them to hire themselves as laborers and other precarious economic circumstances. For this reason, employers paid daily wages to workers. They heeded the command "not let the sun go down on it."

This commandment reiterates God's justice and compassion; it protects vulnerable people from exploitation. It addresses the urgency of workers' needs. Laborers depended on their daily earnings to survive. A delay in payment caused great hardship which led to hunger and suffering.

Any aggrieved persons cry out to the Lord against the offender, the employer. This plea to the Lord was not a mild utterance but a desperate appeal of the oppressed who could only turn God.

In the covenant community, one's vertical relationship with God always intersected with horizontal human relationships. Because God is faithfully passionate about justice, He expects His covenantal people to practice compassion, mercy, and justice.

This sixteenth verse includes family matters. In ancient Israel, specifically, and the Ancient Near East, generally, corporate solidarity of family and larger community was central. The Commandments in Deuteronomy assume personal responsibility of members of the covenant community.

As it relates to social justice, it was possible for entire families to be punished for the crime of one member. Family members in ancient cultures shared jointly in shame and disgrace. Accountability, individually and collectively, subjected everyone to severe punishments including execution.

However, the Law of Moses contested this ancient custom. "Fathers shall not be put to death for their children, nor shall children be put to death for their fathers." That rule departs from the traditional practice within the Law. Each person becomes responsible for his own sins.

The Law next addresses the state of marginalized people: strangers, widows, and fatherless and helpless community members. The Law protected innocent defendants from miscarriages of justice. This protection was more important for these vulnerable ones.

Perversion of the Law and distortion of justice was prohibited. There was evidence of this misfortune among the people whom the Law previously addressed in the nineteenth verse. Bribery and manipulation were means of perverting justice. Three categories of socially disadvantaged lacked any means to bribe officials and were accordingly especially oppressed because of this practice.

Gleaning was one of the practical and social expressions of God's justice for the poor. At harvest time, in picking fields, orchards, or vineyards, they were not to be left clean. Workers were to leave some produce for strangers, widows, and poor people. They were allowed to gather or glean what was left to feed themselves by their own labor. This consideration provided the poor with a means of providing for themselves through their own labor. It also allowed them to maintain their dignity without asking for charity.

The story of Boaz and Ruth is an application of this principle. Ruth was fully aware of her right, as a stranger and a widow, to gather from the fields of anyone with whom she found favor (Ruth 2:2).

II. Generosity in Enslavement (Ephesians 6:5–9)

Paul wrote to the Christians in Ephesus while imprisoned in Rome approximately AD 60–62. He addresses believers who were slaves and their "masters." He urges both groups to treat each other with mutual respect as they obey Christ.

Considered a fundamental institution and indispensable to civilized society, slavery was universally accepted in ancient times. Half of the population in the city of the Rome were slaves. Historians estimate that there were possibly sixty million slaves in the Roman Empire. They included laborers, domestic servants, clerks, teachers, doctors, and other professionals. They were people without rights and worked for the comfort and pleasure of their owners. Undoubtedly, the early Christian churches included slaves among their members.

Along with this passage, parallel ones in Colossians (3:22–4:1), 1 Peter (3:18–22), and Philemon (verse 16), reveal New Testament writers respected the work of slaves and offered comfort to them in their suffering. Moreover, they sought to humanize and regulate slavery among disciples by exhorting Christian masters to treat their slaves with fairness and kindness.

In verse 5, Paul instructs believing slaves to obey their masters according to the flesh. Paul describes the reality of slavery but does not endorse it, however. The master–slave relationship was an earthly arrangement. Obedience resulted from fear and trembling. These words do not express abject terror but rather a solicitous spirit of someone eager to leave no duty undone.

Obedience should be unto the Lord. Hence, servants regarded obedience to earthly masters as Christian duty, a service performed to Christ Himself. This directive contrasts behavior of servants who served with "eyeservice" and tried to be "menpleasers." Eyeservice graphically represents behavior of persons who works only when being watched. "Menpleasers" work with the highest aim to curry favor with their masters.

Paul reminds servants that whatever good they do; they will receive the same from the Lord. Their socio-economic status is irrelevant. God's repayment is an incentive for their obedience.

III. The Worth and Wealth of Generosity (1 Timothy 6:17-19)

Paul writes to his young apprentice Timothy who leads the church in Ephesus. He urges wealthy members of the church to resist arrogance and their hope in uncertain riches rather than in God Almighty. He rather recommends that they be rich in good works, generosity, and willingness to share.

A major port city, Ephesus attracted a diverse population and fostered a wealthy, cosmopolitan society. The wealthy believers, whom Paul addresses, were likely landowners and merchants involved in the lucrative trade associated with the Temple of Artemis, one of the Seven Wonders of the Ancient World. Again, Paul encouraged these disciples to prioritize Christian values, humility and charity inclusive of good deeds and sharing instead of short-sighted reliance upon wealth.

The right disposition of the wealthy, however, is to continue to hope in Almighty God who lavishes all their needs upon His people. God does not give wealth to promote pride. Disciples use and enjoy wealth to glorify God and achieve His will and purposes. This approach promotes gratitude toward God for the benefits He bestows.

Paul then explains good and wise usages of wealth. He first suggests that wealthy people make good use of their riches by doing good things with it. This means they are to use their wealth to create a better society rather than supporting personal luxury. As they measure their wealth abundance, they should measure their good works by abundant generosity.

Wealthy people should be ready to give and willing to share. Interestingly, willingness to share emerges from an inner conviction and compulsion to give. It flows naturally from a generous character and personality.

Generally, Paul's advises Timothy to teach the people that true wealth gives freely and bountifully rather than hoards money for selfish indulgences.

In the nineteenth verse, Paul outlines two truths resulting from generosity. First, he offers that giving generously to those in need stores up future treasure for any faithful giver. "Storing up for themselves" speaks of significant personal benefits. Treasure that accumulates in the life to come is not money, stock portfolios, or real estate. It is spiritual and lasts for eternity.

Eternal treasure, which is the generous and giving life that disciples express in the world, evidences true faith in God and is a firm foundation for entering eternity.

THE LESSON APPLIED

The Apostle Paul's comments here are a great source of debate. Was the great apostle wrong? The horrific and brutal African-American experience with chattel enslavement in the United States certain give pause for reexamination. Are human enslavement and Christianity compatible in the faith?

One African-American theologian stated his reservations regarding Paul's assessment: "As a Black man in America whose history and heritage have been defined significantly by chattel slavery, I appreciate the political implications and hard realities that Paul and the other apostles would have faced had they preached against enslavement in the Roman Empire. Still, their silence undermines the integrity of his message. Paul assumes that Christ's imminent return meant that disciples should focus their preaching and outreach the future hope of the believer's eternal life rather than social justice. However, his short sightedness left the enslaved and other marginalized people in their oppressive situations. Further, Paul's blindness led to centuries of unimaginable cruelty and crimes against humankind."

Generosity is more than good works that disciples who are "blessed and highly favored" do to maintain social respectability in their churches and communities. Genuine willingness to share creates purposeful acts of grace that further social equity. Cultivating generosity is a spiritual discipline wherein disciples encourage each other toward self-realization and achievement individual destiny.

LET'S TALK ABOUT IT...

Discuss the following questions and visit www.rhboyd.com for more information.

- **What do the instructions about leaving gleanings for the poor and the foreigner teach us about God's provision and our responsibility to share? How can we practice this kind of generosity today?**
- **How can serving others "as if serving the Lord" influence our attitude towards generosity and kindness in our daily interactions?**
- **What practical steps can we take to be "rich in good deeds" and generous? How can we cultivate a lifestyle of sharing and helping others?**
- **How does generosity contribute to laying up treasures in heaven and taking hold of "the life that is truly life"? What are some ways we can focus on eternal values in our acts of generosity?**

Get Social
Share your views and tag us
@rhboydco and use #rhboydco

@rhboydco

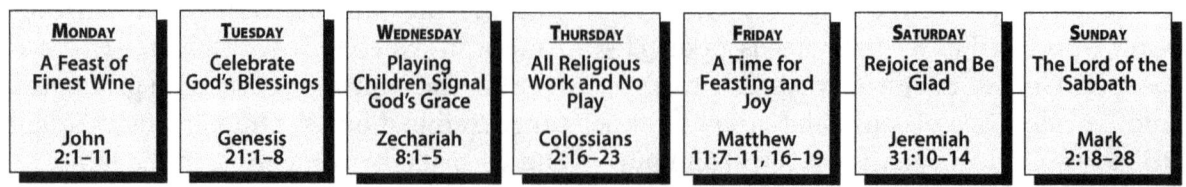

Lesson XIII — **May 24, 2026**

The Christian View of Recreation

Adult Topic: A Well-Earned Rest
Background Scripture: Jeremiah 31:12–13; Zechariah 8:5; Matthew 11:16–19; Mark 2:18–28; 6:30–32; John 2:1–11
Lesson Passage: Mark 2:18–28

MARK 2:18–28

KJV

AND the disciples of John and of the Pharisees used to fast: and they come and say unto him, Why do the disciples of John and of the Pharisees fast, but thy disciples fast not?

19 And Jesus said unto them, Can the children of the bridechamber fast, while the bridegroom is with them? as long as they have the bridegroom with them, they cannot fast.

20 But the days will come, when the bridegroom shall be taken away from them, and then shall they fast in those days.

21 No man also seweth a piece of new cloth on an old garment: else the new piece that filled it up taketh away from the old, and the rent is made worse.

22 And no man putteth new wine into old bottles: else the new wine doth burst the bottles, and the wine is spilled, and the bottles will be marred: but new wine must be put into new bottles.

23 And it came to pass, that he went through the corn fields on the sabbath day; and his disciples began, as they went, to pluck the ears of corn.

24 And the Pharisees said unto him, Behold, why do they on the sabbath day that which is not lawful?

25 And he said unto them, Have ye never read what David did, when he had need, and was an hungred, he, and they that were with him?

26 How he went into the house of God in the days of Abiathar the high priest, and did eat the shewbread, which is not lawful to eat but for the priests, and gave also to them which were with him?

NRSVue

NOW John's disciples and the Pharisees were fasting, and people came and said to him, "Why do John's disciples and the disciples of the Pharisees fast, but your disciples do not fast?"

19 Jesus said to them, "The wedding attendants cannot fast while the bridegroom is with them, can they? As long as they have the bridegroom with them, they cannot fast.

20 The days will come when the bridegroom is taken away from them, and then they will fast on that day.

21 "No one sews a piece of unshrunk cloth on an old cloak; otherwise, the patch pulls away from it, the new from the old, and a worse tear is made.

22 Similarly, no one puts new wine into old wineskins; otherwise, the wine will burst the skins, and the wine is lost, and so are the skins, but one puts new wine into fresh wineskins."

23 One Sabbath he was going through the grain fields, and as they made their way his disciples began to pluck heads of grain.

24 The Pharisees said to him, "Look, why are they doing what is not lawful on the Sabbath?"

25 And he said to them, "Have you never read what David did when he and his companions were hungry and in need of food,

26 how he entered the house of God when Abiathar was high priest and ate the bread of the Presence, which it is not lawful for any but the priests to eat, and he gave some to his companions?"

MAIN THOUGHT: [Jesus] said to [the Pharisees], "The sabbath was made for humankind, and not humankind for the sabbath; so the Son of Man is lord even of the sabbath." (Mark 2:27–28, NRSVue)

MARK 2:18-28

KJV

27 And he said unto them, The sabbath was made for man, and not man for the sabbath:

28 Therefore the Son of man is Lord also of the sabbath.

NRSVue

27 Then he said to them, "The Sabbath was made for humankind and not humankind for the Sabbath,

28 so the Son of Man is lord even of the Sabbath."

LESSON SETTING

Time: AD 1st Century
Place: Galilee
Setting: At the time of this lesson, Jesus' popularity and increasing attention from both followers and critics was at an all-time high. Wherever He went, He drew large crowds expecting Him to do or say something that would change their lives. While much of this notoriety was due to the miracles He performed, it was primarily His teaching that captured the attention of the masses. Jesus was known for teaching doctrine that not only invited a more intimate insight into God as "Father" rather than just Lord but challenged the religious traditions in doing so. This is what attracted critics along with His fans. In this lesson, Jesus is teaching about fasting and its relevance with regard to religion verses relationship.

LESSON OUTLINE

I. The Question of Fasting (Mark 2:18-22)
II. The Question of Sabbath (Mark 2:23-28)

UNIFYING PRINCIPLE

Some people love to work while others love to rest and relax. Why is it important to achieve a balance between work and rest? Are you striving for a work-life (recreation) balance? Additionally, disciples seek balance as it relates to fasting and feasting.

INTRODUCTION

At the beginning of the chapter, Jesus heals a paralytic man and eats with tax collectors. Two new controversies arise in Mark 2:18-28; they relate to ancient Jewish traditions and clear requirements of the Mosaic Law. When is it appropriate to fast? Is it still necessary to keep the Sabbath and other relevant laws?

In both cases, Jesus emphasizes genuine and practical worship over superficial repetition of following tradition. Moreover, he prefers a relationship with God over being religious.

EXPOSITION

I. The Question of Fasting (Mark 2:18-22)

Jesus receives a question about fasting in the eighteenth verse. Mark identifies the people asking the question simply as "they." This intentionally vague characterization indicates a mixed group of disciples of John the Baptist and Pharisees.

The implied phrase "disciples of the Pharisees" probably means "admirers" and "fellow travelers" who were sympathetic to Pharisaic thought and practices. The Pharisees did not have disciples but were disciples of the scribes.

They ask, "Why do the disciples of John and the Pharisees fast, but your disciples do not?" Jesus' practice did not match that of their now imprisoned leader. These disciples of John were sincere but misguided in their inability to understand freedom of spirit which Jesus offers.

The Pharisees interpreted the Law to command fasting. The common people, "sinners," did not practice this spiritual discipline. Jewish tradition required fasting once a year on the Day of Atonement. Observant Jews, however, fasted more frequently. The Pharisees fasted twice a week, on Mondays and Thursdays, usually for twelve hours, from sunrise to sunset. They believed regular fasting confirmed faithfulness to the Law.

Many observers were naturally surprised that Jesus and His disciples did not fast, considering the weekly practices of John's disciples and the Pharisees. These observers might have considered customary fasting to be obligatory.

This pointed, personal and direct question indicted the validity of Jesus' omission and indifference to this sacred ritual.

Jesus utilizes a common analogy to answer the question with one of his own. Referencing the wedding feast, Jesus asks about the worth and appropriateness of fasting. Since engagements were often long, in some cases years, weddings were a time of feasting and great joy. Accordingly, when would it be reasonable to fast?

Specifically, Jesus asks, "Can the friends of the bridegroom fast while the bridegroom is with them?" Two social practices are important in understanding the context and meaning of Jesus' answer. First, in His analogy, Jesus is the bridegroom at the wedding feast. His disciples are friends of the bridegroom. Second, beyond any legal requirement, fasting was an act of repentance. People sought God's forgiveness for sins during periods of fasting. It demonstrated humility and contrition.

People generally fasted during times of mourning and grief. Fasting was an expression of sorrow, personally and communally.

Jews fasted to seek God's guidance and wisdom especially during crises, challenges, and when making important decisions. They draw closer to God and dwelled in His presence to receive His guidance. Fasting increased focus on prayer and spiritual growth by denying physical needs and prioritizing spiritual matters.

If Jesus, in the analogy, represents the bridegroom at a wedding, it is reasonable His friends would celebrate with Him. Fasting would be most inappropriate. Celebrating equated with feasting not fasting.

As long as disciples have the bridegroom with them, they do not need to fast. He provides whatever they seek through fasting. Jesus then speaks of a time when the bridegroom will be taken away. Then, they will fast. His departure begins with a time of grieving and fasting. Such fasting results from the ceremonial rituals of Judaism. Instead, it reflects the genuine purpose of fasting, resolving affliction of the soul by grieving in God's presence and seeking His counsel.

The phrase, "will be taken away," foreshadowed Jesus' death and departure from Earth. This is the first indication in the

Gospel of Mark that Jesus is fully aware of His mission.

The parables of a new patch of cloth being sewn onto an old garment and new wine being poured into in old wineskins demonstrate incompatibility of old religious traditions and rituals with Christ's teachings.

Emphasizing rituals and traditions versus practicing spiritual disciplines to develop a close relationship with God, the teachings and practices of the Pharisees symbolize the old garment and old wineskins.

The new cloth and new wine of the Gospel emerge in Jesus' teaching, preaching and healing which He demonstrates through words, miracles, and compassionate actions.

II. The Question of Sabbath (Mark 2:23–28)

While the Pharisees stressed fasting, they considered strict observance of the Sabbath laws to be more important. Sabbath-keeping was critical to their religious identity. It reflected their commitment to the Law and maintaining a distinctive Jewish way of life.

The Pharisees viewed the Sabbath as a cornerstone of being Jewish. Strict observance of the Sabbath honored God and preserved the sanctity of the day as delineated in the Fourth Commandment.

The laws defined "work" to be avoided on the Sabbath. These rules prohibited activities such as carrying burdens, cooking, and walking certain distances. Detailed regulations were necessary to prevent inadvertent violations.

Jesus challenges the Pharisees' interpretation of Sabbath laws. He underscores the spirit rather than the letter of the Law. He teaches the Sabbath was made for humankind's benefit. God did not intend to burden His people with meaningless ritual observances. Unsurprisingly, many conflicts between Jesus and the Pharisees emerged.

While Jesus and His disciples walk through grain fields on the Sabbath, they picked heads of grain. They rubbed them between their hands to get rid of the chaff before eating it. The Pharisees who witnessed Jesus and His disciples picking and eating the grain viewed it as harvesting, winnowing, threshing, and preparing a meal. They classified Jesus and His disciples as lawbreakers.

Confronting Jesus directly, the Pharisees ask, "Why do they do what is not lawful on the Sabbath?" Again, Jesus answers the question with a question. Citing 1 Samuel 21:1–6, Jesus refers to the actions of King David, "Have you never read what David did when he was in need and hungry, he and those with him?" This passage alludes to the ceremonial practice of presenting the "consecrated bread" in the Tabernacle each Sabbath to symbolize God's presence and provision.

David and his men ate this bread because they were hungry. Jesus establishes the principle that human need supersedes ceremonial laws. Sabbath observance should be more than legalistic restrictions.

Jesus declares in verse 27, "the Sabbath was made for man, and not man for the Sabbath." God intended it to be a free day to rest from labors rather than a day of burdensome rule-keeping. Jesus challenges the legalism of the Pharisees and redefines the meaning and purpose of the Sabbath.

"The Son of Man is also Lord of the Sabbath," Jesus asserts His authority over the Sabbath. He underscores His divine authority to interpret and fulfill the Law. Jesus is not abolishing the Sabbath but reinterpreting its purpose and significance.

The phrase "Son of Man" is deeply rooted in Jewish eschatology. In Daniel 7:13-14 it refers to a heavenly figure endowed with authority, glory, and sovereign power. Jesus aligns Himself with this prophetic vision and indicates His unique role in God's redemptive plan. This title also depicts His humanity and solidarity with humanity thereby making His teachings and ministry relatable and authoritative.

Instituted by God at creation (Genesis 2:2-3) and codified in the Ten Commandments (Exodus 20:8-11), the Sabbath furthered the covenant between God and Israel. It reflected God's rest after creation and His desire for His people's rest and renewal.

The Sabbath became burdensome with numerous legalistic restrictions imposed by the Pharisees and other religious leaders. These additional rules overshadowed the original intent of the Sabbath. Jesus' assertion of His authority over the Sabbath challenges these legalistic interpretations and restores the true purpose of the Sabbath.

Jesus' reinterpretation of the Sabbath posits the principle that God's Laws empower humankind. His teachings suggest mercy, compassion, and human need take precedence over ritualistic observance. This perspective coheres with His broader ministry which Jesus summarizes in Matthew 5:17–20.

Moreover, Jesus' authority over the Sabbath signals His establishment of a new covenant. The focus of religious devotion and worship shifts from strict adherence to rites and rituals to a relationship with God inclusive of grace, love, and mercy. The Sabbath becomes a time for good works, healing, and restoring life.

The focus of the Sabbath becomes nurturing a relationship with God characterized by grace, love, and mercy. Jesus, as the Lord of the Sabbath, embodies this new way of relating to God.

THE LESSON APPLIED

When practicing our faith in daily living, it is important to differentiate between ritual, tradition, and relationship. Mistakenly, some disciples use these terms interchangeably. They, admittedly, relate closely in function and purpose. Rituals preserve the meaning of tradition. As practice and the meaning of tradition evolve with societal shifts, rituals inevitably change as well.

Sadly, this change does not occur in many churches. Like the Pharisees of Jesus' day, many Christians demand strict adherence to rituals without knowing the underlying significance behind the traditions. Whether fasting, Sabbath protocol, or biblical rules relating to Holy Communion, these rituals remain meaningless if disciples are uninformed as it relates to their origins, development, and continuation. It is necessary for disciples to study the history of the Christian faith to equip them to offer a reasonable defense for the faith.

The current weakness and ineffectiveness of countless local churches stems from unimaginable biblical illiteracy in the pews. Disciples know less Scripture than in the years of print Bibles. Nevertheless, it is vital that average disciples develop deep roots in the Christian faith. This type of personal growth and spiritual development emerges from long-term, committed, and sustained study of the Bible and Christian theology and spirituality.

Do average church goers who regularly partake in Holy Communion understand this sacrament and ritual? Are they able to explain to adherents of other faith what it means to be Christian? Can they summarize the beginnings, objectives, purposes, and benefits of baptism, whether infant or immersion, and the tradition of receiving the consecrated elements of the Eucharist? Can they itemize and review the four main distinguishing traditions of their Christian denomination? A lifetime of study is necessary to equip average disciples in favorably answering these questions.

This lesson primarily teaches the importance of limiting reliance upon religious rites, creeds and rituals. You will recall the elder brother in the Parable of the Prodigal Son, through his self-righteousness, squandered the possibility of an intimate communion with the Father. One could suspect that he, like the Rich Young Ruler, perfectly kept the Law from childhood. They followed the rules and demanded recognition because of it. Regrettably, their self-reliance and works righteousness blinded them to learning, growing and living in God's love. What is the worth of perfect Sabbath keeping and church attendance if it does not translate into sharing the Lord's love?

LET'S TALK ABOUT IT...

Discuss the following questions and visit www.rhboyd.com for more information.

How does Jesus' analogy of the bridegroom in Mark 2:19–20 relate to the concept of rest and celebration?

How does the Pharisees' criticism of the disciples plucking grain on the Sabbath highlight their misunderstanding of the purpose of rest?

What does Jesus' reference to David eating the consecrated bread (Mark 2:25–26) teach us about prioritizing human need over strict observance of rest?

How does Jesus' statement, "The Sabbath was made for man, not man for the Sabbath" redefine the purpose of rest in religious practice?

How can we apply Jesus' teachings in Mark 2:18–28 to find balance between work and rest in our own lives?

Get Social

Share your views and tag us
@rhboydco and use #rhboydco

@rhboydco

Home Daily Devotional Readings
May 25–31, 2026

Monday	Tuesday	Wednesday	Thursday	Friday	Saturday	Sunday
Let Us Sing to the Lord	Gladness in the House of the Lord	Members of the Body of Christ	A Holy Day of Rejoicing	Restoring Healthy Relationships	Fellowship through Common Property	Inspiring Love and Good Deeds
Psalm 95	Psalm 122	Romans 12:1–8	Nehemiah 8:9–12	Matthew 18:15–20	Acts 4:32–37	Hebrews 10:19–25

Lesson XIV   May 31, 2026

Fellowship through Worship

Adult Topic: Provoke One Another!
Background Scripture: Nehemiah 8:1–12; Micah 4:1–2; Psalm 122:1–9; Matthew 28:18–20; Hebrews 10:19–25
Lesson Passage: Matthew 28:18–20; Hebrews 10:22–25

MATTHEW 28:18-20; HEBREWS 10:22-25

KJV

AND Jesus came and spake unto them, saying, All power is given unto me in heaven and in earth.

19 Go ye therefore, and teach all nations, baptizing them in the name of the Father, and of the Son, and of the Holy Ghost:

20 Teaching them to observe all things whatsoever I have commanded you: and, lo, I am with you always, even unto the end of the world. Amen.

••• Hebrews 10:22-25 •••

22 Let us draw near with a true heart in full assurance of faith, having our hearts sprinkled from an evil conscience, and our bodies washed with pure water.

23 Let us hold fast the profession of our faith without wavering; (for he is faithful that promised;)

24 And let us consider one another to provoke unto love and to good works:

25 Not forsaking the assembling of ourselves together, as the manner of some is; but exhorting one another: and so much the more, as ye see the day approaching.

NRSVue

AND Jesus came and said to them, "All authority in heaven and on earth has been given to me.

19 Go therefore and make disciples of all nations, baptizing them in the name of the Father and of the Son and of the Holy Spirit

20 and teaching them to obey everything that I have commanded you. And remember, I am with you always, to the end of the age."

••• Hebrews 10:22-25 •••

22 let us approach with a true heart in full assurance of faith, with our hearts sprinkled clean from an evil conscience and our bodies washed with pure water.

23 Let us hold fast to the confession of our hope without wavering, for he who has promised is faithful.

24 And let us consider how to provoke one another to love and good deeds,

25 not neglecting to meet together, as is the habit of some, but encouraging one another, and all the more as you see the Day approaching.

LESSON SETTING

Time: AD 33
Place: Mountains of Galilee

Setting: Known as the Great Commission, Matthew 28:18-20 is set on a mountain in Galilee, where Jesus issues the final and most significant commandment to His disciples that they are to make disciples. This was

MAIN THOUGHT: Let us hold fast to the confession of our hope without wavering, for he who has promised is faithful. (Hebrews 10:23, NRSVue)

their moment of graduation from discipleship into the beginning stages of apostleship. Jesus had finally ascended back to the Father and though He would always be with them in Spirit, He was no longer with them in flesh. But they were not alone because they had each other. Believers being a support for one another is also a common theme in Hebrews 10:20-25. Written to Jewish Christians facing persecution, this passage encourages believers to draw near to God with sincere hearts, hold fast to their faith, and encourage one another. It highlights the importance of community and perseverance in faith, especially in challenging times.

LESSON OUTLINE
I. The Great Commission (Matthew 28:18-20)
II. The Remedy for Persecution (Hebrews 10:20-25)

UNIFYING PRINCIPLE
Today's passages in Matthew and Hebrews depict how community support furthers success in evangelism, worship, and fellowship.

INTRODUCTION

Two texts, Matthew 28:18-20 and Hebrews 10:20-25, encourage believers to support each other especially during times of crisis. These passages emphasize communal aspects of the Christian faith. Believers draw strength from their shared commitment to Christ.

Together, these passages reflect the vital role of community and mutual support in Christian faith. They remind believers of the resources of collective strength and encouragement when they persevere through crises. Unity in the shared mission of Christ provides a foundation for believers to support one another.

EXPOSITION

I. The Great Commission (Matthew 28:18-20)

Matthew provides a brief resurrection account and transitions quickly to a final application of his gospel. This final passage, a resurrection appearance, testifies to the truth of Jesus' resurrection from the dead and provides the cardinal mission for all believers. We designate this passage, "The Great Commission."

These three verses ideally summarize the purpose of the Gospel of Matthew. They rehearse the covenant theme in Matthew 1:1-17. The sacrificial Son of Abraham has completed his redemptive mission. The sovereign Son of David reclaimed his full majesty. The Son of David, the King, deputizes believers to further his mission. As spiritual descendants of Abraham, believers join in fulfilling God's covenant promise; through Abraham, God blesses all the nations of the Earth.

All of Matthew's main themes culminate in this passage: (1) shift from particularism to universalism in the proclamation of the Gospel, (2) discipleship, (3) establishment of the church and (4) Jesus' abiding presence as teacher, Son of God and risen and sovereign Lord.

Within forty days after the resurrection, the eleven disciples and more of Jesus' followers went to Galilee, as He instructed them. He had given them a particular mountain as the meeting place. These obedient followers of the Messiah–King, as the book Acts details, would willingly take any risk to fulfill their Master's instructions.

The eighteenth verse begins the climactic conclusion of the Gospel. Jesus commissions His disciples to build the Kingdom of God on Earth. He promises to be with them forever even as He prepares to return to the Father. Still, Jesus empowers them to accomplish their future mission.

Jesus proclaims, "All authority has been given to Me in heaven and on earth." Earlier, he claimed, "All things have been committed to me by my Father." Those previous words refer to the Father's empowerment of His earthly ministry. Jesus' present claim is transcendent authority like the Son of Man figure in Daniel's vision. He has "authority, glory, and sovereign power [over] all peoples, nations, and people of every language…"

With similar authority, Jesus directs His followers to spread His teachings throughout the world. He further grants them the ability to accomplish the task of making disciples.

The central command is to "go…and make disciples of all the nations." At the heart of the great commission is the reproduction in other people what Jesus produces in the lives of believers. Among the spiritual attributes that disciples acquire are love, faith, acceptance, personal growth, compassion and gratitude. Learners produce more lifelong learners.

In the Greek, the participle, "go," renders "when you have gone." "Going" is one of the three means of fulfilling the command to make disciples. It means more than traveling across geographical boundaries. Believers are to be active, not inactive, in their lifestyle of faith. Simultaneously, to "go" means to cross boundaries to make disciples, to "go" across the street, to "go" to dinner with an unbelieving friend and to "go" into the inner city. It encompasses going beyond one's comfort zone to make the Gospel accessible to the lost. Living life means "going" into each day with purpose.

The goal is to make disciples of "all nations." Earlier instructions limited "to go" are only to the "lost sheep of Israel." Jesus rescinds that directive and replaces it with a universal mission to all peoples. However, the commission does not exclude a mission to Israel; for Israel is now "subordinated and incorporated into the inclusive reference to all nations." Most significantly, Matthew ends his gospel with reference to mission to the Gentiles thereby urging Jewish Christians to abandon their prejudices.

In addition to "going," discipleship requires Jesus' followers to baptize unbelievers of all nations "in the name of the Father and of the Son and of the Holy Spirit." They are to immerse the new believer following the example of Christ, demonstrating His character and emulating his relationship of belonging to the triune God.

According to the twentieth verse, discipleship also includes teaching. The risen Savior instructs his followers to teach people of all nations where they go observe everything He previously taught them.

Unlike commandments of the Jewish law in which obedience was the basic requirement for faithful observance, Jesus' commandments inspired devotion in His followers. Compliance emerges from a willingness to surrender to a heartfelt devotion and relationship rather than a legalistic obligation. He instructs his followers to teach grace, love, and relationship with the Father.

Jesus' followers do not have the latitude of cherry picking among the tenets of His teachings. They cannot choose to teach the parts that they like while ignoring the rest. Life in the Kingdom of God requires total allegiance. Disciples hear and do everything which Jesus commands. His teachings span the life cycle and address the whole person about how to cultivate a lifestyle that pleases God.

Jesus makes a final promise to His disciples, "and behold, I am with you always." Beyond being comforting assurance, this promise necessarily equips disciples for their mission. It complements Jesus' claim to universal authority in Matthew 28:18 and undergirds the believer's confidence in fulfilling the Great Commission.

The Gospel concludes with the promise of the One whom Matthew introduces to readers as "Immanuel" which literally means "God with us." He pledges His abiding presence to His disciples. The Risen Lord will be with His people "until the end of the age." Practically, this means to the end of time and of this world. God thus vindicates His Son. The story ends with assurance of the Son's abiding presence on Earth and anticipation of His direct presence in eschatological glory.

II. The Remedy for Persecution (Hebrews 10:20–25)

This powerful passage, Hebrews 10:20–25, encourages believers with three favorable exhortations: (1) draw near to God with confidence, (2) persevere in their faith, and (3) support each other in their spiritual journey. This section of Hebrews includes a broader context of exhortation and encouragement to Jewish Christians facing fierce persecution and alluring temptation to abandon the Christian faith and return to their old ways.

At best the identity of the author of Hebrews is uncertain; he intended certainly for this letter to be a source for strengthening the faith of his readers. He prioritizes the supremacy of Christ and the new covenant He establishes. Theologically, the author unquestionably errs on the side of "high Christology" similar to the Gospel and Letters of John.

The author explains the role of Christ as the High Priest whose sacrifice has granted access to the Father for those who believe in Him. Jesus' human life and sacrificial death opens the Most Holy Place and enables believers to enter directly into God's presence.

Because of this grace, the author exhorts readers to exercise their freedom to experience God in three specific ways. The twenty-second verse is the first of three exhortations. It invites the reader to approach God with a true heart. At first glance, this exhortation consists of a two–step configuration. First, draw near to God. Second, draw near with a true heart. Actually, a person can only draw near to God with a true heart. Proximity to God is what makes the heart true.

To have a true heart is to have sincere motives. Initiating intimacy with God requires complete surrender to Him and total vulnerability in faith. This process of faith is both unequivocal and unconditional. Note the directive insists the believer draws near to God rather than the reverse. This process indicates God's constant presence and accessibility.

The author qualifies the believer's eligibility to draw near to God. He is to do so with the "full assurance of faith." This confidence results from the believer's knowledge that his heart has been washed or sprinkled by the pure blood of Christ. The blood cleanses an evil conscience and the body from untoward instincts and compulsions. This is another way of saying that the believer has been redeemed. The imagery shows redemption as a process of internal (the conscience) and external (the body) cleansing and change.

The second exhortation, "hold fast the confession of our hope without wavering," appeals to the believer to maintain spiritual consistency. Believers face despondency, discouragement, and distress amidst myriad persecutions of daily living. These afflictions also cause doubt and anxiety. Hence, the author cautions the need to be steadfast as it relates to faith.

First century Christians, to whom the author writes, suffered directly for their faith. As they converted from Judaism or paganism to Christianity, their communities socially ostracized them, and their families and friends often rejected them.

Because of their faith, they were often excluded from trade guilds. They lost their jobs. They even had their property confiscated. Christians could be brought before local magistrates and accused of various crimes. Their refusal to participate in pagan worship or their perceived disloyalty to the Roman Empire led to these frivolous charges. Tragically, some Christians were physically abused and unjustly imprisoned for their beliefs.

Jewish Christians faced additional persecution from their fellow Jews. Considered heretics, they could be expelled from synagogues and excommunicated from religious and social life of their communities. As a remedy for doubt, the author urges his readers to persevere in their conviction. They are to "hold fast to their confession." It is as if they were dangling from a high cliff, and they would not ever willingly let go. They are to remember the assurance they had in God when they first professed their faithfulness to Him. They are to remember that He who promised is unquestionably faithful and unwavering in His commitment to each believer.

The author finally exhorts his readers to consider and respect each other. They encourage and support one another in Christian love and good works. "Consider" is another way of saying "be mindful of" your fellow disciples. Believers are to intentionally cultivate relationships that invite a deeper awareness of each other's needs, character traits, and spiritual gifts. Drawing close to God, as in the first exhortation, practically necessitates drawing close to one another in fellowship, as in this exhortation.

Because many believers were socially ostracized for their faith, they began to avoid public or private gatherings with other believers. The author addresses this social withdrawal by urging believers to do the opposite. He tells them to resist forsaking the assembly of the faith community.

Meeting together was the means to spur other believers forward in the Christian life. Neglecting collective gatherings, however, limits disciples' ability to exchange encouragement toward good works. Regular fellowship with believers was an essential part of Christian growth.

Both the writer and the readers of Hebrews believed that the day of Christ's return was drawing near. Anticipation of the Day of the Lord motivated believers to remain faithful in their confession and diligent in their spiritual practices. The imminent return of Christ underscores the urgency of maintaining a strong and supportive fellowship as believers prepare for the fulfillment of God's promises. Although thousands of years have lapsed since this writing, every believer is charged with living in anticipation of Christ's return, as no one knows the day or the hour (Matthew 24:36).

THE LESSON APPLIED

Understanding the importance of community in cultivating personal faith and an intimate relationship with God is a significant component of discipleship. Experiencing God requires more than a regimented application of biblical principles. True relationship demands intentional engagement with other believers.

Christian community is a unifying theme in both passages in today's lesson. The Great Commission focuses on the collective mission of making disciples and teaching the commandments of Christ. The Hebrews text emphasizes mutual support and encouragement in the community of faith. Together, these passages insist upon believers provoking one another toward love, good deeds, and faithfulness, especially within daily challenges.

LET'S TALK ABOUT IT...

Discuss the following questions and visit www.rhboyd.com for more information.

What parts of the Great Commission imply that believers are to support one another in the community of faith?

In what ways can the assurance of Jesus' presence in Matthew 28:20 inspire believers to support and encourage each other in their faith journeys?

How does the call to "spur one another on toward love and good deeds" in Hebrews 10:24 relate to the mission of making disciples in Matthew 28:18–20?

What practical steps can believers take to ensure they do not "give up meeting together," and how does this foster mutual encouragement?

In what ways can the teachings of Jesus in Matthew 28:18–20 and the exhortations in Hebrews 10:24–25 be applied to create a supportive and dynamic faith community?

Get Social

Share your views and tag us
@rhboydco and use #rhboydco

@rhboydco

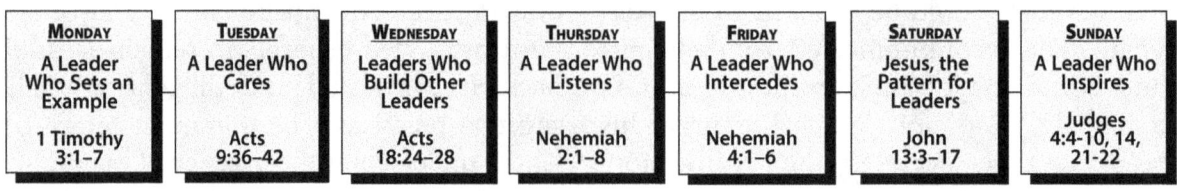

Home Daily Devotional Readings
June 1–7, 2026

Monday	Tuesday	Wednesday	Thursday	Friday	Saturday	Sunday
A Leader Who Sets an Example	A Leader Who Cares	Leaders Who Build Other Leaders	A Leader Who Listens	A Leader Who Intercedes	Jesus, the Pattern for Leaders	A Leader Who Inspires
1 Timothy 3:1–7	Acts 9:36–42	Acts 18:24–28	Nehemiah 2:1–8	Nehemiah 4:1–6	John 13:3–17	Judges 4:4–10, 14, 21-22

FOURTH QUARTER

June
July
August

Lesson material is based on International Sunday School Lessons and International Bible Lessons for Christian Teaching, copyrighted by the International Council of Religious Education, and is used by its permission.

Lesson I — June 7, 2026

Deborah, a Leader in a National Emergency

Adult Topic: Women in Leadership
Background Scripture: Judges 4:1–24
Lesson Passage: Judges 4:4–10, 14, 21–22

JUDGES 4:4-10, 14, 21-22

KJV

AND Deborah, a prophetess, the wife of Lapidoth, she judged Israel at that time.
5 And she dwelt under the palm tree of Deborah between Ramah and Bethel in mount Ephraim: and the children of Israel came up to her for judgment.
6 And she sent and called Barak the son of Abinoam out of Kedeshnaphtali, and said unto him, Hath not the Lord God of Israel commanded, saying, Go and draw toward mount Tabor, and take with thee ten thousand men of the children of Naphtali and of the children of Zebulun?
7 And I will draw unto thee to the river Kishon Sisera, the captain of Jabin's army, with his chariots and his multitude; and I will deliver him into thine hand.
8 And Barak said unto her, If thou wilt go with me, then I will go: but if thou wilt not go with me, then I will not go.
9 And she said, I will surely go with thee: notwithstanding the journey that thou takest shall not be for thine honour; for the Lord shall sell Sisera into the hand of a woman. And Deborah arose, and went with Barak to Kedesh.
10 And Barak called Zebulun and Naphtali to Kedesh; and he went up with ten thousand men at his feet: and Deborah went up with him.

• • • • • •

14 And Deborah said unto Barak, Up; for this is the day in which the Lord hath delivered Sisera into thine hand: is not the Lord gone out before thee? So Barak went down from mount Tabor, and ten thousand men after him.

NRSVue

AT that time Deborah, a prophet, wife of Lappidoth, was judging Israel.
5 She used to sit under the palm of Deborah between Ramah and Bethel in the hill country of Ephraim, and the Israelites came up to her for judgment.
6 She sent and summoned Barak son of Abinoam from Kedesh in Naphtali and said to him, "The Lord, the God of Israel, commands you, 'Position yourself at Mount Tabor, taking ten thousand from the tribe of Naphtali and the tribe of Zebulun.
7 I will draw out Sisera, the general of Jabin's army, to meet you by the Wadi Kishon with his chariots and his troops, and I will give him into your hand.'"
8 Barak said to her, "If you will go with me, I will go, but if you will not go with me, I will not go."
9 And she said, "I will surely go with you; nevertheless, the road on which you are going will not lead to your glory, for the Lord will sell Sisera into the hand of a woman." Then Deborah got up and went with Barak to Kedesh.
10 Barak summoned Zebulun and Naphtali to Kedesh, and ten thousand warriors went up behind him, and Deborah went up with him.

• • • • • •

14 Then Deborah said to Barak, "Up! For this is the day on which the Lord has given Sisera into your hand. Has not the Lord gone out before you?" So Barak went down from Mount Tabor with ten thousand warriors following him.

MAIN THOUGHT: At that time Deborah, a prophet, wife of Lappidoth, was judging Israel. She used to sit under the palm of Deborah between Ramah and Bethel in the hill country of Ephraim, and the Israelites came up to her for judgment. (Judges 4:4–5, NRSVue)

JUDGES 4:4-10, 14, 21-22

KJV
•••••

21 Then Jael Heber's wife took a nail of the tent, and took an hammer in her hand, and went softly unto him, and smote the nail into his temples, and fastened it into the ground: for he was fast asleep and weary. So he died.

22 And, behold, as Barak pursued Sisera, Jael came out to meet him, and said unto him, Come, and I will shew thee the man whom thou seekest. And when he came into her tent, behold, Sisera lay dead, and the nail was in his temples.

NRSVue
•••••

21 But Jael wife of Heber took a tent peg and took a hammer in her hand and went softly to him and drove the peg into his temple, until it went down into the ground—he was lying fast asleep from weariness—and he died.

22 Then, as Barak came in pursuit of Sisera, Jael went out to meet him and said to him, "Come, and I will show you the man whom you are seeking." So he went into her tent, and there was Sisera lying dead, with the tent peg in his temple.

LESSON SETTING

Time: After the death of Joshua and before the birth of Samuel (1050–1000 bc)

Place: Bethel and Ramah; Kedesh; Mount Tabor; Harosheth of the Gentiles; River of Kishon

Setting: It was an extraordinary time of transition as the Israelites began to settle in Canaan. Possessing the land required that they destroy the inhabitants that they found there. As they fought against the various tribes that were living in Canaan, they did not destroy all of them as God commanded. Under Joshua's leadership, they were victorious in getting into Canaan; however, there remained much of the region to overtake. Joshua, their fearless leader, died and another generation rose up that did not know the Lord. After Joshua's death, God sent judges who were also prophets and warrior leaders as His representatives to guide the nation in its new territory. However, the Israelites rejected God's judges, which ushered them through cycles of sinning, punishment, crying out to God for help, and rescue at the hands of the very judges they rejected. Because they failed to drive out all the Canaanites from their land, they allowed their enemies to settle among them. The Israelites intermarried with their enemies and worshiped their gods. This was in direct violation of God's instructions. Their disobedience proved to be devastating, and Israel suffered terrible consequences. God allowed the Canaanites and surrounding nations to revolt against them and to oppress them in order to test their faithfulness to Him. For twenty years, King Jabin of Hazor dominated and oppressed the Israelites. The geopolitical landscape was volatile, and Israel was stuck in a situation that they caused by their own disobedience to the Lord. When they cried to the Lord for help, the Lord raised up a woman judge, prophetess, and warrior named Deborah. She was the only female judge of Israel. She was a talented poet and a courageous warrior whom God used to respond to the national crisis. Through Deborah, God demonstrated that He will often use those who are humble to accomplish His plans. God is not limited by any social constructs of human derivation. The qualifications to be used by God is faithful obedience to Him, as Deborah demonstrated throughout her life of service.

LESSON OUTLINE
  I. God Chose Leaders (Judges 1–3)
 II. God Chose Deborah (Judges 4:4–10)
III. Go! God Has Promised Victory (Judges 4:14; 21–22)

UNIFYING PRINCIPLE
Bad choices often lead to impossible places out of which to climb. How can we achieve rescue when our troubles are too big for us? God empowers Deborah to deliver Israel when they seek God for relief from an oppressive foreign power. Her life reflects God's use of humble, willing, and faithful people.

INTRODUCTION

In this lesson, we examine Israel's plight and God's chosen albeit unconventional servant to deliver His people from a potentially perilous situation. Before delving into the lesson, however, we consider some of the historical events that led to Israel's oppression. Further, we observe how God uses Deborah to deliver Israel from King Jabin of Canaan's oppressive rule.

The book of Judges gives witness to the period in Israel's history after they entered Canaan and before the establishment of the monarchy. As God was their King, the judges were His sanctioned representatives. God empowered men and women judges and military warriors to guide the Israelites through specific crises. These imperfect and very fallible human judges mightily fulfilled God's plans for His people.

Three main military strategies defined Israelite objectives during this period: first, annihilate the enemy; second, gain the territory; and finally, occupy the land.

Joshua led Israel in conquering some strategic strongholds. At the time of his death, a good deal of Canaan territory remained unoccupied. The Israelites were literally and figuratively in bed with their enemies. They intermarried with them and began to worship Canaanite gods. This failure was monumentally devastating and further delayed Israelite conquest of the Canaanites who revolted against the Israelites to restore their power. Within that context, during a time when women were not allowed to assume leadership positions, God raises up Deborah as a mighty warrior to lead His people to victory.

EXPOSITION

I. God Chose Leaders (Judges 1–3)

Before he died, Joshua divided the land of Canaan between the twelve tribes of Israel. However, Philistines, Canaanites, Sidonians, and Hivites remained in the regions that the tribes were to conquer. Judah was the first tribe to continue Israel's conquest of Canaan. The Israelites faced many military, political, and spiritual challenges from their enemies.

Each tribe became autonomous after Joshua's death. Periodically, tribes called upon each other for assistance. The Israelites went through cycles of serving God, disobeying Him, repenting, and then serving Him again. Unsurprisingly, Israel eventually succumbed to the unholy influences of Canaanite culture. Not only did they intermarry with the Canaanites; they also worshiped their gods.

The generation of Israelites that succeeded Joshua did not know the Lord. They, therefore, did what they thought was right in their own eyes. Because of their disobedience, God allowed their oppression by the Canaanites. During this period of early settlement in Canaan, King Jabin ruled. God allowed Jabin to oppress the Israelites to test their faithfulness to Him. The Israelites suffered terribly under the oppressive rule of King Jabin for twenty years. To escape their oppression, strong leadership would be needed. God would call out the right leader for the right time.

According to J.C. Maxwell in *The Maxwell Leadership Bible* (2018), strong leaders possess five characteristics: (1) able to identify a problem; (2) possess confidence and competence to address any situation; (3) cast a vision with passion; (4) persuade others to support the cause; and (5) pursue a strategy to accomplish any goal. Through each of the judges, we see strong godly leadership and the powerful results of their headship.

The first judge of Israel was Othniel, the nephew of Caleb. The Israelites were in servitude for eight years to Chushan-Rishathaim, King of Mesopotamia, and God called Othniel as a judge and warrior to deliver the people. He defeated King Chushan-Rishathaim. Cushan means "man of double wickedness" (Macdonald, W., Farstad, A, 1995. *Believers Bible Commentary*).

After Othniel's valiant victory, Israel lived in peace for forty years.

After Othniel's death, however, the Israelites "did evil again in the sight of the Lord" (Judges 2:13). God allowed Ammon and Malek to overthrow Israel, and for eighteen years, they served Eglon, King of Moab (2:14). God then sent Ehud from the tribe of Benjamin (the smallest tribe) to deliver Israel. Ehud tricked the King of Moab by presenting him with a gift and then killed him by driving a dagger through his belly. After he killed the King of Moab, Ehud led the Israelites to defeat the Moabites. Following this victory, the people and the land rested for fourscore (eighty) years.

Following Ehud, was Shamgar, a judge and warrior who killed 600 Philistines, delivered Israel, and gained control of Philistia. Nevertheless, after escaping this bout of oppression, the children of Israel again did evil in God's sight. Because of their recurring disobedience, the Lord allowed them to be oppressed for twenty years by King Jabin, of Canaan.

II. God Chose Deborah (Judges 4:4–10)

God hand-picked Deborah to serve as the next judge and military leader of Israel to deliver the people from the oppression of King Jabin. The first and only woman judge and military leader of Israel, Deborah's name means "bee" or leader. She was the wife of Lappidoth, whose name means "torch" or "lightning." When the meaning of Deborah's name is combined with the meaning of her husband's name, she can be understood as born a leader possessing lightning or power. She was a strong, powerful leader for God and the light of God was in her. As judge, Deborah's responsibility is to attune herself to hear from the Lord and then tell others how to respond to His word.

Deborah's calling marks a notable exception to the norm of typical male leadership, especially during biblical times. Often,

God uses persons who are considered least among mortals to do His greatest work. Deborah proves fully committed to God and quite capable of handling the task. As the calling of David makes clear, human beings may judge from outward appearances, but God judges the heart (See 1 Samuel 16:7). It is amazing what God accomplishes through people who fully surrender to Him!

Thankfully, God is not bound to human customs and reasonings. In unprecedented fashion, God called and anointed Deborah during a time of spiritual decline and civil oppression. To be called and equipped by God is the highest qualification one can receive. Highly respected, Deborah was sought by her fellow Israelites for direction from God.

III. Go! God Has Promised Victory (Judges 4:14, 21–22)

Deborah commissioned Barak to war against Jabin, King of Hazor. She gave him God's military instructions and assured him that God would deliver Sisera, the captain of Jabin's army, into his hands. Fearing Sisera's army of 900 iron chariots, Barak refused to go into battle without Deborah. She prophesied to him again and assured him he would win the battle; however, the honor of the victory would go to a woman.

Verse 14 represents a pivotal moment in the dialogue between Deborah and Barak, as it encapsulates a profound truth about the sovereignty and power of God in delivering His people. Deborah's strong imperative to Barak to get up and go points us to the initiative and timing of God. Barak's victory is not dependent on Israel's military might, but rather upon God's sovereign plan. The phrase, "Has not the LORD gone before you?" reflects Deborah's God-given authority and God's active presence and leadership. God not only ordains the outcome (victory), He also determines the means (Barak's obedience and faith).

Barak's response—descending Mount Tabor with ten thousand men—demonstrates his faith in God's promise, even in the face of overwhelming odds. His actions indicates his belief that human weakness is no barrier to God's purposes, even though he had refused to go into battle without Deborah. As Paul later writes, "If God is for us, who can be against us?" (Romans 8:31).

The victory belongs to the Lord. Deborah's command could be interpreted as a question, "What are you waiting for? God has already assured the victory!"

Verses 15 reveals that God caused panic and confusion to fall among Sisera's army. The Hebrew verb for "discomfited" (וַיָּהָם, vayyāhām) in the KJV suggests supernatural intervention, reminiscent of God's acts at the Red Sea (Exodus 14:24). God's power is decisive; human effort is secondary and dependent on His initiative.

Sisera ran for his life and Barak pursued him. Sisera sought protection in the tent of Jael, the wife of Heber, who had previously informed Sisera that Barak was planning an attack. Therefore, Sisera understandably assumed Jael and Heber were his allies. Jael urged him to come into her tent, where Sisera immediately fell asleep. Afterward, Jael took a peg from the tent and drove it into his temple. When Barak arrived, Jael showed him Sisera's lifeless body.

God's calling is unique to everyone, based upon gifts, circumstances and His divine plan. From a burning bush, God calls Moses to lead the Israelites out of Egypt (Exodus 3–4). God prepared Samuel and revealed to Jeremiah that he had been chosen as a prophet before he was even born (Jeremiah 1:4–10). God also calls us through divine appointments and circumstances. Esther becomes queen at a critical time to save her people from destruction.

God calls us through the Holy Spirit, who descends at Pentecost, empowering the disciples to preach the Gospel (Acts 2). Paul dramatically sees a vision of Christ on the road to Damascus (Acts 9:1–19). God calls us through burdens and passion for a cause. Nehemiah felt deep sorrow for Jerusalem's ruined walls. He took action to rebuild them (Nehemiah 1–2). God uses unexpected people to accomplish His will. Jael was a non-Israelite woman whose household was at peace with Sisera. The ones we least expect are chosen for great acts of faith.

THE LESSON APPLIED

God's standards for leadership often differ with human standards. Jael appears to be an ordinary woman; however, God uses her to play a pivotal role in Israel's victory. God empowers anyone who trusts in Him, regardless of gender, social status or background.

When God calls us to action, if we feel unqualified, He equips us if we trust Him and move forward, trusting in His plan. Fear restricts us from fully experiencing God's power. Fully trusting God allows us to walk boldly and courageously in His purpose. Fear and hesitation impede opportunities for spiritual victory.

The song of Deborah in Judges 5 celebrates God as the true deliverer. We genuinely rely upon God for success. When He fights for us, God assures victory.

We should always acknowledge and celebrate God's faithfulness. Gratitude deepens our faith and trust and confidence in His purposes and power.

LET'S TALK ABOUT IT...

Discuss the following questions and visit www.rhboyd.com for more information.

How can you know what God is calling you to do?

By what characteristics can you determine a God-called leader?

Have you ever been unenthused about the leadership of someone you doubted was called or sent by God? How was the situation resolved?

Get Social

Share your views and tag us @rhboydco and use #rhboydco

@rhboydco

Lesson II   **June 14, 2026**

Hannah, a Godly Mother

Adult Topic: Wishing and Hoping and Praying
Background Scripture: 1 Samuel 1:1–28; 2:1–11, 18–19; 3:1–18
Lesson Passage: 1 Samuel 1:9–20, 25

1 SAMUEL 1:9–20, 25

KJV

SO Hannah rose up after they had eaten in Shiloh, and after they had drunk. Now Eli the priest sat upon a seat by a post of the temple of the Lord.
10 And she was in bitterness of soul, and prayed unto the Lord, and wept sore.
11 And she vowed a vow, and said, O Lord of hosts, if thou wilt indeed look on the affliction of thine handmaid, and remember me, and not forget thine handmaid, but wilt give unto thine handmaid a man child, then I will give him unto the Lord all the days of his life, and there shall no razor come upon his head.
12 And it came to pass, as she continued praying before the Lord, that Eli marked her mouth.
13 Now Hannah, she spake in her heart; only her lips moved, but her voice was not heard: therefore Eli thought she had been drunken.
14 And Eli said unto her, How long wilt thou be drunken? put away thy wine from thee.
15 And Hannah answered and said, No, my lord, I am a woman of a sorrowful spirit: I have drunk neither wine nor strong drink, but have poured out my soul before the Lord.
16 Count not thine handmaid for a daughter of Belial: for out of the abundance of my complaint and grief have I spoken hitherto.
17 Then Eli answered and said, Go in peace: and the God of Israel grant thee thy petition that thou hast asked of him.
18 And she said, Let thine handmaid find grace in thy sight. So the woman went her way, and did eat, and her countenance was no more sad.

NRSVue

AFTER they had eaten and drunk at Shiloh, Hannah rose and presented herself before the Lord. Now Eli the priest was sitting on the seat beside the doorpost of the temple of the Lord.
10 She was deeply distressed and prayed to the Lord and wept bitterly.
11 She made this vow: "O Lord of hosts, if only you will look on the misery of your servant and remember me and not forget your servant but will give to your servant a male child, then I will set him before you as a nazirite until the day of his death. He shall drink neither wine nor intoxicants, and no razor shall touch his head."
12 As she continued praying before the Lord, Eli observed her mouth.
13 Hannah was praying silently; only her lips moved, but her voice was not heard; therefore Eli thought she was drunk.
14 So Eli said to her, "How long will you make a drunken spectacle of yourself? Put away your wine."
15 But Hannah answered, "No, my lord, I am a woman deeply troubled; I have drunk neither wine nor strong drink, but I have been pouring out my soul before the Lord.
16 Do not regard your servant as a worthless woman, for I have been speaking out of my great anxiety and vexation all this time."
17 Then Eli answered, "Go in peace; the God of Israel grant the petition you have made to him."
18 And she said, "Let your servant find favor in your sight." Then the woman went her way and ate and drank with her husband, and her countenance was sad no longer.

MAIN THOUGHT: In due time Hannah conceived and bore a son. She named him Samuel, for she said, "I have asked him of the LORD." (1 Samuel 1:20, NRSVue)

1 SAMUEL 1:9–20, 25

KJV

19 And they rose up in the morning early, and worshipped before the Lord, and returned, and came to their house to Ramah: and Elkanah knew Hannah his wife; and the Lord remembered her.

20 Wherefore it came to pass, when the time was come about after Hannah had conceived, that she bare a son, and called his name Samuel, saying, Because I have asked him of the Lord.

• • • • •

25 And they slew a bullock, and brought the child to Eli.

NRSVue

19 They rose early in the morning and worshiped before the Lord; then they went back to their house at Ramah. Elkanah knew his wife Hannah, and the Lord remembered her.

20 In due time Hannah conceived and bore a son. She named him Samuel, for she said, "I have asked him of the Lord."

• • • • •

25 Then they slaughtered the bull and brought the child to Eli.

LESSON SETTING

Time: Approx. 1105–1000 BC
Place: Ramah, Palestine
Setting: The books of 1 and 2 Samuel cover a significant period in Israel's history. From the Exodus to their settlement in Canaan and beyond, God Himself was the King of Israel. However, He appointed judges as His earthly representatives to lead Israel and serve as military commanders. God also communicated with the Israelites through the judges. During their settlement and conquest of Canaan, the Israelites fought many nations who were under a monarchy. They noticed that the other nations had kings. The Israelites thought that having an earthly king would strengthen their political power in the region; therefore, they asked God to change their governmental leadership structure from that of the judges (theocracy) to that of kings (monarchy). Judges led Israel for 200 years; however, when the people demanded a king, God listened and gave them what they asked for. God used the family circumstances and faith of Hannah who was living in a painful and impossible family situation, to bring Samuel into the world. He raised Samuel to serve as the last judge of Israel and guide them through the big change of establishing a monarchy.

LESSON OUTLINE

I. Hannah's Faith Under Fire (1 Samuel 1:9–11)
II. Hannah's Encounter with Eli (1 Samuel 1:12–18)
III. The Lord Remembers Hannah (1 Samuel 1:19–20, 25)

UNIFYING PRINCIPLE

Everyone has experienced fears that his or her dreams and hopes for the future may not be realized. How do we seek reassurance that our hopes and dreams may yet come true? Hannah turned to prayer, confident that the Lord would fulfill her hopes for conceiving a child.

INTRODUCTION

Elkanah, a righteous and loving man, married two women, Hannah and Peninnah. Although he dearly loves Hannah, she was barren. His second wife, Peninnah, gave him several sons and daughters, but he still favored Hannah more. Jealous of her husband's affection for Hannah, Peninnah relentlessly attempted to leverage Hannah's infertility to her favor. Compounding Hannah's pain was the prevalent social stigma that infertility was the woman's fault and a curse from God. Peninnah's harassment became unbearable for Hannah. In the midst of her despair, she turns to God.

Family dysfunction can be extremely painful. Hannah's story highlights adversity that families face. God transforms and redeems adversities to achieve His purposes. Despite the painful situation that she faced with Peninnah, Hannah's prayer life exhibited extraordinary faith and resilience.

Hannah's story also reveals how God mysteriously and majestically uses the infertility of a woman to perform the miracle of Samuel's birth. Her son became one of the greatest leaders of Israel. Samuel guides the people to worship Almighty God and assists in transitioning the governance for the nation.

EXPOSITION

I. Hannah's Faith Under Fire (1 Samuel 1:9–11)

While the Israelites dwelled in Egypt, they adopted some of the customs of idol worship. After their settlement in Canaan, Joshua died and there arose another generation that felt no need to obey the first Commandment (Exodus 20:3) given to them by the God who had delivered their forebears from bondage. Throughout the years of conquest in Canaan, they adopted the idols of their enemies. The Israelites intermingled worship of Yahweh with that of other gods. The Israelites' worship of Baal, Asherah, and other Canaanite deities, wherein they made sacrifices to demons, greatly displeased Almighty God. Their idolatry led to military setbacks and yielded oppression at the hands of their enemies. The judges exhorted the people to rebuke idolatry and return to worshiping the God of their forebears. God ironically selects an infertile, humble woman as His vessel to raise up one of the nation's greatest leaders.

Verses 9–20 narrate the pivotal moment in Israel's history when Hannah, out of the pain of her barrenness, prays fervently to the Lord and is granted a son, Samuel, who will become a prophet and judge. This passage is foundational for understanding the themes of divine sovereignty, answered prayer, and the birth of prophetic leadership in Israel. The narrative highlights God's compassion and power while it also models faith, persistence in prayer, and the fulfillment of God's redemptive purposes.

Elkanah taking his family on their annual pilgrimage to Shiloh (1 Samuel 1) typifies Israelite religious life during the period of the judges. The text mentions Elkanah's regular journeys to "worship and sacrifice to the Lord Almighty at Shiloh" (1 Sam. 1:3), raising questions about the specific festival(s) involved and the significance of these observances. Among the major Israelite feasts, the Feast of Tabernacles (*Sukkot*) is often named in relation to such pilgrimages.

The Feast of Tabernacles, also known as Sukkot (סֻכּוֹת, booths), is one of the three major pilgrimage festivals in the Torah, alongside Passover (*Pesach*) and Weeks (*Shavuot*). The festival is described in Leviticus 23:33–43, Numbers 29:12–38, and Deuteronomy 16:13–17. In Leviticus

23:34 (NRSVue), God mandates that "On the fifteenth day of this seventh month and lasting seven days, there shall be the Festival of Booths to the LORD."

Sukkot commemorates Israel's wilderness wanderings, when God's chosen people dwelled in temporary shelters after the Exodus (Lev. 23:42–43). According to *myjewishlearning.com*, "Beginning five days after Yom Kippur, Sukkot is named after the booths or huts (*sukkot* in Hebrew) in which Jews are supposed to dwell during this week-long celebration. According to rabbinic tradition, these flimsy *sukkot* represent the huts in which the Israelites dwelt during their forty years of wandering in the desert after escaping from slavery in Egypt.

During the observance, Elkanah gave portions of the sacrificial meat to Peninnah and her children, "But to Hannah he gave a double portion because he loved her…" This sacrifice was a thank offering, which allowed the worshipers to eat the part that was not offered to God. The "double" portion means "to show the face." Elkanah showed his face to Hannah, indicating that she was worthy and that he cared deeply for her. In that culture, honored guests were given a "super-sized" meal, but it had to be difficult for Hannah to eat food that was associated with being thankful, especially when she was so distressed about her barrenness and the torture it yielded.

By this point, Hannah is spiritually disturbed, socially disgraced, and emotionally depressed. This broken woman rises after the sacrificial meal at Shiloh and enters the house of the Lord, where Eli the priest is seated by the doorpost (v. 9). In "bitterness of soul," (KJV) Hannah weeps and prays, vowing that if God grants her a son, she will dedicate him to God as a Nazirite (vv. 10–11; cf. Numbers 6:1–21).

A Nazirite (Hebrew: נָזִיר, nazir, "one set apart, consecrated") is an Old Testament follower of God who takes a vow of separation and dedication to the LORD. The primary biblical legislation concerning Nazirites is found in Numbers 6:1–21. The Nazirite vow could be taken by men or women, usually for a specified period, though in rare cases (e.g., Samson, Samuel, John the Baptist) it was lifelong. The key elements of the Nazirite vow included abstinence from wine and all grape products (Num. 6:3–4); no razor touching one's hair (Num. 6:5); and avoidance of ritual defilement by corpses (Num. 6:6–7). Although not explicitly stated in Scripture, Samuel is traditionally considered to have taken a Nazirite vow.

Hannah's weeping leads to worship as her tears mingle with her prayers. The kind of prayer that arises from the bitterness of the soul is far different than the perfunctory prayers of normalcy. When tears are in our eyes, our prayers are offered from the heart.

Her petition to God as "the Lord of Hosts" refers to all the armies of heaven. The Lord Almighty has all the hosts of heaven ready to do His bidding. Hannah appeals to God's power and authority because she knows there is nothing she can do. Having struggled through years of barrenness and the associated stigmas and issues, Hannah realizes a very important truth: children are not just for parents; they are for the Lord. As God's creatures, nothing we have truly belongs to us. That includes children; they're on loan to parents, to shepherd and to train them for the Lord's work.

II. Hannah's Encounter with Eli (1 Samuel 1:12–18)

Hannah's prayer is marked by persistence and intensity: "As she continued praying before the Lord, Eli observed her mouth"

(v. 12). The Hebrew verb for "continued" (hirbah, הִרְבְּה) conveys prolonged, earnest supplication. Her silent prayer—moving her lips but making no sound—was unusual for the time, as public prayer was typically vocal (cf. Psalm 142:1). Hannah's silent, heartfelt communication with God anticipates the New Testament's emphasis on praying "in the Spirit" (Ephesians 6:18).

Hannah did not offer a quick or superficial prayer. Hers was a repeated request, bathed in tears. She prayed secretly, not wanting to draw any attention to herself. Yet her quiet prayer had an unfortunate consequence when Eli, the priest, accused her of drunkenness. Because a great celebration was going on, many people may have over indulged in the various libations offered. Eli thought she was one of them.

Hannah's response is respectful yet honest: "I am a woman deeply troubled... I have been pouring out my soul before the Lord" (v. 15). The phrase "pouring out my soul" (*eshpokh et-nafshi*, יִשְׁפָּנַ־תִאָ פִּשְׁאָ) evokes the imagery of a drink offering, symbolizing total surrender and vulnerability before God.

Her sombre testimony must have convinced Eli, as he offers a blessing and message of divine affirmation to her. His words (v. 17) serve as a turning point in Hannah's journey toward motherhood. Though Eli does not know the specifics of Hannah's request, his words function as a priestly benediction, affirming God's attentiveness.

Hannah's transformation is immediate: "her countenance was sad no longer" (v. 18). This shift from anguish to peace illustrates the power of prayer and the assurance of God's presence, even before the answer is manifested. She is a faithful servant of God who longs for a child, yet she knows that if she has a child she must relinquish him to the Lord for safekeeping.

III. The Lord Remembers Hannah (1 Samuel 1:19–20, 25)

Verse 18 tells us that it was not conceiving Samuel in her womb that changed her countenance. Hannah's disposition changed after she prayed, and the prayer must have changed her because she believed in God. And because she believed she left the manifestation to God. She trusted the Almighty God whom they went to Shiloh to serve. This passage tells us they had gone to Shiloh to serve YHWH. There were many gods around that people served. The writer of Samuel wants it clear that they went to worship the Almighty God who had committed many mighty acts over the course of history.

Hannah believed that YHWH was able. So assured was she that "she went away and ate something, and her face was no longer downcast." Her outward circumstances had not changed, but Hannah had changed.

More than desiring a son, Hannah longed for spiritual wholeness and peace with God. It was God's desire for her to feel whole, and in the process, Samuel was born. What changed for Hannah was her relationship with God. She did not turn to Samuel and try to live through him because he had made her whole. She gave him up. Because her focus was on God and not Samuel, God blessed her with five more children.

Hannah went to God with her desires and prayed for deliverance, but we do not know how long the fulfillment took. Scripture simply tells us that the Lord remembered her and "over time" she conceived.

Once again, they got up early the next morning and worshiped before the Lord (v. 19). This was their practice, not something they did just once in a while. Then they went back home. A short time later, Hannah conceived and gave birth to a son, naming him Samuel. The common evangelical and scholarly interpretation is that Samuel means "God has heard" or "name of God." Every time Hannah said his name, she was reminded of his origin and destiny.

God answered Hannah's prayer, but not simply so she could have a baby. God needed a special prophet through whom He could work. He allowed a time of barrenness in Hannah's life to bring a greater blessing than she could ever imagine.

After Samuel was born, Elkanah returned to Shiloh to worship. Hannah decided to wait until Samuel was weaned, which would have been at around age three. She dedicated herself to her child, knowing that she will eventually present him to the Lord, and he will live there always."

Many people make promises to God, only to forget them once time passes or circumstances are no longer convenient. Hannah fully intended to keep her promise because she knew that Samuel did not belong to her.

THE LESSON APPLIED

In ancient Israel culture, barrenness was often seen as a sign of divine displeasure or a lack of blessing. Despite her anguish, Hannah turned to God in earnest prayer, demonstrating unwavering faith and dependence on Him. Our personal despairs and longings can open a door for God's Kingdom to advance.

Hannah's physical barrenness symbolizes spiritual barrenness both in her own life and in the nation of Israel. The nation was spiritually stagnant and fruitless because of their idolatry. When we humble ourselves before God and seek Him wholeheartedly, we can experience revival and renewal of our faith in Him.

Often, we may not see God at work. God's blessing of a son came to Hannah in His perfect timing. Let us trust God's timing, hold onto hope, and not give up, even when it seems as though God is not answering our prayers.

LET'S TALK ABOUT IT...

Discuss the following questions and visit www.rhboyd.com for more information.

What can we learn from Hannah's prayer that will help us to go through times of deep pain and how can we support others who are going through similar situations?

Get Social

Share your views and tag us
@rhboydco and use #rhboydco

@rhboydco

Home Daily Devotional Readings
June 15–21, 2026

Monday	Tuesday	Wednesday	Thursday	Friday	Saturday	Sunday
Encouraging Each Other's Faith	Choose Your Friends Wisely	A Friend Closer than a Brother	Friends When All Is Lost	The Greatest Love	Fierce and Faithful Friends	A Death in the Family
Romans 1:8–12	1 Corinthians 15:30–34	Proverbs 18:19–24	Ruth 1:11–18	John 15:9–17	1 Samuel 20:16–17, 32–34, 42	2 Samuel 1:17, 19–27

Lesson III   **June 21, 2026**

Jonathan and David, a Noble Friendship

Adult Topic: A Forever Bond
Background Scripture: 1 Sam. 18:1–4; 19:1–7; 20:1–42; 2 Sam. 1:17–27; 21:7
Lesson Passage: 1 Samuel 18:1–4; 20:16–17, 32–34, 42; 2 Samuel 1:26–27; 21:7

1 SAMUEL 18:1-4; 20:16-17, 32-34, 42; 2 SAMUEL 1:26-27; 21:7

KJV	NRSVue
AND it came to pass, when he had made an end of speaking unto Saul, that the soul of Jonathan was knit with the soul of David, and Jonathan loved him as his own soul.	WHEN David had finished speaking to Saul, the soul of Jonathan was bound to the soul of David, and Jonathan loved him as his own soul.
2 And Saul took him that day, and would let him go no more home to his father's house.	2 Saul took him that day and would not let him return to his father's house.
3 Then Jonathan and David made a covenant, because he loved him as his own soul.	3 Then Jonathan made a covenant with David because he loved him as his own soul.
4 And Jonathan stripped himself of the robe that was upon him, and gave it to David, and his garments, even to his sword, and to his bow, and to his girdle.	4 Jonathan stripped himself of the robe that he was wearing and gave it to David and his armor and even his sword and his bow and his belt.
• • • • • •	• • • • • •
16 So Jonathan made a covenant with the house of David, saying, Let the Lord even require it at the hand of David's enemies.	16 Thus Jonathan made a covenant with the house of David, saying, "May the Lord seek out the enemies of David."
17 And Jonathan caused David to swear again, because he loved him: for he loved him as he loved his own soul.	17 Jonathan made David swear again by his love for him, for he loved him as he loved his own life.
• • • • • •	• • • • • •
32 And Jonathan answered Saul his father, and said unto him, Wherefore shall he be slain? what hath he done?	32 Then Jonathan answered his father Saul, "Why should he be put to death? What has he done?"
33 And Saul cast a javelin at him to smite him: whereby Jonathan knew that it was determined of his father to slay David.	33 But Saul threw his spear at him to strike him, so Jonathan knew that it was the decision of his father to put David to death.
34 So Jonathan arose from the table in fierce anger, and did eat no meat the second day of the month: for he was grieved for David, because his father had done him shame.	34 Jonathan sprang up from the table in fierce anger and ate no food on the second day of the month, for he was grieved for David and because his father had disgraced him.
• • • • • •	• • • • • •
42 And Jonathan said to David, Go in peace, forasmuch as we have sworn both of us in the name	42 Then Jonathan said to David, "Go in peace, since both of us have sworn in the name of the

MAIN THOUGHT: Jonathan said to David, "Go in peace, since both of us have sworn in the name of the LORD, saying, 'The LORD shall be between me and you, and between my descendants and your descendants, forever.'" (1 Samuel 20:42, NRSVue)

1 SAMUEL 18:1–4; 20:16–17, 32–34, 42; 2 SAMUEL 1:26–27; 21:7

KJV

of the Lord, saying, The Lord be between me and thee, and between my seed and thy seed for ever. And he arose and departed: and Jonathan went into the city.

• • • 2 Samuel 1:26-27 • • •

26 I am distressed for thee, my brother Jonathan: very pleasant hast thou been unto me: thy love to me was wonderful, passing the love of women.
27 How are the mighty fallen, and the weapons of war perished!

• • • 2 Samuel 21:7 • • •

7 But the king spared Mephibosheth, the son of Jonathan the son of Saul, because of the Lord's oath that was between them, between David and Jonathan the son of Saul.

NRSVue

Lord, saying, 'The Lord shall be between me and you and between my descendants and your descendants forever.' " He got up and left, and Jonathan went into the city.

• • • 2 Samuel 1:26-27 • • •

26 I am distressed for you, my brother Jonathan; greatly beloved were you to me; your love to me was wonderful, passing the love of women.
27 How the mighty have fallen,

• • • 2 Samuel 21:7 • • •

7 But the king spared Mephibosheth, the son of Saul's son Jonathan, because of the oath of the Lord that was between them, between David and Jonathan son of Saul.

LESSON SETTING

Time: 1025 BC
Place: Bethlehem, Jerusalem
Setting: Through unlikely circumstances, the friendship between Jonathan and David emerges at the end of one of the most repeated biblical stories of all time—the story of David and Goliath. First Samuel 18 begins with David standing before King Saul and Jonathan, Prince of Israel. David has just killed Goliath. Jonathan, a fearless warrior and faithful servant of the Lord, admires David, who is also a fearless and humble servant of God. They share much in common, and discover this in the moment. Jonathan's heart was knit with David's on the heels of David's victory over Goliath. Later in this story, we see Saul's declining mental condition and flawed leadership, which is unleashed upon David. The bond of friendship between David and Jonathan would prove to be divinely directed as Jonathan's loyalty to David helps to save David's life and ensure his ascension to the throne.

LESSON OUTLINE

I. Divine Destiny in the Making of a King (Background)
II. A Covenant Friendship (1 Samuel 18:1–4; 20:16–17)
III. Loyalties Tested (1 Samuel 19:1–7)
IV. The Covenant Friendship Endures the Test of Time (2 Samuel 1:26–27; 21:7)

UNIFYING PRINCIPLE

Amid danger and distress, we desire support from a trustworthy friend. How does a friend prove trustworthy in difficult situations? Jonathan demonstrates genuine friendship to David despite King Saul's paranoia. David later honors their friendship with provision for Mephibosheth, Jonathan's son.

INTRODUCTION

In 1 Samuel 18, David is no longer a shepherd boy but rather a warrior whom Samuel (Hannah's son) anoints to be the next king of Israel. In this study we also encounter Jonathan, a son of King Saul, Israel's first monarch. Amid a battle with the Philistines, as Saul's mental stability declines and leadership fails, Jonathan and David form an eternal bond of friendship. Their covenant friendship was determinative in David's ascension to the throne as Israel's second king.

EXPOSITION

I. Divine Destiny in the Making of a King (Background)

As Samuel was anointing David, the Spirit of the Lord departs from Saul. An evil spirit infuses and terrorizes him. God permits Saul to suffer mental illness which probably would be diagnosed as manic-depressive disorder today. God's rejection of Saul creates an opportunity for David. Realizing Saul's mental instability, Saul's servants suggest music on the harp to calm him down.

Saul sends for David who plays the harp whenever an evil spirit arrests Saul. Through his service to Saul, David becomes an armor bearer and observes firsthand the life of a king. David remains a humble and loyal servant of Saul.

Meanwhile, Goliath, standing nearly nine feet tall, relentlessly challenges Israel for forty days to a fighting match. Fear paralyzes Israel's army and King Saul. One day, Jesse sends David to take food to his brothers who were serving in Saul's army. When David hears Goliath's threats against Israel and becomes angry. He volunteers to fight Goliath, though he had no military training. God's Spirit infuses David with courage to fight Goliath.

David single-handedly destroys Goliath using a shepherd's sling shot and stones. David appears before Saul with Goliath's head. This valiant victory leads to Prince Jonathan and David becoming best friends. God uses their friendship to save David's life and help him ascend to the throne.

Interestingly, friendship plays a pivotal role in divine and personal destiny. Many famous and successful people owe their achievements to good and loyal friends. No one succeeds at anything without gracious and empowering assistance from family, friends, or even kind strangers. David owes his kingship partly to Jonathan's faithfulness to God. As you study this lesson, consider the ways your friendships have furthered your personal destiny.

II. A Covenant Friendship (1 Samuel 18:1–4; 20:16–17)

It was a glorious day for Israel when David defeats Goliath. A young lad killing a giant would have been impossible by anyone's standards except God's. The Spirit of the Lord empowers David to kill Goliath and position the Israelites to overthrow the Philistines. David becomes an instant national hero! David appears before Saul and Jonathan. An immediate connection between Jonathan and David occurs. Their souls knit together. Often translated from Hebrew (*nephesh*) and Greek (*psyche*), "soul" refers to the innermost being of a person's mind, emotions, heart and will. It is the essence of personality, desires and relational capabilities. Jonathan and David share a divinely ordained spiritual connection. The Lord aligns their hearts, faith, values and destiny to accomplish His will.

A deep friendship and godly affection exist between Jonathan and David. Jonathan's love for David is not superficial or fleeting. Its covenantal nature exceeds personal gain or self-interest. From its origin, their friendship reflects loyalty, mutual respect, and common purpose.

Jonathan is the hereditary successor to the throne. However, he recognizes that God has chosen David to be Israel's next king. He affirms God's choice by giving his clothing and armor to David. Jonathan loves David "as his own soul" which indicates a Christlike selflessness and sacrificial consideration. Jonathan willingly lays aside his rights as heir and acknowledges David as God's chosen king.

Jonathan and David model true friendship. Principles determine their loyalty. They share the common belief and commitment to obeying God's will. Sacrificing his right to the throne because he accepts God's plan, Jonathan steps aside to allow David to become king. We marvel at Jonathan's ability to obey God rather than pursue any self-seeking objectives. Willing to defy his father, King Saul, to further God's plan, Jonathan protects David's life while risking his own life. In response for God's favor as evident in Jonathan's longstanding commitment, David demonstrates the importance of gratitude. Friends are usually equally situated in life. They do not need, nor do they ask anything of each other. Showing appreciation for loyalty and reliability is significant. After Jonathan's death, David demonstrates the enduring nature of heartfelt thanksgiving. Forever grateful that Jonathan's kindness laid the foundation for his ascension to the throne, David as King of Israel gives a permanent place at his table to Jonathan's son, Mephibosheth.

III. Loyalties Tested (1 Samuel 19:1–7)

At the start of chapter 20, David flees from Naioth at Ramah and seeks Jonathan, desperate to know why Saul wants to kill him (v. 1): "What have I done? What is my guilt? (NRSVue). Jonathan, unwilling to believe his father would kill David without telling him, agrees to test Saul's intentions during the upcoming New Moon festival, a time when David's absence would be conspicuous. The two friends devise a plan: Jonathan will gauge Saul's reaction to David's absence and communicate the outcome to David by shooting arrows as a covert signal (vv. 18–23).

At the festival, Saul notices David's absence, and by the second day, Saul's anger boils over. When Jonathan explains that David has gone to Bethlehem, Saul erupts in rage, hurling insults and even a spear at his own son (vv. 30–33). Saul's fury exposes his intent to kill David and his willingness to harm his own flesh and blood for siding with David.

Jonathan's questions are a plea for justice and reason, exposing Saul's irrational hatred of David. Saul's violent response, throwing his spear at Jonathan, is a shocking act that severs the father-son bond and confirms Saul's intent to kill David when given the opportunity. Jonathan's anger and grief are palpable; he is "grieved for David and because his father had disgraced him." The Hebrew word for "disgraced" (klm) can mean "shamed" or "dishonored," indicating Saul's actions have brought public and personal shame to their family.

After secretly warning David, Jonathan meets him for a final, emotional farewell. Jonathan's words, "Go in peace, since both of us have sworn in the name of the Lord," recall the covenant of loyal love (*hesed*) they have made (cf. 1 Sam 18:3; 20:16–17). The phrase, "The Lord shall be between me and you, and between my descendants and your descendants, forever," affirms a bond that transcends personal loss and political upheaval. Their covenant is not merely a private pact, but also a solemn commitment before God, ensuring mutual care for their families even after death (fulfilled in 2 Samuel 9).

Jonathan's selfless and righteous actions highlight the cost of covenant faithfulness, the pain of divided loyalties, and the sustaining power of godly friendship. Jonathan's willingness to confront injustice and embrace loss for the sake of righteousness models Christlike love (John 15:13). The enduring covenant points to God's faithfulness, even amid human brokenness and betrayal.

IV. The Covenant Friendship Endures the Test of Time (2 Samuel 1:26-27; 21:7)

The closing chapter of 1 Samuel details the tragic conclusion of Saul's reign. In 1 Samuel 31, Saul and his sons, including Jonathan, are killed in battle against the Philistines on Mount Gilboa. News of their deaths reaches David at Ziklag through an Amalekite messenger (2 Sam 1:1-10). David, who has been living as a fugitive from Saul, responds not with profound grief. He composes a lament known as the "Song of the Bow" (2 Sam 1:17-27), to honor Saul and Jonathan. This elegy is a poetic tribute to their bravery and a public expression of mourning for Israel's loss.

David's tribute to Jonathan is deeply personal. Their friendship, forged in faith and tested by Saul's hostility, was marked by covenant loyalty (1 Sam. 18:1-4; 20:16-17). David's grief is not only for a fallen comrade, but for a covenant brother whose love and faithfulness surpassed all others.

David's lament for Jonathan is one of the most poignant expressions of love and loss in Scripture. "Your love to me was wonderful, passing the love of women" (v. 26) speaks to the depth of their covenant bond—a relationship built on mutual trust, loyalty, and faith in God's promises. The repeated phrase, "How the mighty have fallen," is both a cry of anguish and a recognition of the costliness of leadership and war.

The refrain, "How the mighty have fallen" (v. 27), echoes throughout the lament, underscoring the tragedy of Israel's loss and the end of an era.

Decades after Jonathan's death, David's loyalty to his friend endures. When Israel is faced with famine, David, who has long been crowned king, seeks an answer from the Lord. God reveals that the famine is a consequence of Saul's earlier attempt to annihilate the Gibeonites, violating Israel's oath of protection to them (see Joshua 9). To atone, David asks the Gibeonites what must be done. They request the execution of seven of Saul's male descendants. David consents, but with one crucial exception: "But the king spared Mephibosheth, the son of Saul's son Jonathan, because of the oath of the Lord that was between them, between David and Jonathan son of Saul." David spares Mephibosheth, Jonathan's disabled son, out of loyalty rooted in the covenant David and Jonathan made (1 Sam. 20:14-17, 42), wherein David promised to show steadfast love (*hesed*) to Jonathan's house forever.

David's actions contrast sharply with Saul's disregard for covenant (as seen in his violence against the Gibeonites). David's sparing of Mephibosheth is an embodiment of godly faithfulness, even when it is costly or countercultural.

The deep and abiding friendship between Jonathan and David highlights the enduring power of covenant love and faithfulness. David's grief for Jonathan models authentic lament, while his protection of Mephibosheth demonstrates the gospel principle of steadfast love and keeping one's word (cf. Psalm 15:4; Matthew 5:37). The narrative points to Christ, who fulfills God's covenant promises and embodies perfect faithfulness to His people.

THE LESSON APPLIED

In 1624, English poet John Donne wrote, "No man is an island." When we discover loyal friends, we honor and value those relationships as expressions of God's unfailing love. Jonathan and David's friendship is a witness to God's love. Their bond endures as one of the most powerful examples of selfless friendship in the Bible.

True friends will seek the good of each other regardless of personal cost or sacrifice. Jonathan embodies selflessness which strengthens relationships. He willingly yields the throne to David because he accepts God's choice of David to be the next heir to the throne. True friends celebrate each other's successes without envy.

Trust is the foundation of all strong relationships. Jonathan risks his life to warn David about Saul's intentions to kill him.

True friends advocate for each other. Jonathan spoke up for David to his own father, a powerful king, no less (1 Samuel 19:4–5). Friends defend each other in difficult situations.

Godly friendships encourage faith. Jonathan encourages David to stay strong in his faith in God during challenging times (1 Samuel 23:16–17). A godly friend strengthens your faith and encourages you to trust in God's plan.

The story of Jonathan and David teaches us the beauty of selfless, sacrificial, and God-centered friendships. It reminds us of the kind of friends we should strive to be and have.

LET'S TALK ABOUT IT...

Discuss the following questions and visit www.rhboyd.com for more information.

When confronted by pressures that test our loyalty in friendships, what lessons can we learn from the friendship of Jonathan and David?

Get Social
Share your views and tag us
@rhboydco and use #rhboydco

@rhboydco

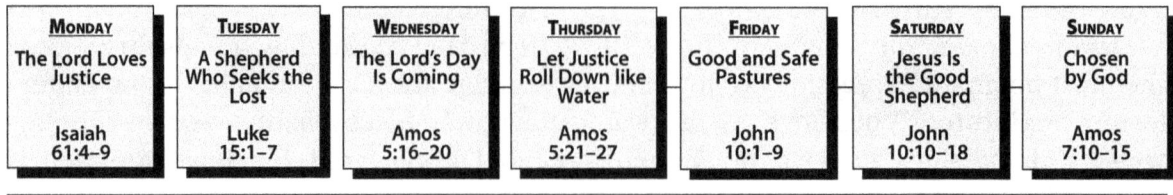

Lesson IV June 28, 2026

Amos, a Herdsman Called of God to Be a Prophet

Adult Topic: Standing Up to the Powerful
Background Scripture: Amos 1:1; 2:11-12; 3:7-8; 7:10-15
Lesson Passage: Amos 1:1; 2:11-12; 3:7-8; 7:10-15

AMOS 1:1; 2:11-12; 3:7-8; 7:10-15

KJV

THE words of Amos, who was among the herdmen of Tekoa, which he saw concerning Israel in the days of Uzziah king of Judah, and in the days of Jeroboam the son of Joash king of Israel, two years before the earthquake.

• • • • • •

11 And I raised up of your sons for prophets, and of your young men for Nazarites. Is it not even thus, O ye children of Israel? saith the Lord.

12 But ye gave the Nazarites wine to drink; and commanded the prophets, saying, Prophesy not.

• • • Amos 3:7–8 • • •

7 Surely the Lord God will do nothing, but he revealeth his secret unto his servants the prophets.

8 The lion hath roared, who will not fear? the Lord God hath spoken, who can but prophesy?

• • • Amos 7:10–15 • • •

10 Then Amaziah the priest of Bethel sent to Jeroboam king of Israel, saying, Amos hath conspired against thee in the midst of the house of Israel: the land is not able to bear all his words.

11 For thus Amos saith, Jeroboam shall die by the sword, and Israel shall surely be led away captive out of their own land.

12 Also Amaziah said unto Amos, O thou seer, go, flee thee away into the land of Judah, and there eat bread, and prophesy there:

13 But prophesy not again any more at Bethel: for it is the king's chapel, and it is the king's court.

NRSVue

THE words of Amos, who was among the shepherds of Tekoa, which he saw concerning Israel in the days of King Uzziah of Judah and in the days of King Jeroboam son of Joash of Israel, two years before the earthquake.

• • • • • •

11 And I raised up some of your children to be prophets and some of your youths to be nazirites. Is it not indeed so, O people of Israel? says the Lord.

12 But you made the nazirites drink wine and commanded the prophets, saying, "You shall not prophesy."

• • • Amos 3:7–8 • • •

7 Surely the Lord God does nothing without revealing his secret to his servants the prophets.

8 The lion has roared; who will not fear? The Lord God has spoken; who can but prophesy?

• • • Amos 7:10–15 • • •

10 Then Amaziah, the priest of Bethel, sent to King Jeroboam of Israel, saying, "Amos has conspired against you in the very center of the house of Israel; the land is not able to bear all his words.

11 For thus Amos has said, 'Jeroboam shall die by the sword, and Israel must go into exile away from his land.' "

12 And Amaziah said to Amos, "O seer, go, flee away to the land of Judah, earn your bread there, and prophesy there,

13 but never again prophesy at Bethel, for it is the king's sanctuary, and it is a temple of the kingdom."

MAIN THOUGHT: "The LORD took me from following the flock, and the LORD said to me, 'Go, prophesy to my people Israel.'" (Amos 7:15, NRSVue)

AMOS 1:1; 2:11-12; 3:7-8; 7:10-15

KJV

14 Then answered Amos, and said to Amaziah, I was no prophet, neither was I a prophet's son; but I was an herdman, and a gatherer of sycomore fruit:

15 And the Lord took me as I followed the flock, and the Lord said unto me, Go, prophesy unto my people Israel.

NRSVue

14 Then Amos answered Amaziah, "I am no prophet nor a prophet's son, but I am a herdsman and a dresser of sycamore trees,

15 and the Lord took me from following the flock, and the Lord said to me, 'Go, prophesy to my people Israel.'

LESSON SETTING

Time: 765–755 BC during the reign of Jeroboam II
Place: Bethel, Samaria
Setting: The Book of Amos is set during the 8th century BC, specifically around 760–750 BC. This was a time of prosperity and political stability for both the Northern Kingdom of Israel and the Southern Kingdom of Judah. Under the rule of Jeroboam II, the Northern Kingdom of Israel experienced great economic growth and territorial expansion. Amos primarily directed his prophecy towards the Northern Kingdom of Israel. Uzziah was the King of Judah during this time. His reign was also marked by stability and growth. Amos was from Tekoa, a small town in Judah in the Southern Kingdom. During this period, the regional powers such as Assyria were gaining strength, but had not yet become a direct threat to Israel or Judah. This relative peace allowed for economic growth, but also complacency among the people. The wealth of the time led to increased luxury for the elite, while the poor were oppressed. Social injustice, exploitation, and neglect of the covenant with God were rampant. Religious practices became empty rituals, with the people engaging in outward worship but ignoring God's moral requirements. Amos' prophecies reference places in Israel, such as Bethel, Samaria, and Gilgal, which were significant religious and political centers.

LESSON OUTLINE

I. An Unlikely Prophet (Amos 1:1)
II. Speaking Truth to Power (Amos 2:11-12; 3:7-8)
III. Confronting Israel's Religious Complacency (Amos 7:10-15)

UNIFYING PRINCIPLE

Intimidation is always possible when speaking the truth to people in positions of authority. How do we boldly speak the truth when people are not inclined to receive our message? Amos, a humble shepherd, faced rejection when God called him to prophesy to powerful kings and priests.

INTRODUCTION

The Book of Amos offers a moving and provocative message of justice, righteousness, and accountability. Amos was a shepherd and fig grower from Tekoa, which was a small village in Judah. This prophetic book primarily addresses the Northern Kingdom of Israel during the eighth century BC. It pronounces God's judgment against the Syrians, Philistines, Tyrians, Edomites, Moabites and the Ammonites for oppressing God's people.

Lacking status as a professional prophet or priest, Amos answers God's call and delivers a sober message of judgment and hope to a nation that had lost its priorities and principles. Amos speaks during a time of relative peace and prosperity under the reigns of King Jeroboam II in Israel and King Uzziah in Judah. However, widespread social injustice, moral decay, and religious hypocrisy coincided with this prosperity. Empty rituals and idolatry have corroded worship of God.

The central themes of Amos detail God's concern for justice and righteousness. Amos emphasizes that true worship accompanies ethical living and care for vulnerable people. His most quoted declaration, "Let justice roll on like a river, righteousness like a never-failing stream" (Amos 5:24), timelessly aligns faith with action. The prophet's words were invoked by the Rev. Dr. Martin Luther King, Jr. in various speeches; most notably during his "I Have a Dream" speech on August 28, 1963, at the March on Washington for Jobs and Freedom. In the speech, Dr. King declared: "We will not be satisfied until justice rolls down like waters and righteousness like a mighty stream."

Amos courageously delivers harsh warnings of God's judgment to people in power. Amos offers glimpses of hope and promises of restoration. He envisions future renewal for God's people wherein His blessings will overflow. Amos reminds us of God's ultimate purpose in redemption and restoration even amidst judgment.

The book's relevance transcends time and urges us to align our hearts with God's will and seek a righteous and just world.

EXPOSITION

I. An Unlikely Prophet (Amos 1:1)

The name Amos means "burden bearer." This prophet of God assumes the thankless burden of serving as God's prophet to warn God's people of His coming judgment. God gives Amos a vision of what will happen to the Northern Kingdom of Israel and their enemies. Amos emerges from obscurity to pronounce this strong warning within Israel's divided kingdom and equally divided loyalty to God.

The Northern Kingdom of Israel and Southern Kingdom of Judah often contested each another. Amid these tensions, Amos traveled between kingdoms to deliver God's warning. Amos' boldness is remarkable given Northerners were unwelcoming to the Southerners. Regardless of social, economic, and political tensions, God's prophets and agents must obey Him.

The division of the United Kingdom is a water shed moment in biblical history. It resulted in political, religious, and social tensions that emerged over generations. From the monarchical division to the reign of Uzziah, King of Judah (792–740 BC) and Jeroboam II, king of Israel (793–753 BC), the two kingdoms coexisted for nearly two centuries. Although Uzziah and Jeroboam brought economic expansion and military strength to their kingdoms, they also presided over a period of spiritual decline, which prophets, Amos, Hosea, and Isaiah, condemned.

Amos' ministry occurs during a time of apparent prosperity but deep spiritual and social corruption. His oracles confront Israel's complacency, injustice, and religious hypocrisy, and they highlight God's unwavering commitment to justice and covenant faithfulness. God calls Amos to confront the ruling elite of Israel and demand their repentance.

II. Speaking Truth to Power (Amos 2:11–12; 3:7–8)

These two passages bring into focus the themes of prophetic calling, Israel's wholesale rejection of God's words of warning, and the necessity of divine revelation.

God reminds Israel that He had raised up prophets and Nazirites from among them. Prophets were God's mouthpieces, used to call the nation back to covenant faithfulness, while Nazirites were specially consecrated to God, marked by vows of abstinence and holiness (cf. Numbers 6:1–21). Both were signs of God's ongoing engagement with His people. Yet, Israel not only ignored these gifts but rather, actively opposed them, forcing Nazirites to break their vows and silencing the prophets.

Israel's rejection is not merely a refusal of God-sent messengers, but also a direct affront to God's redemptive initiative. As evangelical scholar Douglas Stuart notes, "Israel's sin is compounded by their deliberate suppression of the very means God provided for their spiritual renewal" (*Word Biblical Commentary: Hosea-Jonah*, Vol. 31. Thomas Nelson, 1987).

Amos 3:1–8 emphasizes Israel's unique relationship with God and the inevitability of His judgment. Verses 7–8 are especially significant in understanding the prophetic office. Here, Amos asserts a foundational principle: God's actions in history are always preceded by revelation to His prophets. The word "secret" (*sôd*, סוֹד) refers to God's counsel or plan, shared with His trusted servants (cf. Psalm 25:14). This underscores both the privilege and responsibility of the prophetic vocation.

The imagery of the lion's roar in verse 8 is striking. Just as the roar of a lion provokes fear and demands attention, so the word of the Lord compels the prophet to speak. Amos, as a true prophet sent by God, cannot remain silent in the face of divine revelation. Biblical commentators such as J. Alec Motyer stress that "The prophet's compulsion is not self-generated but arises from the overwhelming reality of God's word" (*The Message of Amos: The Bible Speaks Today Series*, 1974).

These two passages offer several important insights. First is that of God's persistent grace. God continually raises up witnesses—prophets and consecrated individuals—to call His people back to Himself. So, the rejection of these messengers is a rejection of God's grace.

Second, these verses highlight the authority of prophetic revelation. God's purposes are made known through His word. The principle that "the Lord God does nothing, without revealing his secret to his servants the prophets" (Amos 3:7) amplifies the trustworthiness and necessity of divine revelation. For Christians, this finds its fullness in the ultimate revelation of God through Jesus Christ (Hebrews 1:1–2). Finally, Amos' inability to remain silent is a model for all who are entrusted with God's message. The Gospel compels believers to speak truth, especially truth to power, even when the message is unpopular or personally costly (cf. Acts 4:20).

Together, Amos 2:11–12 and 3:7–8 reveal the tragic consequences of Israel's rejection of God's prophetic voice and the unyielding necessity of God's revelation. Nevertheless, God's love is seen in His persistent outreach to a stubborn and disobedient people, while His justice is seen in the certainty of judgment when His word is ignored. For the church today, these verses call us to a renewed attention to God's word, a willingness to heed His messengers, and a boldness to proclaim His truth in a world that often resists it or openly rebukes it.

III. Confronting Israel's Religious Complacency (Amos 7:10–15)

The opening verses of chapter 7 reveal visions of judgment—locusts, fire, and a plumb line—each underscoring God's resolve to punish Israel's persistent sin. Amos' intercessions delay but ultimately do not avert the imminent disaster. It is in this context that Amaziah, priest of the royal sanctuary at Bethel, enters the narrative.

Alarmed by Amos' prophetic pronouncements, Amaziah accuses the prophet of conspiracy and sedition. In reporting the matter to King Jeroboam, Amaziah frames Amos' message as a political threat rather than a divine warning. The charge is serious: to predict the king's death and national exile is, in the eyes of authorities, treasonous.

Amaziah tells Amos, 'O seer, go, flee away to the land of Judah, earn your bread there, and prophesy there; but never again prophesy at Bethel, for it is the king's sanctuary, and it is a temple of the kingdom.'" His words are dripping with irony and contempt. Calling Amos "seer" (a term for prophets, but here most likely an expression of mocking), he commands Amos to return to Judah and apply his trade there. Bethel, as the royal sanctuary, is off-limits to such troubling messages. Amaziah's concern is for institutional stability and royal favor, not for the strength and truth of God's word.

Amos' response to the priest is both humble and arresting. He disavows any professional or hereditary claim to the prophetic office: "I am no prophet, nor a prophet's son" (v. 14). In the ancient Near East, prophetic guilds or schools existed (cf. 1 Samuel 10:5; 2 Kings 2:3), but Amos insists he is not part of such a tradition. He is a mere layman—a herdsman and a caretaker of sycamore-fig trees. His authority does not derive from institutional credentials but rather from the direct call of God (v. 15).

Amos' call underscores that God chooses whom He wills, often persons from unlikely backgrounds. God's messengers are not always products of religious establishments, but rather, are called and empowered by His Spirit (cf. 1 Corinthians 1:26–29).

Interestingly, Amos faces opposition not from pagans, but from the religious hierarchy itself. The temptation for religious leaders to prioritize institutional preservation over prophetic truth is perennial. Evangelical Christians are reminded that faithfulness to God's word may bring conflict with established powers, even within the church. This prioritization of the institutional church persists even today. Many church leaders have hidden scandals and corruption within the organizational structure, or deeds committed at the hands of trusted, and often revered, authorities.

Amos' bold testimony echoes the experience of other biblical prophets (e.g., Jeremiah 1:4–9; Isaiah 6:8–9) who are compelled by God's word to speak, regardless of personal cost or social acceptance. The authenticity of prophetic ministry is measured not by institutional endorsement but rather by obedience to God's call.

Amaziah's Bethel was a major religious center but had become spiritually corrupt. The passage warns against mistaking religious tradition or national identity for true covenant faithfulness.

THE LESSON APPLIED

The division of Israel illustrates the consequences of the nation's spiritual compromise and disobedience and reflects ways that political division contributed to Israel's failure to remain faithful to God. Jeroboam II's reign in the Northern Kingdom of Israel was successful economically and politically, but disastrous spiritually.

Ironically, Amos' prophecy remains as relevant in the twenty-first century as it was for his original audience. He condemns injustices of the wealthy toward the poor. Many wealthy nations today face the challenges of establishing justice amid prosperity, corruption, and spiritual decline.

Prophets are rarely revered during their lifetime. Amos speaks against idolatry, immorality, false worship, and exploitation and subjugation of poor people. He steadfastly pronounces God's judgment to correct these injustices.

It is sometimes forgotten or outright ignored by contemporaries that, at the time of his assassination, Dr. King's message was quite unpopular among large swaths of Americans, including some Black people. He lost supporters due to his stance against the Vietnam War and his support for the sanitation workers in Memphis, Tenn. By the time he died, Dr. King also had become more vocal about how poverty in America impacts all races. While many laud snippets of his messages today, often extracting them for their own purposes, Dr. King accepted the mantle God put upon him and spoke truth to power. Ultimately, his obedience to God cost his life.

LET'S TALK ABOUT IT...

Discuss the following questions and visit www.rhboyd.com for more information.

What does it look like for a common person, an everyday citizen, to speak truth to power? Consider the faith-driven courage of Fannie Lou Hamer and Nat Turner.

Get Social

Share your views and tag us
@rhboydco and use #rhboydco

@rhboydco

Home Daily Devotional Readings
June 29–July 5, 2026

Monday	Tuesday	Wednesday	Thursday	Friday	Saturday	Sunday
A Light to the Nations	May All Nations Serve the Lord	God Makes Us Alive through Christ	Strangers Brought Near through Christ	Arise, Shine; Your Light Has Come	The Coastlands Await God's Light	A Banquet Spread for All
Isaiah 49:1–6	Psalm 72:1–13	Ephesians 2:1–10	Ephesians 2:11–22	Isaiah 60:1–8	Isaiah 60:9–14	Matthew 8:5–13

Lesson V — July 5, 2026

The Believing Centurion, a Gentile Whose Faith Jesus Commended

Adult Topic: Don't Judge a Book (or a Person) by Its Cover
Background Scripture: Matthew 8:5–13
Lesson Passage: Matthew 8:5–13

MATTHEW 8:5–13

KJV

AND when Jesus was entered into Capernaum, there came unto him a centurion, beseeching him,

6 And saying, Lord, my servant lieth at home sick of the palsy, grievously tormented.

7 And Jesus saith unto him, I will come and heal him.

8 The centurion answered and said, Lord, I am not worthy that thou shouldest come under my roof: but speak the word only, and my servant shall be healed.

9 For I am a man under authority, having soldiers under me: and I say to this man, Go, and he goeth; and to another, Come, and he cometh; and to my servant, Do this, and he doeth it.

10 When Jesus heard it, he marvelled, and said to them that followed, Verily I say unto you, I have not found so great faith, no, not in Israel.

11 And I say unto you, That many shall come from the east and west, and shall sit down with Abraham, and Isaac, and Jacob, in the kingdom of heaven.

12 But the children of the kingdom shall be cast out into outer darkness: there shall be weeping and gnashing of teeth.

13 And Jesus said unto the centurion, Go thy way; and as thou hast believed, so be it done unto thee. And his servant was healed in the selfsame hour.

NRSVue

WHEN he entered Capernaum, a centurion came to him, appealing to him

6 and saying, "Lord, my servant is lying at home paralyzed, in terrible distress."

7 And he said to him, "I will come and cure him."

8 The centurion answered, "Lord, I am not worthy to have you come under my roof, but only speak the word, and my servant will be healed.

9 For I also am a man under authority, with soldiers under me, and I say to one, 'Go,' and he goes, and to another, 'Come,' and he comes, and to my slave, 'Do this,' and the slave does it."

10 When Jesus heard him, he was amazed and said to those who followed him, "Truly I tell you, in no one in Israel have I found such faith.

11 I tell you, many will come from east and west and will take their places at the banquet with Abraham and Isaac and Jacob in the kingdom of heaven,

12 while the heirs of the kingdom will be thrown into the outer darkness, where there will be weeping and gnashing of teeth."

13 And Jesus said to the centurion, "Go; let it be done for you according to your faith." And the servant was healed in that hour.

MAIN THOUGHT: When Jesus heard him [the centurion], he was amazed and said to those who followed him, "Truly I tell you, in no one in Israel have I found such faith." (Matthew 8:10, NRSVue)

LESSON SETTING

Time: Between AD 60 and 65
Place: Bethlehem, Jerusalem, Capernaum, Galilee, Judaea
Setting: Matthew was once a despised tax collector who became one of Jesus' closest disciples, as he was one of the Twelve. The book of Matthew connects the Old Testament with the New Testament by emphasizing the prophecies of old and the fulfillment of those prophecies in Jesus. Matthew traced the genealogy of Jesus to provide evidence to his fellow Jews that Jesus was indeed the Messiah. Although the Jews had long awaited the fulfillment of the prophecies of the Messiah, they overlooked that He would be humble, rejected, and killed. In the end, they rejected the very Messiah that they looked for. Despite the opposition that Jesus faced, He remained faithful to the plan of salvation for humanity—even to His death on the cross and His resurrection. Throughout His ministry, Jesus healed many people. On this occasion, a Roman centurion demonstrates great faith in Jesus to heal his servant who had been paralyzed. Jesus intervenes and his servant is healed that same hour. The extraordinary faith of this Gentile military commander is a striking contrast to the rejection and opposition of the Jews toward Jesus. His response to the centurion demonstrated the inclusive nature of His mission to save humanity.

LESSON OUTLINE

I. A Centurion Asks Jesus for Help (Matthew 8:5-7)
II. Understanding Authority (Matthew 8:8-9)
III. Jesus Confesses Amazement (Matthew 8:10-13)

UNIFYING PRINCIPLE

We do not expect our enemies to trust us and ask for our help. When someone we previously considered our enemy asks us for help, how do we respond? Jesus responds favorably to the extraordinary faith of the centurion, made even more remarkable because of his ties to the evil Roman government.

INTRODUCTION

Jesus leaves his home, Nazareth, and begins His public ministry in Capernaum, located near the Sea of Galilee. It was an agricultural region consisting mainly of fishing and farming. Jesus chooses local fishermen from the region as His first disciples. Both Jewish towns and Gentile populations comprised Galilee, although Jews regarded Gentile Galileans as an inferior class and held prejudices against them.

The prophets had declared the Kingdom of heaven was at hand. Their consistent message anticipated a Messiah who would establish God's reign and relieve them of Roman oppression.

Rather than amassing military might or political influence, Jesus goes to the people, deliberately positioning Himself among the disenfranchised and hurting. In Capernaum, Jesus teaches crowds of people, heals the sick and restores sight to the blind, expanding His messianic mission through the Galileans. As word spread of His miraculous power and His message of encouragement and hope, crowds gather to see, hear, and receive Him.

The story of Jesus' encounter with a Roman officer is one of the most compelling demonstrations of faith in all the Gospels. Even more ironic is the fact that this unwavering faith in Jesus comes from a Gentile, a Roman centurion. These verses contain a profound lesson in the nature of true faith, humility, and the boundless reach of Jesus' authority and grace.

As Jesus enters Capernaum, a bustling town on the northern shore of the Sea of Galilee and the center of much of His ministry, He is approached by a centurion. In an era when Roman soldiers were often resented and Gentiles were considered outsiders to God's covenant, the centurion's approach is compelling for its humility and compassion.

EXPOSITION

I. A Centurion Asks Jesus for Help (Matthew 8:5–7)

As Jesus enters Capernaum, a Roman centurion (captain of a military unit of one hundred soldiers), approaches and pleads with Him on behalf of his servant, who is ill. Strikingly, the centurion says, "Lord, my servant lies at home paralyzed, suffering terribly." This statement reflects the centurion's concern, humility and recognition of Jesus' authority.

Jesus offers to visit the centurion's home to heal the servant. Responding with great faith, the centurion declines Jesus' offer but requests that He simply speak the word and his servant would be healed. Jesus had not seen such great faith in Israel.

This narrative depicts faith, humility, and the inclusive nature of Christ's ministry. It portrays Jesus' miraculous healing power and the centurion's remarkable faith. This story is one of multiple contrasts: consider Jesus' miracle in comparison with the people surrounding the centurion's servant and compare the centurion's faith with that of the Jewish people. These comparisons yield a greater understanding of grace as evident in miracles and faith as embodied in a Roman military officer.

Further, the centurion's compassion for his servant is atypical of military leaders. His decision to ask Jesus for help is remarkable given the cultural and social dynamics of the day. A representative of the Roman occupying force in Judea, these officers lived in daily tension among the local Jewish population. But this centurion defied stereotypes. His concern for his servant's well-being reflected a level of empathy not commonly associated with military leaders of his time. The centurion's willingness to seek Jesus' help demonstrates his belief that Jesus' authority transcended cultural and religious boundaries.

Then, contrast the centurion's military authority to his spiritual humility. He challenges preconceived notions about who can approach and receive God's grace. His actions further highlight the universal scope of Jesus' ministry, which extends beyond ethnic and social divides.

According to Luke's account (Luke 7:1–10), the centurion does not directly approach Jesus, but rather sends Jewish elders to intercede on his behalf. Therein, he avoids offending their leadership and respects Jewish customs. These elders praise the centurion to Jesus, acknowledging his regard for the Jewish nation. Their intercession indicates the centurion's positive relationship with the local Jewish community and its authorities.

Although he holds a position of power and prestige, the centurion approaches Jesus with humility, addressing Him as "Lord." This title respects and recognizes Jesus' divine authority. It contrasts starkly with many Jewish leaders who often questioned or rejected Jesus' identity.

In seeking Jesus' help for his servant, the centurion exemplifies the role of an intercessor. He channels his faith, humility and compassion for his servant into spiritual advocacy. His genuine care for his servant demonstrates love and grace driven intercession. By acknowledging his unworthiness to have Jesus come under his roof, the centurion reflects an intercessor's posture of humility before God.

II. Understanding Authority (Matthew 8:8–9)

Jesus agrees to visit the centurion, who sends friends with a follow-up message of extraordinary faith and humility. "Lord, don't trouble yourself, for I do not deserve to have you come under my roof. That is why I did not even consider myself worthy to come to you. But say the word, and my servant will be healed." With this humble statement, the centurion faithfully acknowledges Jesus' divine nature and healing power.

The centurion acknowledges Jesus' authority to heal apart from physical distance: "But just say the word…" (v. 8). The centurion, a man of considerable earthly authority, perceives in Jesus a kind of authority that surpasses even his own. "For I also am a man under authority…" (v. 9).

The centurion understands that his own authority is effective only because he himself is under the authority of Rome. Accustomed to giving commands and expecting immediate obedience, the centurion recognizes a parallel in Jesus' spiritual authority. He concludes Jesus' word alone suffices to heal.

He perceives that Jesus' authority comes from His unique relationship with a higher authority, God the Father. Understanding what it means to simply speak a word of power, he knows Jesus does not need to be physically present exert His healing power. His word alone is sufficient, because He speaks with the authority of God.

Unlike Jewish teachers or miracle workers who might need to be physically present, the Gentile commander unequivocally accepts that Jesus can heal with a mere word. The centurion's faith in Jesus' spoken command reveals a belief in the limitless scope of Christ's authority—over sickness, distance, and even cultural boundaries. Jesus' authority is not confined by geography, ritual, or tradition. He reigns over all creation, and His power is effective wherever His word is received with faith.

The centurion uses his authority not for self-advancement but to seek help for his suffering servant. Jesus, who has the authority and power of Almighty God, in turn, responds willingness and compassion. This models a biblical understanding of authority as service, not domination (cf. Mark 10:42–45).

The miraculous healing of the centurion's servant indeed occurs at a distance, emphasizing Jesus' authority over space and physical constraints.

III. Jesus Confesses Amazement (Matthew 8:10–13)

Verses 10–13 record Jesus' response to the Roman centurion's extraordinary faith and the subsequent healing of the centurion's servant. This passage offers insight into the nature of faith, the scope of God's Kingdom, and the authority of Christ's word. Moreover, Jesus' interaction with the centurion challenges assumptions about who can belong to the family of God and invites a deeper trust in Jesus' sovereign power.

Notably, Jesus is amazed by the Gentile military officer's open expression of confidence that He can heal the servant using only His words, without even coming near his house. But as amazing as the centurion's statement of faith is, so is Jesus' response. The Greek verb (thaumazō) conveys wonder or astonishment. Nowhere else in Matthew's gospel does Jesus marvel at someone's faith. The centurion, an outsider to Israel's covenant community, demonstrates a depth of trust that surpasses anything Jesus has encountered among the Jewish people. The Gentile man's faith is not based on religious heritage or ritual, but rather on a clear recognition of Jesus' authority.

Biblical scholar R.T. France observes, "The centurion's faith is remarkable not for its quantity but for its quality: it is a faith that takes Jesus at his word and recognizes his authority as absolute" (*The Gospel of Matthew: New International Commentary on the New Testament*. Eerdmans, 2007).

Jesus then turns to the listening crowd and offers a prophetic vision of the Kingdom's inclusivity (vv. 11–12). People from all nations ("east and west") will join the patriarchs at the messianic banquet—a symbol of eternal salvation and fellowship with God (cf. Isaiah 25:6–9). This is a radical statement for Jesus' Jewish audience, who would have expected the Kingdom to be reserved primarily for Israel. But Jesus warns that "the heirs of the kingdom," those who presume upon their religious heritage, may find themselves excluded if they lack authentic faith.

The imagery of "outer darkness" and "weeping and gnashing of teeth" is a recurring motif in Matthew (cf. 22:13; 25:30), signifying judgment and separation from God. The point here is not ethnic exclusion, but rather the necessity of faith in Jesus as the criterion for entrance into the Kingdom.

Craig Blomberg notes, "Jesus' words are both a warning and an invitation: the kingdom is open to all who believe, but closed to those who rely on privilege rather than faith" (*The New American Commentary: Matthew*. Broadman Press, 1992).

The episode concludes with Jesus addressing the centurion (v. 13): "…Go; let it be done for you according to your faith.' And the servant was healed in that hour" (v. 13, NRSVue)

Jesus' word is sufficient to heal, even at a distance. The servant's healing is immediate and complete, demonstrating the efficacy of faith and the boundless reach of Jesus' authority. The centurion's faith is not a magical force that summons healing. His faith is rooted in his trust in the person and power of Jesus, the Son of God.

The centurion's simple yet strong declaration of what he believed Jesus could do underscores the importance of faith that rests on Christ's word and character, not on visible signs or religious status. It also affirms the global scope of the Gospel: all who trust in Jesus, regardless of background, are welcomed into God's family.

THE LESSON APPLIED

Genuine faith is the most reliable method to access God's miraculous power and gracious blessings. The centurion's faith confirms that ethnicity, social status or religious background are not determinative. Jesus' declaration that many will come from the east and west to take their places in the Kingdom of heaven (see Matthew 8:11) reinforces the inclusive nature of salvation. This exchange reminds us of Jesus' authority over the created order. Unlike earthly rulers whose power is limited by proximity, Jesus demonstrates that His word alone accomplishes His will.

The centurion's humility and faith contrast sharply with the pride and self-righteous nature of many of the religious leaders. His recognition of his own unworthiness serves as a model for approaching God with a contrite heart.

By responding to the faith of a Gentile, Jesus affirms His mission extends to all people. He foreshadows the Great Commission to preach the Gospel to all nations and charts the early church's outreach to the Gentiles.

The centurion's affection for his servant coupled with his willingness to humble himself before Jesus affirms the selflessness inherent in intercessory acts. His plea is not for personal gain, but offered for the well-being of another, a servant whose condition may not have mattered to some. The centurion's example challenges us to intercede for others with bold faith, humility and resolute trust in God's power. He further teaches us to care for the vulnerable among us, the meek and lowly. He was willing to use his voice for the voiceless.

Intercessory prayer is a vital Christian spiritual discipline. An act of love and faith, it testifies to God's favorable intervention in response to faithful prayer. Through intercessory prayer, we participate in God's redemptive work. We trust that He answers our prayers according to His will. Intercession transcends social and cultural barriers, thereby uniting people in collective faith and dependence on God.

LET'S TALK ABOUT IT...

Discuss the following question(s) and visit www.rhboyd.com for more information.

How can we, like the centurion, stand in the gap for those who are suffering?

This passage reveals one of the few occasions when Jesus was amazed or pleasantly surprised by the actions of another person. Why was Jesus amazed by the centurion?

How does the centurion embody the expression that those who lead must first be able to follow?

Get Social

Share your views and tag us
@rhboydco and use #rhboydco

@rhboydco

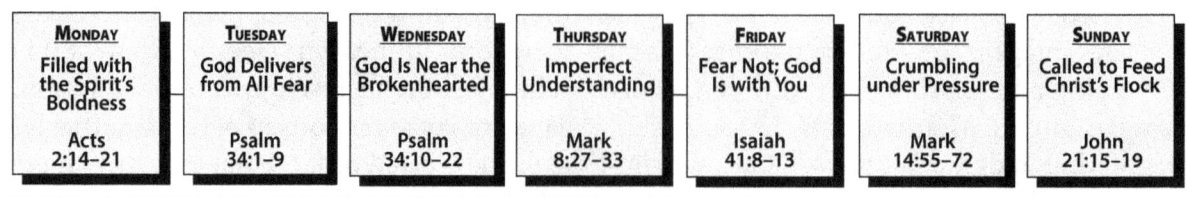

Lesson VI   July 12, 2026

Simon Peter, from Weakness to Strength

Adult Topic: From a Rock to a Hard Place
Background Scripture: Mark 8:27–29; Luke 22:31–34; John 18:25–27; 21:15–17
Lesson Passage: Mark 8:27–29; Luke 22:31–34; John 18:25–27; 21:15–17

MARK 8:27–29; LUKE 22:31–34; JOHN 18:25–27; 21:15–17

KJV

AND Jesus went out, and his disciples, into the towns of Caesarea Philippi: and by the way he asked his disciples, saying unto them, Whom do men say that I am?

28 And they answered, John the Baptist; but some say, Elias; and others, One of the prophets.

29 And he saith unto them, But whom say ye that I am? And Peter answereth and saith unto him, Thou art the Christ.

• • • Luke 22:31–34 • • •

31 And the Lord said, Simon, Simon, behold, Satan hath desired to have you, that he may sift you as wheat:

32 But I have prayed for thee, that thy faith fail not: and when thou art converted, strengthen thy brethren.

33 And he said unto him, Lord, I am ready to go with thee, both into prison, and to death.

34 And he said, I tell thee, Peter, the cock shall not crow this day, before that thou shalt thrice deny that thou knowest me.

• • • John 18:25–27 • • •

25 And Simon Peter stood and warmed himself. They said therefore unto him, Art not thou also one of his disciples? He denied it, and said, I am not.

26 One of the servants of the high priest, being his kinsman whose ear Peter cut off, saith, Did not I see thee in the garden with him?

27 Peter then denied again: and immediately the cock crew.

NRSVue

JESUS went on with his disciples to the villages of Caesarea Philippi, and on the way he asked his disciples, "Who do people say that I am?"

28 And they answered him, "John the Baptist; and others, Elijah; and still others, one of the prophets."

29 He asked them, "But who do you say that I am?" Peter answered him, "You are the Messiah."

• • • Luke 22:31–34 • • •

31 "Simon, Simon, listen! Satan has demanded to sift all of you like wheat,

32 but I have prayed for you that your own faith may not fail, and you, when once you have turned back, strengthen your brothers."

33 And he said to him, "Lord, I am ready to go with you to prison and to death!"

34 Jesus said, "I tell you, Peter, the cock will not crow this day until you have denied three times that you know me."

• • • John 18:25–27 • • •

25 Now Simon Peter was standing and warming himself. They asked him, "You are not also one of his disciples, are you?" He denied it and said, "I am not."

26 One of the slaves of the high priest, a relative of the man whose ear Peter had cut off, asked, "Did I not see you in the garden with him?"

27 Again Peter denied it, and at that moment the cock crowed.

MAIN THOUGHT: He said to him the third time, "Simon son of John, do you love me?" Peter felt hurt because he said to him the third time, "Do you love me?" And he said to him, "Lord, you know everything; you know that I love you." Jesus said to him, "Feed my sheep." (John 21:17, NRSVue)

MARK 8:27–29; LUKE 22:31–34; JOHN 18:25–27; 21:15–17

KJV
••• John 21:15-17 •••

15 So when they had dined, Jesus saith to Simon Peter, Simon, son of Jonas, lovest thou me more than these? He saith unto him, Yea, Lord; thou knowest that I love thee. He saith unto him, Feed my lambs.

16 He saith to him again the second time, Simon, son of Jonas, lovest thou me? He saith unto him, Yea, Lord; thou knowest that I love thee. He saith unto him, Feed my sheep.

17 He saith unto him the third time, Simon, son of Jonas, lovest thou me? Peter was grieved because he said unto him the third time, Lovest thou me? And he said unto him, Lord, thou knowest all things; thou knowest that I love thee. Jesus saith unto him, Feed my sheep.

NRSVue
••• John 21:15-17 •••

15 When they had finished breakfast, Jesus said to Simon Peter, "Simon son of John, do you love me more than these?" He said to him, "Yes, Lord; you know that I love you." Jesus said to him, "Feed my lambs."

16 A second time he said to him, "Simon son of John, do you love me?" He said to him, "Yes, Lord; you know that I love you." Jesus said to him, "Tend my sheep."

17 He said to him the third time, "Simon son of John, do you love me?" Peter felt hurt because he said to him the third time, "Do you love me?" And he said to him, "Lord, you know everything; you know that I love you." Jesus said to him, "Feed my sheep.

LESSON SETTING

Time: AD 60–65
Place: Caesarea Philippi
Setting: During this period, the Roman Empire was under the rule of Tiberius Caesar. Caesarea Phillipi, an ancient city in northern Israel at the foot of Mount Hermon, was known for the many Greek gods worshiped there. This coastal city was named after Caesar, emperor of Rome, and Phillip, ruler of Caesarea. As in many coastal areas, fishing was a key economic engine. Ironically, it was near this seat of idolatry that Peter the fisherman clearly identified Jesus as the promised Messiah, Son of the Living God.

LESSON OUTLINE

I. Who Do You Say I Am? (Mark 8:27–29)
II. From Faith to Failure (Luke 22:31-34; John 18:25–27)
III. Restored (John 21:15–17)

UNIFYING PRINCIPLE

It often seems impossible to overcome one's failures and regain respect. How might one be restored from the shame and dishonor of personal failure? Aware of Peter's shame and remorse for his betrayal of him, Jesus forgave Peter and commissioned him to "feed my sheep."

INTRODUCTION

Peter, also known as Cephas and Simon Peter, was one of the most prominent figures in the New Testament, and one of the foremost leaders within Jesus' innermost circle of disciples. He was a passionate follower of the Messiah, an apostle, and an early church pillar. In many ways, Peter represents the fullness of what it means to be a Christ follower. Although he was a devout disciple, Peter was also strong-willed, impulsive, and prejudiced. A native of Bethsaida who lived in Capernaum, he was married (1 Corinthians 9:5) and was a partner of James and John in the fishing industry (Luke 5:10).

As a follower of Jesus, Peter's life was marked by faith, failure, redemption, and leadership. His journey from a simple fisherman to a foundational leader of the early church provides valuable insights and lessons of discipleship. Throughout the Gospels, Peter's personality shines through as bold, passionate, and sometimes impulsive. His eagerness to follow Jesus often leads him to take risks, some of which resulted in great faith-filled moments.

Peter's life is documented in the Gospels, Acts, and some of his own letters (1 and 2 Peter). At birth, he was named Simon; however, Jesus gave him the name Cephas (Aramaic for "rock," translated as Peter in Greek). His new name symbolized his future role in establishing the early church. He witnessed the miracles of Jesus and was the only disciple who walked on water. He was bold about proclaiming his faith. His life depicts for us: how to live in faith; our vulnerability to failure; the redemption of Christ; and transformation that comes when we are completely restored to a right relationship with God.

On a journey to Caesarea Philippi, a well-known stronghold of idolatrous activity, Jesus uses this opportunity to teach His disciples what it means to follow Him. Peter emerged as one who knew Jesus' true identity. Later, Peter's confidence in Christ would be tested. During Christ's crucifixion, He would face enormous pressures to deny Christ.

Like Peter, we may be eager to follow Christ, and we may often face pressures to deny Him. In our cosmopolitan, technically driven age, who do you say Jesus in? Do you recognize Him among the gods of this age?

EXPOSITION

I. Who Do You Say I am? (Mark 8:27–29)

On this occasion, before His crucifixion, Jesus and His disciples were on their way to Caesarea Philippi, when He initiated a conversation about His identity. His first objective was to help His disciples to know who He is. Located at the base of Mount Hermon in northern Israel, Caesarea Philippi was a center of pagan worship and a stronghold of demonic activity. Many gods were worshiped there, including the most prominent, Pan, the Greek god of shepherds, wild nature, and fertility.

Caesarea Philippi was home of a large cave sanctuary (Grotto of Pan) also known as the gates of Hades, which was believed to be an entrance to the underworld. Many rituals, animal sacrifices, and possibly sacrifices of humans were offered to Pan to gain favor. Other gods of Caesarea Philippi included Zeus, the god of the Greek pantheon, Nemesis, the goddess of divine retribution and justice, Ba'al, the god of storm and fertility, and the Emperor (the worship of Caesar as a part of the imperial cult).

This setting was significant because it is where Jesus wants to distinguish Himself to His disciples. First, Jesus asks them, 'Who do people say that I am? (see Matthew 16:13–19). The disciples mention the names of a few highly regarded prophets. While these identifications are respectful and even complimentary, they all fall short of Jesus' true identity. People recognized something special about Jesus, but their understanding was incomplete. They placed Him within familiar categories—a prophet, a forerunner, a moral teacher—but missed His true significance.

Jesus then asks, "Who do you say that I am?" (see Matthew 16:13-20). This was a call for them recognize Him as the Son of God even though they are surrounded by many other gods. Peter wastes no time offering: "You are the Christ, the Son of the living God." Jesus commends him, affirming that no person on earth (flesh and blood) had revealed this information to him.

By declaring Jesus as "Son of the Living God," Peter is rejecting the false gods of the region and affirming that Jesus was the true Messiah. This setting, with its backdrop of pagan worship, makes Peter's confession striking. Jesus wants His disciples to not only be curious about Him, but also that they move from curiosity to commitment to Him. His crucifixion was soon to come, and Jesus, knowing that their faith would be tested, wanted them to be confident in His identity.

In asking these two critical questions, Jesus amplifies the fact that personal commitment matters. He distinguishes between reporting others' opinions and stating personal beliefs. Faith must be personal. No matter what the crowds would say about Him, Jesus wanted His closest followers to be certain of His identity. Peter's Spirit-led confession became the foundation upon which Christ would build His Church.

II. From Faith to Failure (Luke 22:31-34; John 18:25-27)

Despite his devotion to Christ, Peter experiences significant failures throughout his life. However, each misstep proves to be a step in his growth and his ultimate restoration. During the Last Supper, Jesus tells His disciples that they will all fall away that very night. Peter strongly disagrees, saying; "Even if all fall away on account of you, I never will." (Matthew 26:33). Peter is insistent in his declaration of devotion; however, he is unaware that he is already set up for failure.

All four Gospels recount that during the meal Jesus foretells Peter's denial three times before the rooster's morning crow (Luke 22:31-34). To deny means to say something is not true, to disown or disclaim association with someone or something.

In the Upper Room, as Jesus prepares His disciples for the coming ordeal, He singles out Simon Peter with a double address, "Simon, Simon," signaling both affection and urgency. Jesus reveals a cosmic dimension to Peter's coming trial: "Satan has demanded to sift all of you like wheat." The metaphor of sifting evokes the image of violent shaking, separating grain from chaff. Peter's impending denial is not merely a personal failing but also part of a larger spiritual conflict.

Yet, Jesus' words are not only a warning but also a comfort: "I have prayed for you that your own faith may not fail." Jesus' intercession does not prevent Peter's failure, but it ensures that his faith will not be utterly destroyed. The promise of restoration, "when once you have turned back, strengthen your brothers," anticipates Peter's future role as a leader and encourager in the early church.

Peter's response is bold but naïve: "Lord, I am ready to go with you to prison and to death!" His self-confidence is sincere, yet Jesus knows the truth. His prediction is precise, underscoring both Jesus' foreknowledge and Peter's vulnerability.

After their final meal together, Jesus takes Peter, James, and John to pray with Him in the Garden of Gethsemane. However instead of praying with Jesus, the disciples fall asleep. After Jesus is arrested, the disciples flee, including Peter (Matthew 26:56).

Peter's fear of human authorities overpowers his faith in Jesus. At the third denial of Jesus, a group confronts Peter, saying; "Surely you are one of them; your accent gives you away." Peter begins to curse and swear, saying; "I don't know the man!" Immediately, a rooster crows. Jesus turns and looks at Peter (Luke 22:61). The moment the rooster crows, Peter realizes he has done exactly what Jesus foretold, and he weeps "bitterly."

When confronted with his failure, Peter is broken with remorse. Jesus looks at him, not with condemnation, but with love and sorrow. Peter is indeed guilty, but still loved by God, who still had plans for His disciple. Unlike Judas, who fell into self-destruction, Peter's remorse led him to restoration. Although Peter betrayed Christ, God still used him mightily. Failures do not disqualify the faithful from God's calling. Peter's denial of Jesus blends the consequences of both human weakness and God's grace.

III. Restored (John 21:15–17)

At the post-resurrection appearance of Jesus to the disciples by the Sea of Galilee, Peter has returned to his former vocation as a fisherman (John 21:1–14). The exchange begins with Jesus posing a penetrating question: "Do you love me more than these?" The Greek verb used here for "love" is *agapao*, which denotes a deep, sacrificial affection. Jesus' use of this term, rather than the more casual *phileo*, suggests He is probing the depth of Peter's devotion.

"These" in Jesus' question is likely a reference to the other disciples or perhaps the fishing equipment, alluding to the possibility that other priorities or attachments had eclipsed Peter's love for Christ. This connects to Peter's earlier boast that he would never desert Jesus, even if all the others did (Mark 14:29). But now, rather than confidently affirming a superior love, Peter humbly acknowledges Jesus' omniscience, appealing to the Lord's own knowledge of his heart. His self-awareness and humility contrast with his previous overconfidence.

Jesus' reply, "Feed my lambs," is both a reinstatement of Peter's pastoral calling and a challenge to demonstrate his love through sacrificial service. The imagery of feeding lambs evokes the role of a shepherd, which was a common metaphor for spiritual leadership in the ancient Near East. Jesus is entrusting Peter with the care of His flock, a weighty responsibility that will require unwavering devotion.

In the second exchange, Jesus again poses the question, probing deeper into the state of Peter's love. The repetition suggests the importance of this issue and Jesus' desire to fully restore Peter's relationship with Him. Jesus' command to "Tend my sheep" reinforces the pastoral metaphor, but with a more active and supervisory nuance. The Greek word *poimaino* means "to shepherd" or "to pastor," implying not just feeding but also guiding, protecting, and providing overall care for the flock.

Jesus is entrusting the weighty responsibility of spiritual leadership to Peter. He is being called to assume a role of influence and authority within the community of believers, with the understanding that he will be held accountable for the welfare of Christ's "sheep."

Jesus questions Peter's love a third time, but this time using the less intense *phileo* instead of *agapao*. This subtle shift may have resonated with Peter, who had previously declared his *phileo* (affectionate) love for Jesus, even as he denied knowing Him three times (John 18:15–27).

Peter's response indicates his grief over Jesus' repeated questioning, perhaps because it stirred painful memories of his failures. Yet, he reaffirms his love, once more appealing to Jesus' omniscience as the basis for his claim.

Jesus' final instruction, "Feed my sheep," reinforces the pastoral calling He has placed upon Peter. The shift from "lambs" to "sheep" suggests a broader scope of responsibility, encompassing the entire flock of God's people—not just the young or vulnerable, but the mature as well.

This threefold commission to "feed" and "tend" the sheep is significant in light of Peter's previous three denials of Christ. The repetition mirrors the earlier denials, symbolically restoring Peter to fellowship and ministry. Just as he had publicly disowned Jesus three times, now he is publicly reinstated and entrusted with the sacred task of shepherding Christ's beloved people and leading them further in the faith.

THE LESSON APPLIED

Peter's life is a testimony to God's grace and power. He started as a fisherman, struggled in his faith, but became a pillar of the early church. Often, God will use our trials and mistakes as object lessons to help us to grow in faith. When we fail, we should see our shortcomings as opportunities to reaffirm our faith in Christ.

Peter was a passionate follower of Christ; however, his denial of Christ at such a crucial moment shows us that even the strongest believers can fall. But after Jesus restored Peter, he became a bold leader in the early church. The past need not define anyone. We are defined by God's calling. He will use our weaknesses for His glory. The journey from failure to faithfulness can take time. Peter's story encourages us to stay humble, prayerful, and dependent on the Lord. Peter's life shows us God's grace and the power of His forgiveness to transform our lives.

LET'S TALK ABOUT IT...

Discuss the following questions and visit www.rhboyd.com for more information.

How do believers handle personal failure? Do we allow it to shape us, transform us, or do we let it define us?

Get Social

Share your views and tag us @rhboydco and use #rhboydco

@rhboydco

Home Daily Devotional Readings
July 13–19, 2026

Monday	Tuesday	Wednesday	Thursday	Friday	Saturday	Sunday
God Calls for Restitution	God Desires Justice for the Oppressed	Blessings and Woes	Love, Hospitality, and Contentment	Meeting Needs through God's Love	The Righteous Are Generous Givers	Salvation Has Come to This House
Exodus 22:1–6	Isaiah 58:3–7	Luke 6:20–26	Hebrews 13:1–6	1 John 3:14–18	Psalm 37:1–5, 18–22	Luke 19:1–10

Lesson VII   July 19, 2026

Zacchaeus, the Publican

Adult Topic: Climbing a Tree, What Will I See?
Background Scripture: Luke 19:1–10
Lesson Passage: Luke 19:1–10

LUKE 19:1-10

KJV	NRSVue
AND Jesus entered and passed through Jericho. 2 And, behold, there was a man named Zacchaeus, which was the chief among the publicans, and he was rich. 3 And he sought to see Jesus who he was; and could not for the press, because he was little of stature. 4 And he ran before, and climbed up into a sycomore tree to see him: for he was to pass that way. 5 And when Jesus came to the place, he looked up, and saw him, and said unto him, Zacchaeus, make haste, and come down; for to day I must abide at thy house. 6 And he made haste, and came down, and received him joyfully. 7 And when they saw it, they all murmured, saying, That he was gone to be guest with a man that is a sinner. 8 And Zacchaeus stood, and said unto the Lord; Behold, Lord, the half of my goods I give to the poor; and if I have taken any thing from any man by false accusation, I restore him fourfold. 9 And Jesus said unto him, This day is salvation come to this house, forsomuch as he also is a son of Abraham. 10 For the Son of man is come to seek and to save that which was lost.	HE entered Jericho and was passing through it. 2 A man was there named Zacchaeus; he was a chief tax collector and was rich. 3 He was trying to see who Jesus was, but on account of the crowd he could not, because he was short in stature. 4 So he ran ahead and climbed a sycamore tree to see him, because he was going to pass that way. 5 When Jesus came to the place, he looked up and said to him, "Zacchaeus, hurry and come down, for I must stay at your house today." 6 So he hurried down and was happy to welcome him. 7 All who saw it began to grumble and said, "He has gone to be the guest of one who is a sinner." 8 Zacchaeus stood there and said to the Lord, "Look, half of my possessions, Lord, I will give to the poor, and if I have defrauded anyone of anything, I will pay back four times as much." 9 Then Jesus said to him, "Today salvation has come to this house, because he, too, is a son of Abraham. 10 For the Son of Man came to seek out and to save the lost."

LESSON SETTING

Time: AD 63 or 64
Place: Jericho

MAIN THOUGHT: When Jesus came to the place, he looked up and said to him, "Zacchaeus, hurry and come down; for I must stay at your house today." (Luke 19:5, NRSVue)

Setting: Jericho, located in the plains of the Jordan Valley near the Jordan River and the Dead Sea, and about fifteen miles from Jerusalem, one of the oldest inhabited cities in the world. It was a thriving center of trade and commerce that attracted the wealthy. Its tropical climate, date palm trees, balsam groves, sycamore trees, and fig and olive trees provided an oasis for aristocrats during ancient times. After the children of Israel entered Canaan, Joshua conquered Jericho. By the time of the New Testament, Judea and surrounding regions were under Roman control. During the reign of Herod, the Great, Jericho was beautified after the Romans plundered it. The Romans financed their empire by levying heavy taxes on all the nations that it conquered. The taxes helped fund the Roman military, infrastructure, and imperial governance. Jericho was a prosperous trade route hub, a place where tax collection was very significant. Tax collectors played a significant, complex, and often controversial role within Jewish society. Jesus traveled through Jericho during His ministry, to get to other locations in the region, including Jerusalem. He was baptized by John the Baptist in the Jordan River, which as located near Jericho. Jesus is on the final segment of His earthly ministry. The crowds following Jesus at this point are very large, as His fame has grown. He meets Zacchaeus, a Jew and chief tax collector, despised by the Jews for his dishonest gains through tax collection. Through His encounter with Zacchaeus, we learn Jesus' mission—to seek and save the lost. We also learn that no one is beyond redemption.

LESSON OUTLINE

   I. Hungry for More (Luke 19:1–4)
   II. An Invitation to Change (Luke 19:5–7)
   III. Transformed by His Grace (Luke 19:8–10)

UNIFYING PRINCIPLE

An unexpected encounter with someone we've never met before can result in a transforming experience. What is it about a new relationship that opens up the possibility of transformation in our lives? When Zacchaeus opens his home to Jesus as his special guest, he is transformed by the experience and becomes a follower of Jesus who does more than the Law required.

INTRODUCTION

The story of Zacchaeus (Luke 19:1–10), is one of the most compelling narratives of transformation in the Gospel of Luke. A chief tax collector in Jericho, Zacchaeus is both wealthy and despised due to his occupation, which was often associated with corruption and extortion. However, his encounter with Jesus leads to a radical transformation that demonstrates the power of divine grace, the depth of true repentance, and the call to restorative justice.

Through this study of a man who was small in stature but large in humility, we will explore what Luke wants his audience to understand about healing, conversion, restoration, and justice, and what can be gleaned from Zacchaeus' enthusiasm to follow Jesus. The study also addresses Jesus' mission to seek and save the lost.

EXPOSITION

I. Hungry for More (Luke 19:1–4)

Luke records the life of Jesus with detail and order unlike the other Gospel writers. He wants his audience to understand Jesus' mission and message of healing, conversion, restoration, and justice. In Jesus' final journey to Jerusalem, where He will be crucified, He meets two men whose lives are forever changed. His encounters with them teach us the importance and focus of Jesus' mission to save the lost, the least of these.

As He nears Jericho, Jesus meets a blind beggar known as blind Bartimaeus (cf. Mark 10:46). He recognizes a once-in-a-lifetime opportunity is before him. The beggar cries out for Jesus to have mercy on him, and he is healed at that very moment.

Continuing His journey, Jesus enters the city of Jericho, when He meets Zacchaeus, a Jew, and a chief tax collector who was despised by the Jews for his dishonest tax collection practices. This encounter is not about his profession or collecting taxes, neither is it about his small stature. This exchange is a microcosm representing what Jesus came to do in this world.

The backstory of Zacchaeus helps us to understand why his encounter with Jesus is so significant. Rome required taxes from its conquered territories, and used a system known as "tax farming," where private individuals bid for the right to collect taxes in a specific area.

Zacchaeus (a Jew) had contracted with a Roman official to be the chief tax collector in his district. In Bible times, chief tax collectors held an important and often controversial position in society. Their role went beyond collecting money; the position they held was tied to political power, personal wealth, and significant social stigma. Chief tax collectors often bought the rights to collect taxes in a certain area from Roman authorities. For their compensation, they were allowed to collect more than the fixed tax amount. This was part of the Roman tax farming system. They would then hire local tax collectors to do the actual collecting, while keeping a portion of the proceeds for themselves. Chief tax collectors oversaw revenue collection of customs duties on goods and trade, toll taxes on bridges and road, property taxes, and income taxes. They ensured that Rome received its share and kept anything above Rome's share as their profit.

Jewish tax collectors were considered traitors among the Jews. Their work was both administrative and political, and they were eyed with deep suspicion and contempt by the Jewish public. They were often accused of dishonesty and collusion with Roman oppression.

Tax collecting was generally viewed as a shady business because the system was structured to support their greed and extortion. They often negotiated or bribed Roman officials for more favorable contracts. They also added their own fee on top of the tax. Because there were few rules or transparency, corruption was rampant.

One of the remarkable aspects of Zacchaeus' story is his eagerness to see Jesus. Despite his immense wealth and status, he clearly seeks more. In an effort to obtain what he needs, the tax collector humbles himself in a way that is uncommon for someone of his position. Luke tells us that Zacchaeus was "small in stature" (Luke 19:3), and because he could not see over the crowd, he runs ahead and climbs a sycamore tree.

Luke mentions Zacchaeus' height to show us his "smallness" in the eyes of society. He is a chief tax collector, despised by his own people, regarded as a traitor, and aligned with Roman oppressors. The reference to his height also shows that Zacchaeus is physically and spiritually marginalized. He is looked down upon literally and figuratively. As corrupt as Zacchaeus is perceived to be, however, when he gets word that Jesus is near, he quickly finds a place where he can get a glimpse of the Man he has heard so much about.

II. An Invitation to Change (Luke 19:5-7)

Spiritually, Zacchaeus is in a state of disconnect from his community. But as he watches Jesus approach from his position spot in a sycamore tree, he receives a life-changing invitation. Jesus does not wait for Zacchaeus to approach Him. Instead, He stops, looks up at Zacchaeus, and invites Himself to Zacchaeus' house.

Jesus takes the initiative; Jesus declaring, "for I must (δεῖ / dei) stay at your house today." The Greek word δεῖ expresses divine necessity, suggesting that this encounter is part of God's sovereign plan for Zacchaeus' life. Jesus, who is on His way to Jerusalem to fulfill His redemptive mission, pauses for Zacchaeus. No person is beyond the reach of God's grace, and His timing is perfect.

Zacchaeus' reaction is immediate and unreserved (v. 4), and his joy gives testament to the transformative power of encountering Christ.

The crowd considers Jesus' actions scandalous. They murmur, "He has gone to be the guest of a sinner" (v. 7). The onlookers grumble (Greek: *diegongyzon*), a term often used in Luke to describe the Pharisees' disapproval of Jesus' association with sinners (e.g., Luke 5:30; 15:2). Their complaint reveals their self-righteous nature as well as their blindness to their own need for grace. Believers must guard against pride and the temptation to judge others. The crowd's reaction reflects the tension that often exists between religious tradition and divine grace. Christians are called to emulate Jesus' compassion for the lost rather than adopt a posture of condemnation.

Jesus' appears oblivious to the crowd's response, or perhaps He is even amused by it. Whatever the case, His response to Zacchaeus is not based upon the crowd's estimation of His dealings with the tax collector or the man himself. Jesus extends acceptance for Zacchaeus by personally addressing him and acknowledging his humanity and worth by going to his house. In a society where he is despised, Jesus' act of public recognition brings emotional and social healing.

The Greek word for "received" (*hypedexato*) implies a warm and hospitable welcome. Zacchaeus, once a man defined by greed, now opens his home and heart to Jesus. This is the fruit of genuine repentance—a heart turned toward God with joy (Acts 2:28).

Jesus offers grace to Zacchaeus. His self-invitation reflects the divine initiative in God's salvation plan. God seeks the lost before they even realize their need for Him. By dining with Zacchaeus, Jesus shatters the cultural and religious norms that dictated who is considered worthy of fellowship. This act of inclusion reinforced Jesus' mission: "For the Son of Man came to seek and to save the lost" (Luke 19:10). Jesus wanted Zacchaeus to know that He was loved and accepted, and that God's forgiveness and salvation was for him also.

III. Transformed by His Grace (Luke 19:8-10)

Having been extended immeasurable grace, Zacchaeus' transformation is immediate and dramatic. His heart is changed instantly and he makes a tangible demonstration of the change that has occurred within. The utter generosity of Zacchaeus' actions reveal the depth of his repentance; "Look, half of my possessions, Lord, I will give to the poor, and if I have defrauded anyone of anything, I will pay back four times as much" (v. 8).

Before his encounter with Jesus, Zacchaeus' wealth had been an instrument of exploitation. Now it becomes a means of generosity and justice. Without prompting from Jesus, Zacchaeus indicates his desire to make things right with those whom he has cheated. "If I have cheated anybody out of anything, I will pay back four times the amount" (v. 8).

For him, true repentance means measurable change. First, he pledges to give half of his goods to the poor. The man who was consumed by greed is now immersed in generosity. His actions align with the biblical call to care for the marginalized (Proverbs 19:17; James 1:27). In addition to support for the poor, Zacchaeus vows to repay anyone he has defrauded—fourfold—exceeding the Old Testament requirement (Leviticus 6:5; Numbers 5:7). His offer of restitution reflects genuine remorse, and a desire to make amends, and a heart that certainly wants to change.

Zacchaeus also acknowledges Jesus as Lord. In so doing, Zacchaeus demonstrates that his faith is not only intellectual but also transformative. For him, "Lord" acknowledges Jesus' authority and his submission to it. His every action confirms the sincerity of his faith.

Jesus responds to Zacchaeus' repentance with a declaration that must have been most unexpected (v. 9): "Today salvation has come to this house." His words are rich in theological significance. Zacchaeus' salvation is immediate ("Today"), emphasizing the present reality of God's Kingdom (Luke 4:21; 2 Corinthians 6:2). Not only is the once unscrupulous tax collector blessed, but also "this house." Jesus' blessing extends beyond Zacchaeus to his entire household, reflecting the communal nature of God's grace (Acts 16:31).

In deliberately using the term "Son of Abraham", to refer to Zacchaeus, Jesus acknowledges his inclusion in the covenant community, despite his past. This concept of inclusion is further explained in Paul's teaching that faith, not ethnicity or works, defines the true children of Abraham (see Romans 4:16; Galatians 3:7).

Jesus concludes with a summary of His earthly mission "to seek and to save the lost" (v. 10). This verse is the thematic heart of Luke's Gospel and the entire biblical narrative:

The words "seek" and "save" encapsulate His mission. Jesus actively pursues sinners, as seen in His encounter with Zacchaeus. His mission contrasts with that of religious leaders who avoided "unclean" people (Luke 5:30–32) and believe the Law justified their doing so.

"The lost" encompasses all who are spiritually alienated from God, regardless of their social or moral status (Luke 15:4–7). The "lost" people of the world are the target of the Great Commission (Matthew 28:19–20), which calls believers to participate in Jesus' mission of seeking the lost.

Zacchaeus, though previously alienated, is publicly confirmed as a member of God's covenant people. Jesus' affirmation countered the community's negative perception of Zacchaeus. That day a great lesson was learned by everyone—no one is beyond redemption in God's sight.

THE LESSON APPLIED

Jesus boldly declares His mission through His experience at Zacchaeus' house—to save the least and the lost. One does not need to look very far or very long to find the least of these—those who are social outcasts or who have been forgotten by society. These persons may be wealthy or poor, young or old, genius level or intellectually challenged. Jesus came to save them all. He came to save the forgotten, those who are social outcasts, and those who are desperate to meet Him. Broadly speaking, "the lost" symbolizes those who are vulnerable, marginalized, or in need—those who are rejected, forgotten, and hungry for deeper meaning in life.

Zacchaeus' salvation experience is rich with spiritual lessons that speak to the heart of Jesus' mission and our response to His call. His story teaches us about the healing power of divine acceptance, the necessity of genuine conversion, the importance of restorative justice, and the joy of following Jesus with enthusiasm. Through Zacchaeus, Luke shows us that salvation is available to all, and a true encounter with Jesus results in tangible, measurable life changes that can include generosity, restitution, integrity, and justice.

Although the crowd judges Zacchaeus and tries to block his view as Jesus is passing by, he does not let naysayers hinder keep him from seeing Jesus or accepting His invitation. People may doubt another person's worthiness, but their opinions should never impede the progress of one who is seeking to know Christ.

Through Zacchaeus, Jesus demonstrates that grace comes before change. Jesus invites Himself into Zacchaeus' home and heart before Zacchaeus promises to change.

Zacchaeus was small in stature, but Jesus saw his spiritual hunger. God doesn't measure people by outward appearance or social status. He looks at the heart and sees what we can become in Him.

LET'S TALK ABOUT IT...

Discuss the following questions and visit www.rhboyd.com for more information.

Is there a place in your life where failure still speaks louder than grace? Will you allow Jesus to transform your life today?

Get Social

Share your views and tag us
@rhboydco and use #rhboydco

@rhboydco

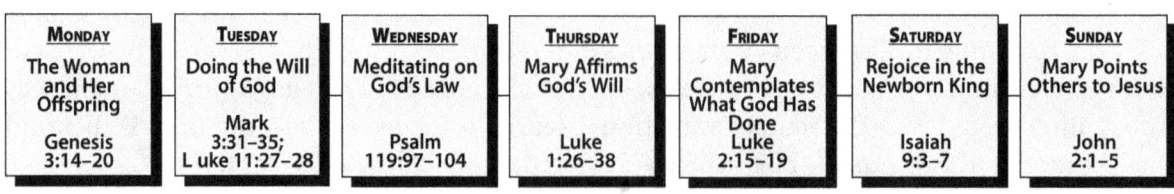

Lesson VIII   **July 26, 2026**

Mary, the Mother of Jesus

Adult Topic: Living with What You Didn't Ask For
Background Scripture: Luke 2:15–19; John 2:1–5; 19:25–27
Lesson Passage: Luke 2:15–19; John 2:1–5; 19:25–27

LUKE 2:15-19; JOHN 2:1-5; 19:25-27

KJV

AND it came to pass, as the angels were gone away from them into heaven, the shepherds said one to another, Let us now go even unto Bethlehem, and see this thing which is come to pass, which the Lord hath made known unto us.
16 And they came with haste, and found Mary, and Joseph, and the babe lying in a manger.
17 And when they had seen it, they made known abroad the saying which was told them concerning this child.
18 And all they that heard it wondered at those things which were told them by the shepherds.
19 But Mary kept all these things, and pondered them in her heart.

••• John 2:1–5 •••

1 And the third day there was a marriage in Cana of Galilee; and the mother of Jesus was there:
2 And both Jesus was called, and his disciples, to the marriage.
3 And when they wanted wine, the mother of Jesus saith unto him, They have no wine.
4 Jesus saith unto her, Woman, what have I to do with thee? mine hour is not yet come.
5 His mother saith unto the servants, Whatsoever he saith unto you, do it.

••• John 19:25–27 •••

25 Now there stood by the cross of Jesus his mother, and his mother's sister, Mary the wife of Cleophas, and Mary Magdalene.

NRSVue

WHEN the angels had left them and gone into heaven, the shepherds said to one another, "Let us go now to Bethlehem and see this thing that has taken place, which the Lord has made known to us."
16 So they went with haste and found Mary and Joseph and the child lying in the manger.
17 When they saw this, they made known what had been told them about this child,
18 and all who heard it were amazed at what the shepherds told them,
19 and Mary treasured all these words and pondered them in her heart.

••• John 2:1–5 •••

1 On the third day there was a wedding in Cana of Galilee, and the mother of Jesus was there.
2 Jesus and his disciples had also been invited to the wedding.
3 When the wine gave out, the mother of Jesus said to him, "They have no wine."
4 And Jesus said to her, "Woman, what concern is that to me and to you? My hour has not yet come."
5 His mother said to the servants, "Do whatever he tells you."

••• John 19:25–27 •••

25 And that is what the soldiers did. Meanwhile, standing near the cross of Jesus were his mother, and his mother's sister, Mary the wife of Clopas, and Mary Magdalene.

MAIN THOUGHT: Mary treasured all these words and pondered them in her heart. (Luke 2:19, NRSVue)

LUKE 2:15–19; JOHN 2:1–5; 19:25–27

KJV

26 When Jesus therefore saw his mother, and the disciple standing by, whom he loved, he saith unto his mother, Woman, behold thy son!

27 Then saith he to the disciple, Behold thy mother! And from that hour that disciple took her unto his own home.

NRSVue

26 When Jesus saw his mother and the disciple whom he loved standing beside her, he said to his mother, "Woman, here is your son."

27 Then he said to the disciple, "Here is your mother." And from that hour the disciple took her into his own home.

LESSON SETTING

Time: AD 30
Place: Nazareth
Setting: Mary, the mother of Jesus, lived during the late Second Temple period, around 4 BC to AD 30 in Roman-occupied Judea (modern-day Israel/Palestine). She was from Nazareth, a small, seemingly insignificant village in Galilee, far from the powerful cities of Jerusalem and Rome. At the time of the birth of Jesus, Judea was under Roman rule, led by Herod the Great and later by his son, Herod Antipas. Jewish people lived under heavy taxation, political oppression, and religious tension. While they were allowed to maintain their faith and Temple practices, they longed for liberation—the promised Messiah who would restore Israel and defeat their enemies. Nazareth was a secluded town in Galilee, south of the Lebanon Mountain range. It was close to the trade routes of Palestine. Situated in a basin between steep hills, Nazareth was secluded from nearby trade routes. It was not considered important to national and religious life of Israel. Nazareth had somewhat of a bad reputation for its morals and religion. The name Nazareth in Aramaic means watchtower. Mary lived in a time of political oppression, economic hardship, and deep spiritual longing. The Jewish people were waiting for a Messiah, a Savior who would redeem them from Roman rule and restore the Kingdom of Israel. In the middle of this tension and uncertainty, God chose a young girl from Nazareth to play a central role in His redemptive plan.

LESSON OUTLINE

I. Mary and the Shepherds (Luke 2:15–19)
II. Mary at the Wedding Feast (John 2:1–5)
III. Mary at the Foot of the Cross (John 19:25–27)

UNIFYING PRINCIPLE

We are faced with many choices throughout our lives, but it is impossible to commit to everything. How do we prioritize our commitments? We see Mary's commitment to Jesus at significant moments throughout his life—from the announcement of His birth to His first miracle, to His crucifixion.

INTRODUCTION

Mary, the mother of Jesus, is one of the most revered and significant personalities in the Bible. Her life of humility, faith, and obedience plays a central role in God's redemptive plan for the world. As a young Jewish girl, Mary would have been reared in a religious household, deeply familiar with the Hebrew Scriptures. Girls were typically betrothed around the age of 12–14, so Mary was likely very young when the angel Gabriel visited her (Luke 1:26–38). She lived in a patriarchal society with limited social mobility, yet she played a pivotal role in God's redemptive plan.

For centuries, the descendants of Abraham held onto prophecies of a coming Savior—the Messiah—who would redeem the world; However, because they were under Roman rulership, they believed their Messiah would redeem Israel from Roman oppression and economic hardship. Mary would have been taught the prophesies of a coming Messiah as part of her faith development—such as that found in Isaiah 7:14, where Isaiah prophesied the Messiah would be born of a virgin.

When the angel Gabriel appears to her, he greets her saying, "Greetings, you who are highly favored! The Lord is with you" (Luke 1:28). Mary finds favor with God, not because of her status or accomplishments, but because of her purity of heart. She loved God and trusted Him, even when His plans defied logic or social expectations.

Mary's ready response to God's call is one of the most convicting statements of surrender in Scripture. "Here am I, the servant of the Lord; let it be with me according to your word."(Luke 1:38 NRSVue). In saying yes to God, Mary shows her deep commitment to God's purpose, even though she did not fully understand the future.

This lesson examines three of her critical encounters as the mother of the long-awaited Messiah and the joys and sorrows she endured along the journey.

EXPOSITION

I. Mary and the Shepherds (Luke 2:15–19)

Luke's record of the shepherds' encounter with the heavenly host, and later, Joseph, Mary, and Jesus, is a well-known and endearing narrative that captures the wonder of the first Christmas. This story not only highlights the humble beginnings of Jesus' earthly life but also underscores the miracles associated with His birth and the transformative power of an encounter with the Messiah at any age of His human development and growth.

Luke the physician meticulously records the events surrounding Jesus' birth, emphasizing the fulfillment of prophecy and the inclusivity of God's salvation plan. The shepherds' encounter with the angels is a moment of divine interruption. The phrase "Let us go over to Bethlehem and see this thing that has happened" reflects their immediate faith and obedience. Unlike the religious elite of the time, the shepherds did not hesitate to act on God's word. These shepherds, who are marginalized in Jewish society due to their thankless and mundane occupation, become unlikely recipients of divine revelation. They are the first to receive the good news, and their inclusion in the Nativity story demonstrates God's heart for the lowly and His desire to reveal His glory to all people, regardless of social standing.

The shepherds find the Messiah humbly lying in a manger—a feeding trough for animals—rather than in a palatial setting as one might expect. This stark contrast between the heavenly proclamation and the earthly reality underscores the humility of Christ's incarnation. After witnessing the Christ child, the shepherds "made known what had been told them about this child." Their testimony elicits amazement among all who hear what they have to say.

The passage concludes with a poignant observation about Mary, the mother of Jesus: "Mary treasured all these words and pondered them in her heart." The Greek verbs συνετήρει (sunetērei/treasured) and συμβάλλουσα (symballousa/pondered) convey a sense of deep reflection and contemplation, as Mary sought to make sense of the extraordinary circumstances surrounding her son's birth. Mary receives their words in quiet contemplation. By this point in the unfolding Christmas story, young Mary's life has changed dramatically in a short period—from the divine announcement of her pregnancy to their visit from a group of strangers offering a divine message about her newborn Son. She likely has no words in the moment to express what the men have just revealed to her.

II. Mary at the Wedding Feast (John 2:1–5)

The setting of a wedding feast in Cana is also rich in symbolic meaning. In the ancient Near Eastern culture, weddings were celebrated as joyous communal events, often lasting for several days. The fact that Jesus was invited to this wedding, along with His disciples, suggests that He was already gaining recognition and influence within the community.

The narrative then pivots to what is seemingly the central issue of the story: the wine runs out. This normally mundane problem takes on deeper significance when considering the cultural and social implications of such a shortage. At a traditional Jewish wedding celebration, the depletion of wine would have been a major embarrassment for the host family, potentially damaging their reputation and position of honor within the community.

Mary informs Jesus, "They have no wine." But she is not merely giving Him information. Her words are a veiled plea for Jesus to intervene and resolve the crisis. The Greek word here for wine (οἶνον/oinon) can also be understood metaphorically as a symbol of joy, abundance, and the blessings of God's Kingdom.

Jesus' reply to His mother, "Woman, what does this have to do with me? My hour has not yet come," may initially seem cryptic or even dismissive. However, a closer examination of the Greek text reveals profound theological significance. The term (γύναι/gunai, "woman") is not a sign of disrespect as Jesus uses it here, but rather a formal address that points to Mary's elevated role as the mother of the Messiah. More importantly, Jesus' statement, "My hour has not yet come," is a reference to the crucial moment of His crucifixion and resurrection, the ultimate fulfillment of His messianic mission. Despite His apparent hesitation, Mary's faith and trust in her Son's divine power is unwavering. Her instruction to the servants, "Do whatever He tells you" (v. 5), demonstrates her confidence in Jesus' ability to resolve the crisis and reveals her role as a model of obedient discipleship.

The Johannine record of Jesus' first miracle highlights His divinity, as it "revealed his glory" (John 2:11) and Himself as the long-awaited Messiah. This miraculous act foreshadows the greater work of redemption that Jesus will accomplish through His death and resurrection. Secondly, the passage emphasizes the importance of faith and obedience in the face of seemingly insurmountable challenges. Mary's trust in Jesus' divine power, even when the outcome was not yet clear, serves as an inspiring example for believers to follow. Thirdly, the narrative demonstrates Jesus' compassionate nature, a God who cares about the practical needs and concerns of His people. The miracle of turning water into wine at Cana is a reminder that our Lord is neither aloof nor distant. He is intimately involved in the details of human lives, ready to intervene and provide for the needs of His people.

III. Mary at the Cross (John 19:25-27)

John's Gospel, with its unique theological depth and narrative artistry, brings us to an intimate yet heart-wrenching moment at the foot of the cross. As Jesus endures the agony of crucifixion, the Evangelist draws his readers' attention to those who remain with Him in His final hours, especially the woman who gave birth to Him.

Mary's presence at the cross is the culmination of a journey that began with angelic announcements, prophetic songs, and the marvel of shepherds and Magi. At Jesus' birth, Simeon had prophesied to Mary, "a sword will pierce your own soul too" (Luke 2:35, NRSVue). Throughout Jesus' ministry, Mary had to ponder, question, and ultimately yield to the mysterious and sometimes painful unfolding of her Son's mission (Luke 2:19; John 2:4-5).

Now, at the cross, Mary's journey of faith and motherhood reaches its most excruciating point. She stands amid the chaos, not as a passive observer, but rather as a faithful disciple and a suffering mother, witnessing the apparent defeat of her Son. The cross is the place where Mary's faith is tested and refined; it is also where her relationship with Jesus is transformed.

Mary's presence at the cross exemplifies steadfast faith in the face of suffering and loss. She does not abandon her Son and her Teacher, even when all seems lost. Perhaps as He hung on the cross she recalls the words offered to her by the shepherds and the prophetic voices of Simeon (Luke 2:35) and Anna (Luke 2:36-38). Through her steadfast devotion, Mary paints the picture of one who is a model of persevering faith, trust, and obedience.

Meanwhile, as Jesus hangs on the cross, His concern for His mother is striking. He addresses her not as "mother," but as "woman," a term of respect that also signals a new relationship. Jesus entrusts the woman who carried Him in her womb and nurtured Him into adulthood to the care of the "disciple whom he loved" (traditionally understood as John), saying, "Woman, here is your son." To the disciple, Jesus says, "Here is your mother." In doing so, Jesus creates a new family unit, not based on blood but on faith, obedience, and discipleship.

This act fulfills Jesus' filial duty and His messianic mission. Even in agony, Jesus cares for those He loves. His concern for Mary and the beloved disciple reflects His ongoing care for His people. While taking some of His last breaths, Jesus honors God's commandment to care for one's parents (Exodus 20:12), even in His dying moments. Yet, He also points beyond biological ties to the new faith community formed by His death and resurrection. As D.A. Carson notes, "Jesus' words are simultaneously an act of human kindness and a theological declaration about the new family of God" (*The Gospel According to John, PNTC*, 1991). Jesus' words to Mary and the beloved disciple signify the birth of the Church as a new family. In Christ, believers are united by faith, not blood, and are called to care for one another as brothers and sisters (cf. Galatians 6:10). The cross is the foundation of this new community.

Mary's faith is most deeply tested and most fully realized at the cross. There, the promises, prophecies, and ponderings of her heart converge in the mystery of redemptive suffering. This passage challenges all disciples to stand with Mary at the foot of the cross—to embrace both the cost and the hope of discipleship, to care for one another as Christ commands, and to trust that in moments of deepest sorrow, Jesus is present and faithful. Her journey is an example to all believers that following Jesus includes both joy and sorrow. The sword that pierced her soul is emblematic of the suffering that often accompanies faithfulness. Yet, at the cross, suffering is transformed into hope, and loss into new relationships.

THE LESSON APPLIED

Saying yes to God, as Mary did when Gabriel came to her, requires that disciples believe Him and trust His plan. We may not always understand what He is doing, but we can trust that He is always at work. Mary was chosen by God. Her willingness to say "yes" to God's plan, despite its cost and uncertainty, challenges us today to trust in God's purpose for our lives. Mary and Joseph were faithful and obedient to God regardless of the social constructs of their time.

Mary's unwavering presence throughout Jesus' life, even in His darkest moments, inspires us to remain steadfast in faith, even when faced with pain and loss. Her example of selfless love and care for her Son reminds us to extend this same love to others, especially the vulnerable and suffering.

LET'S TALK ABOUT IT...

Discuss the following questions and visit www.rhboyd.com for more information.

What is God asking you to say yes to?

How can we stay committed through the good times and bad?

What are some examples of consistency in the Bible and elsewhere?

Get Social

Share your views and tag us @rhboydco and use #rhboydco

@rhboydco

Home Daily Devotional Readings
July 27–August 2, 2026

Monday	Tuesday	Wednesday	Thursday	Friday	Saturday	Sunday
Seek the Lord; Call on God	Have Mercy on Those Who Doubt	How Can We Know the Way?	Call on the Lord	Seek God with Heart and Soul	So I Send You	My Lord and My God!
Isaiah 55:6–11	Jude 20–25	John 14:1–7	Psalm 50:7–15	Deuteronomy 4:27–31	John 20:19–23	John 20:24–29

Lesson IX — August 2, 2026

Thomas, the Honest Doubter

Adult Topic: I'll See It When I Believe It
Background Scripture: John 11:14–16; 14:5–8; 20:24–29; 21:1–2
Lesson Passage: John 11:14–16; 14:5–8; 20:24–29; 21:1–2

JOHN 11:14–16; 14:5–8; 20:24–29; 21:1–2

KJV

THEN said Jesus unto them plainly, Lazarus is dead.
15 And I am glad for your sakes that I was not there, to the intent ye may believe; nevertheless let us go unto him.
16 Then said Thomas, which is called Didymus, unto his fellowdisciples, Let us also go, that we may die with him.

• • • • • •

5 Thomas saith unto him, Lord, we know not whither thou goest; and how can we know the way?
6 Jesus saith unto him, I am the way, the truth, and the life: no man cometh unto the Father, but by me.
7 If ye had known me, ye should have known my Father also: and from henceforth ye know him, and have seen him.
8 Philip saith unto him, Lord, show us the Father, and it sufficeth us.

• • • • • •

24 But Thomas, one of the twelve, called Didymus, was not with them when Jesus came.

25 The other disciples therefore said unto him, We have seen the Lord. But he said unto them, Except I shall see in his hands the print of the nails, and put my finger into the print of the nails, and thrust my hand into his side, I will not believe.
26 And after eight days again his disciples were within, and Thomas with them: then came Jesus,

NRSVue

THEN Jesus told them plainly, "Lazarus is dead.

15 For your sake I am glad I was not there, so that you may believe. But let us go to him."

16 Thomas, who was called the Twin, said to his fellow disciples, "Let us also go, that we may die with him."

• • • • • •

5 Thomas said to him, "Lord, we do not know where you are going. How can we know the way?"
6 Jesus said to him, "I am the way and the truth and the life. No one comes to the Father except through me.
7 If you know me, you will know my Father also. From now on you do know him and have seen him."
8 Philip said to him, "Lord, show us the Father, and we will be satisfied."

• • • • • •

24 But Thomas (who was called the Twin), one of the twelve, was not with them when Jesus came.

25 So the other disciples told him, "We have seen the Lord." But he said to them, "Unless I see the mark of the nails in his hands and put my finger in the mark of the nails and my hand in his side, I will not believe."

26 A week later his disciples were again in the house, and Thomas was with them. Although

MAIN THOUGHT: [Jesus] said to Thomas, "Put your finger here and see my hands. Reach out your hand and put it in my side. Do not doubt but believe." (John 20:27, NRSVue)

JOHN 11:14-16; 14:5-8; 20:24-29; 21:1-2

KJV	NRSVue
the doors being shut, and stood in the midst, and said, Peace be unto you. 27 Then saith he to Thomas, Reach hither thy finger, and behold my hands; and reach hither thy hand, and thrust it into my side: and be not faithless, but believing. 28 And Thomas answered and said unto him, My Lord and my God. 29 Jesus saith unto him, Thomas, because thou hast seen me, thou hast believed: blessed are they that have not seen, and yet have believed. • • • • • • 1 After these things Jesus shewed himself again to the disciples at the sea of Tiberias; and on this wise shewed he himself. 2 There were together Simon Peter, and Thomas called Didymus, and Nathanael of Cana in Galilee, and the sons of Zebedee, and two other of his disciples.	the doors were shut, Jesus came and stood among them and said, "Peace be with you." 27 Then he said to Thomas, "Put your finger here and see my hands. Reach out your hand and put it in my side. Do not doubt but believe." 28 Thomas answered him, "My Lord and my God!" 29 Jesus said to him, "Have you believed because you have seen me? Blessed are those who have not seen and yet have come to believe." • • • • • • 1 After these things Jesus showed himself again to the disciples by the Sea of Tiberias, and he showed himself in this way. 2 Gathered there together were Simon Peter, Thomas called the Twin, Nathanael of Cana in Galilee, the sons of Zebedee, and two others of his disciples.

LESSON SETTING

Time: AD 30
Place: Judea
Setting: The authorship of the Gospel of John has been a topic of scholarly debate for centuries. While tradition attributes the writing to John the Apostle, one of Jesus' twelve disciples, modern scholarship often questions this view. Nevertheless, John's narrative depicts the nature of many Jews then and Christians today who struggle with a double mind. They are like the disciple called twin—they want to have faith yet still have doubts. Thomas' interactions with Jesus take place in the region of Judea. The setting for Thomas' faith journey starts in Bethany, where he witnesses the resurrection of Lazarus. Then, in Jerusalem where Jesus affirms His Messianic work and ends by the Sea of Tiberius where doubting Thomas grows into believing Thomas.

LESSON OUTLINE

I. Overcoming Negativity (John 11:14–16)
II. Overcoming Uncertainty (John 14:5–8)
III. Overcoming Sight-based Belief (John 20:24–29)
IV. Learning to Believe (John 21:1–2)

UNIFYING PRINCIPLE

In the face of doubts many people will seek out solid evidence or proof. What source of evidence is persuasive enough to address our doubt? John indicated that after Thomas received evidence from Jesus, his doubts were relieved, and his faith restored.

INTRODUCTION

Jesus had the most impactful discipleship ministry on earth. He called his followers and taught them the ways of faith through word and deed. In this lesson, Jesus works with His twelve disciples with a particular emphasis on Thomas. He is molding their character from doubters to deliverers. It is a process, but every act of Jesus is designed to grow their faith. The key for Thomas and the others is to stay close to the Lord. As they follow Him, the disciples realize that every experience is another building block in their faith.

Students should take note of the intentionality of Jesus, which reveals that nothing took place by happenstance. As the Lord works miracles, teaches unequivocal faith, and is raised from the dead, all His life affirms Him as the promised Messiah. The lesson also emphasizes that followers of Christ must not allow doubt to undermine their faith. Jesus is the Son of God who came to save the world from their sins. He has all authority to both forgive and to cleanse humanity of sin.

Studying this lesson should inspire an unwavering confidence in the divinity of Christ. He is God incarnate, and every knee shall bow and tongue confess that He is Lord. Initially, Thomas and the other disciples have a hard time accepting this truth, but as they encounter the Lord in these passages their doubts turn into belief.

EXPOSITION

I. Overcoming Negativity (John 11:14–16)

Jesus was teaching in the region of Perea, which is on the eastern side of the Jordan River. His cousin, John the Baptist, baptized in this area and now Jesus spent time there as He made His way to Jerusalem. The people followed the Lord into the area which afforded Him the opportunity to heal and minister to the people. The ministry in Perea went well for many came to believe in the Lord. However, belief was not the same as committed discipleship. Jesus understood this principle. In John 11:3, the atmosphere changed when Jesus received word that his dear friend Lazarus was sick. The Lord had known Lazarus for many years and likely met him on his journey to Passover at the age of twelve. Lazarus may have been Jesus' best friend. The Lord knew that not only was Lazarus sick, but dead. This situation created a good opportunity to teach his disciples about overcoming the negative trait of skepticism.

In the verses prior to 14, the disciples are trying to understand Lazarus' condition. They think their friend was simply sleeping. Thomas listens to the conversation trying to ascertain the facts. After a few moments of their dialogue, Jesus informs them Lazarus is dead (v. 14). It is time for them to leave Perea and go back into Judea to see about him. Thomas and the others knew the danger of going back, for their enemies planned to kill Jesus there. Jerusalem of Judea had a bad reputation for killing prophets. Zechariah was stoned in the court of God's house in 2 Chronicles 24:21. Urijah (Uriah) was killed in the holy city by King Jehoiakim (Jeremiah 26:23). Jesus was almost stoned in John 8:59 when He declared that He predated Abraham.

Thomas ponders these things in his mind as Jesus tells them of His intent. He uses Lazarus' death as an opportunity to display the glory of God. Jesus' words (v. 15) convey the greater plan of His ministry. He has not come simply to keep people from dying or healing everyone that was sick. His Messianic work is designed to increase faith in God. Waiting four days before getting to Lazarus allow for circumstances to unfold where Christ will show His power over death. Thomas and the other disciples need this experience because they are still burdened by doubts.

Bethany is about two miles from Perea, so it takes a couple of hours to walk to the village. During that time, Thomas considers that they may die (v. 16), but he is willing to follow Jesus to the point of death. Thomas wants to be hopeful, but skepticism dogs him. He probably wonders whether they are on a death march. But for Jesus, the journey to see Lazarus proves to be a training march toward overcoming doubt. They need a live experience of a resurrection to help them believe that Jesus is God who has power over death. He uses the experience to teach them that when one dies, it does not mean he or she will remain dead forever. These discipleship principles are vital and must not be overshadowed by negativity. After Jesus raises Lazarus from the dead (v. 44), the witnesses gain a critical piece in their faith treasury. Thomas learns that Jesus has come to bring life, but it is not yet time for him to die with the Lord.

II. Overcoming Uncertainty (John 14:5–8)

After leaving Bethany, Jesus triumphantly enters Jerusalem and resides at a house with an upper room to intensively teach his disciples. The Bible does not identify the owner of the house, but tradition suggests that it belongs to Mary, the mother of John Mark (Upper Room traditional site). This section of Scripture is part of the Upper Room Discourse consisting of John 13–17. The Lord engages in several activities and lessons designed to stimulate His disciples' faith and overcome doubt. In chapter 13, he washes their feet along with the foretelling of his betrayer. In chapter 14, the Messiah prophesies His return to the Father. Then, Thomas listens to Jesus talk about going to his Father's house. As he listened, seeds of uncertainty must have been budding in Thomas' mind. He has questions.

Thomas may have been thinking about the house where they presently stayed. Could Jesus be speaking of a house on earth? The Lord's messaging is very conflicting for a typical Jewish man's train of thought. When Jesus says He is going to prepare a place, the language He uses typically is reserved for a bridegroom preparing to leave his father's house to obtain a house fit for his new wife.

The disciples are perplexed. These mansions or rooms indicate a very spacious area. From Thomas' view, if Jesus is alluding to heaven, how can he imagine heaven in his mind? If Jesus means a place on earth, then living in something as large as His description would certainly attract undesired attention for a man under the threat of being killed. These thoughts must have been overwhelming for Thomas. In verse 5 he questions where Jesus is going and how can the disciples know the way to follow Him?

The disciples should understand because the Master has been teaching them about His death and resurrection for three years. Yet, it is clear that they do not understand the depth of his teaching. Jesus wants His followers to think in a spiritual vein rather than a natural mind. His words indicate that He will soon die, but it is part of a larger plan to prepare the way for believers to have eternal life. Therefore, he tells them not to feel troubled. They will have difficult days ahead, but if they maintain their faith, they will join Jesus in the place He is preparing for them.

Jesus takes Thomas through the process of overcoming uncertainty. It requires him to stop doubting and trust the process. The Lord then reveals himself to be the conduit between humanity and God (v. 6). If the faithful want to go to heaven, they must reach God through faith in Christ.

Philip (v. 7) asks to see the Father. Jesus made it clear that when they follow and believe in the life and work of Christ, they experience the presence of God among them on earth. The upper room discourse reveals that His disciples can be confident in Christ no matter what they would encounter in the coming days.

III. Overcoming Sight-based Belief (John 20:24–29)

The scene has changed to after the resurrection of Jesus. The disciples secretly gathered in a house in Jerusalem still afraid that they too might be arrested and killed. Thomas is not present during this first meeting (v. 24). He may have drifted off due to his grief about Jesus' death. The other disciples were more hopeful because they had seen the risen Lord that Sunday evening (vv. 19–23). When Thomas shows up, the other disciples tell him they have seen the Lord. But Thomas' response (v. 25) reveals a negative consequence of missing evening service. He refused to believe it. Thomas has missed a grand opportunity and comes into the assembly late, resulting in him still burdened by unbelief.

Thomas wants to see Jesus with his own eyes before he will believe in the resurrection. The problem of sight-based faith is it will not allow one to embrace the spiritual aspects of God. John 4:24 conveys that God is a Spirit requiring worshipers to encounter Him spiritually. Thomas has to transition to trusting the Word of the Lord. However, his doubts did not cause him to desert the other disciples. If one has doubts about the faith, staying among other believers is the key to overcoming those challenges. Eight days later, Jesus appears again and this time Thomas is there. Jesus gives him the privilege of touching His nail imprinted hands and side.

In verse 27, the Lord exhorts Thomas to stop doubting and start believing. This phrase in the grammatical Greek is in the imperative mood, which means Jesus commands Thomas to stop disbelieving and start believing. The Lord is engaged in a type of casting out of an ungodly spirit. And Thomas receives his deliverance because he responded with words of worship (v. 28). If Christianity is to be meaningful in one's life, it is required to believe in Jesus by faith.

Verse 29 reveals a blessing for those who believe by faith rather than sight. Not only will these believers have eternal life, they will do even greater things in the Kingdom of God. Tradition suggests that Thomas' ministry later expands to India. Christians today who believe have an expanse of ministry that can touch the entire world.

IV. Learning to Believe (John 21:1–2)

At each stage of Thomas' journey, the Lord has discipled him to grow in faith. In John 11, Thomas was a skeptical doubter but by chapter 21, he has matured into a man of faith. These verses convey that faith development was a process. Chapter 21 starts with, "After these things," indicating that everything the disciples experienced helped them increase their faith. Jesus appearing to them at the Sea of Tiberias also affirms that the Lord never left His disciples, even. when they could not see Him. At the Sea of Tiberias, also known as the Sea of Galilee, the disciples have returned to fishing. Verse 2 names all but two of the disciples who witness the risen Lord.

By looking at their experiences, each one had an encounter with the Lord designed to stimulate their belief. Thomas struggled with a double mind. He had a twin conscious, wanting to believe yet still not believing. Jesus commands him to come out of his double consciousness. The names of the other disciples are not given, but every Christian can place his or her name as one of the others so, each one can be delivered from doubt to embrace the greater blessings of Jesus Christ.

THE LESSON APPLIED

The decision to follow Christ can be one of the hardest or the simplest of choices, depending upon one's faith. Christianity can be difficult in the sense that faith requires one to maintain hope when things do not appear to be going well. Consider the crucifixion of Christ, Jesus tells His disciples that He is going away to prepare mansions for them. A few days later they do not see mansions but their beloved Savior hangs on a cross. It appears as if their hopes have been devastated. Yet, Jesus' training of their faith is activated to get them to trust despite what they see. The disciples must remember their experiences with the Lord and rely upon that to keep trusting despite the situation.

If today's Christians use the same principle, then we will discover how easy it is to be a believer. If we forget all of what the Lord has done, then devastating situations can cause one to drift like Thomas. The word "remember" is used over 250 times in the Bible. The repetitive rituals of Passover and other Mosaic Law instructions are designed to keep God's activities at the forefront of the mind. God knows that it is the key to overcoming doubt. Fear and doubt should not be impediments to faith. Jesus promises to be with His people always, even unto the end of the world.

LET'S TALK ABOUT IT...

Discuss the following questions and visit www.rhboyd.com for more information.

What are some doubts that you have about faith in Jesus Christ?

What are some lived experiences that you have witnessed that strengthened your confidence in Jesus Christ?

Get Social

Share your views and tag us
@rhboydco and use #rhboydco

@rhboydco

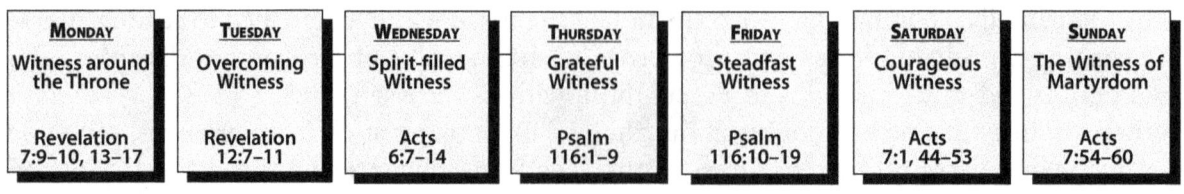

Home Daily Devotional Readings
August 3–9, 2026

Monday	Tuesday	Wednesday	Thursday	Friday	Saturday	Sunday
Witness around the Throne	Overcoming Witness	Spirit-filled Witness	Grateful Witness	Steadfast Witness	Courageous Witness	The Witness of Martyrdom
Revelation 7:9–10, 13–17	Revelation 12:7–11	Acts 6:7–14	Psalm 116:1–9	Psalm 116:10–19	Acts 7:1, 44–53	Acts 7:54–60

Lesson X   **August 9, 2026**

Stephen, an Early Interpreter of Christianity

Adult Topic: A Dirty Job
Background Scripture: Acts 6:1–7:60
Lesson Passage: Acts 6:7-10; 7:54-60

ACTS 6:7-10; 7:54-60

KJV

AND the word of God increased; and the number of the disciples multiplied in Jerusalem greatly; and a great company of the priests were obedient to the faith.

8 And Stephen, full of faith and power, did great wonders and miracles among the people.

9 Then there arose certain of the synagogue, which is called the synagogue of the Libertines, and Cyrenians, and Alexandrians, and of them of Cilicia and of Asia, disputing with Stephen.

10 And they were not able to resist the wisdom and the spirit by which he spake.

• • • • • •

54 When they heard these things, they were cut to the heart, and they gnashed on him with their teeth.

55 But he, being full of the Holy Ghost, looked up stedfastly into heaven, and saw the glory of God, and Jesus standing on the right hand of God,

56 And said, Behold, I see the heavens opened, and the Son of man standing on the right hand of God.

57 Then they cried out with a loud voice, and stopped their ears, and ran upon him with one accord,

58 And cast him out of the city, and stoned him: and the witnesses laid down their clothes at a young man's feet, whose name was Saul.

59 And they stoned Stephen, calling upon God, and saying, Lord Jesus, receive my spirit.

60 And he kneeled down, and cried with a loud voice, Lord, lay not this sin to their charge. And when he had said this, he fell asleep.

NRSVue

THE word of God continued to spread; the number of the disciples increased greatly in Jerusalem, and a great many of the priests became obedient to the faith.

8 Stephen, full of grace and power, did great wonders and signs among the people.

9 Then some of those who belonged to the synagogue of the Freedmen (as it was called), Cyrenians, Alexandrians, and others of those from Cilicia and Asia, stood up and argued with Stephen.

10 But they could not withstand the wisdom and the Spirit with which he spoke.

• • • • • •

54 When they heard these things, they became enraged and ground their teeth at Stephen.

55 But filled with the Holy Spirit, he gazed into heaven and saw the glory of God and Jesus standing at the right hand of God.

56 "Look," he said, "I see the heavens opened and the Son of Man standing at the right hand of God!"

57 But they covered their ears, and with a loud shout all rushed together against him.

58 Then they dragged him out of the city and began to stone him, and the witnesses laid their coats at the feet of a young man named Saul.

59 While they were stoning Stephen, he prayed, "Lord Jesus, receive my spirit."

60 Then he knelt down and cried out in a loud voice, "Lord, do not hold this sin against them." When he had said this, he died

MAIN THOUGHT: Stephen, full of grace and power, did great wonders and signs among the people. (Acts 6:8, NRSVue)

LESSON SETTING

Time: AD 31
Place: Jerusalem
Setting: The Lord Jesus returns to heaven after He ascends from Mt. Olive. On that day, His followers gaze into heaven, watching the Son of God go back to His Father. Some people react to His departure by continuing to promote the work of Christ, while others go back to their regular routines. One hundred and twenty disciples continue the faith by meeting in Jerusalem to wait for the promised Holy Spirit. God's Spirit descends upon Jesus' disciples on the Day of Pentecost. They are empowered to witness as they start sharing the Gospel out of the mother church in Jerusalem. The number of disciples multiply in Jerusalem, creating both good and bad consequences. More souls are being saved in the name of Jesus Christ, but the church is challenged as it becomes more diverse, leading to cultural clashes and complaints of discrimination. Out of this context, Stephen, a man full of faith, becomes a church leader. He ministers to the needs of the early church but also powerfully proclaims the divinity of Christ. The religious leaders in Jerusalem take note of Stephen's activities and deem his boldness offensive. Consequently, Stephen is brought before the Sanhedrin Council. The setting of Stephen's trial is significant because it shows that the clash between Jewish religiosity and Christian faith is front and center in Jerusalem. In this confrontation, Christ wins, igniting the spread of the Gospel throughout the world.

LESSON OUTLINE

I. Faithful to the Gospel (Acts 6:7–10)
II. Faithful unto Death (Acts 7:54–60)

UNIFYING PRINCIPLE

People may hesitate to speak up and take action even when their beliefs are called into question. What sparks a readiness to act on and speak the truth? Stephen, full of grace and the power of the Spirit, was equipped to defend his faith and speak the truth of God's Word.

INTRODUCTION

This lesson highlights the ministry of Stephen, a man known to be full of faith and power. He emerges as a leader of the early church (Acts 6:5), where he and six others are set apart to settle a dispute between the Hebrew and Hellenistic members. Although the Bible does not identify these peacekeepers as deacons, Stephen serves in this role within the congregation. This man of faith reveals that deacons are active participants in spreading the Gospel. Stephen models the commitment and boldness required to be a witness for Jesus. He preaches during a time when he can be killed for his faith. Yet, he does not allow that danger to stop him from declaring that Jesus is the fulfillment of God's plan of salvation. When Stephen died for his faith, a unique thing took place. Jesus stood to receive this him into the Kingdom of Heaven. It is the only occasion in the Bible where Jesus gives a standing reception.

EXPOSITION

I. Faithful to the Gospel (Acts 6:7–10)

Verse 7 underscores the results of the Gospel of Jesus Christ. Despite the persecution that the early church experienced, the Word of God continues to spread. Luke, the author of Acts, particularly describes the growth of Christianity is tied to the propagation of God's word. The first group of disciples numbered 120, but after being filled with the Holy Spirit, their numbers grew to more than 3000. However, these early church believers meet secretly in Jerusalem because they faced threats against their lives. Preaching and teaching doctrine of Jesus Christ is offensive to the Jewish religious leaders, resulting in the church facing great persecution.

The faithful also faces internal challenges. People join the church in droves, and they bring into the congregation their cultural differences, which leads to disunity. The church consists of Hebraic disciples who live in Jerusalem as well as the Hellenistic believers who live outside of the city. This diversity leads to distrust and discrimination over resources to help those in need. To address these problems, Stephen and six other godly men are chosen to ensure fair distribution. These men possess good reputations, empowered by the Holy Spirit, and wise. These servant leaders calm the confusion and the church continues to grow.

Stephen was likely a Hellenistic member of the church due to his name being derived from Grecian origin. It meant crown depicting him as a leader (The Bible Dictionary®/Stephen). Hellenistic Christians are viewed as less adherent to the Jewish traditions. They are considered outsiders although their numbers outpaced the Jewish Christians. Stephen understands the importance of unity. So, he takes leadership using prayer and the Word of God to keep the church together.

Verse 7 also emphasizes that some Jewish priests embraced Christianity. First Chronicles 24 described the twenty-four divisions of priests who served in the Temple each day, many of whom frequented Jerusalem and accepted the Gospel. Their conversion was no small matter because they were trained in the Hebrew Scriptures. Yet, the sincerity of these early believers and their faithfulness impressed upon these priests to submit to Christ as Lord. The key to the extensive growth of the church related to the study of the Word and the godly examples of those who believed it. Stephen was indicative of both, which inspired his magnificent witness for Jesus Christ.

Stephen accomplishes great wonders and signs as he proclaims the Gospel (v. 8). His effectiveness is tied to being full of faith and power. The word "faith" (Greek: *charitos*), which meant grace, gift, or favor (*Interlinear Bible*: faith) speaks to Stephen as being a favored gift from God. The Lord's gift of Stephen proves so valuable that his ministry exhibits divine intervention or power. Often, the world views ministers as offensive, eerie money seekers. The religious leaders who heard Stephen viewed him in that way. Yet, the text highlights that a minister operating under the anointing of God is truly a gift from above.

Stephen performs amazing deeds. Scripture does not specify them, but one that stands out is his ability to affirm Jesus as the fulfillment of prophecy. He interprets Christianity within the framework of Jesus as Messiah and Savior of the world.

Those in the Synagogue of the Freedmen (v. 9) are opponents of Stephen's assertions. These were Hellenistic Jews who followed Judaism and had matriculated from throughout the ancient near eastern world. The diversity within this synagogue indicates that many had come to Jerusalem during the Passover and gathered in religious groups with like-minded Jews, including North Africans, Egyptians, and Asians.

They reject Stephen's message (v. 10) and consider it blasphemy against Judaism. These freedmen are formerly enslaved people within the Roman Empire. They believed that their strict interpretation of the Jewish religion was an important reason why God gad granted their liberty. Therefore, Stephen's claims of Jesus being the fulfillment of the Law of Moses threatened traditions, customs, and even their freedom. They report him to the Jewish authorities. Nevertheless, Stephen stands firm in his convictions. He is accused of being an instigator of religious apostasy and is sentenced to be stoned for his crime. Stephen remains faithful to the Gospel even in the face of death.

II. Faithful unto Death (Acts 7:54–60)

Revelation 2:10 admonishes the Church to be faith unto death. The early Christians believe that willingness to endure a literal death is a part of faithfulness. Stephen is brought before the Sanhedrin Council because of his fidelity to the Gospel.

Acts 7:1–54 provides the scenario of Stephen's testimony before the Sanhedrin Council, brought into the matter after the crowd stirs against Stephen and his message. The council is the highest Jewish religious authority, comprised of seventy-one respected religious leaders from among the Pharisees, Sadducees, scribes, and elders in the community. When a matter could not be settled in a small group or a synagogue, the next step was to take the accused before the Sanhedrin. The council had the final authority in religious disputes.

Caiaphas is the high priest at the time of Stephen's case and was also involved in Jesus' trial; therefore, the stakes are against Stephen as they listen to his testimony. He begins with how God called Abraham and made a covenant with him to be the father of Israel. God preserved them through challenges because their destiny centered on providing the world with a Savior. Stephen also explains how the Hebrews were enslaved in Egypt and out of their experience God raised Moses to be their deliver.

The freedmen certainly could relate to the struggles of enslavement, yet they are not convinced by Stephen's interpretation of Jewish history. He points out that Moses, whom the Jews revere as their deliverer, prophesied that another Prophet would come as the ultimate Savior (Deuteronomy 18:15). Stephen tells the Sanhedrin that the prophets were rejected, Moses' leadership was misunderstood, and the covenant promise to Abraham was misinterpreted. Stephen directly charges their ancestors and them for being stiff-necked. The word "stiff-necked" or stubborn. He further raises their fury by charging their fathers and them with killing God's prophet and Jesus Christ.

Stephen's message (v. 53) reveals his holy boldness and proves to be the final straw leading to him being stoned. Stephen is focused on heaven rather than the hatred of men on earth. As he looks upward (v. 55), he sees Jesus standing at the right hand of God. The council is focused on killing the man of God who, in turn, is focused on his entrance into heaven. Stephen transitions to a higher and deeper level of faith, one that empowers him to see Jesus standing with him while the council stood against him. His vision (v. 56) of Jesus standing at the right hand of God confirmed his testimony before the council.

The people refuse to hear more. They push Stephen out of the Temple courts and force him out of Jerusalem. Leviticus 24:13–16 calls for the stoning of a person who blasphemes against God. So, in the eyes of the council, his execution is justified. Stephen exemplifies what it means to be an offense to the world (1 Peter 2:7–8). He is rejected by the world but accepted by Christ.

It should be noted that Saul of Tarsus is present to observe these horrific proceedings. Verse 58 indicates that he kept the clothes of those who disrobed themselves so they could throw the stones.

Saul does not believe Stephen's testimony, although he has heard his claims, and the seeds of the Gospel were planted. One never knows the impact that faithfulness has upon others.

As Stephen is dying, he calls on Jesus to receive his spirit. His final words depict how genuine Christianity transforms a person's heart. In the same manner as Jesus on the cross, Stephen asks that God forgive his executioners for their sin. Luke purposefully uses the phrase, "he fell asleep" (v. 60). Stephen transitioned from earth to heaven in a peaceful way. He completed his work and received his eternal reward.

THE LESSON APPLIED

Was it really necessary for Stephen to give his life for the faith? Believers answer in the affirmative. Rev. Dr. Martin Luther King, Jr. alludes to unearned suffering as being redemptive ("Suffering and Faith," 1960). It brings one closer to God, and it has a way of convicting those who witness the unjustified suffering. Stephen accomplishes both through his suffering. Christians should not entice persecution, but if it is required, they should not surrender their faith.

LET'S TALK ABOUT IT...

Discuss the following questions and visit www.rhboyd.com for more information.

How can the people of God maintain boldness in their faith?

Get Social

Share your views and tag us @rhboydco and use #rhboydco

@rhboydco

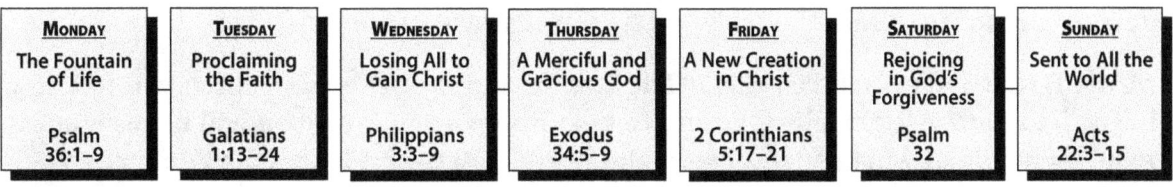

Lesson XI   **August 16, 2026**

Saul of Tarsus, How a Pharisee Became a Christian

Adult Topic: Tell Me What You Know
Background Scripture: Acts 22:3-15
Lesson Passage: Acts 22:3-15

ACTS 22:3-15

KJV

I AM verily a man which am a Jew, born in Tarsus, a city in Cilicia, yet brought up in this city at the feet of Gamaliel, and taught according to the perfect manner of the law of the fathers, and was zealous toward God, as ye all are this day.
4 And I persecuted this way unto the death, binding and delivering into prisons both men and women.
5 As also the high priest doth bear me witness, and all the estate of the elders: from whom also I received letters unto the brethren, and went to Damascus, to bring them which were there bound unto Jerusalem, for to be punished.

6 And it came to pass, that, as I made my journey, and was come nigh unto Damascus about noon, suddenly there shone from heaven a great light round about me.
7 And I fell unto the ground, and heard a voice saying unto me, Saul, Saul, why persecutest thou me?
8 And I answered, Who art thou, Lord? And he said unto me, I am Jesus of Nazareth, whom thou persecutest.
9 And they that were with me saw indeed the light, and were afraid; but they heard not the voice of him that spake to me.
10 And I said, What shall I do, Lord? And the Lord said unto me, Arise, and go into Damascus; and there it shall be told thee of all things which are appointed for thee to do.

NRSVue

"I AM a Jew born in Tarsus in Cilicia but brought up in this city at the feet of Gamaliel, educated strictly according to our ancestral law, being zealous for God, just as all of you are today.

4 I persecuted this Way up to the point of death by binding both men and women and putting them in prison,
5 as the high priest and the whole council of elders can testify about me. From them I also received letters to the brothers in Damascus, and I went there in order to bind those who were there and to bring them back to Jerusalem for punishment.
6 "While I was on my way and approaching Damascus, about noon a great light from heaven suddenly shone about me.

7 I fell to the ground and heard a voice saying to me, 'Saul, Saul, why are you persecuting me?'

8 I answered, 'Who are you, Lord?' Then he said to me, 'I am Jesus of Nazareth whom you are persecuting.'
9 Now those who were with me saw the light but did not hear the voice of the one who was speaking to me.
10 I asked, 'What am I to do, Lord?' The Lord said to me, 'Get up and go to Damascus; there you will be told everything that has been assigned to you to do.'

MAIN THOUGHT: [Ananias] said, "The God of our ancestors has chosen you to know his will, to see the Righteous One and to hear his own voice; for you will be his witness to all the world of what you have seen and heard." (Acts 22:14-15, NRSVue)

ACTS 22:3-15

KJV

11 And when I could not see for the glory of that light, being led by the hand of them that were with me, I came into Damascus.
12 And one Ananias, a devout man according to the law, having a good report of all the Jews which dwelt there,
13 Came unto me, and stood, and said unto me, Brother Saul, receive thy sight. And the same hour I looked up upon him.
14 And he said, The God of our fathers hath chosen thee, that thou shouldest know his will, and see that Just One, and shouldest hear the voice of his mouth.
15 For thou shalt be his witness unto all men of what thou hast seen and heard.

NRSVue

11 Since I could not see because of the brightness of that light, those who were with me took my hand and led me to Damascus.
12 "A certain Ananias, who was a devout man according to the law and well spoken of by all the Jews living there,
13 came to me, and standing beside me, he said, 'Brother Saul, regain your sight!' In that very hour I regained my sight and saw him.
14 Then he said, 'The God of our ancestors has chosen you to know his will, to see the Righteous One, and to hear his own voice,
15 for you will be his witness to all the world of what you have seen and heard.

LESSON SETTING

Time: AD 59
Place: Jerusalem (Setting of Paul's arrest and speech)
Setting: The Apostle Paul's ministry encompasses three missionary journeys. This lesson depicts him at the end of his third trip. He travels from Antioch of Syria, throughout Asia Minor and Greece then Paul a ship that carries him across the Mediterranean Sea where he ultimately reaches the setting for this lesson, Jerusalem. At every stop of his travels, Paul proclaims the Gospel message of Christ. When Paul arrives in Jerusalem, a city of people from diverse backgrounds, they listen to his sermons, but most consider him either a troublemaker or a blasphemer deserving death. This lesson details his speech to the Jerusalem crowd. He has been arrested and accused of speaking against the teachings of Judaism. Jews from Asia claim that he desecrates the sanctity of the Law of Moses and the holy Temple. They also accuse him of bringing a Gentile into the Temple area set apart for Jews. These accusations stir up such a ruckus that the mob wants to stone him like they did Stephen.

LESSON OUTLINE

I. A Misguided Journey (Acts 22:3-5)
II. A Journey Toward Deliverance (Acts 22:6-11)
III. A Witnessing Journey (Acts 22:12-15)

UNIFYING PRINCIPLE

It's sometimes difficult to believe that change in a person is authentic. What convinces us of the authenticity of the changes a person claims to have made? Paul testifies to his faith in Christ to convince Christians that he had truly repented of his former convictions and violent actions against believers.

INTRODUCTION

This lesson explores the experience of the apostle Paul as he concludes his third missionary journey. Paul is arrested in Jerusalem and stands before a hostile crowd. He tries to defend himself by giving a testimony of his conversion on the road to Damascus (Acts 9:1-19). Paul explains to the Jerusalem mob that he is no different from them other than having been converted by Jesus Christ. His life reveals that when one truly meets Jesus, he or she will never be the same.

EXPOSITION

I. A Misguided Journey (Acts 22:3–5)

The Jews from Asia have grown disgusted with Paul's ministry. They likely encountered Paul in Ephesus or one of the other cities of Asia Minor and are enraged by his teachings about Jesus. These conservative Jews have no tolerance for challenges to their understanding of the Laws of Moses. Paul's teaching claimed that Jesus is the Messiah and the fulfillment of the Law, doctrine that was considered a curse against God and worthy of the death penalty. When the Jews recognize Paul in the Temple, they rail against him, accusing him of being a heretic. They accuse him of bringing a Gentile named Trophimus into the sacred Jewish Temple area. Trophimus is a man of great faith who has taken the risk of becoming a religious companion of Paul. The Bible does not confirm their accusation, but Paul's opponents are willing to use any controversy to discredit him.

The mob's uproar against Paul is so intense that it leads to his arrest. Paul stands (v. 3) before the crowd and offers his defense. He is neither a blasphemer nor a troublemaker. He gives his ancestry, identifying himself as a Jew from Tarsus of Cilicia, as are many of his accusers. Cilicia was a city in Asia Minor (Turkey). He has been taught by a highly esteemed Orthodox Jewish scholar, Gamaliel. Therefore, accusing him of being a blasphemer of the Mosaic Law was ridiculous. He was reared as a fervent student of that Law. Jewish boys were educated on three levels—Bet Sefer, Bet Talmud, and Bet Midrash (Steve Corn, *Jewish Educational System*). Paul's study under Gamaliel falls under the Bet Midrash classification, the highest level of preparation for Jewish young men to become religious scholars. The apostle spent five to seven years with Gamaliel, learning the Jewish traditions and Law. He tells the skeptical crowd that his zeal for obeying the Law of Moses is as strict as those who charged him with heresy. Prior to his conversion, Paul held the same level vitriol toward Christians as his accusers.

His reference to them as followers of the "Way" (v. 4) indicates how early Christians were identified at that time. This name signifies that these disciples believe Jesus was the only way to God (see also Acts 9:2, 19:9, 19:23, 24:14, 24:22). Paul expresses his initial disdain for the people of the Way because they had deviated from traditional Jewish teachings. Paul (v. 5) calls out the high priest and other officials on the Sanhedrin Council. His defense was a mirror of who they are as religious leaders. Paul's defense makes it difficult for the crowd to stone him; he was one of them. Paul is as committed to the Law as anyone; however, his misunderstanding has been corrected by his encounter with Jesus.

II. A Journey Toward Deliverance (Acts 22:6–11)

The apostle continues to assert his innocence by telling the crowd what happened on his journey to Damascus. The fact that Paul had voluntarily chosen to make the journey 135-mile journey from Jerusalem to Damascus highlighted his once intense determination to stop the Christian movement. Damascus had emerged as a hub for Christianity. There were several synagogues were in the city (Acts 9:20), and out of them people were converting to the Way. Paul had been determined to cut off this developing network.

Paul's focus drastically changed when he saw a great light from heaven (v. 6). It was about noon on the road to Damascus. The intensity of the light was so powerful that it knocked Paul to the ground. Scripture reveals light as a sign of God's intervention on earth. Since Paul was a student of the scriptures, he immediately knew that this was a divine encounter.

Verses 7 and 8 show that Jesus viewed Paul's activities as a personal attack. This reflective question revealed the bondage of Paul's struggle. As Paul describes this quagmire to the Jerusalem crowd, the majority brush it off as gibberish. But his experience causes some hearers to examine themselves. Paul heard the Lord identify himself as Jesus of Nazareth. The use of the hometown of Jesus showed his humanity.

The beauty of Paul's testimony centers on Christ not leaving him in his predicament. His traveling companions saw the light, but they did not hear the voice. Verse 9 underscores his conversion. Paul had to personally respond to the voice of Jesus. The Lord's method of transforming Paul applies to every person who is converted. Individuals must experience Jesus for themselves and choose to follow Him. Verse 10 confirms that Paul made up his mind to submit to Christ as Lord and Savior. The grammatical Greek of this question indicated Paul's open-ended commitment to doing whatever the Lord commanded. The missionary was ready for action. He had no reservations or conditions upon his service.

The crowd, who listens to Paul's defense, probably wondered why he would put himself in so much jeopardy for his religious convictions. The scoffers pondered why this man would not just practice his religion privately like most normal Jews. But Paul operated under higher authority. His missionary work was inspired by the Lord Jesus Christ.

Verse 11 indicates Paul's willingness to go on to Damascus to receive further instructions and commission. Paul tells the Jerusalem crowd that life changed for him on the road to Damascus. He no longer desired to bind folks in a prison of Jewish legalism. He labored to set people free through a genuine faith in Jesus Christ.

III. A Witnessing Journey (Acts 22:12–15)

Before his Damascus Road experience, Paul lacked a clear spiritual purpose. When Paul reached Damascus, his companions led him into the city. Ironically, those who were following Paul when he was en route to persecute the Christians became his guides. Paul had to learn to submit to leadership. He was no longer the hunter. Now, he was the prey. Yet, God sent Ananias to guide and protect him as this convert transitioned into his new mission (vv. 12–13). The name Ananias means Jehovah is gracious. One can see the grace of God in Paul's experience, for he was very vulnerable in Damascus.

Paul already had a reputation of being a dangerous man. Therefore, anyone in Damascus could have taken the opportunity to harm this blind man. He was like a wounded lion and had it not been for Ananias, Paul likely would have been killed. The crowd possibly thinks Paul's story is fabricated to gain sympathy. The commander who had arrested Paul after the temple commotion also listened but none of them were persuaded.

Paul received his commission through Ananias (v. 14). As Ananias ministered to Paul, he spoke to him as being a part of the Christian family. Paul was no longer a threat but now a fellow brother in the Lord. The use of "the God of our father" showed that both men have the same ancestral heritage. The Christian way was not a deviation from Judaism but the proper extension of it through Jesus Christ. Ananias helped Paul to make those historical connections, but the crowd rejects them.

Finally, in verse 15, Paul receives his God ordained purpose. His assignment centers on being a witness to all people. Acts recounts Paul's testimony in Acts 9:1-16, 22:1-21, and 26:12-18. The common thread of each account was Paul's message, and ministry came from the Lord. In the same way that Jesus converted Paul, salvation was available for everyone. Ananias believed in the Lord's plan and so did Paul. The mob in Jerusalem had no interest. They shouted the apostle down and called for his death.

THE LESSON APPLIED

Paul's confrontations with the Jerusalem crowd came because of their envy, ignorance, unbelief, and hatred. Paul stood firm in his faith and always remembered that except by the grace of God, he was just like these unbelievers. Often the target of the missionary's outreach does not receive the gospel, yet saints must not lose hope. Ananias' ministry to Paul in Damascus proves to be prophetic for Paul and for present-day missionaries.

LET'S TALK ABOUT IT...

Discuss the following questions and visit www.rhboyd.com for more information.

Did you have a conversion experience? How is your conversion similar or different from Paul's testimony?

Has there been a time in your life when you needed to stand in the faith? Why did others oppose you?

Get Social

Share your views and tag us
@rhboydco and use #rhboydco

@rhboydco

Home Daily Devotional Readings
August 17–23, 2026

Monday	Tuesday	Wednesday	Thursday	Friday	Saturday	Sunday
A Protégé with Promise	Listen to Wise Instruction	Learn from Father and Mother	A Worthy and Trusted Minister	Make God Known to Future Generations	Thankful for Established Faith	Continue in What You Have Learned
Acts 16:1-5	Proverbs 1:1-9	Proverbs 23:22-26	Philippians 2:19-24	Deuteronomy 4:9-13	2 Timothy 1:1-16	2 Timothy 3:10-11, 14-16

Lesson XII August 23, 2026

Timothy, the Influence of Home Training

Adult Topic: Home Is Where the Heart Is
Background Scripture: Acts 16:1–3; Philip. 2:19–22; 2 Timothy 1:1–6; 3:14–16
Lesson Passage: 2 Timothy 1:1–6; 3:14–16

2 TIMOTHY 1:1-6; 3:14-16

KJV

PAUL, an apostle of Jesus Christ by the will of God, according to the promise of life which is in Christ Jesus,

2 To Timothy, my dearly beloved son: Grace, mercy, and peace, from God the Father and Christ Jesus our Lord.

3 I thank God, whom I serve from my forefathers with pure conscience, that without ceasing I have remembrance of thee in my prayers night and day;

4 Greatly desiring to see thee, being mindful of thy tears, that I may be filled with joy;

5 When I call to remembrance the unfeigned faith that is in thee, which dwelt first in thy grandmother Lois, and thy mother Eunice; and I am persuaded that in thee also.

6 Wherefore I put thee in remembrance that thou stir up the gift of God, which is in thee by the putting on of my hands.

• • • 3:14–16 • • •

14 But continue thou in the things which thou hast learned and hast been assured of, knowing of whom thou hast learned them;

15 And that from a child thou hast known the holy scriptures, which are able to make thee wise unto salvation through faith which is in Christ Jesus.

16 All scripture is given by inspiration of God, and is profitable for doctrine, for reproof, for correction, for instruction in righteousness:

NRSVue

PAUL, an apostle of Christ Jesus by the will of God, for the sake of the promise of life that is in Christ Jesus,

2 To Timothy, my beloved child: Grace, mercy, and peace from God the Father and Christ Jesus our Lord.

3 I am grateful to God—whom I worship with a clear conscience, as my ancestors did—when I remember you constantly in my prayers night and day.

4 Recalling your tears, I long to see you so that I may be filled with joy.

5 I am reminded of your sincere faith, a faith that lived first in your grandmother Lois and your mother Eunice and now, I am sure, lives in you.

6 For this reason I remind you to rekindle the gift of God that is within you through the laying on of my hands,

• • • 3:14–16 • • •

14 But as for you, continue in what you have learned and firmly believed, knowing from whom you learned it

15 and how from childhood you have known sacred writings that are able to instruct you for salvation through faith in Christ Jesus.

16 All scripture is inspired by God and is useful for teaching, for reproof, for correction, and for training in righteousness,

MAIN THOUGHT: I am reminded of your sincere faith, a faith that lived first in your grandmother Lois and your mother Eunice and now, I am sure, lives in you. (2 Timothy 1:5, NRSVue)

LESSON SETTING
Time: AD 67
Place: Rome
Setting: The Apostle Paul writes to Timothy, his son in the ministry, while incarcerated under Roman authority. Timothy receives this letter while serving as a pastor in Ephesus. Paul knows his death is near, and he urges Timothy to come for a visit.

LESSON OUTLINE
I. Remember the Godly Heritage (2 Timothy 1:1–6)
II. Remember the Scriptures (2 Timothy 3:14–16)

UNIFYING PRINCIPLE
People closest to us can influence us either positively or negatively. How can we discern the positive influences from the negative influences in our lives? Paul reminds Timothy of the genuine faith of his mother and grandmother and encourages him to see in them models for his own faith.

INTRODUCTION

If a person knew that they only had one week to live, what are the key things that he or she would do with those last days? Paul uses his last days to inspire the next generation to continue the work of God. His letter to Timothy reveals a determined man who is faithful to his calling until his last breath. When Pope Francis died in 2025, he expressed his thankfulness to God and to his caretaker for bringing him back to the square at the Vatican ("Revealing the Last Words of Pope Francis Before Dying." CiberCuba, April 22, 2025). Paul expresses gratitude for his service to the Lord. Then, the apostle prays that Timothy will also remain faithful. However, saints understand that being faithful in Christian service can be easier said than done. The persecution against the believers is intense during Paul's time. His zeal literally cost him his life.

Therefore, the question of how to be faithful is central in this lesson. Paul conveys three keys to being faithful unto death. Believers must have a commitment to Jesus Christ within their hearts. They must continue to exercise their Christian training. And the faithful must learn and apply the God's inspired word as the ultimate standard of conduct. Timothy's instructions are to fulfill all the above. It is not certain whether the young pastor sees Paul again after receiving this letter. But his words are planted like seeds in Timothy which still inspire the next generation of Christian leaders today.

EXPOSITION

I. Remember the Godly Heritage (2 Timothy 1:1–6)

Paul greets Timothy warmly and calls the younger man's attention to his maternal heritage. He highlights that his ministry originated from a divine call from Jesus Christ. Therefore, his message was not shallow suggestions for his son in the ministry to blow off. Paul's words were divinely inspired that applied from one generation to the next. The apostle knew that he would soon be executed for the cause of Christ. So, he wanted Timothy to take seriously the important message of what to do and how to carry on the Gospel of Jesus Christ as pastor in the church at Ephesus. Writing from Rome, Paul was many miles from Timothy and the letter was perhaps carried to him by Tychicus referred to in 2 Timothy 4:12.

Even with death staring Paul in the face, he did not allow his circumstances to keep him from speaking life into Timothy. Paul exemplified a great model of mentorship. He understood how to motivate his son to remain faithful to the Lord's call. Young Timothy had to remember several key principles as he ministered for the Lord. Verse 2 identified him as Paul's son. Although not his biological son, they had a spiritual kinship. In verse 2, Paul emphasized his spiritual paternity to help his son remember that he had a divine connecting cord that came from Christ, to Paul, and into Timothy.

The divine virtues of grace, mercy, and peace flowed down the spiritual feeding cord. Timothy had an eternal nourishment that he was to rely upon as he did his work. This divine connection is important for modern day pastors and Christian leaders. Often, the saints struggle with becoming burned out while doing the work of Christ. People can be mean and reject the Gospel. These responses can cause even the most faithful to become tired and frustrated. Paul certainly knew of these challenges and understood that his spiritual son faced those hindrances. So, he told him that the Lord Jesus Christ was continuously sustaining him with favor, kindness, and peace.

Whenever the opposition tried to stop Timothy's ministry, he could draw on grace. When the people were unkind, Timothy could rebuff it with God's supernatural affinity. Peace was a tranquility about life and death. Timothy could minister without fear knowing that whatever happened to him, he was safe in the arms of God. Paul's greeting was more than a simple introduction. It was Paul's way of assuring him that even if he was not there physically, he was present spiritually.

In verses 3–6, Timothy is directed to remember the faith of his grandmother and mother. They were a part of that cloud of witnesses both living and deceased who were pulling for him. One can imagine movies where a key figure is facing a challenge, and the movie does a flashback where the actor remembers something or someone significant to urge him forward. Paul wanted Timothy to know that he had that same type of spiritual backing in his corner.

Verse 5 indicates that Timothy's grandmother and mother also played an important role in stimulating his calling. Paul called Timothy's attention to them because he wanted him to remember their faith. The loyalty to Christ shown by Lois and Eunice was also within Timothy. When things got tough, Paul implored him to act on what God put in him through his heritage and by way of the Holy Spirit. Paul's admonition in verse 6 to stir up the gift meant to rekindle all the spiritual seeds that were already implanted. He had everything necessary to be a great pastor. Paul gave Timothy more than a superficial affirmation of his ministry. He reminded him of his divine supply line of faith, three virtues to rely upon, the power of vision, and a heritage of God-fearing ancestors.

II. Remember the Scriptures (2 Timothy 3:14–16)

In the earlier verses of chapter 3, Paul did not want his spiritual son disillusioned about ministry. Their ministry took place during perilous times. Men and women rejected God and had become lovers of themselves. His work in Ephesus entailed trying to lead a very self-centered people to faith in Jesus Christ. The worship of the goddess Artemis proved to be a major challenge for Timothy. The people came to Ephesus and participated in festivals giving homage to idols. Sexual perversion was a part of the worship with temple prostitutes exploiting patrons. Moreover, if one tried to condemn the pagan religions it could lead to death. For this religion was tied to folks making money and gaining social status. If one was a trader, complying with the activities of Artemis worship afforded that person a more lucrative status. Timothy's preaching against paganism put him in direct confrontation with both the financial and spiritual institutions in the city.

Paul spent more than three years ministering in Ephesus visiting them during his second and third missionary journeys. So, he knew the kind of people that Timothy faced. They were evil and opportunist men and women who hated and envied someone like the young pastor. Therefore, the apostle instructed him to remember his training in verse 14. When undermined by false teachers such as Hymenaeus and Philetus, who doubted the return of Christ, Timothy had to stand firm on Paul's teachings about the second coming of Jesus. To survive, it was important for Timothy to study the examples of his parents, Paul, and the Word.

Verse 15 reveals that his grandmother Lois and mother Eunice gave him a strong moral foundation. One can imagine that Timothy watched Eunice pray to the one true God of Abraham, Isaac, and Jacob. This experience reinforced in him that making sacrifices to idols was prohibited. He likely also heard the story from Grandmother Lois about Paul's resilience in Lystra. Some psychologists suggest that a child's moral development is formed between three months to six years. Timothy's moral formation served him well, for he had a strong moral compass to guide his decisions.

When Timothy learned about Paul's life experiences such as him being beaten in Lystra and still continuing to teach, this recollection conveyed to him that being rejected was no excuse to forsake the cause. Verse 15 emphasizes that these lifestyle traits of his parents and Paul were grounded in their faithfulness to the Holy Scriptures. When Paul referred to them, he primarily spoke of the Law, prophets, and writings in the Old Testament. The New Testament Scriptures were not yet written, so Timothy could still read the godly lifestyle of Paul as a model. All of this in total gave the pastor wisdom and a context for salvation.

Verse 16 reveals that his most effective tool for ministry was the inspired Word of God. The word *inspiration* used in the text literally means "God-breathed." By preaching and teaching the word, the pastor had God's oxygen sustaining him. The scriptures were not just words on parchment but living seeds designed to promote salvation.

Paul understood that believers had a tendency to receive the word and then fall away from the faith. Therefore, a continued rehearsal of the tenets of the Word were essential to maintain steadfastness. The end results of adhering to the Word was a perfect finish. The Holy Scriptures provided a complete finish for Timothy. If the people lived by the Word, their lives would have a perfect finish like a diamond with no blemishes. Timothy had every tool necessary for a successful ministry. He simply needed to remember what God gave him and apply it based upon the Scriptures.

THE LESSON APPLIED

A man was eating with friends and ordered a bottle of water before stepping away from the table for a few minutes. He did not know that the water cost a dollar. He consumed the refreshment, giving no thought to the bill. When presented with the bill, he struggled trying to figure out how to pay the tab. His friends quickly stepped in a paid the cost with no questions. The thirst-quenched man was so relieved by the generosity of his friends. He did not realize that he had more than enough supply sitting at his table.

Paul conveys a similar lesson to his protégé, young Timothy, who faces an uphill struggle trying to lead the Ephesians to Christ. Paul assures the young pastor that he already has what he needs to be effective in ministry. There was nothing to fear and no need to worry about failure. Timothy was more than ready to meet the challenge.

God's supplies the needs of those He calls to ministry. He gives a heritage of faith, mentors, and God-inspired Scripture. No matter how terribly the people may conduct themselves, Christians overcome the world through the power of Jesus Christ.

LET'S TALK ABOUT IT...

Discuss the following questions and visit www.rhboyd.com for more information.

What can Christians do to carry on God's ministry when they are not blessed with godly parentage like Timothy?

How can we recognize God's supply when things feel stressed?

What are some things we can do to maintain a steadfast faith?

Identify some of the attributes that a spiritual and/or physical parent should intend to pass on to children.

How can we ensure a strong moral compass is instilled to guide our spiritual and/or physical children?

Get Social

Share your views and tag us
@rhboydco and use #rhboydco

@rhboydco

Home Daily Devotional Readings
August 24–30, 2026

Monday	Tuesday	Wednesday	Thursday	Friday	Saturday	Sunday
Stewards of God's Good Gifts	God Sees and Rewards Hospitality	A Capable, Entrepreneurial Woman	Good and Trustworthy Servants	Blessed Are the Risk-takers	The Righteous Provide to Others	An Eager, Hospitable Disciple
1 Peter 4:7–11	2 Kings 4:8–17	Proverbs 31:10–22	Matthew 25:14–23	Matthew 25:24–30	Job 31:16–28	Acts 16:11–15, 40

Lesson XIII　　　　　　　　　　　　　　　　　　　　　　　　　　**August 30, 2026**

Lydia, Judged to Be Faithful

Adult Topic: All Are Welcome
Background Scripture: Acts 16:11–40
Lesson Passage: Acts 16:11–15, 40

ACTS 16:11–15, 40

KJV

THEREFORE loosing from Troas, we came with a straight course to Samothracia, and the next day to Neapolis;

12 And from thence to Philippi, which is the chief city of that part of Macedonia, and a colony: and we were in that city abiding certain days.

13 And on the sabbath we went out of the city by a river side, where prayer was wont to be made; and we sat down, and spake unto the women which resorted thither.

14 And a certain woman named Lydia, a seller of purple, of the city of Thyatira, which worshipped God, heard us: whose heart the Lord opened, that she attended unto the things which were spoken of Paul.

15 And when she was baptized, and her household, she besought us, saying, If ye have judged me to be faithful to the Lord, come into my house, and abide there. And she constrained us.

• • • • • •

40 And they went out of the prison, and entered into the house of Lydia: and when they had seen the brethren, they comforted them, and departed.

NRSVue

WE therefore set sail from Troas and took a straight course to Samothrace, the following day to Neapolis,

12 and from there to Philippi, which is a leading city of the district of Macedonia and a Roman colony. We remained in this city for some days.

13 On the Sabbath day we went outside the gate by the river, where we supposed there was a place of prayer, and we sat down and spoke to the women who had gathered there.

14 A certain woman named Lydia, a worshiper of God, was listening to us; she was from the city of Thyatira and a dealer in purple cloth. The Lord opened her heart to listen eagerly to what was said by Paul.

15 When she and her household were baptized, she urged us, saying, "If you have judged me to be faithful to the Lord, come and stay at my home." And she prevailed upon us.

• • • • • •

40 After leaving the prison they went to Lydia's home, and when they had seen and encouraged the brothers and sisters there, they departed.

LESSON SETTING

Time: AD 49
Place: Phillipi
Setting: A few years after the death of Emperor Julius Caesar, a Roman civil war battle takes place near the city of Phillipi. After the battle, the Romans take control of the city and began to infiltrate their influence with the Greek culture already in the region. At the time of this lesson, Philippi, a Roman territory,

MAIN THOUGHT: When she and her household were baptized, she urged us, saying, "If you have judged me to be faithful to the Lord, come and stay at my home." And she prevailed upon us. (Acts 16:15, NRSVue)

has a population of nearly 15,000 people. A small population of Jews also live in Philippi who are monotheistic and reject the notion of Caesar being God. They must maintain a low profile or face punishment. Within this context, Paul enters this city preaching a Gospel that threatens the status quo.

LESSON OUTLINE

I. Going to Macedonia (Acts 16:11–12)
II. Sharing the Gospel in Philippi (Acts 16:13–14)
III. Turning the Message into a Ministry (Acts 16:15, 40)

UNIFYING PRINCIPLE

We question the sincerity of others when their words are not backed up with their actions. How do our actions show that we are genuine? Paul and his companions accepted Lydia's hospitality after her household showed their faith and were baptized.

INTRODUCTION

This lesson is part of Paul's second missionary journey to the regions of Asia minor and Macedonia. Paul and his fellow missionaries progressively move the message of the Gospel in a westerly direction. Paul discovers that God intends for him to focus his ministry on the Gentiles. In Acts 9:15, Jesus assigns Paul to carry His name to the Gentile world.

He wants to do mission work in Asia such as Bithynia, but the Holy Spirit forbids him. The restrictions raised by the Holy Spirit, as Paul tries to find his field of ministry, affirm that Jesus will say no. Although saints may not want to hear that answer, they must still trust in the plan of God rather than their own. Paul yields to the Holy Spirit and goes into the region of Macedonia where he meets Lydia.

Servants of God must always keep an open mind when it comes to ministry. Scripture reveals that the Lord directs His missionaries into places not desired but still needed for the sake of the Kingdom. Paul's kingdom-minded perspectives pave the way for not only Lydia to be saved but all those who follow her in the western world.

EXPOSITION

I. Going to Macedonia (Acts 16:11–12)

In Acts 16:8, Paul, Silas, Luke, and Timothy came to a place called Troas. Today, Troas is in modern Turkey. Paul received a vision of a man in Macedonia saying, "come over to Macedonia and help us." This spiritual encounter was his confirmation to depart from ministering in Asia and move to Macedonia. This region was a part of Europe. Although controlled by the Romans, a diversity of people lived there totaling over 10,000 in population. It was a new field for Paul. But he immediately obeyed the Holy Spirit and made the two-day trip.

As he left Troas, verse 11 indicates that they went directly to Samothrace. The trip took about a day. Paul's determination to go to Macedonia was evident because he did not take detours. This direct course modeled how believers should respond. They must stay focused on the call and not allow last-minute circumstances to take them off course. When responding to God's call, one can be assured that Satan will try to offer detours. Examples of Satan's detours include fleshly desires, the lack of resources, idol talkers, and the lure of selfish gain. Paul understood that all these things were potential distractions. But his direct course showed that he refused to give the devil a chance to change his mind. He had a divine date with destiny, which motivated him to steadfastly head to Macedonia. He moved immediately and directly, allowing him to reach the port city of Neapolis in two days.

Neapolis was a port city consisting of several thousand people. When Paul landed, he encountered Romans, Greeks, sailors, and merchants. He continued his journey eight miles inland until he arrived at Philippi. It too had a diverse population, for the writer of Acts labeled it a foremost city in verse 12. Philippi was uniquely located on the Via Egnatia which was a famous Roman road that fostered trade, travel, and for Paul the dispersion of the Gospel into Europe. As Paul followed the Holy Spirit, the Lord guided him to the target of his witness.

II. Sharing the Gospel in Philippi (Acts 16:13–14)

When Paul arrived in a city to witness, he practiced a pattern of starting his mission in the Jewish synagogues. He preached his first sermon in the synagogue of Damascus in Acts 9:20. When he went into Cyprus and Antioch of Pisidia, he used the same strategy in Acts 13. The difference with Phillipi was it did not have a Jewish synagogue. The Jewish population numbered too small for a synagogue. On this Sabbath day in verse 13, Paul, Silas, Luke and Timothy went to the river for their worship service. In Jewish history, waters represented divine emphases. They served as transition points between the realm of man and the realm of God. When the Hebrew children passed through the Red Sea, it was a deliverance from Egyptian slavery to God's liberty. When Israel crossed the Jordan River, it signified that they crossed over from bondage into the Lord's Promised Land. Therefore, it fit Jewish tradition to view the river as a place for worship.

In Philippi, the walk from the city down to the river took about 30–45 minutes, because it was outside of the city gates. Paul and his co-laborer's desire to go there displayed the sincerity of their worship. It was not enough for them to remain at home and pray. The time and effort sacrificed to go to a specific place of worship revealed the importance of their service to God. Believers should be doing more than looking for a church home like shopping for something in the mall. This lesson teaches a different perspective. Missionaries must sacrifice to encounter God. They must put forth effort to carry out His mission.

As Paul and Silas went to the river, they encountered Lydia and other women in verse 14. They were also worshiping God but not in the same way as the missionaries. Lydia had some commitment to Judaism since she and the others prayed on the Sabbath. But she was more of a businesswoman than a devout Jew. She had relocated some 300 miles from Thyatira to open a purple dye trade in Philippi. She understood the nature of taking risks.

Thyatira was a hub for selling valuable purple dye used especially for clothes worn by the rich and royalty. The dye was derived from the mucus of murex snails. The rarity of the dye and the labor needed to produce it made purple very expensive. Lydia took a venture to offer the product in Philippi. The city contained wealthy citizens but there was no guarantee of a continuous successful trade. Lydia had a lot of reasons to pray. She had to maintain a house, employees, servants, and family. Although she was a woman of means, she still faced challenges. Her biggest challenge centered on her relationship with the Lord. Paul immediately recognized his contact with Lydia as an opportunity to share the Gospel.

III. Turning the Message into a Ministry (Acts 16:15, 40)

Not being distracted by Lydia's purple dyes, Paul focused on his primary reason for coming to Philippi. He spoke to her about salvation through Jesus Christ. Lydia understood that she was to remember the Sabbath and keep it holy. But Paul explained to her why it was holy. Jesus is the Lord of the Sabbath. Paul helped Lydia to see that the Gospel of Jesus Christ opens the door for all to be forgiven of sins and receive eternal life.

Lydia once again showed her willingness to break from the norm and opened her heart to Paul's Gospel message. With Lydia being a rich woman from another city, she already had a lot of peculiarities that created barriers for her life in Philippi. Her decision to become a Christian would be one more reason why some people would shun her. Nevertheless, she made a good business decision concerning her soul to receive Jesus as Lord.

The verses in this section of the lesson reveal the activity of the Holy Spirit. Lydia accepted Christ because of the inspiration of God. She, along with Paul and the others, allowed the Holy Spirit to bring about the first conversion in Europe. At times, humans want to put their fingers on the scales trying to manipulate a person to accept Christ. This methodology always leads to superficial faith. Philippi was a Roman colony with many retired Roman soldiers living there. They certainly believed in the imperial cult system where everyone pledged allegiance to Caesar as God. The Jewish population did not believe in it, but they still had to superficially show some homage to the Roman emperor. Lydia willingly accepted Christ under the leadership of the Holy Spirit and not the dictates of an idol system. Her salvation affirmed that the Gospel alone has its own saving power.

Verse 15 reveals the results of receiving the Gospel. She and her household were baptized. This act indicates that Lydia was likely the head of her house. The text does not speak of a husband, but her openness to the Gospel was so influential that everyone associated with her also accepted Christ. Moreover, she led the household in a public baptism where others at the river saw the event. She was not shy about her conversion, making it clear that she was not ashamed of the Gospel. Lydia turned the Gospel message into a ministry. Her family got saved. Her baptism turned into a public witness, and Paul could clearly see her sincerity.

The natural inclination of Paul was to finish his sharing and move on to the next assignment. However, Lydia refused to allow him to disconnect that easily. She urged him to come to her house and receive the hospitality of a new sister in the Lord. Paul and Silas knew the trouble that their presence brought to fellow co-laborers. Their tenacity for the Gospel made them a magnet for trouble. Lydia did not care nor was she afraid of what might happen to her. She joined the family of God and would not allow her mentors to fend for themselves. Her spirit of hospitality modeled for believers how they should treat each other as one body in Christ. Lydia understood that a vital part of salvation included fellowship. Christians need a close relationship with the Lord, but they also need a loving network.

Verse 40 reveals that Lydia proved herself faithful by turning her house into a gathering place for the first Philippian church. After Paul and Silas were imprisoned in Philippi for witnessing for Jesus, the Lord sent a miraculous earthquake which allowed them to be set free. Paul and Silas' impact disturbed the city so much that the missionaries were forced to leave. Lydia once again showed her commitment and took care of them before they departed Philippi. Luke, the writer of Acts, was a part of the missionary team and likely remained in Philippi while Paul, Silas, and Timothy continued to Thessalonica. Lydia and the saints of Philippi played an important role in leading more souls to Christ and many of those souls came to know Jesus within her house.

THE LESSON APPLIED

Lydia proves to be a unique person. She takes a leap of faith by leaving Thyatira and moving to Philippi. Her responsibilities are great being the head of the household. Yet, she still attends to her spirituality. Most importantly, she chooses to join a persecuted religion by giving her life to Christ. Lydia's example is a good pattern for Christians. She sincerely believes in the Lord and uses all her influences to lead others to Jesus. Christians today tend to separate their spiritual lives from their personal lives. Lydia displays that giving one's life to Christ is a total sacrifice. Being faithful to the Lord is more than what takes place on Sunday; it includes a lifestyle of following the Holy Spirit.

LET'S TALK ABOUT IT...

Discuss the following questions and visit www.rhboyd.com for more information.

How much of a risk are you willing to take as a follower of Jesus Christ?

How can you foster a lifestyle of following the Holy Spirit?

If there was one thing getting in the way of your relationship with God, would you remove it from your life? How?

Can you recognize the work of the Holy Spirit in your life? What are the signs that a situation has the fingerprints of God on it?

What is one thing that draws people to God?

Get Social

Share your views and tag us
@rhboydco and use #rhboydco

@rhboydco

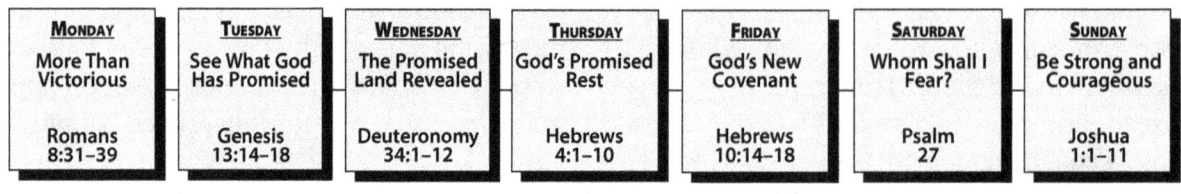

Home Daily Devotional Readings
August 31–September 6, 2026

Monday	Tuesday	Wednesday	Thursday	Friday	Saturday	Sunday
More Than Victorious	See What God Has Promised	The Promised Land Revealed	God's Promised Rest	God's New Covenant	Whom Shall I Fear?	Be Strong and Courageous
Romans 8:31–39	Genesis 13:14–18	Deuteronomy 34:1–12	Hebrews 4:1–10	Hebrews 10:14–18	Psalm 27	Joshua 1:1–11

*PARTIAL BIBLIOGRAPHY

Duvall, J. S. and Hays, J. D. (2020). The Baker Illustrated Bible Background Commentary. Baker Books, Grand Rapids, MI.

Evans, T. (2019). Th Tony Evans Bible Commentary. Advancing God's Kingdom Agenda. Holman. Nashville, TN.

MacDonald, W. and Farstad, A. (1989). Believer's Bible Commentary, 2nd ed. Thomas Nelson. Nashville, TN.

Pfeiffer, C.F. and Harrison, E.F. (1990). Wycliffe Bible Commentary. Moody Press. Chicago, IL.

Stanley, C.F. (2009). The Charles F. Stanley Life Principles Bible, NASB. Thomas Nelson, Nashville, TN.

The Life Application Study Bible, 3rd ed, KJV (2018). Tyndale House Publishers. Carol Stream, IL.

Youngblood, R. F., Bruce, F.F., and Harrison, R.K. (2014). Nelson's Illustrated Bible Dictionary New and Enhanced Edition. Thomas Nelson. Nashville, TN.

Anderson, N.T. (2020).Victory Over the Darkness: Realize the Power of Your Identity in Christ. Bethany House Publishers, Bloomington, MN, p. 22.

Baker, W. (2013). Hebrew-Greek Key Word Study Bible, ESV. AMG Publishers. Chattanooga, TN.

Duvall, J. S. and Hays, J. D. (2020). The Baker Illustrated Bible Background Commentary. Baker Books, Grand Rapids, MI.

Evans, T. (2019). The Tony Evans Bible Commentary. Advancing God's Kingdom Agenda. Holman. Nashville, TN.

MacDonald, W. and Farstad, A. (1989). Believer's Bible Commentary, 2nd ed. Thomas Nelson. Nashville, TN.

Pfeiffer, C.F. and Harrison, E.F. (1990). Wycliffe Bible Commentary. Moody Press. Chicago, IL.

Stanley, C.F. (2009). The Charles F. Stanley Life Principles Bible, NASB. Thomas Nelson, Nashville, TN.

The Life Application Study Bible, 3rd ed, KJV (2018). Tyndale House Publishers. Carol Stream, IL.

Youngblood, R. F., Bruce, F.F., and Harrison, R.K. (2014). Nelson's Illustrated Bible Dictionary New and Enhanced Edition. Thomas Nelson. Nashville, TN.

Baker, W. (2013). Hebrew-Greek Key Word Study Bible, ESV. AMG Publishers. Chattanooga, TN.

Duvall, J. S. and Hays, J. D. (2020). The Baker Illustrated Bible Background Commentary. Baker Books, Grand Rapids, MI.

Evans, T. (2019). The Tony Evans Bible Commentary. Advancing God's Kingdom Agenda. Holman. Nashville, TN.

MacDonald, W. and Farstad, A. (1989). Believer's Bible Commentary, 2nd ed. Thomas Nelson. Nashville, TN.

Pfeiffer, C.F. and Harrison, E.F. (1990). Wycliffe Bible Commentary. Moody Press. Chicago, IL.

Stanley, C.F. (2009). The Charles F. Stanley Life Principles Bible, NASB. Thomas Nelson, Nashville, TN.

The Life Application Study Bible, 3rd ed, KJV (2018). Tyndale House Publishers. Carol Stream, IL.

Youngblood, R. F., Bruce, F.F., and Harrison, R.K. (2014). Nelson's Illustrated Bible Dictionary New and Enhanced Edition. Thomas Nelson. Nashville, TN.

Baker, W. (2013). Hebrew-Greek Key Word Study Bible, ESV. AMG Publishers. Chattanooga, TN.

Duvall, J. S. and Hays, J. D. (2020). The Baker Illustrated Bible Background Commentary. Baker Books, Grand Rapids, MI.

Evans, T. (2019). Th Tony Evans Bible Commentary. Advancing God's Kingdom Agenda. Holman. Nashville, TN.

MacDonald, W. and Farstad, A. (1989). Believer's Bible Commentary, 2nd ed. Thomas Nelson. Nashville, TN.

Pfeiffer, C.F. and Harrison, E.F. (1990). Wycliffe Bible Commentary. Moody Press. Chicago, IL.

Stanley, C.F. (2009). The Charles F. Stanley Life Principles Bible, NASB. Thomas Nelson, Nashville, TN.

The Life Application Study Bible, 3rd ed, KJV (2018). Tyndale House Publishers. Carol Stream, IL.

Youngblood, R. F., Bruce, F.F., and Harrison, R.K. (2014). Nelson's Illustrated Bible Dictionary New and Enhanced Edition. Thomas Nelson. Nashville, TN.

"Acts 6:8 Interlinear: And Stephen, Full of Faith and Power, Was Doing Great Wonders and Signs among the People,." Accessed May 14, 2025. https://biblehub.com/interlinear/acts/6-8.htm.

Ali, Muhammad. News Conference in London. United Press International (UPI), November 30, 1974. Quoted in The Port Arthur News, p. 11.

Bibledictionarytoday. "Stephen: Biblical Meaning and Origin of This Name in the Bible." Accessed May 3, 2025. https://bibledictionarytoday.com/biblical-names/stephen/#google_vignette.

Blue Letter Bible. "G739 – Artios & exartizo - Strong's Greek Lexicon (Nasb20)." Accessed May 29, 2025. https://www.blueletterbible.org/nasb20/gen/1/1/s_1001.

CiberCuba Editorial Team. 2025. "Revealing the Last Words of Pope Francis Before Dying." CiberCuba, April 22, 2025. https://en.cibercuba.com/noticias/2025-04-22-u1-e199894-s27061-nid301414-revelan-ultimas-palabras-papa-francisco-morir.

Coptic Orthodox Diocese of the Southern United States. "The Upper Room." Accessed May 3, 2025. https://www.suscopts.org/resources/interesting-facts/8/the-upper-room/.

"Golgotha Chap 11: Where Was the Sanhedrin Located?" n.d. PDF, accessed May 3, 2025.

https://www.askelm.com/golgotha/Golgotha%20Chap%2011.pdf.

Kassinger, Ruth G. (6 February 2003). Dyes: From Sea Snails to Synthetics. 21st century. ISBN 0-7613-2112-8.

"Moral Development in Children: How Values Are Formed • Teachers Institute," December 27, 2023. https://teachers.institute/facilitating-growth-development/moral-development-in-children-values-formed/.

Patten, Arthur Bardwell. Faith of Our Mothers. Accessed May 27, 2025. Hymnary.org.

Smithsonian Channel. The Fishy Reason This Ancient Roman City Was so Wealthy, 2019. https://www.youtube.com/watch?v=tGqiJmJ-m_g.

STEVE. "Jewish Educational System." Stevecorn.Com, 1 Nov. 2010, https://stevecorn.com/2010/11/01/jewish-educational-system/.

"Strong's Greek: 3624. Οἶκος (Oikos) — House, Household, Home, Family." Accessed June 4, 2025. https://biblehub.com/greek/3624.htm.

"Suffering and Faith." The Christian Century, https://www.christiancentury.org/article/suffering-and-faith. Accessed 17 May 2025.

www.ingramcontent.com/pod-product-compliance
Lightning Source LLC
Chambersburg PA
CBHW080222170426
43192CB00015B/2720